SWORD ART ONLINE
PROGRESSIVE
006

SWORD ART ONLINE PROGRESSIVE 002

CONTENTS

ART: KISEKI HIMURA
ORIGINAL STORY: REKI KAWAHARA
CHARACTER DESIGN: abec

#006: Partner

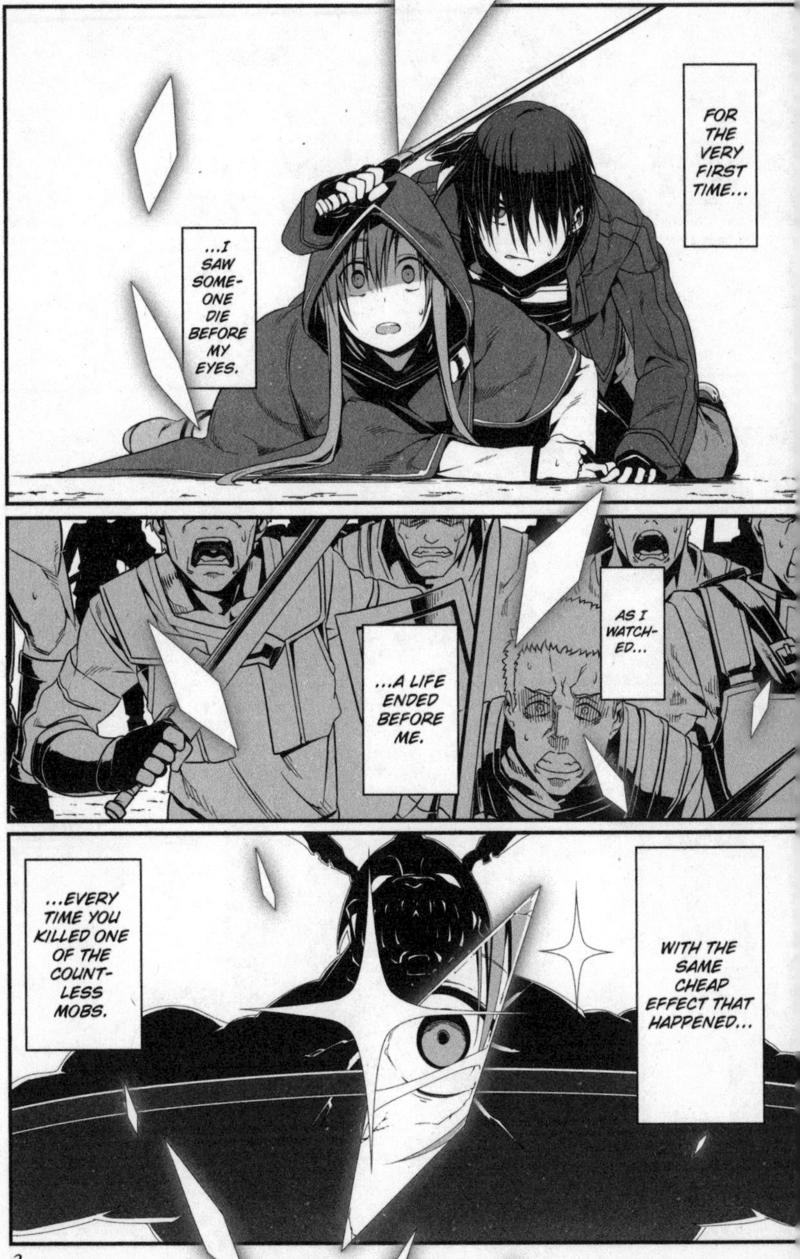
FOR THE VERY FIRST TIME...
...I SAW SOMEONE DIE BEFORE MY EYES.
AS I WATCHED...
...A LIFE ENDED BEFORE ME.
WITH THE SAME CHEAP EFFECT THAT HAPPENED...
...EVERY TIME YOU KILLED ONE OF THE COUNTLESS MOBS.

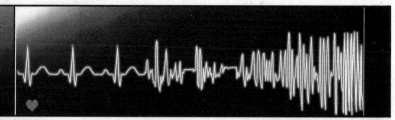

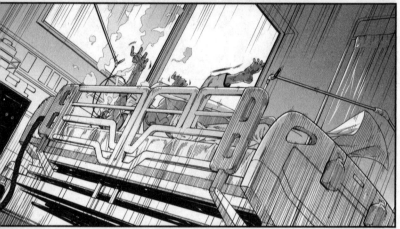

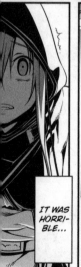

IT WASN'T FAIR.
CARDIAC ARREST
HR
SpO2
SYS
bpm
##
IT WAS HORRI-BLE...

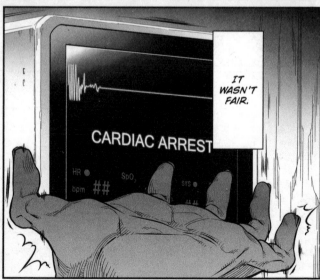

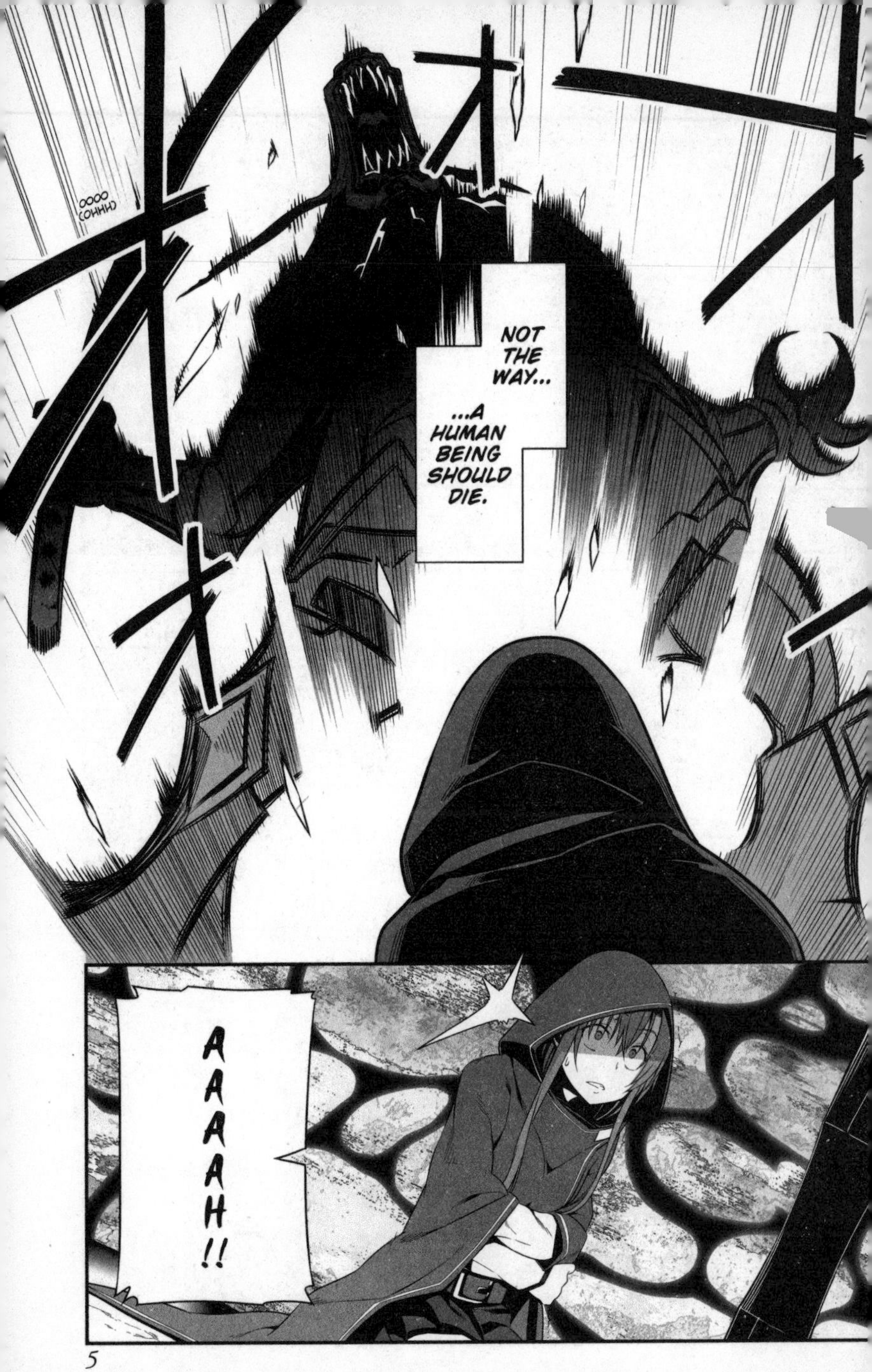
OOOO (OHHH)
NOT THE WAY...
...A HUMAN BEING SHOULD DIE.
AAAAAH!!

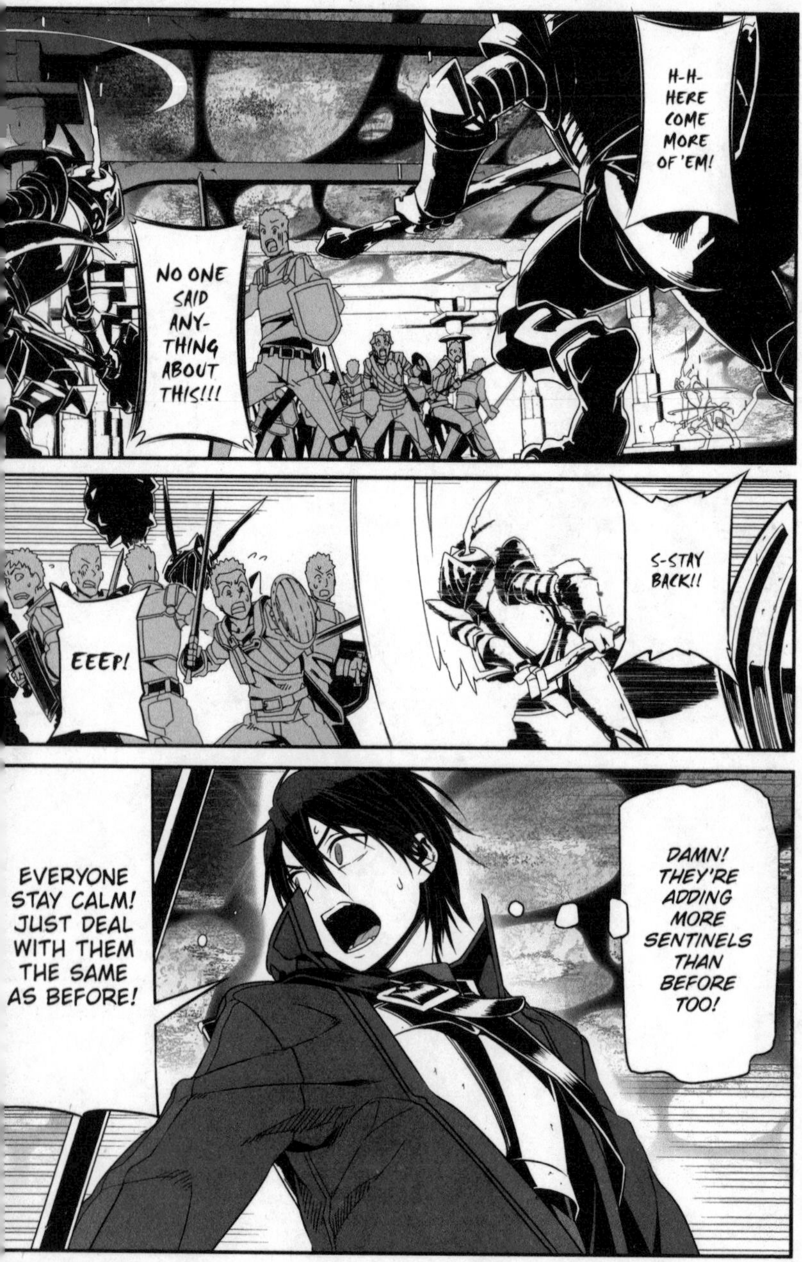
H-H-HERE COME MORE OF 'EM!
NO ONE SAID ANY-THING ABOUT THIS!!!
S-STAY BACK!!
EEEP!
DAMN! THEY'RE ADDING MORE SENTINELS THAN BEFORE TOO!
EVERYONE STAY CALM! JUST DEAL WITH THEM THE SAME AS BEFORE!

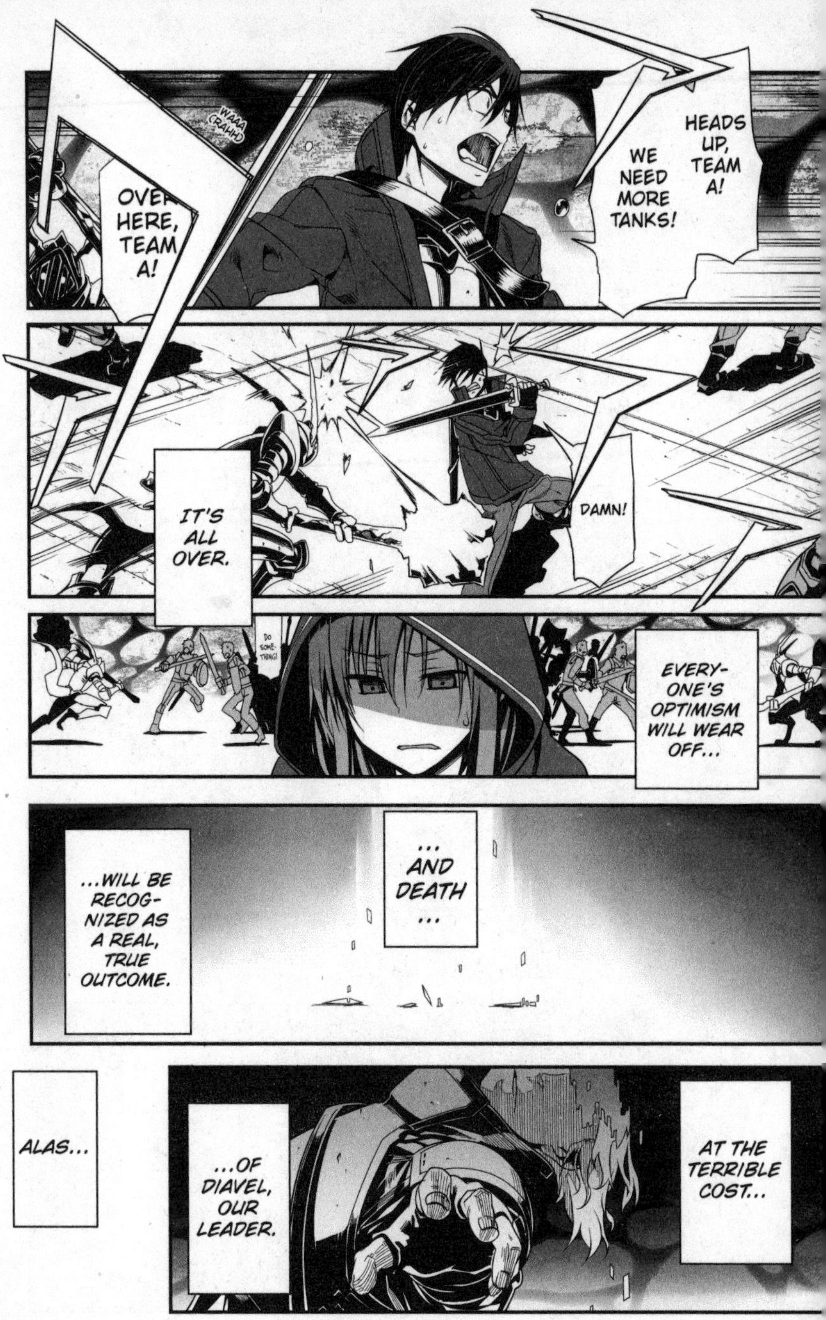
HEADS UP, TEAM A!
WE NEED MORE TANKS!
WAAA CRAHH
OVER HERE, TEAM A!
DAMN!
IT'S ALL OVER.
EVERY-ONE'S OPTIMISM WILL WEAR OFF...
DO SOME-THING!
...AND DEATH...
...WILL BE RECOG-NIZED AS A REAL, TRUE OUTCOME.
AT THE TERRIBLE COST...
...OF DIAVEL, OUR LEADER.
ALAS...

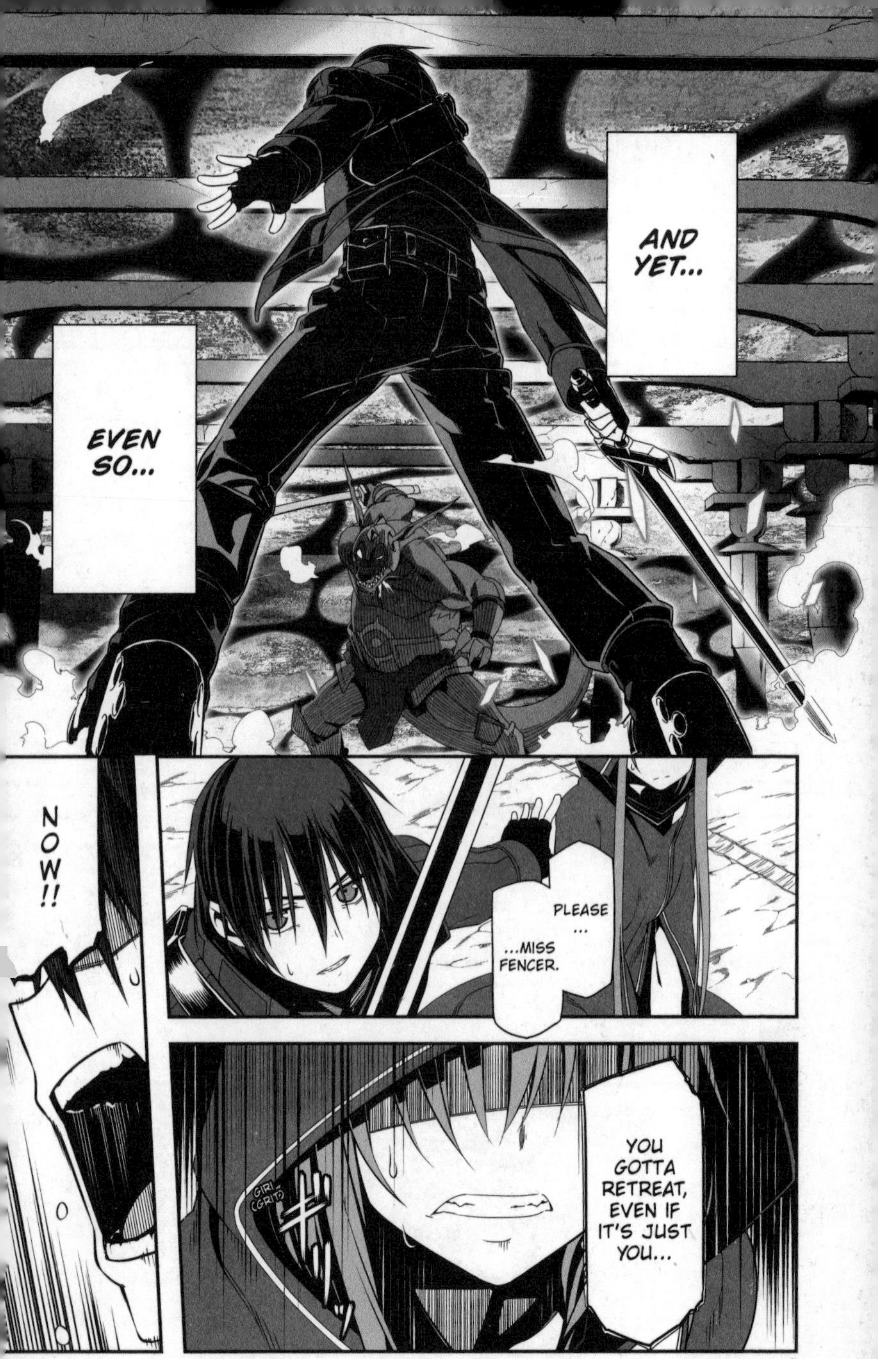
AND YET...
EVEN SO...
PLEASE ... ...MISS FENCER.
YOU GOTTA RETREAT, EVEN IF IT'S JUST YOU...
GIRI (GRIT)
NOW!!

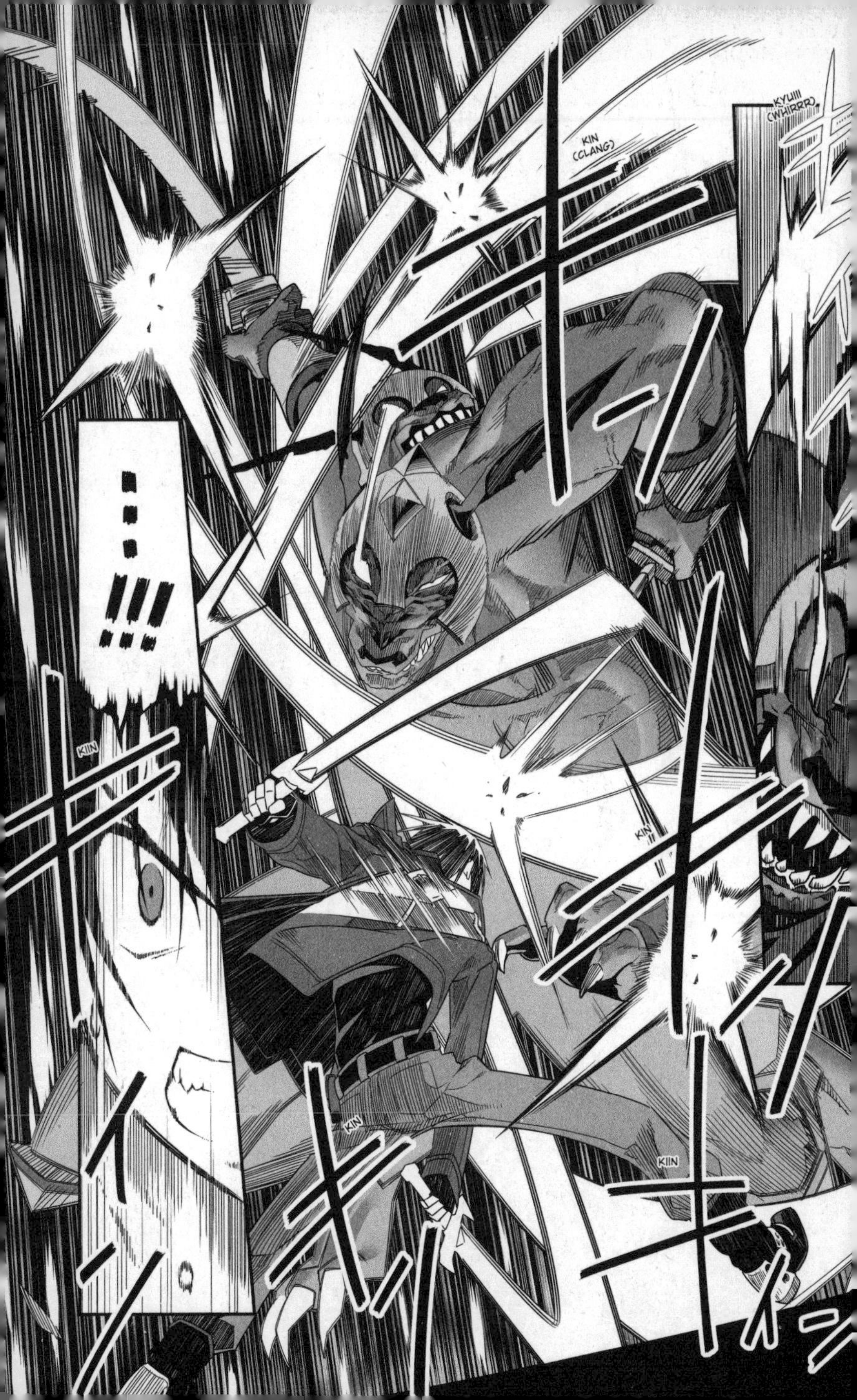
KYUIII (WHIRRR)
KIN (CLANG)
...!!!
KIN
KIIN
KIN
KIIN

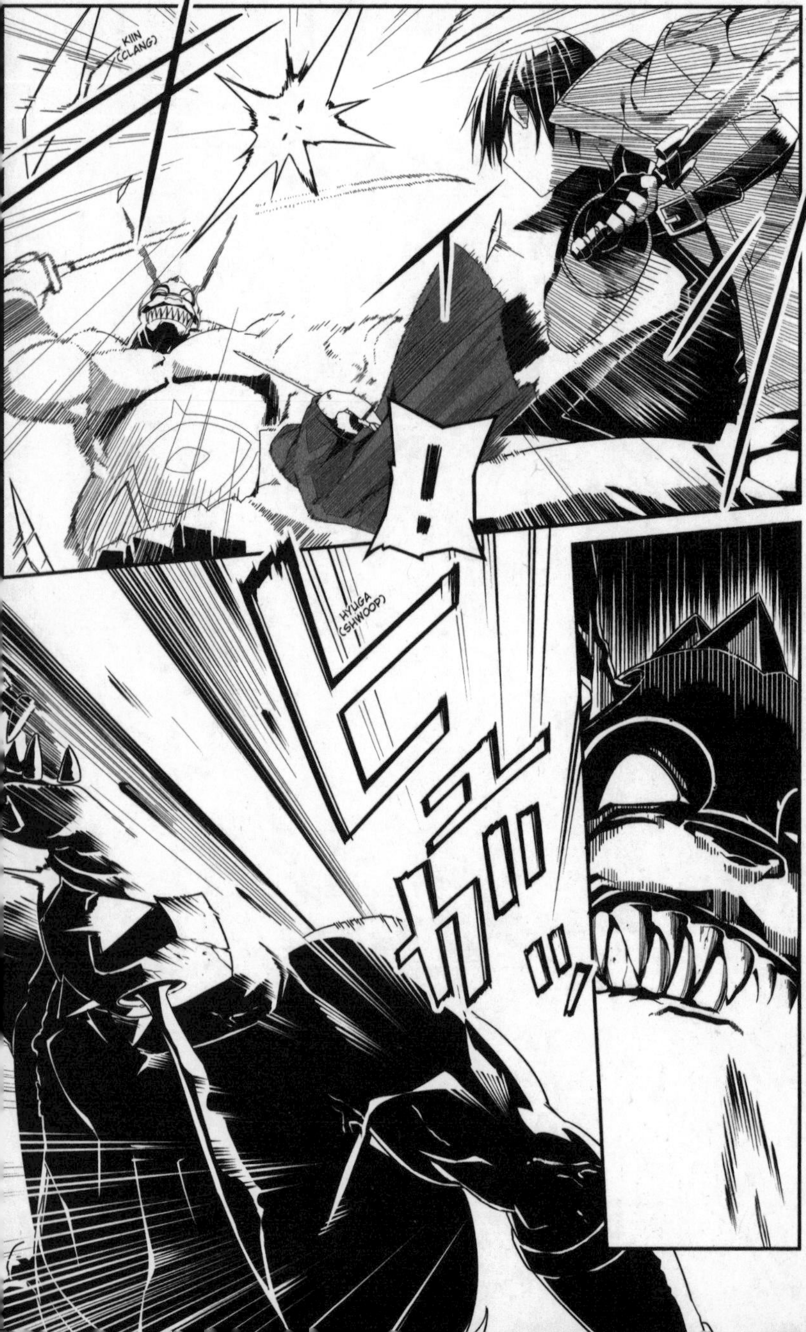
KIIN (CLANG)
!
HYUGA (SHWOOP)

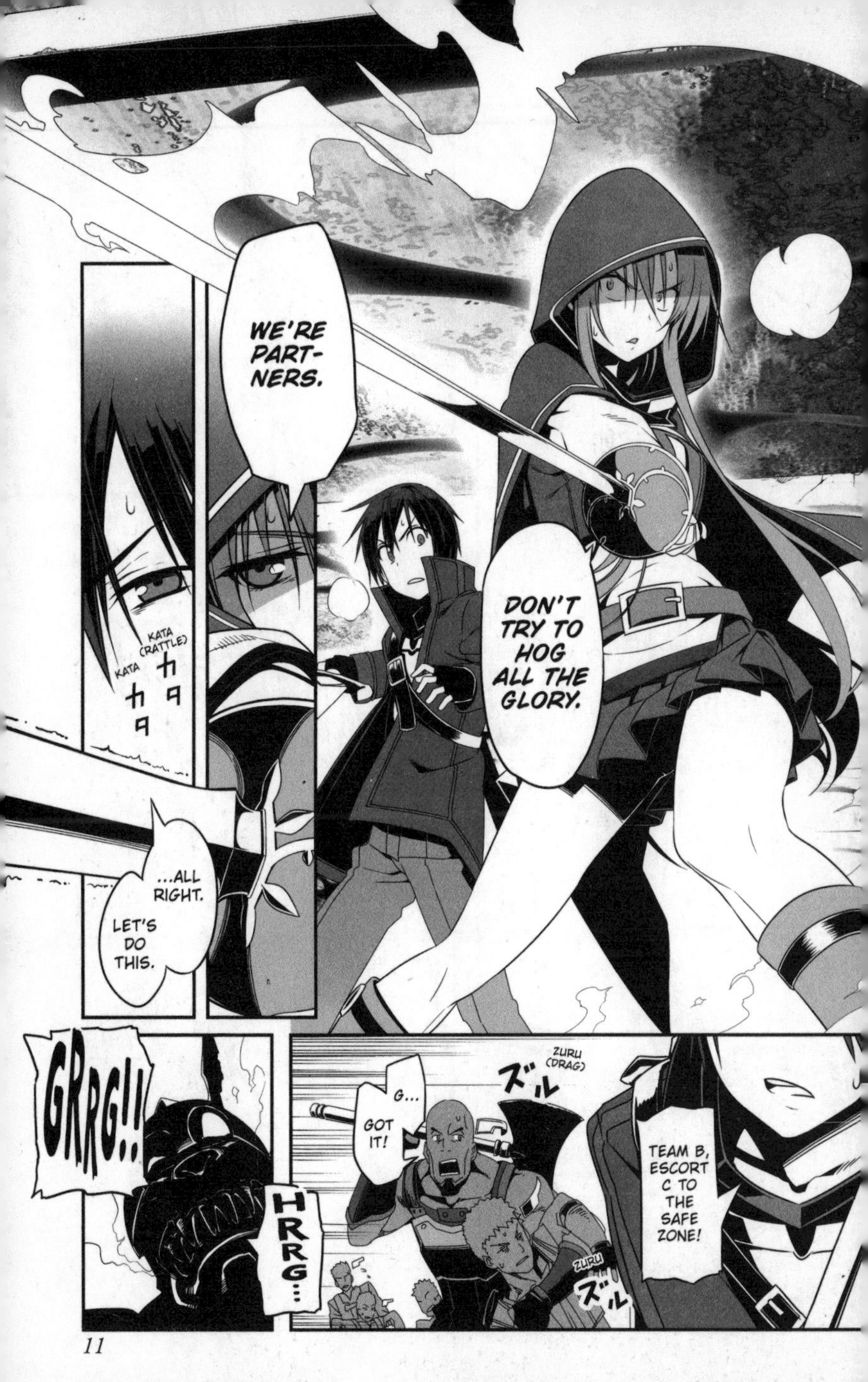
WE'RE PARTNERS.
DON'T TRY TO HOG ALL THE GLORY.
KATA KATA
KATA (RATTLE)
カタカタ
...ALL RIGHT.
LET'S DO THIS.
TEAM B, ESCORT C TO THE SAFE ZONE!
ZURU (DRAG)
ズル
G...
GOT IT!
ZURU
ズル
GRRG!!
HRRG...

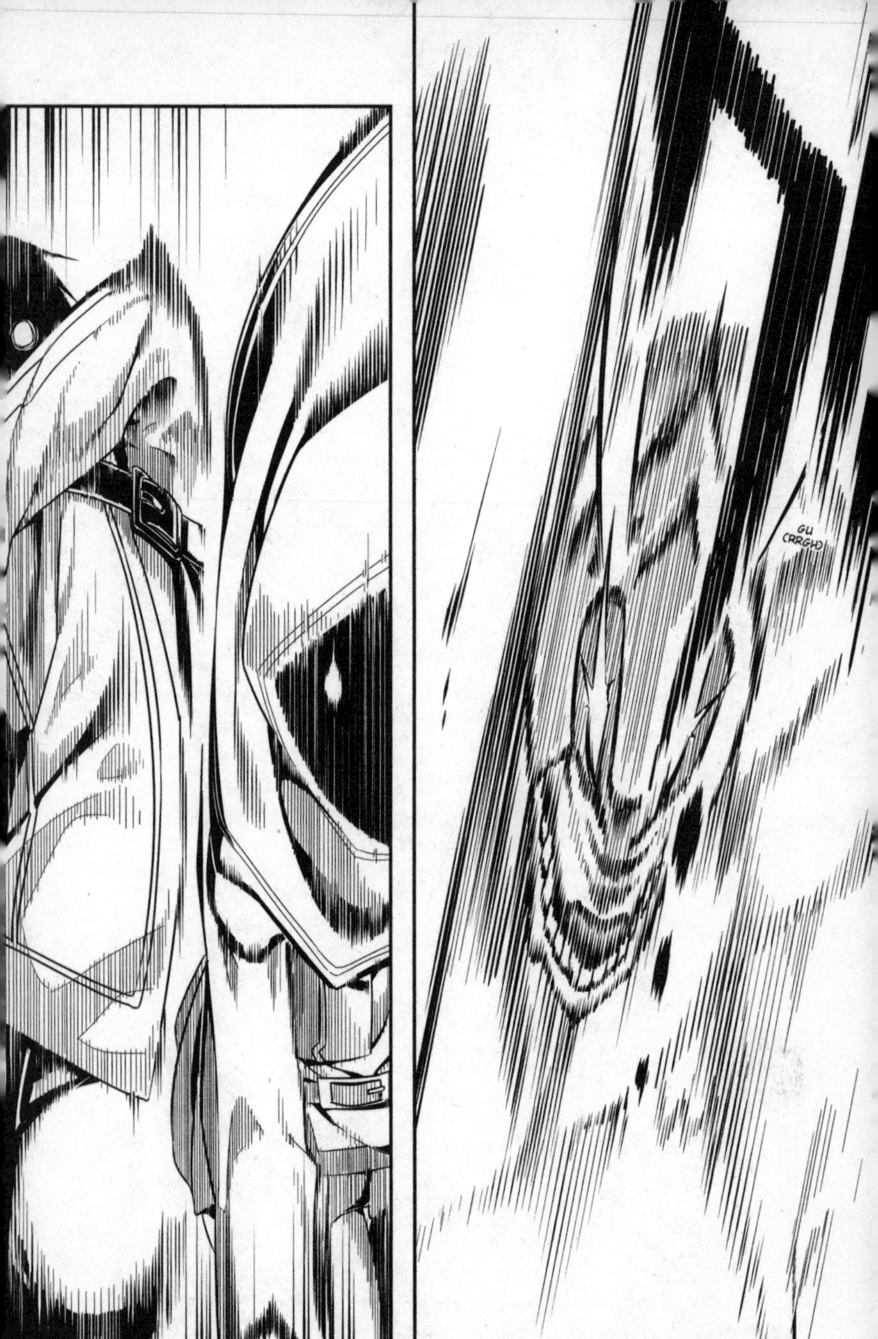
GU
(RRGH)

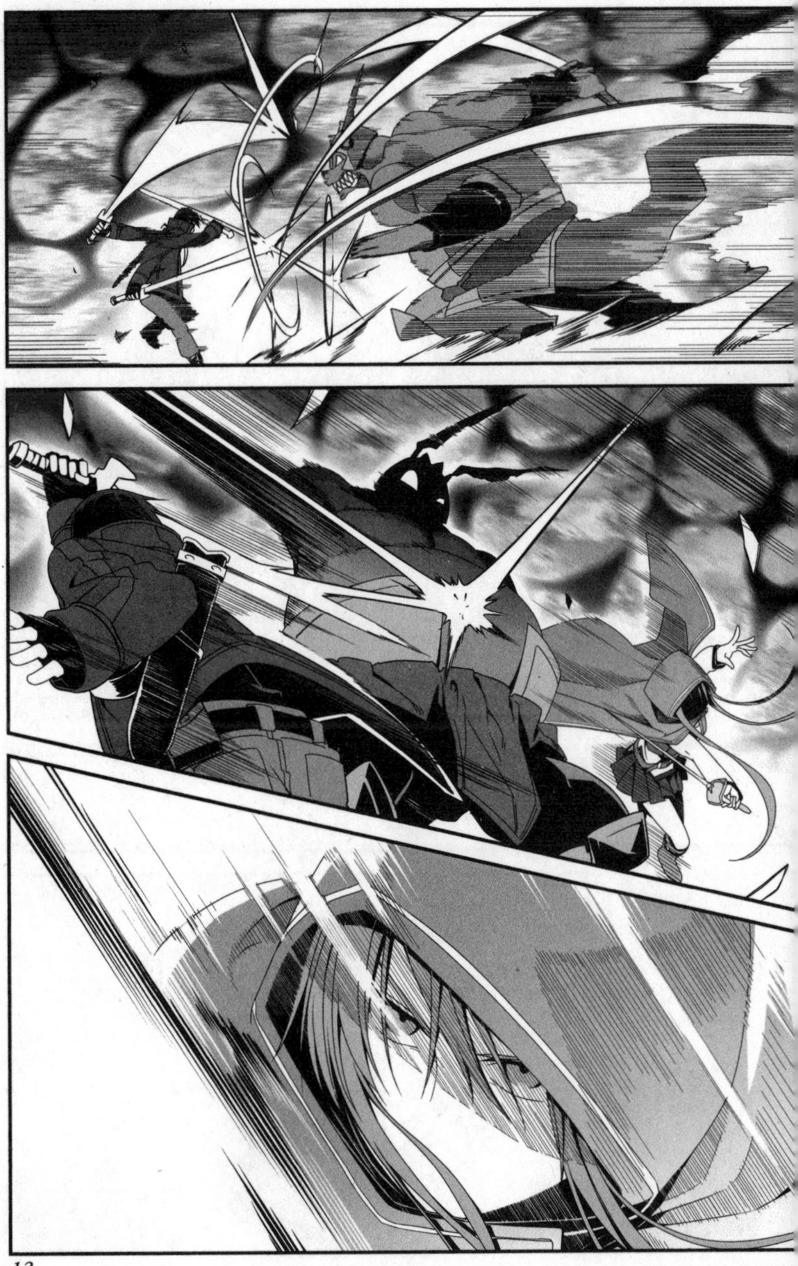

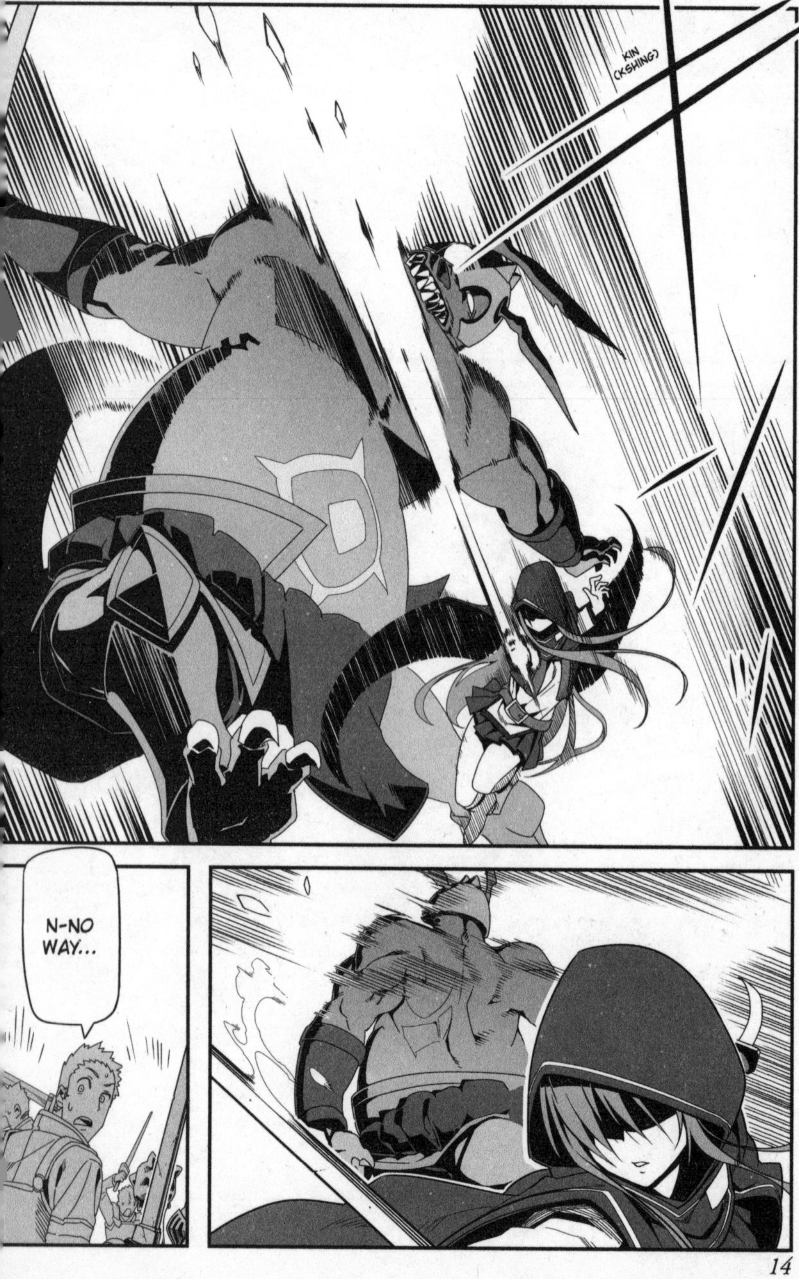
KIN (KSHING)
N-NO WAY...

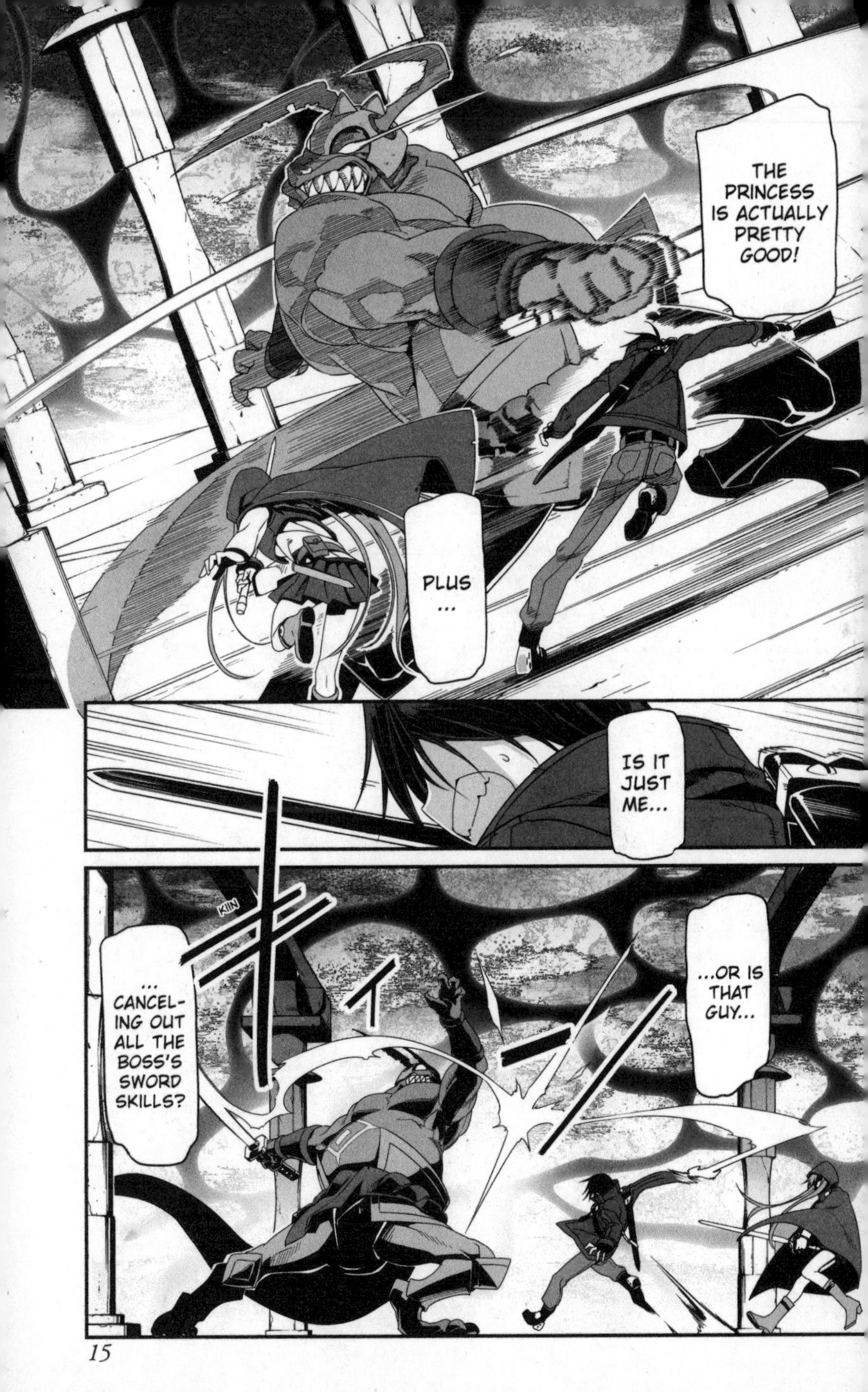
THE PRINCESS IS ACTUALLY PRETTY GOOD!
PLUS ...
IS IT JUST ME...
...OR IS THAT GUY...
KIIN
... CANCEL-ING OUT ALL THE BOSS'S SWORD SKILLS?

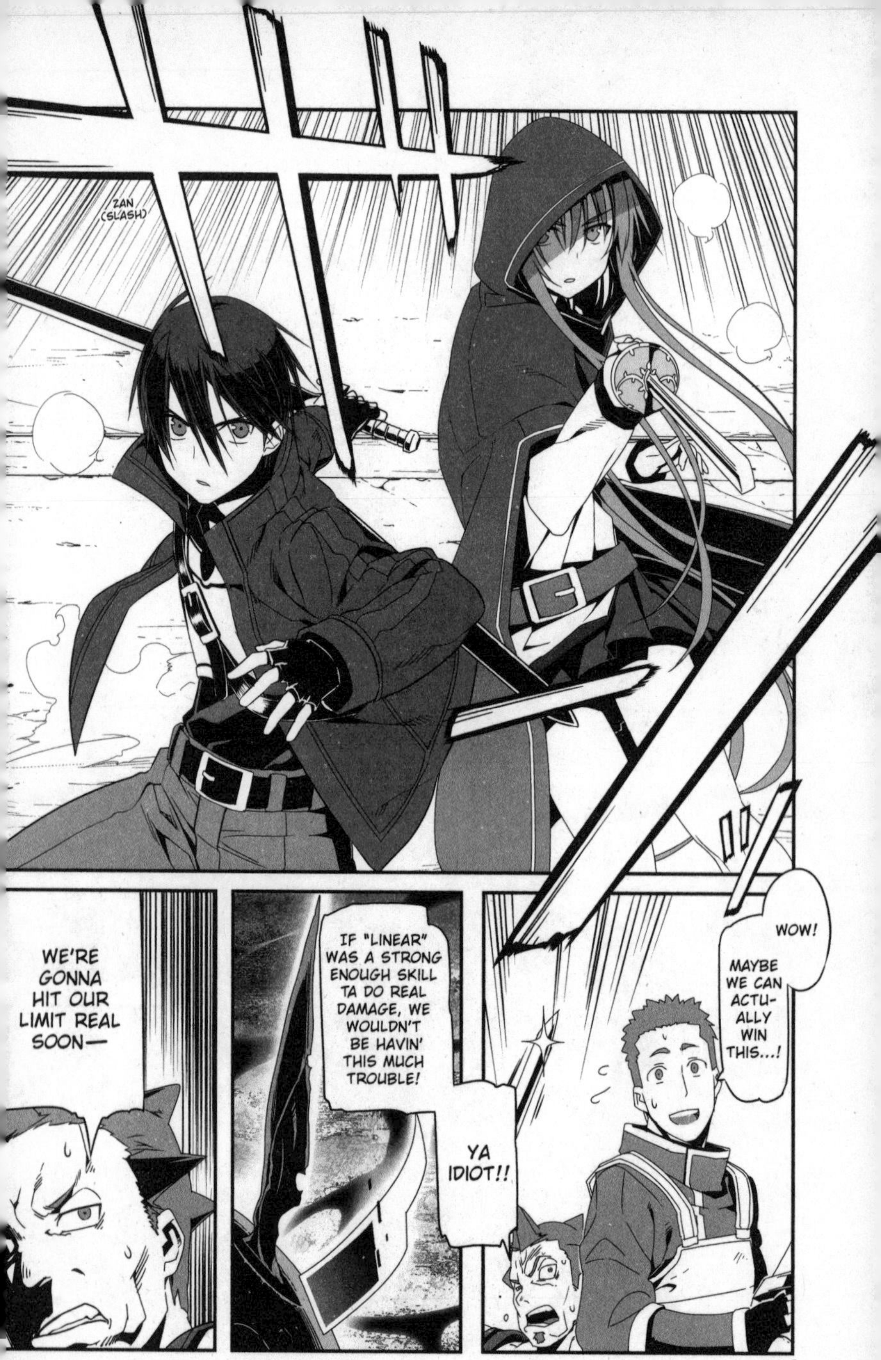
ZAN (SLASH)
WOW!
MAYBE WE CAN ACTU-ALLY WIN THIS...!
YA IDIOT!!
IF "LINEAR" WAS A STRONG ENOUGH SKILL TA DO REAL DAMAGE, WE WOULDN'T BE HAVIN' THIS MUCH TROUBLE!
WE'RE GONNA HIT OUR LIMIT REAL SOON—

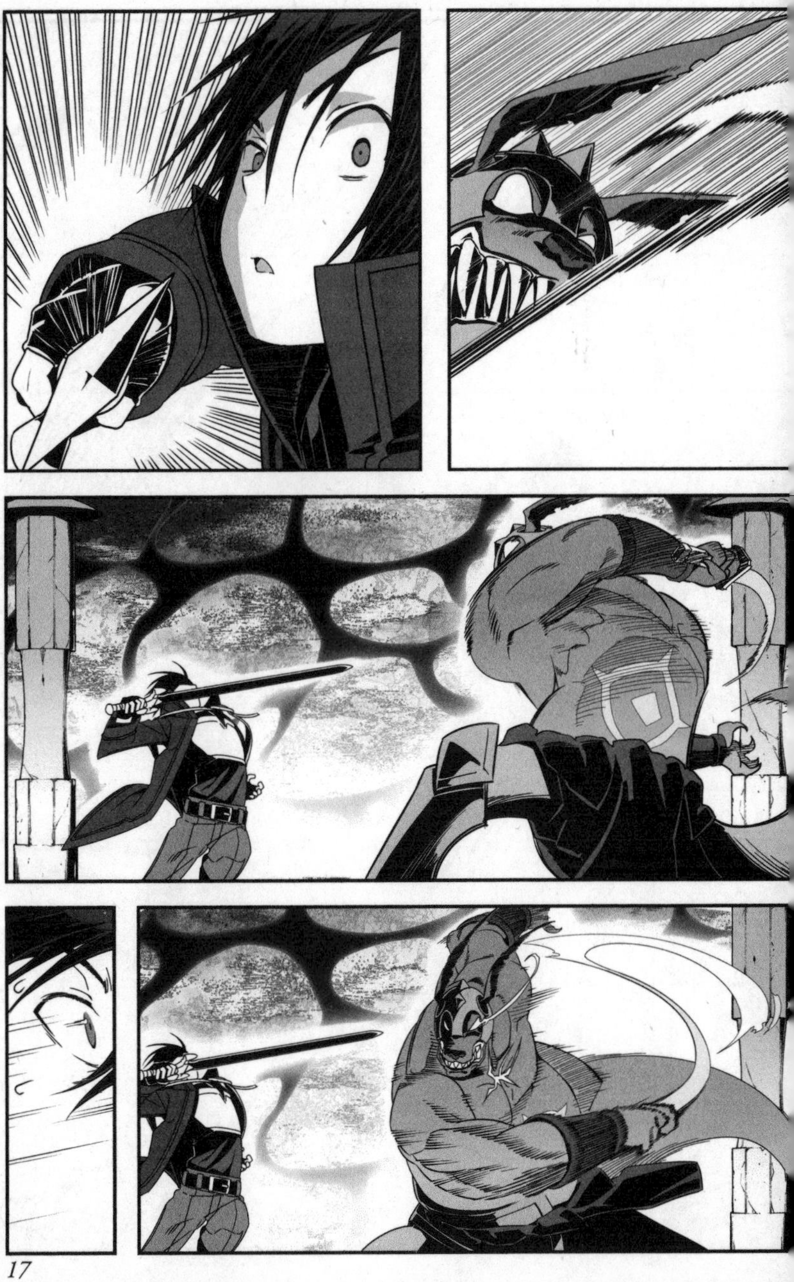

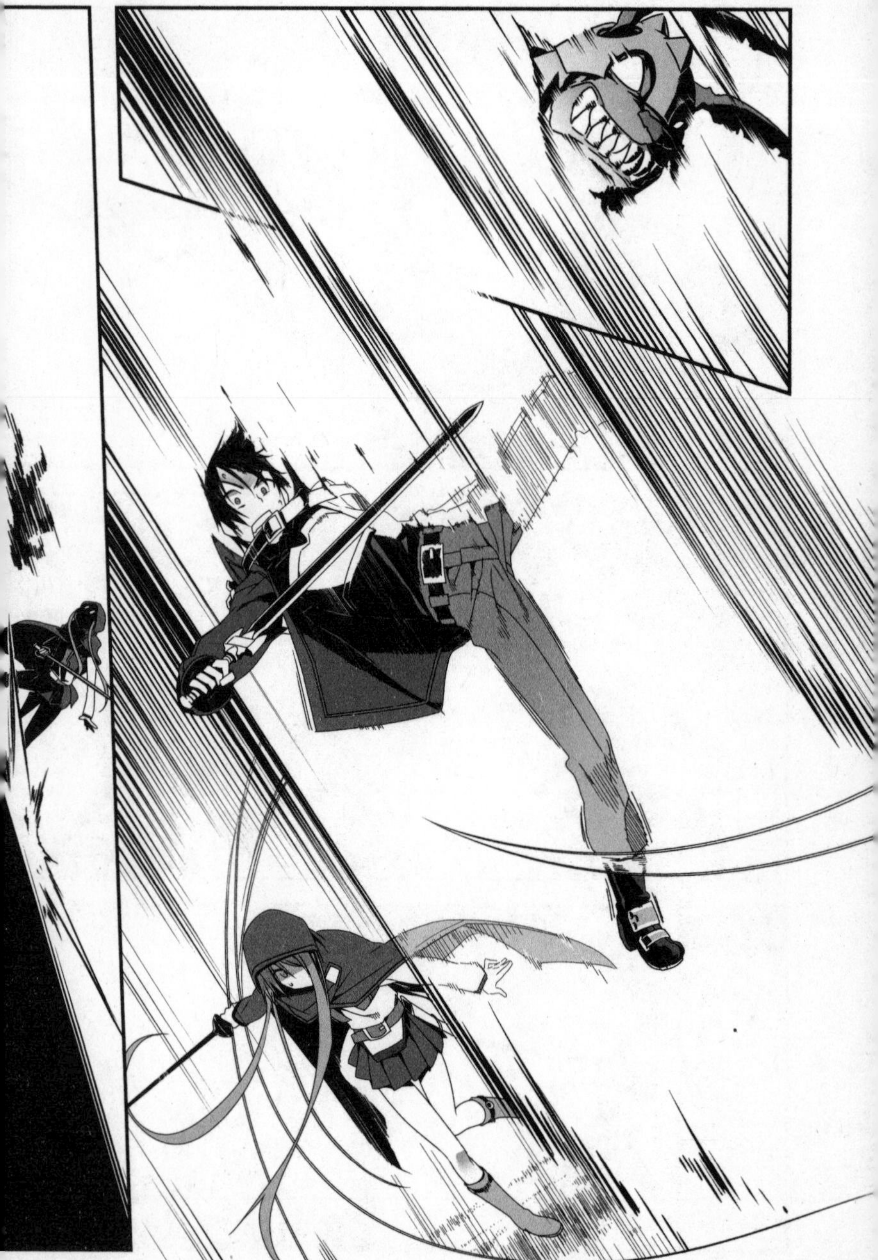

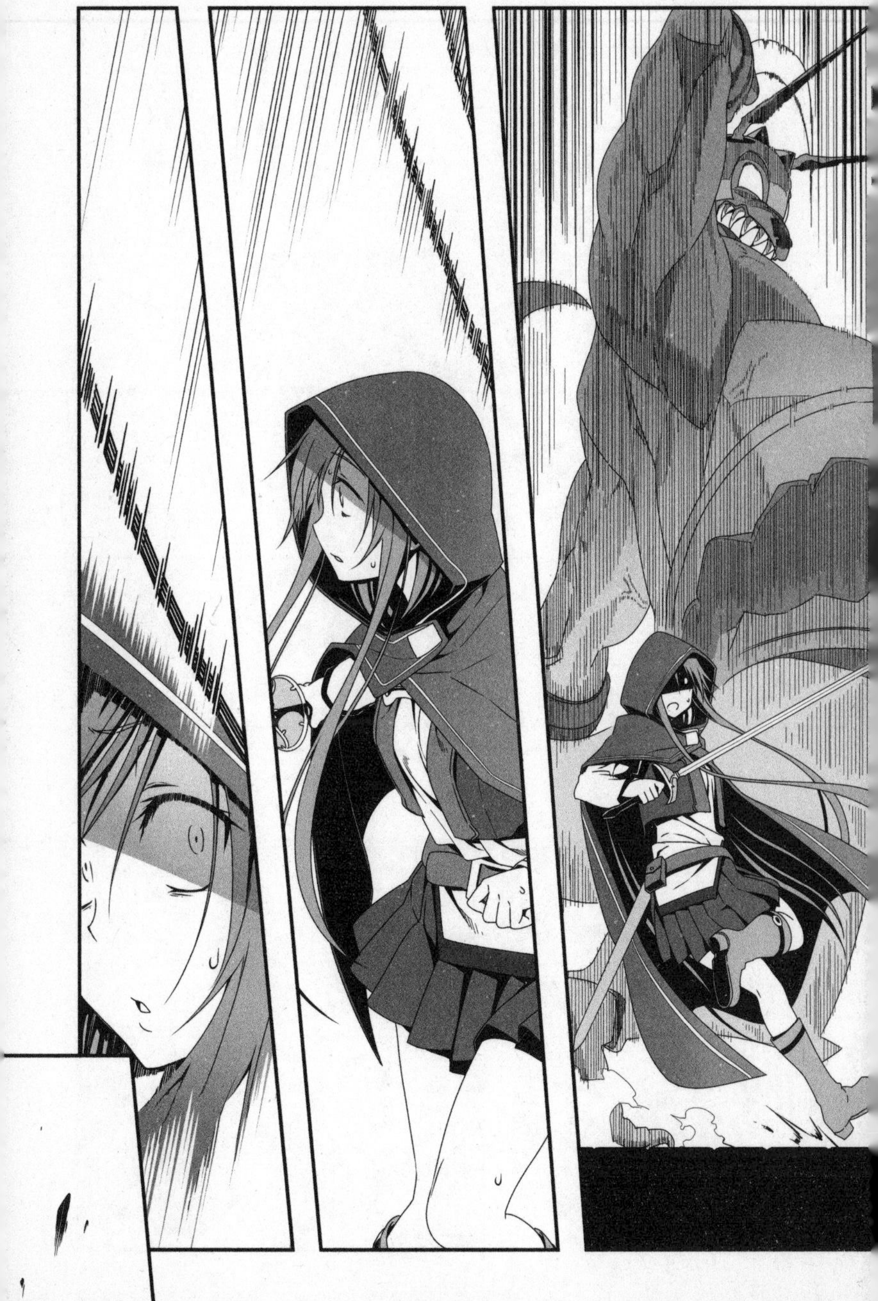

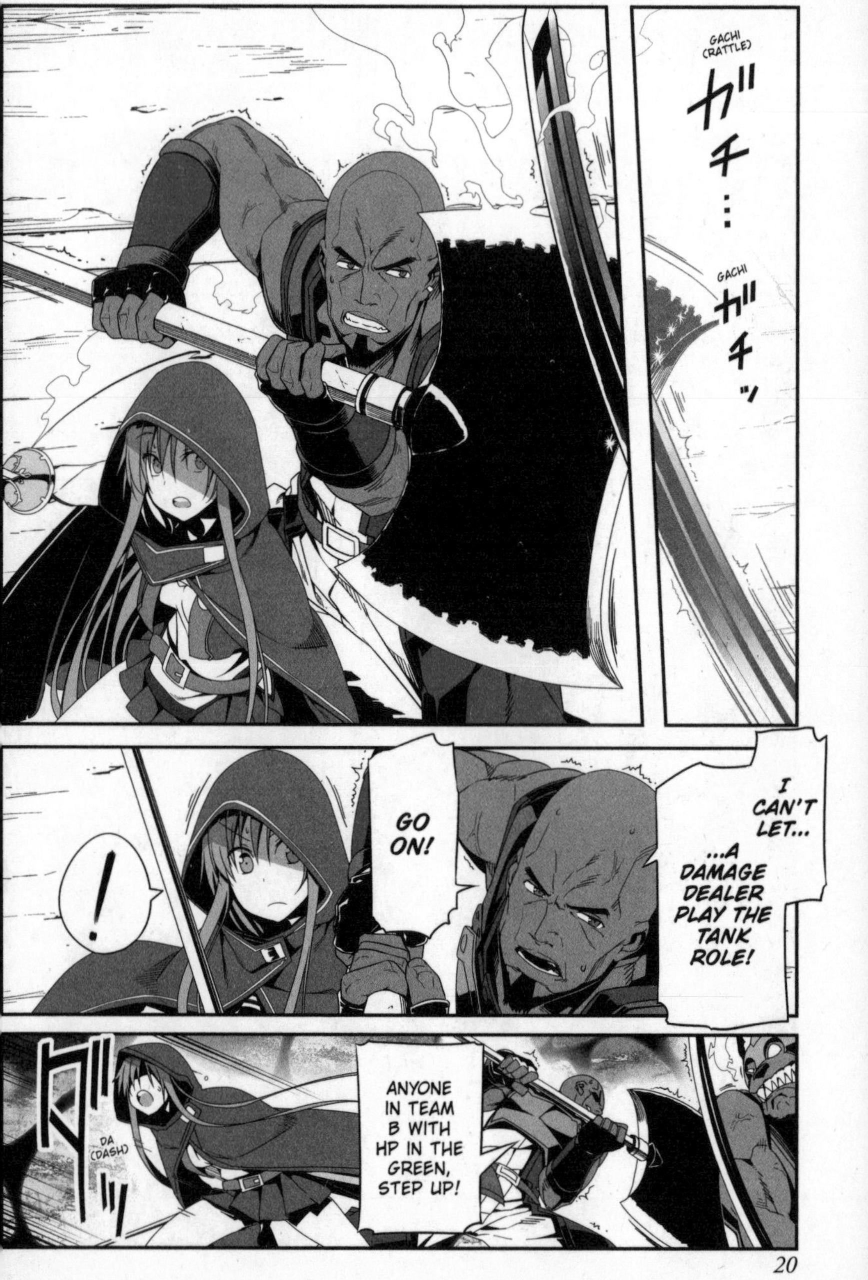
GACHI (RATTLE)
ガチ…
GACHI
ガチッ
I CAN'T LET...
...A DAMAGE DEALER PLAY THE TANK ROLE!
GO ON!
!
ANYONE IN TEAM B WITH HP IN THE GREEN, STEP UP!
DA (DASH)
ダッ

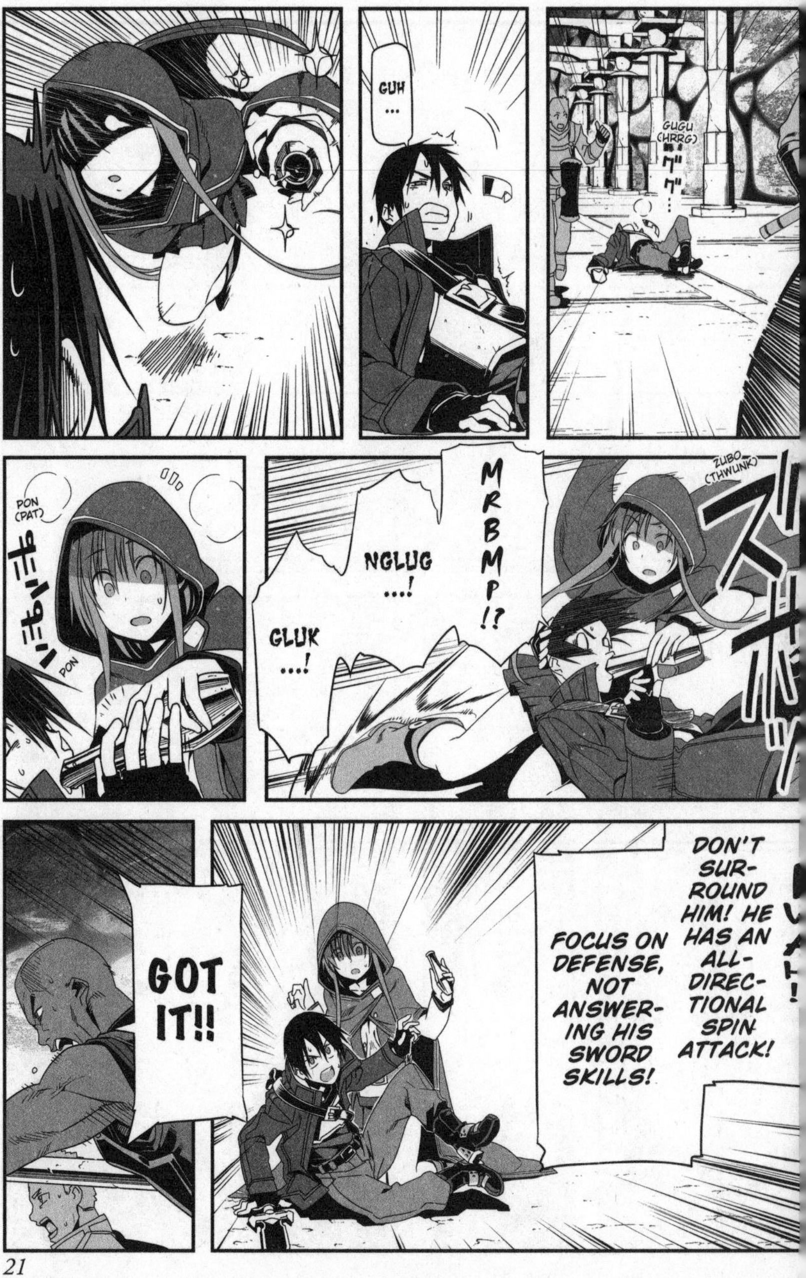
GUGU (HRRG)
GUH ...
ZUBO (THWUNK)
MRBMP!?
NGLUG ....!
GLUK ....!
PON (PAT)
PON
DON'T SURROUND HIM! HE HAS AN ALL-DIRECTIONAL SPIN ATTACK!
FOCUS ON DEFENSE, NOT ANSWERING HIS SWORD SKILLS!
GOT IT!!

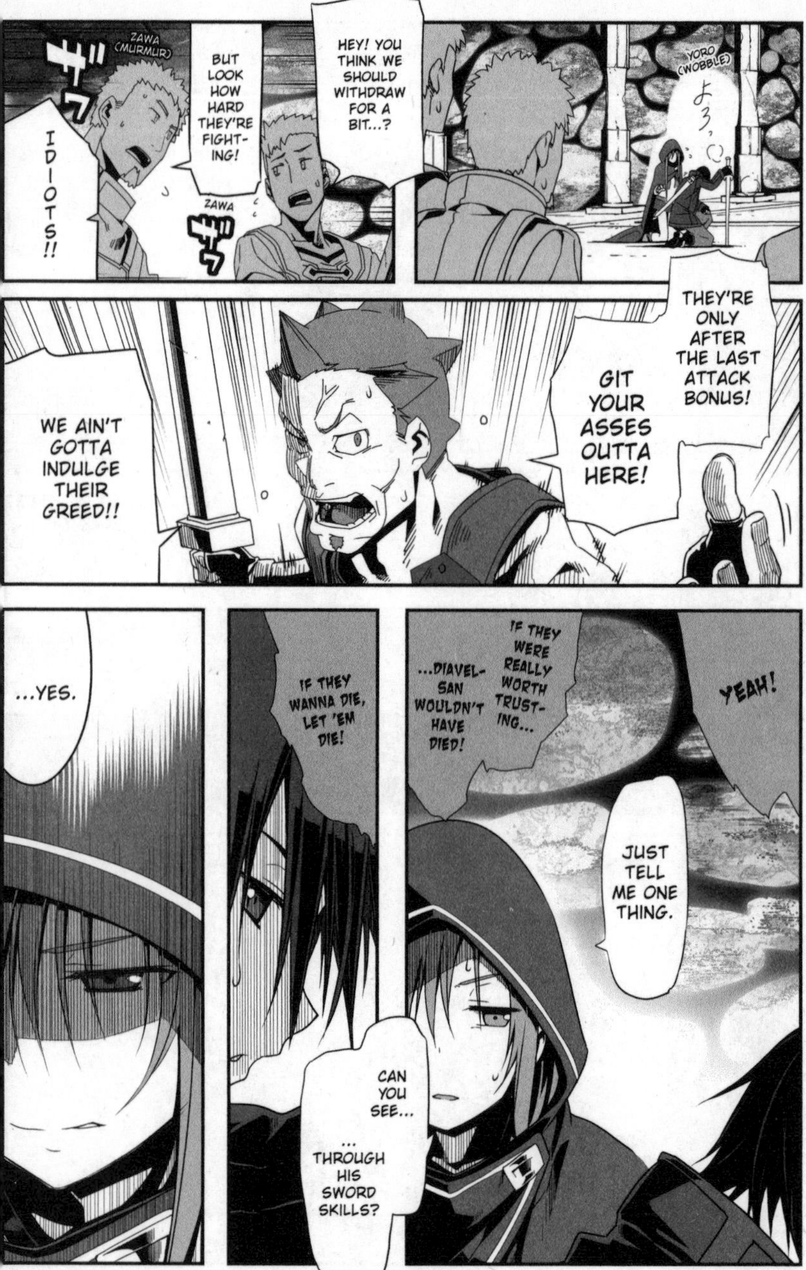

YORO (WOBBLE)
HEY! YOU THINK WE SHOULD WITHDRAW FOR A BIT...?
BUT LOOK HOW HARD THEY'RE FIGHT-ING!
ZAWA
ZAWA (MURMUR)
IDIOTS!!
THEY'RE ONLY AFTER THE LAST ATTACK BONUS!
GIT YOUR ASSES OUTTA HERE!
WE AIN'T GOTTA INDULGE THEIR GREED!!
YEAH!
IF THEY WERE REALLY WORTH TRUST-ING...
...DIAVEL-SAN WOULDN'T HAVE DIED!
JUST TELL ME ONE THING.
CAN YOU SEE...
... THROUGH HIS SWORD SKILLS?
IF THEY WANNA DIE, LET 'EM DIE!
...YES.

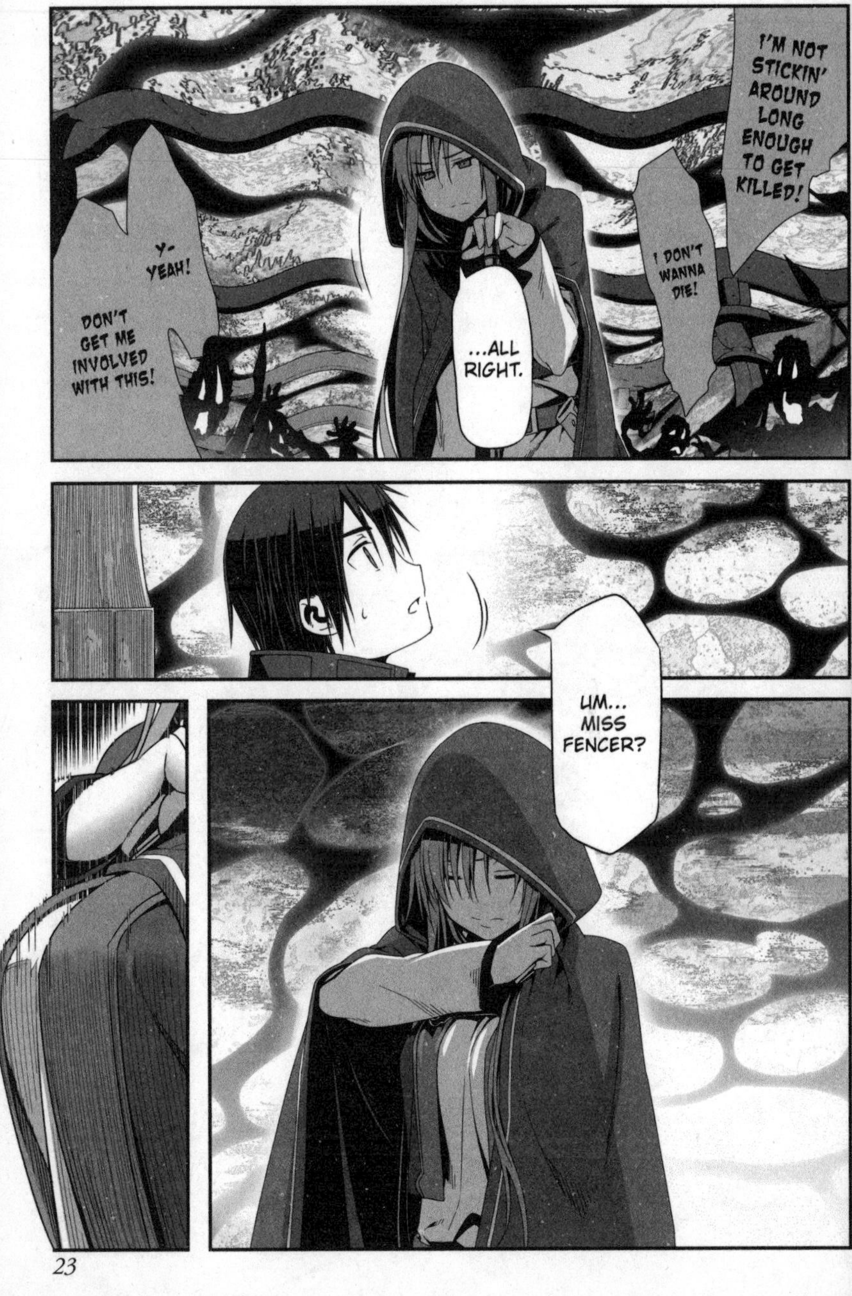
I'M NOT STICKIN' AROUND LONG ENOUGH TO GET KILLED!
I DON'T WANNA DIE!
...ALL RIGHT.
Y-YEAH!
DON'T GET ME INVOLVED WITH THIS!
UM... MISS FENCER?

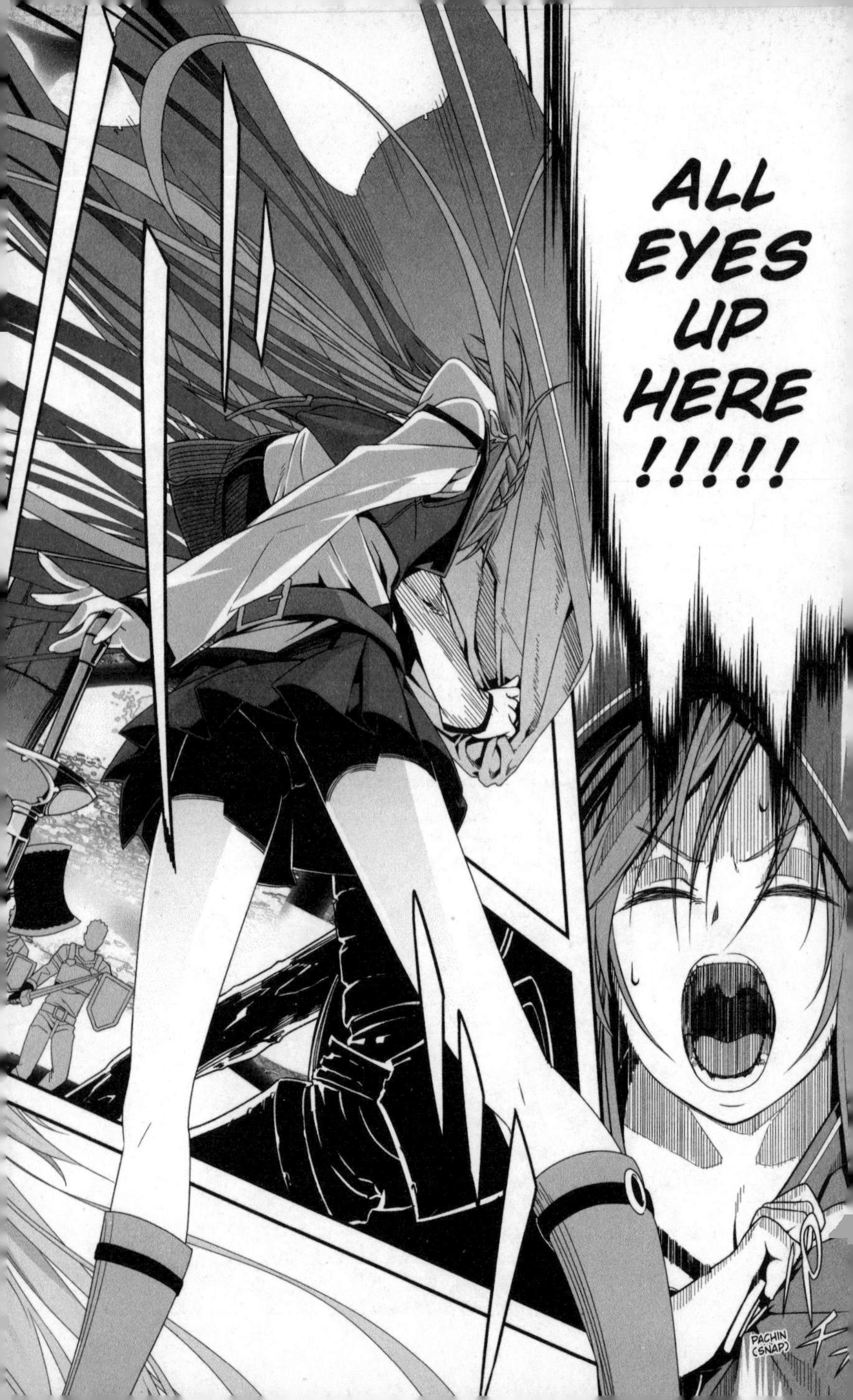
ALL EYES UP HERE!!!!!
PACHIN (SNAP)

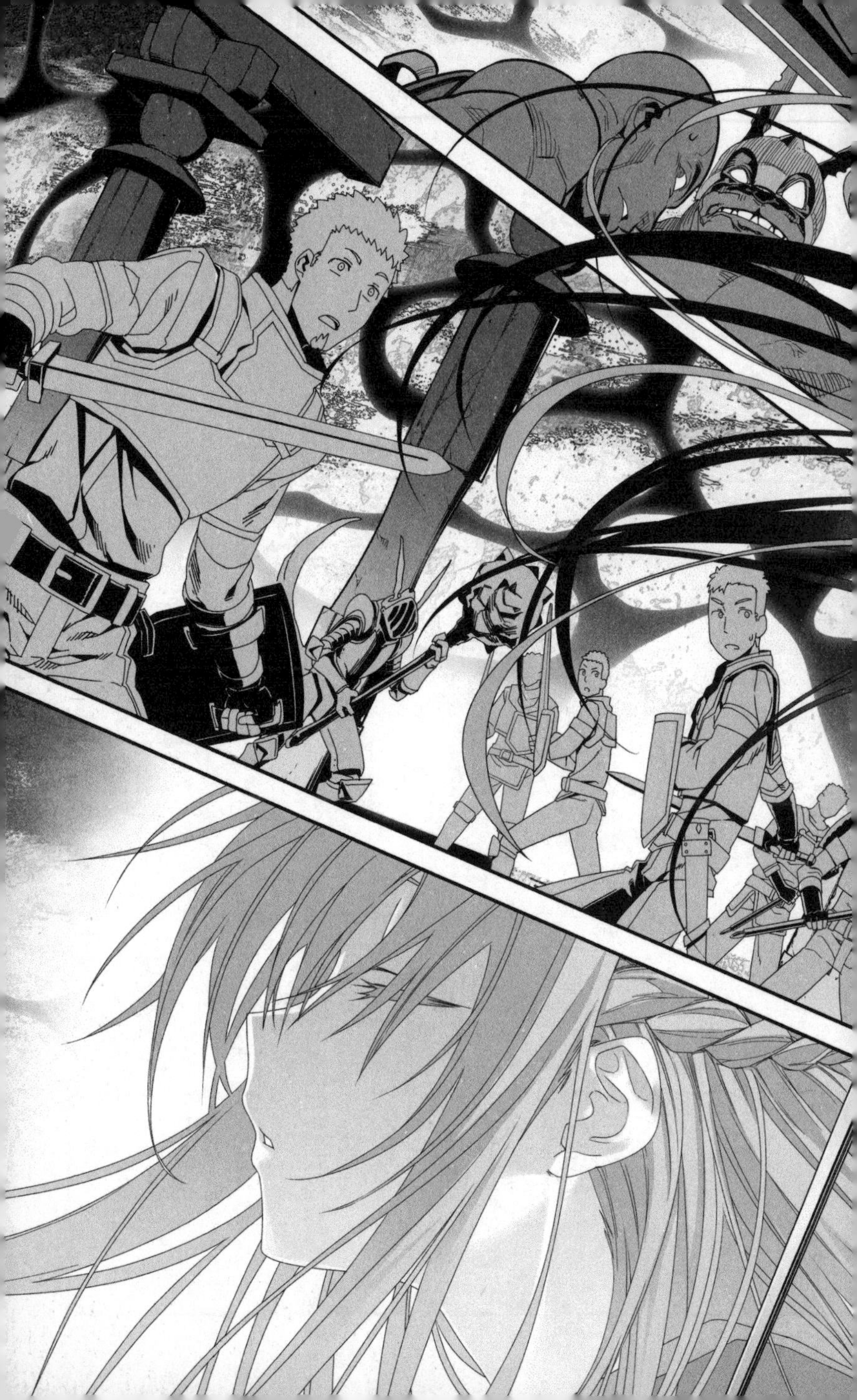

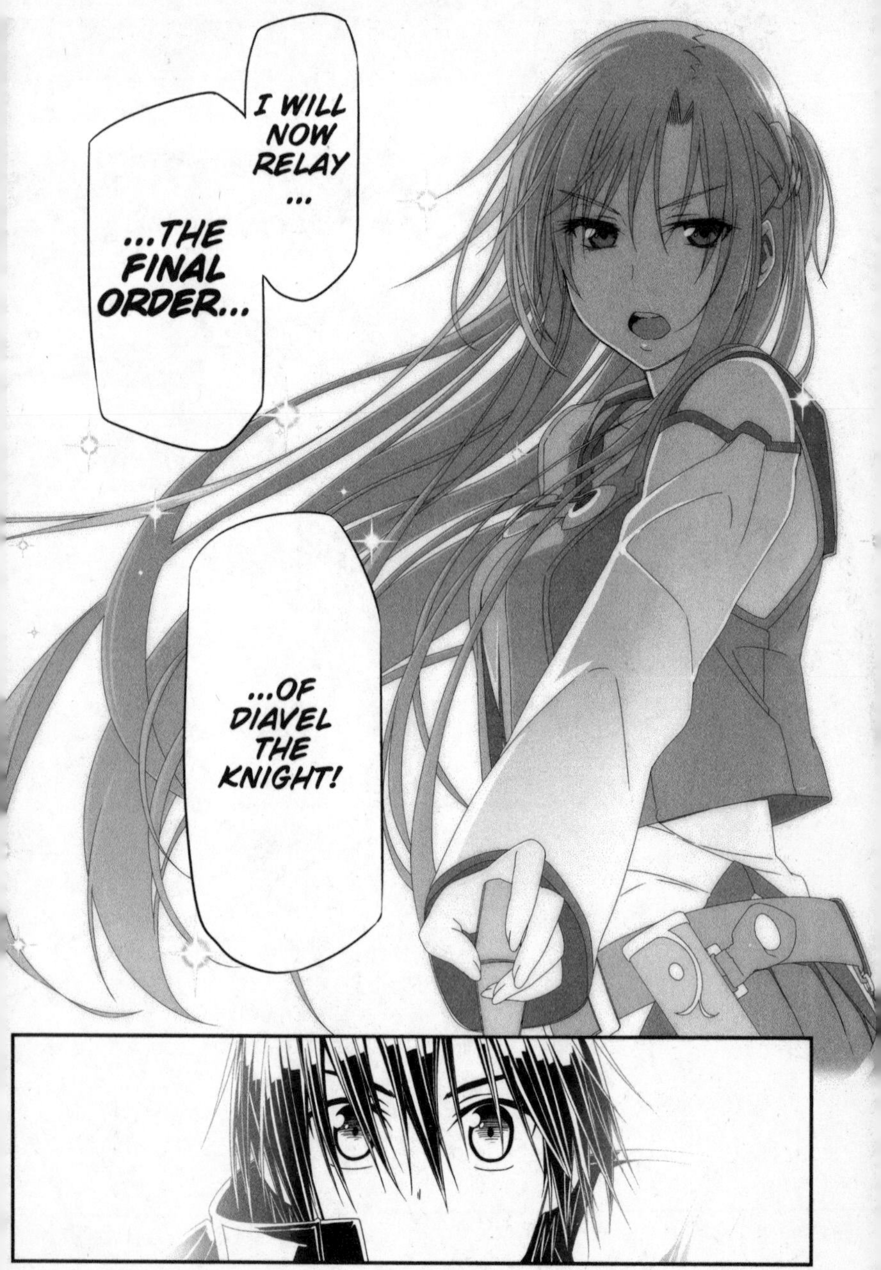
I WILL NOW RELAY ...
...THE FINAL ORDER...
...OF DIAVEL THE KNIGHT!

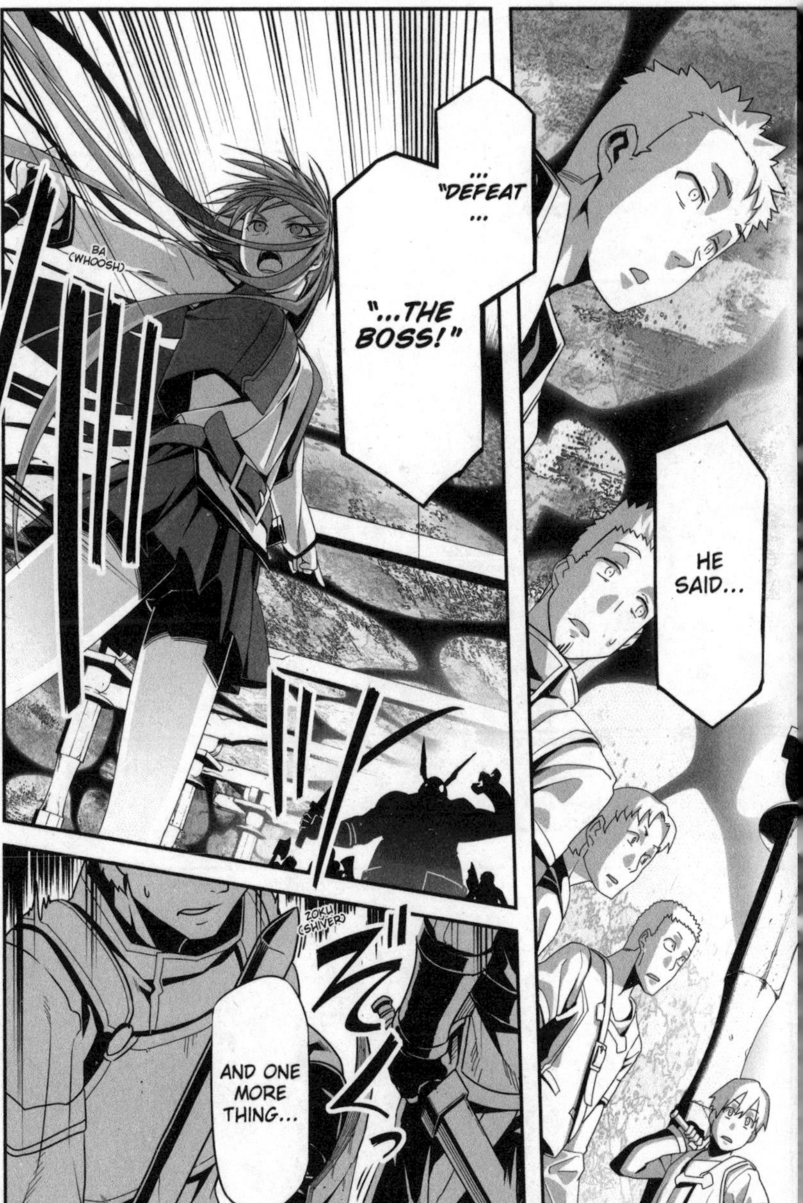
HE SAID...
..."DEFEAT...
"...THE BOSS!"
BA (WHOOSH)
ZOKU (SHIVER)
AND ONE MORE THING...

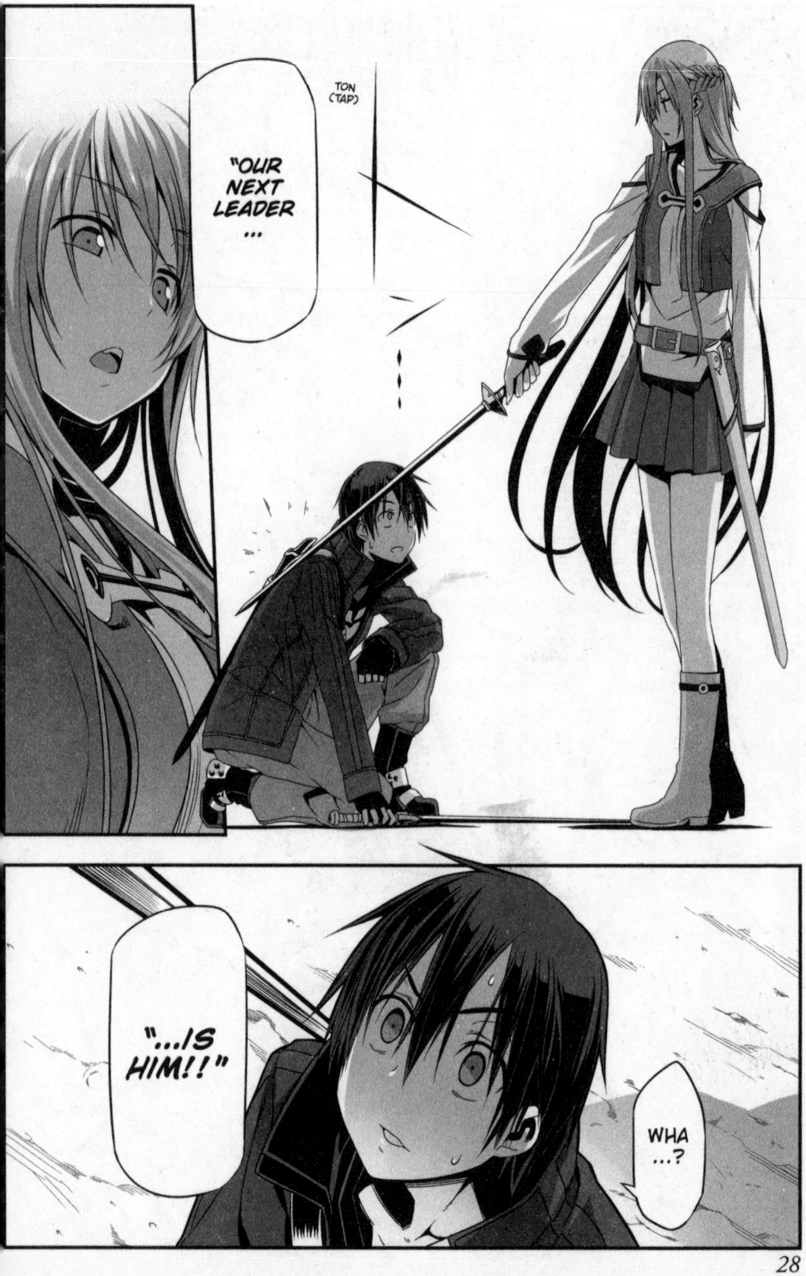
TON (TAP)
"OUR NEXT LEADER ...
"...IS HIM!!"
WHA ...?

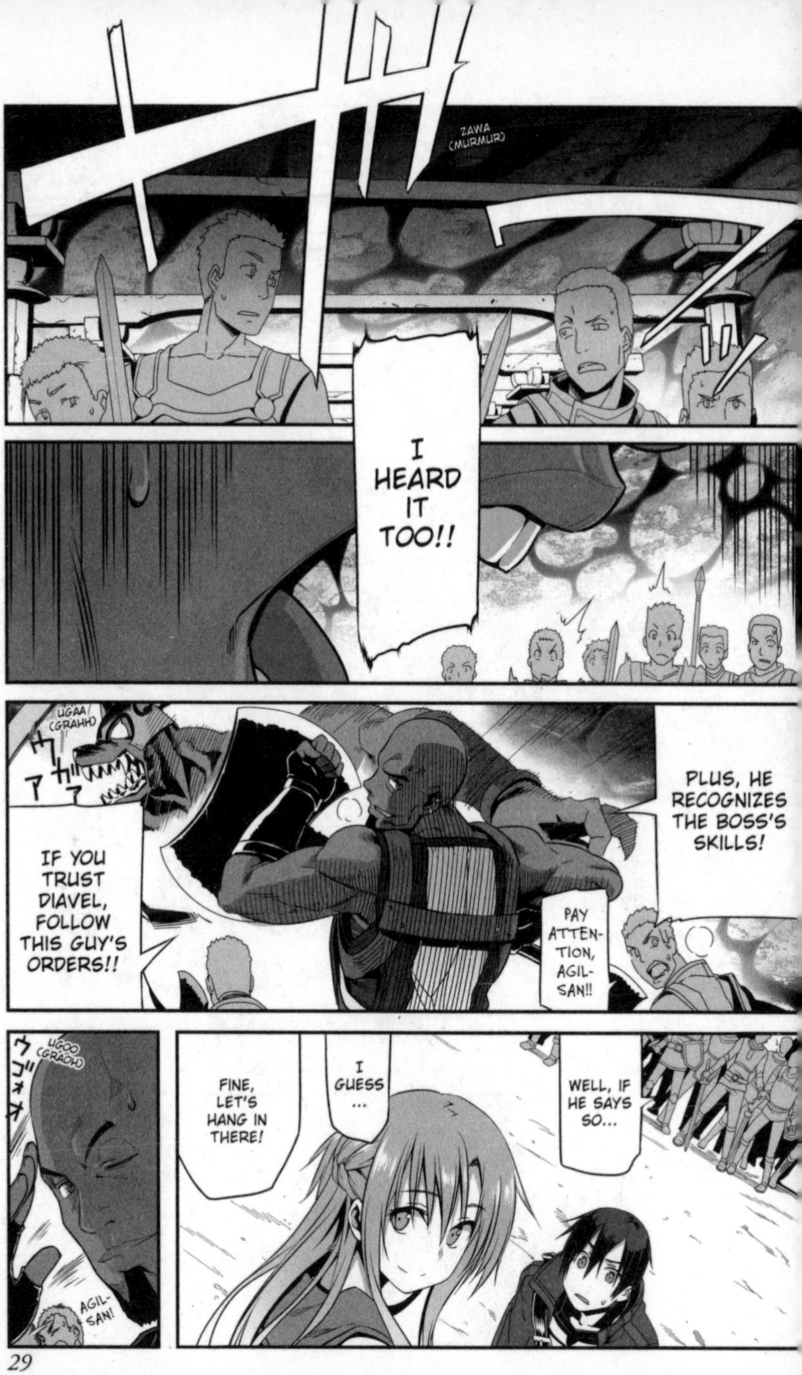
ZAWA (MURMUR)
I HEARD IT TOO!!
PLUS, HE RECOGNIZES THE BOSS'S SKILLS!
PAY ATTENTION, AGIL-SAN!!
IF YOU TRUST DIAVEL, FOLLOW THIS GUY'S ORDERS!!
UGAA (GRAHH)
WELL, IF HE SAYS SO...
I GUESS ...
FINE, LET'S HANG IN THERE!
UGOO (GRAOH)
AGIL-SAN!

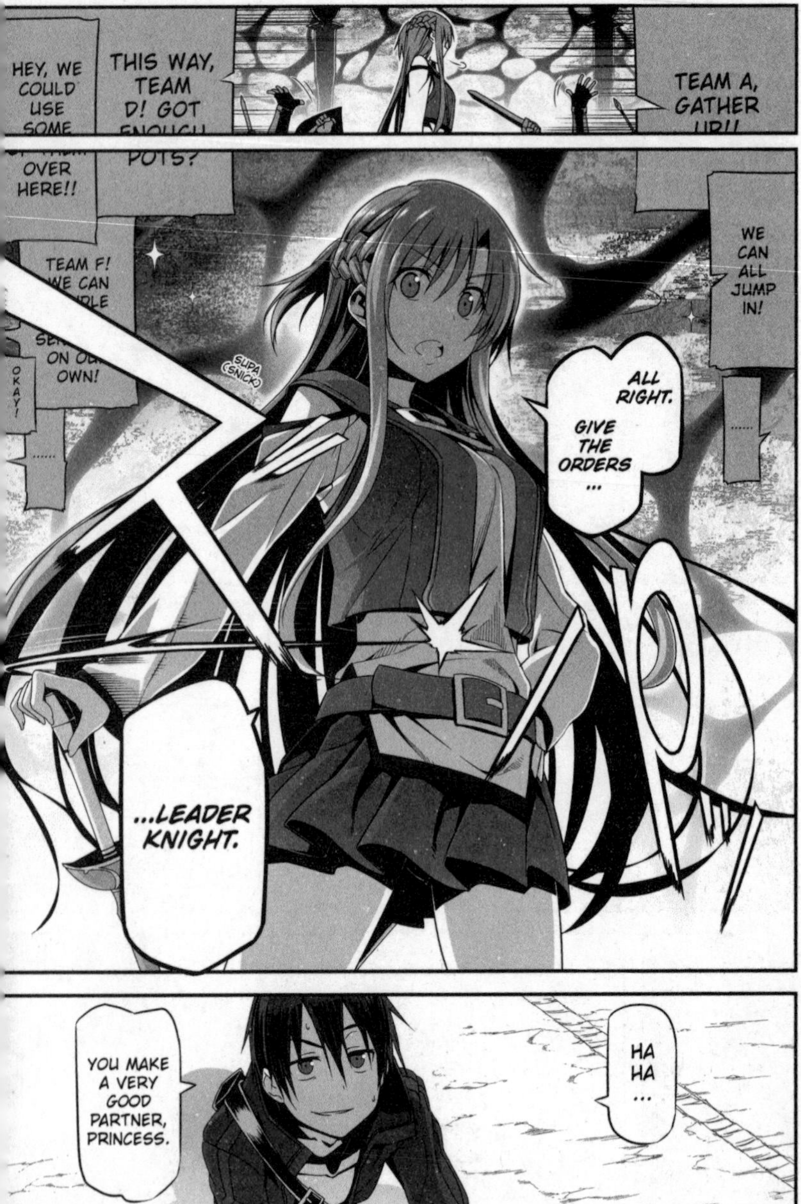

TEAM A, GATHER UP!!
THIS WAY, TEAM D! GOT POTS?
HEY, WE COULD USE SOME OVER HERE!!
WE CAN ALL JUMP IN!
......
ALL RIGHT. GIVE THE ORDERS ...
SUPA (SNICK)
TEAM F! WE CAN ON OUR OWN!
OKAY!
......
...LEADER KNIGHT.
HA HA ...
YOU MAKE A VERY GOOD PARTNER, PRINCESS.

#006.5: Scapegoat

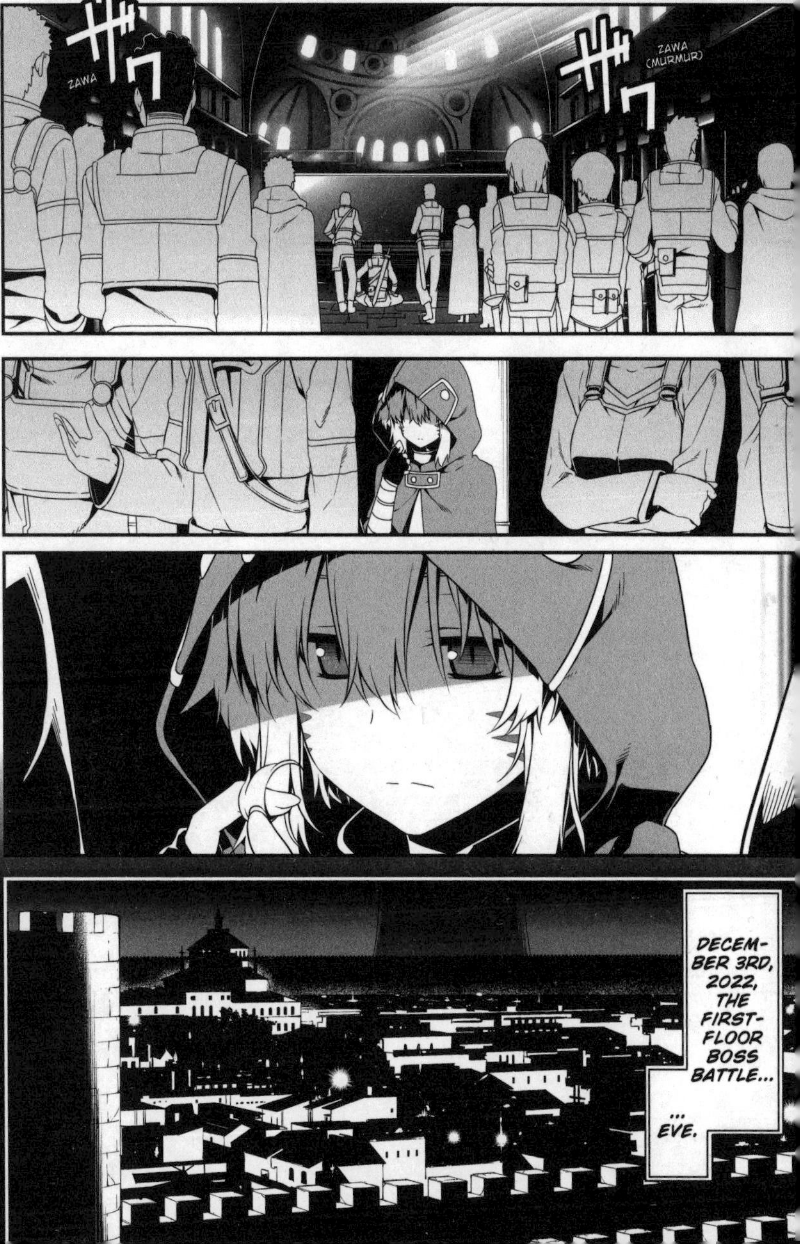
ザワ
ZAWA (MURMUR)
ザワ
ZAWA
DECEMBER 3RD, 2022, THE FIRST-FLOOR BOSS BATTLE...
...EVE.

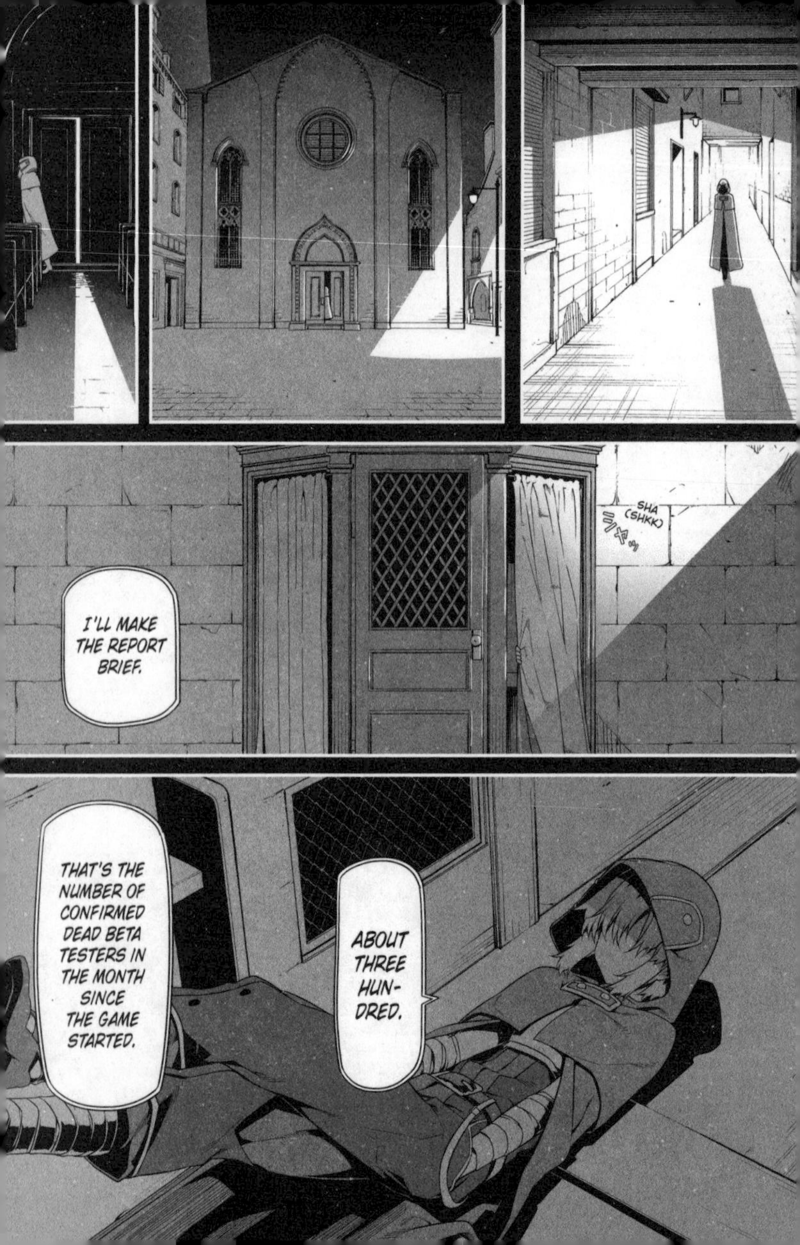
シャッ
SHA (SHKK)
I'LL MAKE THE REPORT BRIEF.
ABOUT THREE HUN-DRED.
THAT'S THE NUMBER OF CONFIRMED DEAD BETA TESTERS IN THE MONTH SINCE THE GAME STARTED.

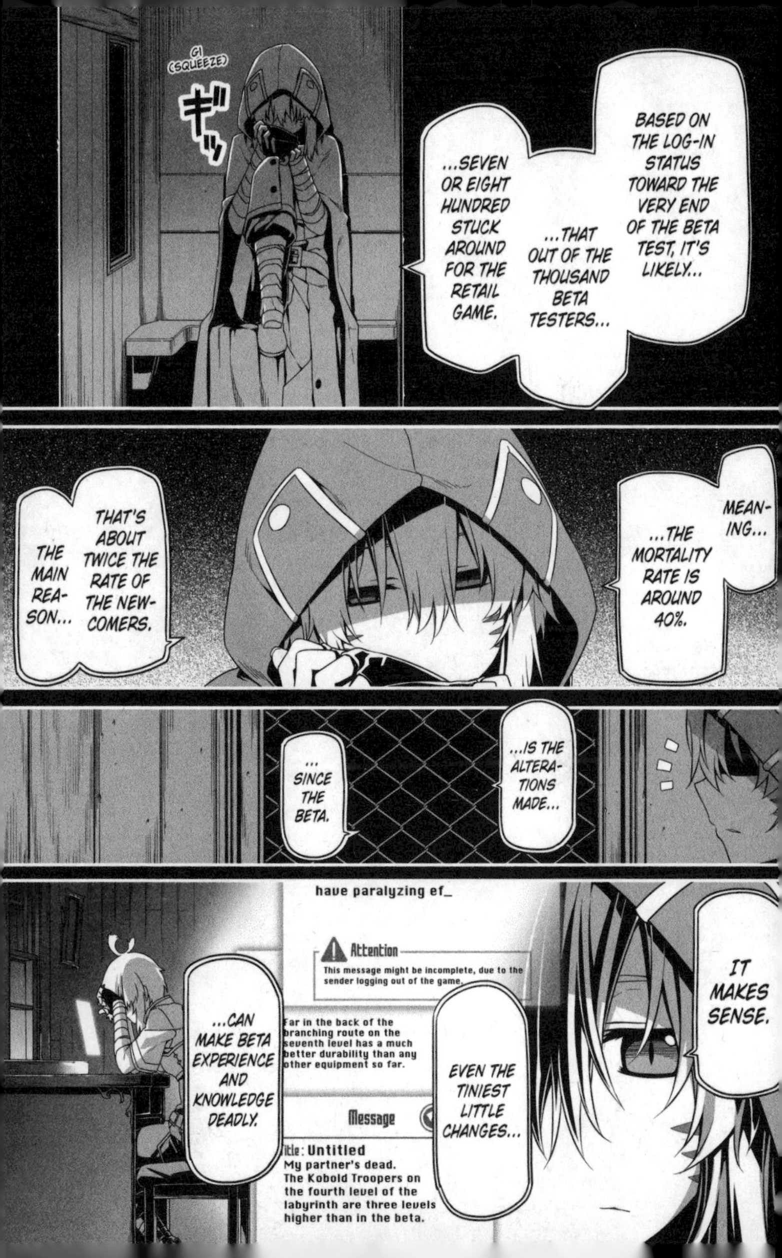
BASED ON THE LOG-IN STATUS TOWARD THE VERY END OF THE BETA TEST, IT'S LIKELY...
...THAT OUT OF THE THOUSAND BETA TESTERS...
...SEVEN OR EIGHT HUNDRED STUCK AROUND FOR THE RETAIL GAME.
GI (SQUEEZE)
ギッ
MEAN-ING...
...THE MORTALITY RATE IS AROUND 40%.
THAT'S ABOUT TWICE THE RATE OF THE NEW-COMERS.
THE MAIN REA-SON...
...IS THE ALTERA-TIONS MADE...
...SINCE THE BETA.
IT MAKES SENSE.
have paralyzing ef_
Attention
This message might be incomplete, due to the sender logging out of the game.
EVEN THE TINIEST LITTLE CHANGES...
Far in the back of the branching route on the seventh level has a much better durability than any other equipment so far.
Message
itle: Untitled
My partner's dead. The Kobold Troopers on the fourth level of the labyrinth are three levels higher than in the beta.
...CAN MAKE BETA EXPERIENCE AND KNOWLEDGE DEADLY.

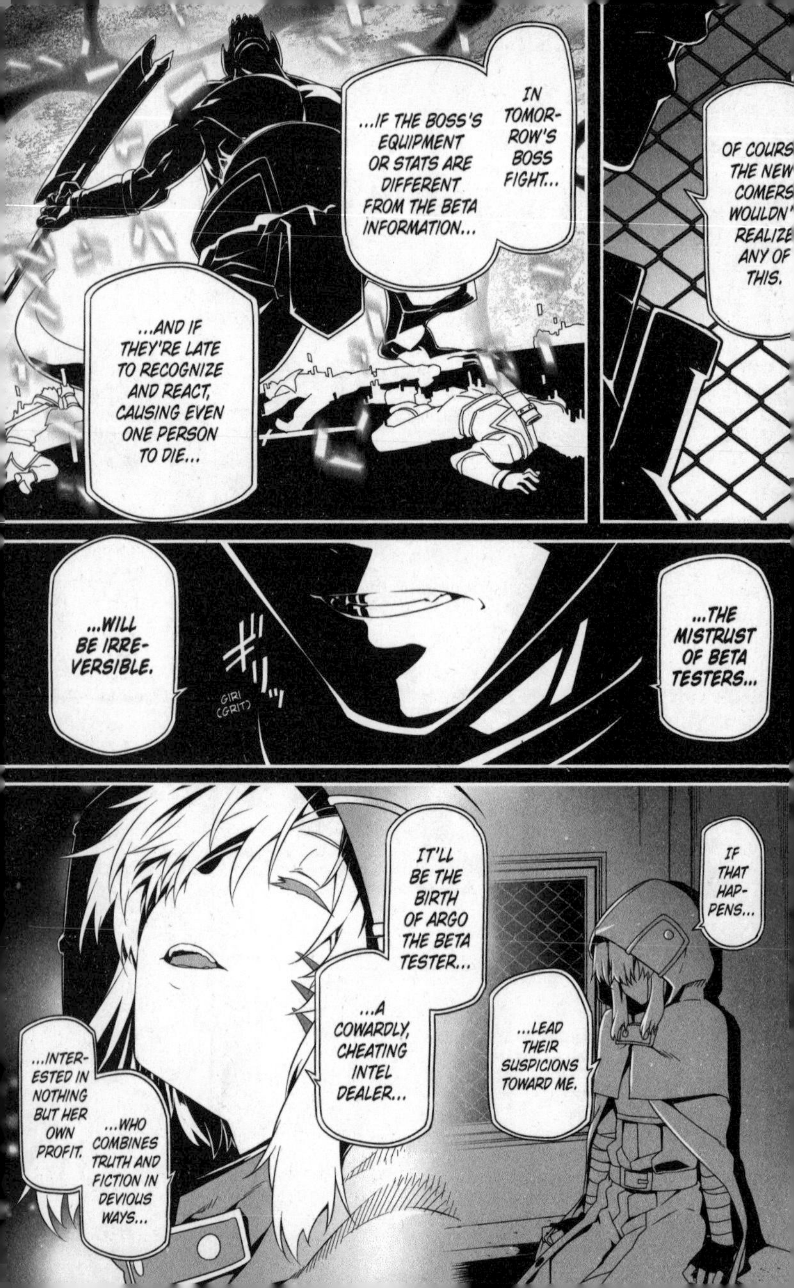
OF COURS THE NEWCOMERS WOULDN' REALIZE ANY OF THIS.
IN TOMORROW'S BOSS FIGHT...
...IF THE BOSS'S EQUIPMENT OR STATS ARE DIFFERENT FROM THE BETA INFORMATION...
...AND IF THEY'RE LATE TO RECOGNIZE AND REACT, CAUSING EVEN ONE PERSON TO DIE...
...THE MISTRUST OF BETA TESTERS...
GIRI (GRIT)
...WILL BE IRREVERSIBLE.
IF THAT HAPPENS...
...LEAD THEIR SUSPICIONS TOWARD ME.
IT'LL BE THE BIRTH OF ARGO THE BETA TESTER...
...A COWARDLY, CHEATING INTEL DEALER...
...INTERESTED IN NOTHING BUT HER OWN PROFIT.
...WHO COMBINES TRUTH AND FICTION IN DEVIOUS WAYS...

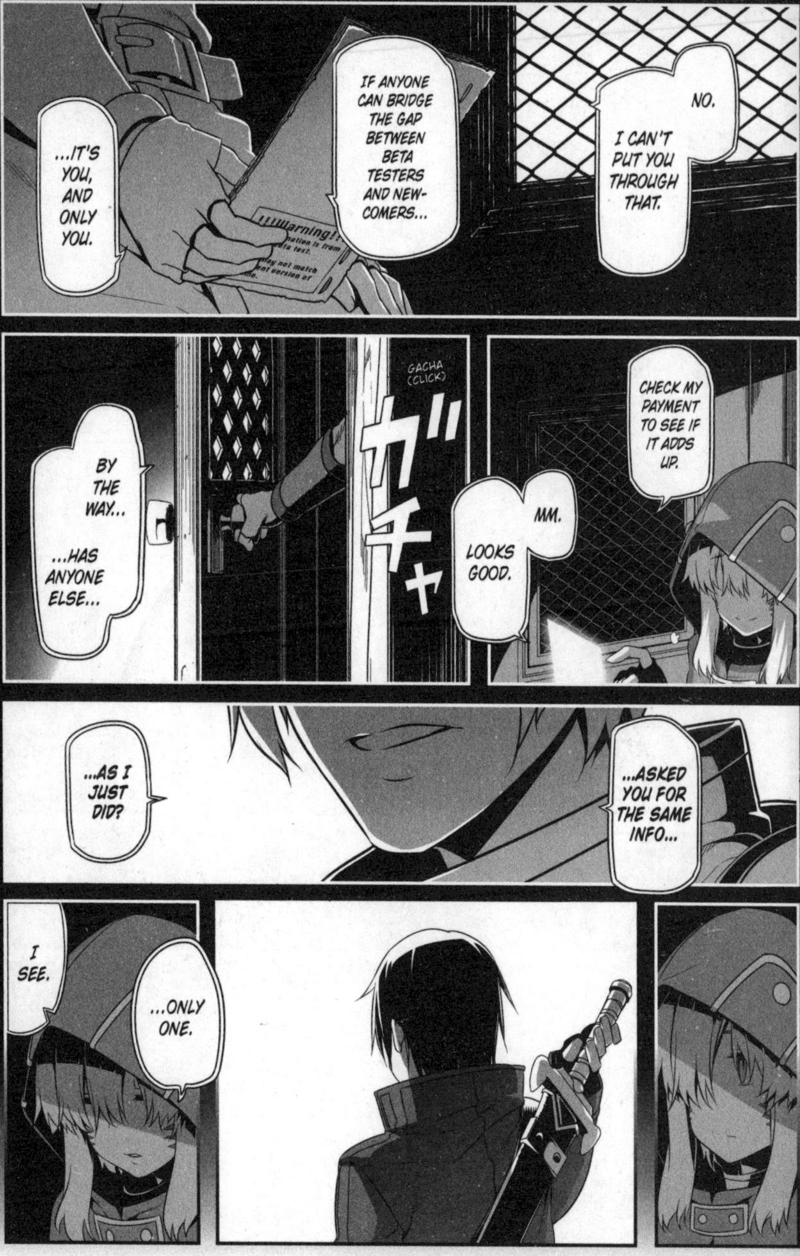
NO.
I CAN'T PUT YOU THROUGH THAT.
IF ANYONE CAN BRIDGE THE GAP BETWEEN BETA TESTERS AND NEW-COMERS...
...IT'S YOU, AND ONLY YOU.
CHECK MY PAYMENT TO SEE IF IT ADDS UP.
MM.
LOOKS GOOD.
ガチャ
GACHA (CLICK)
BY THE WAY...
...HAS ANYONE ELSE...
...ASKED YOU FOR THE SAME INFO...
...AS I JUST DID?
...ONLY ONE.
I SEE.

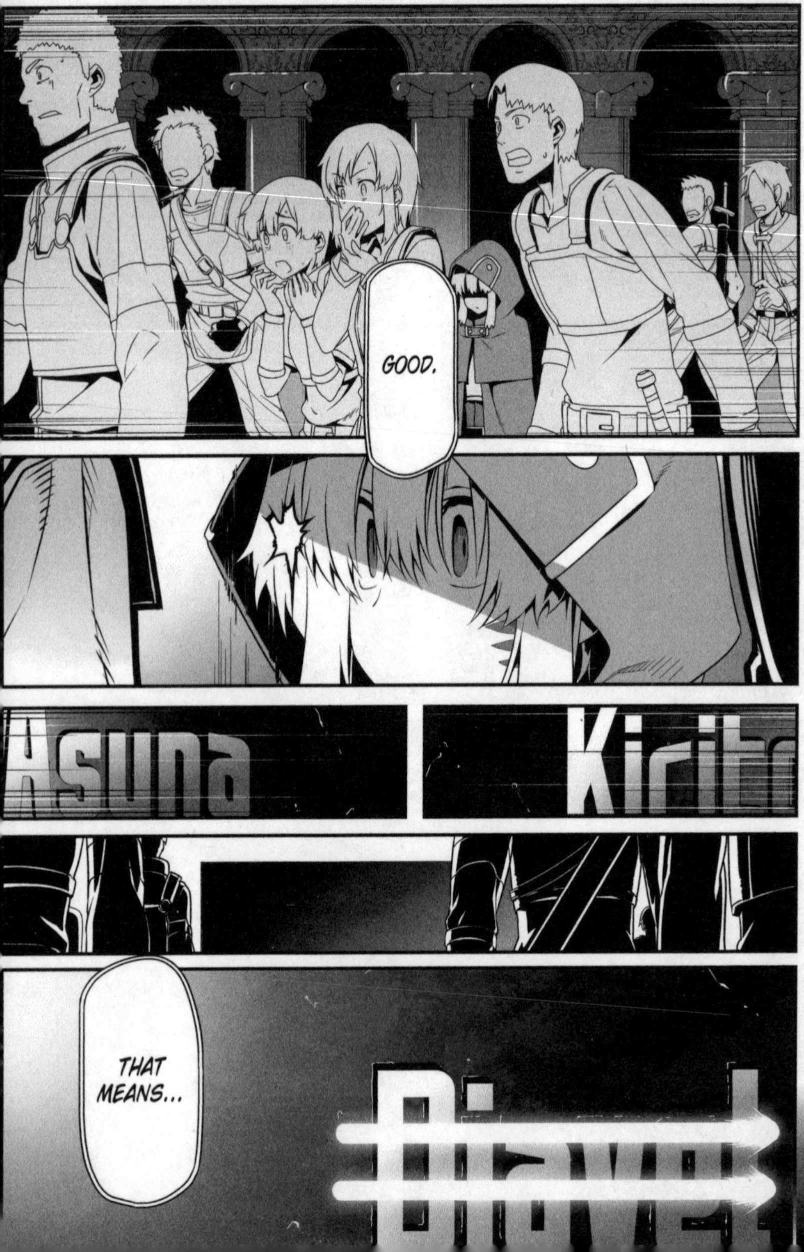
GOOD.
Kirit
Asuna
THAT MEANS...
Diavel

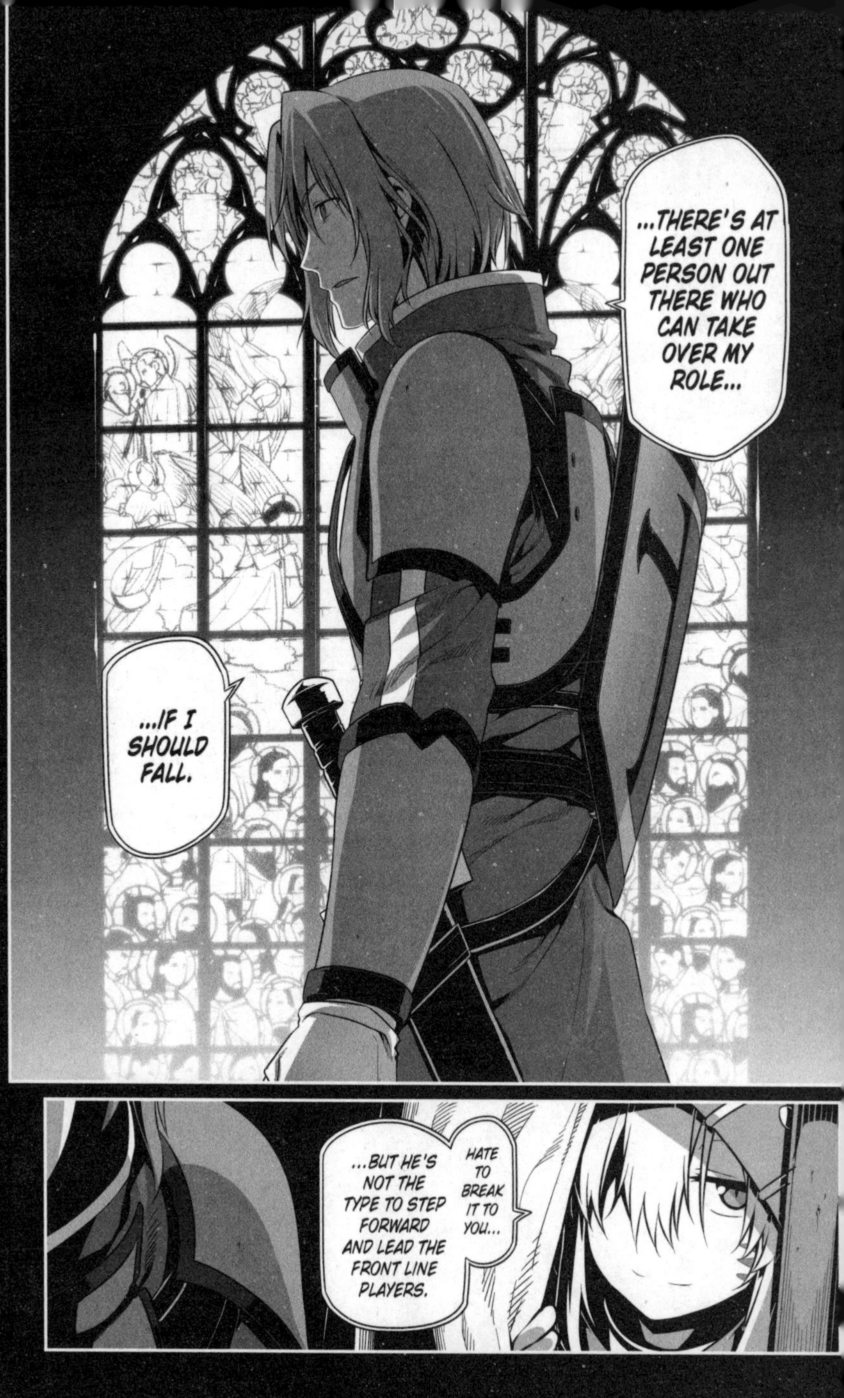
...THERE'S AT LEAST ONE PERSON OUT THERE WHO CAN TAKE OVER MY ROLE...
...IF I SHOULD FALL.
HATE TO BREAK IT TO YOU...
...BUT HE'S NOT THE TYPE TO STEP FORWARD AND LEAD THE FRONT LINE PLAYERS.

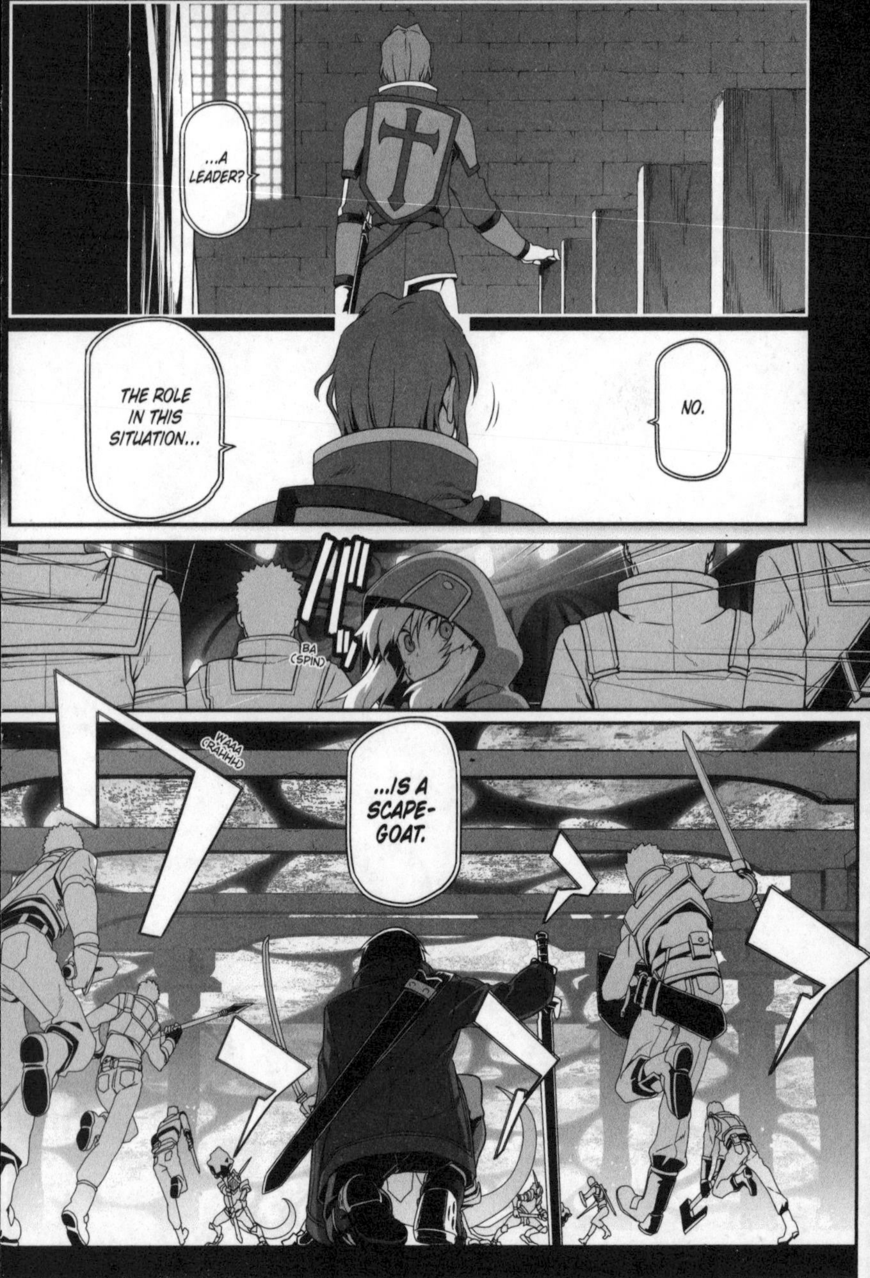
...A LEADER?
NO.
THE ROLE IN THIS SITUATION...
BA (SPIN)
...IS A SCAPE-GOAT.
WAAA (RAHHH)

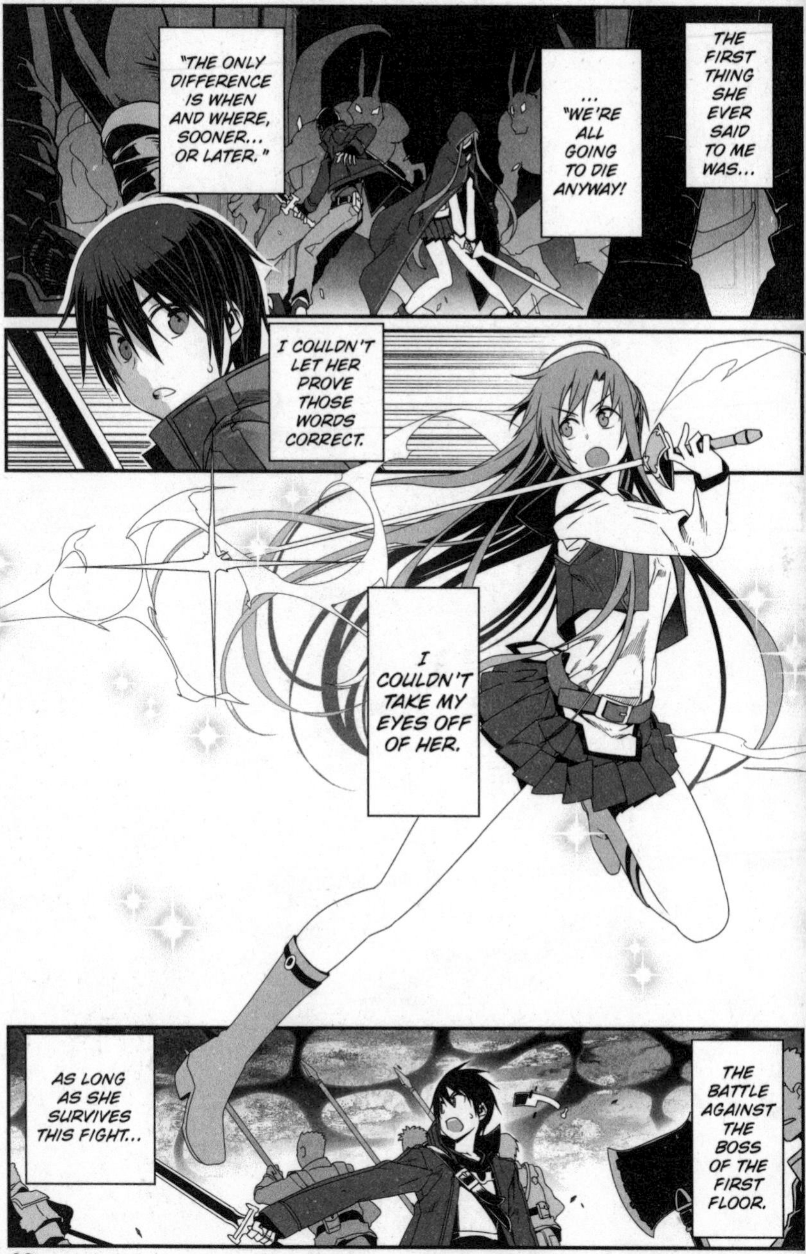
THE FIRST THING SHE EVER SAID TO ME WAS...
... "WE'RE ALL GOING TO DIE ANYWAY!
"THE ONLY DIFFERENCE IS WHEN AND WHERE, SOONER... OR LATER."
I COULDN'T LET HER PROVE THOSE WORDS CORRECT.
I COULDN'T TAKE MY EYES OFF OF HER.
THE BATTLE AGAINST THE BOSS OF THE FIRST FLOOR.
AS LONG AS SHE SURVIVES THIS FIGHT...

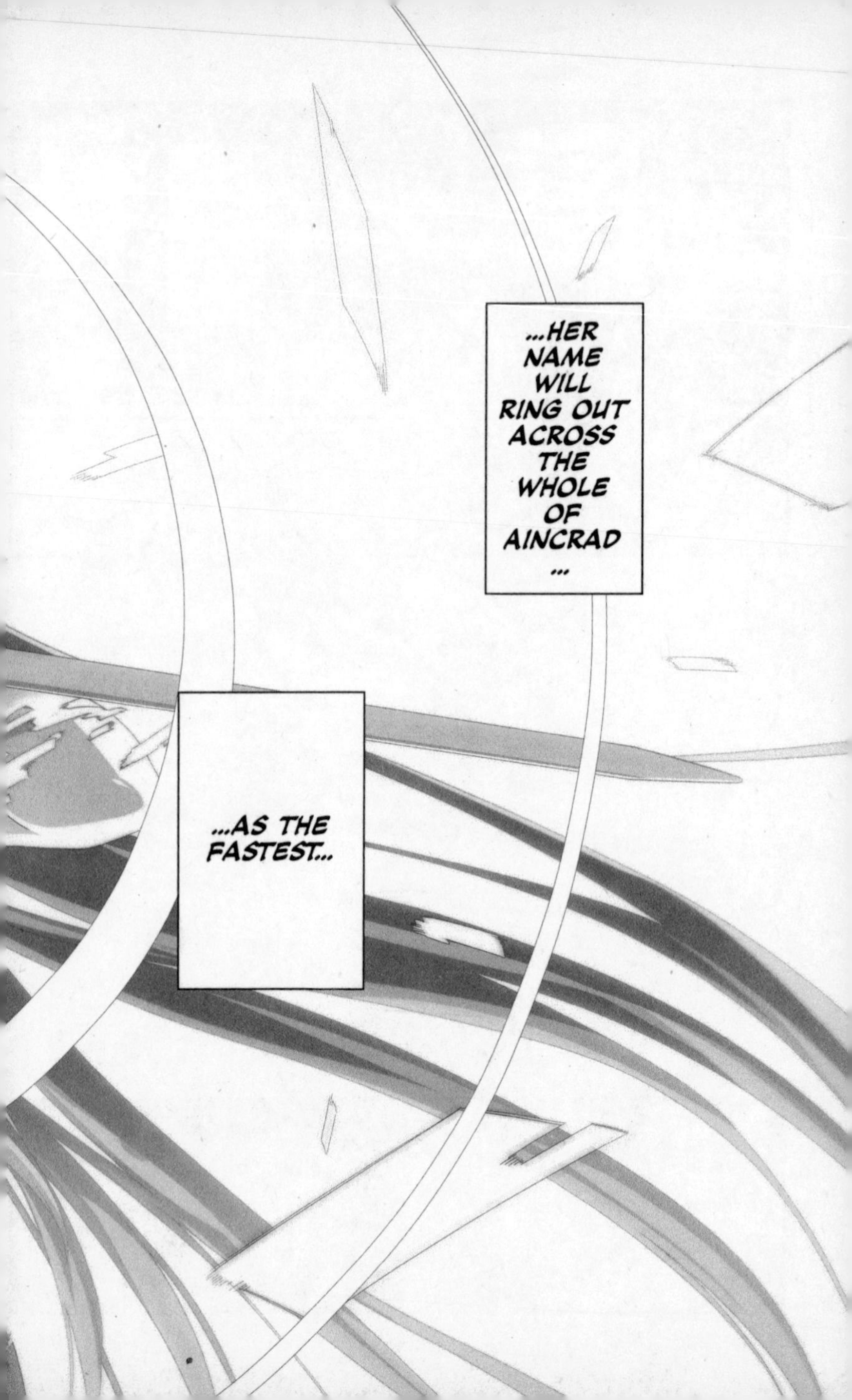
...HER NAME WILL RING OUT ACROSS THE WHOLE OF AINCRAD ...
...AS THE FASTEST...

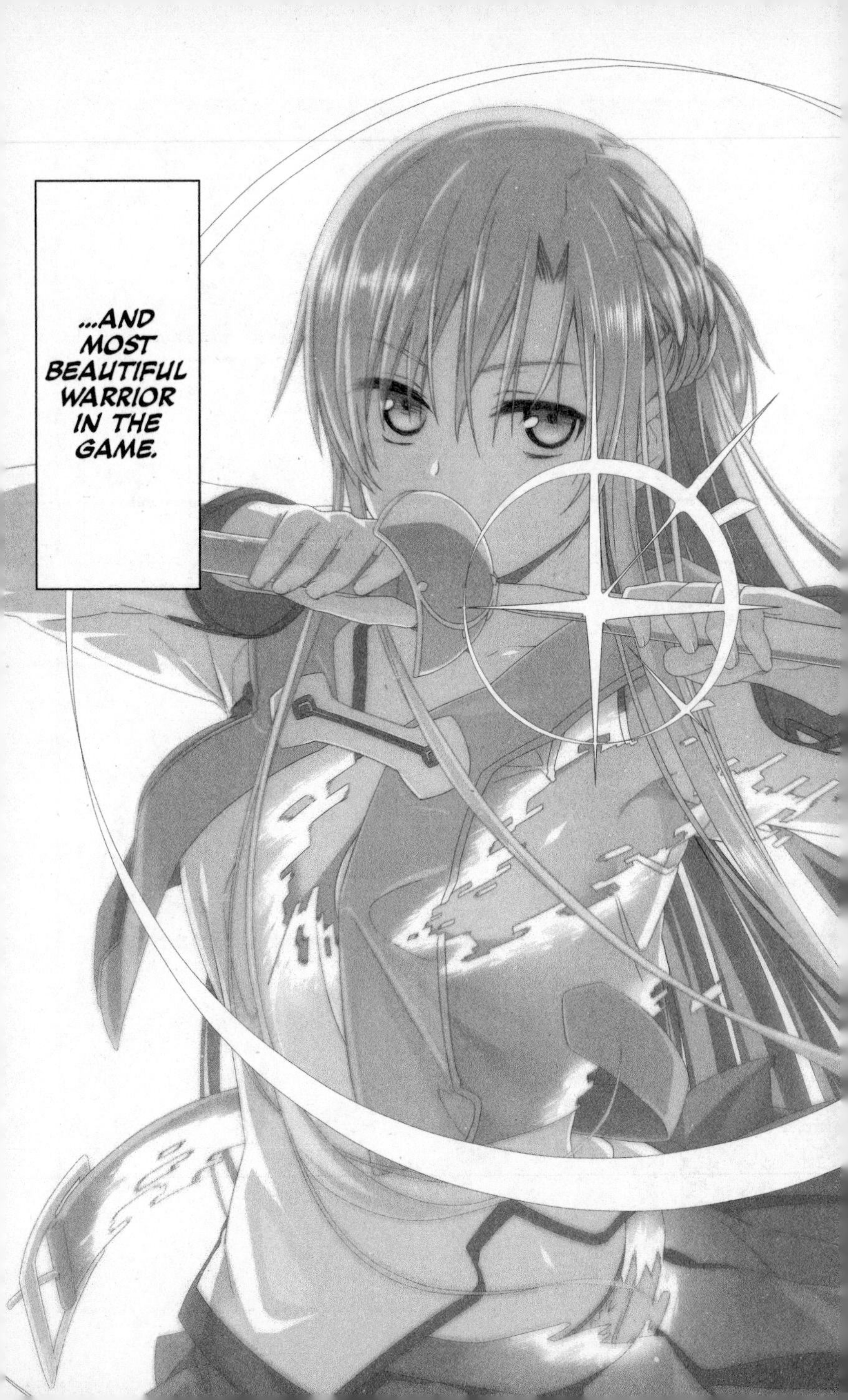
...AND MOST BEAUTIFUL WARRIOR IN THE GAME.

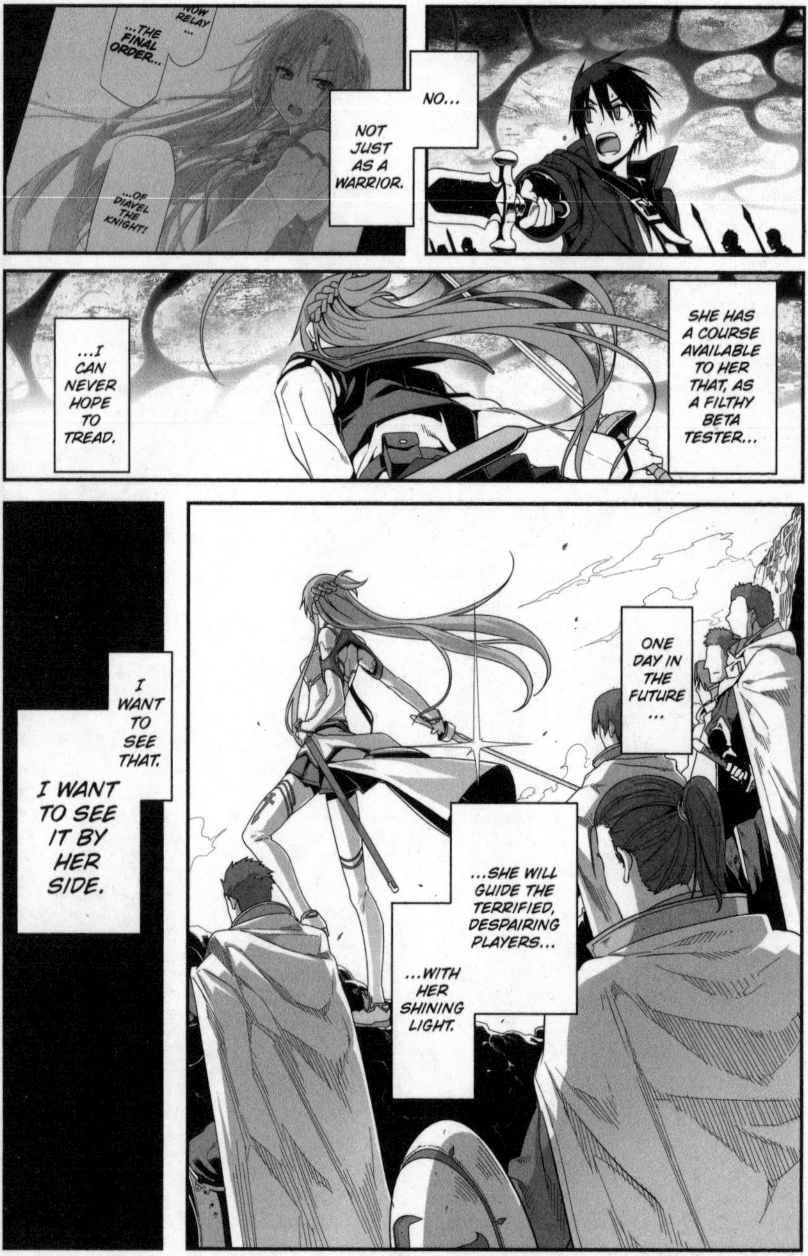
NO...
NOT JUST AS A WARRIOR.
NOW RELAY ...
...THE FINAL ORDER...
...OF DIAVEL THE KNIGHT!
SHE HAS A COURSE AVAILABLE TO HER THAT, AS A FILTHY BETA TESTER...
...I CAN NEVER HOPE TO TREAD.
ONE DAY IN THE FUTURE ...
...SHE WILL GUIDE THE TERRIFIED, DESPAIRING PLAYERS...
...WITH HER SHINING LIGHT.
I WANT TO SEE THAT.
I WANT TO SEE IT BY HER SIDE.

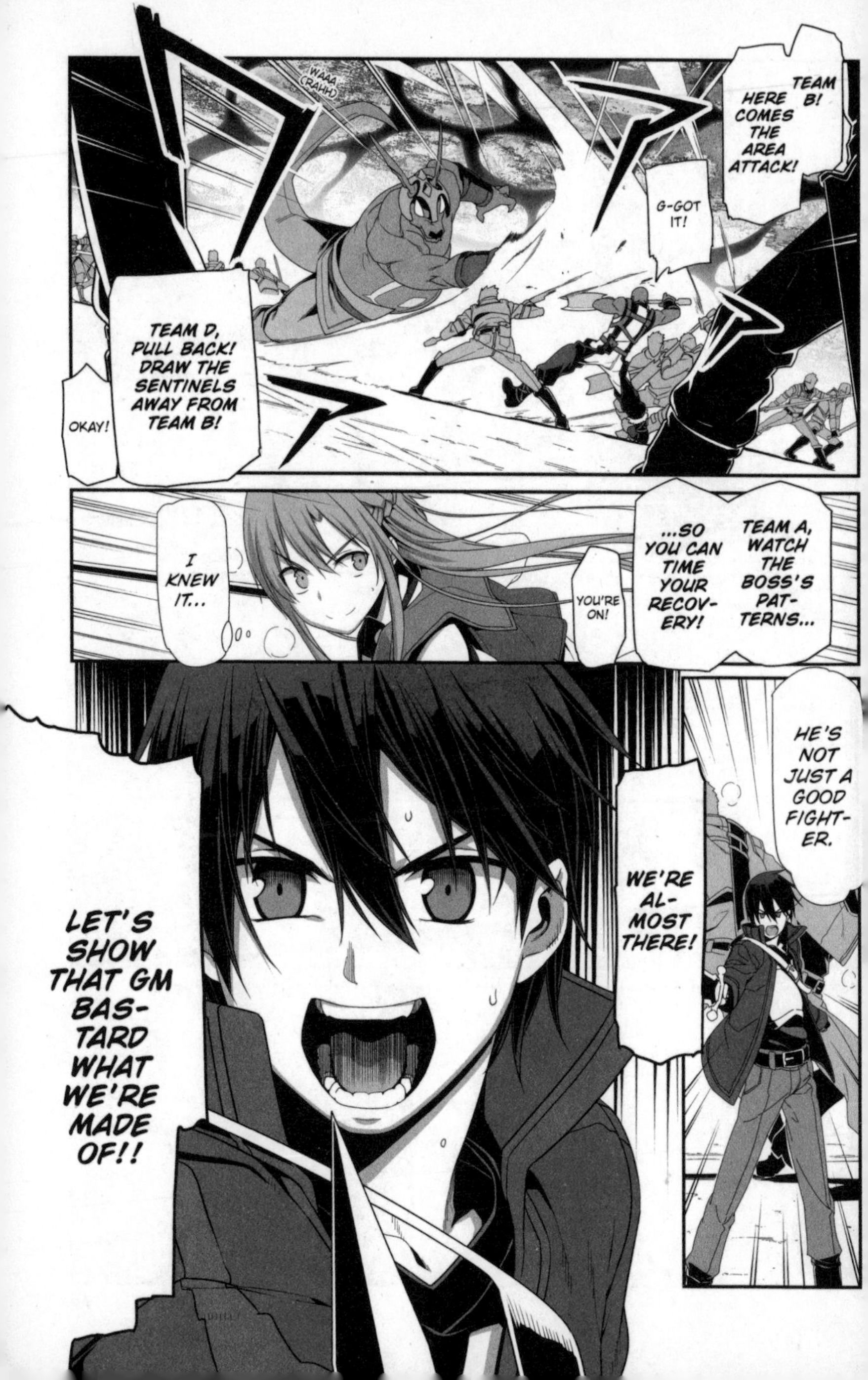
TEAM B! HERE COMES THE AREA ATTACK!
G-GOT IT!
WAAA (RAHH)
TEAM D, PULL BACK! DRAW THE SENTINELS AWAY FROM TEAM B!
OKAY!
TEAM A, WATCH THE BOSS'S PAT-TERNS...
...SO YOU CAN TIME YOUR RECOV-ERY!
YOU'RE ON!
I KNEW IT...
HE'S NOT JUST A GOOD FIGHT-ER.
WE'RE AL-MOST THERE!
LET'S SHOW THAT GM BAS-TARD WHAT WE'RE MADE OF!!

IN YOUR FACE, GM!!!!

......

THINKS HE'S SUCH A BIG SHOT...

LITTLE TURD.

OOOO (RAHH)

HMM? WHAZ-ZAT?

GET TEAM E BACK!!

KIBA-OU!

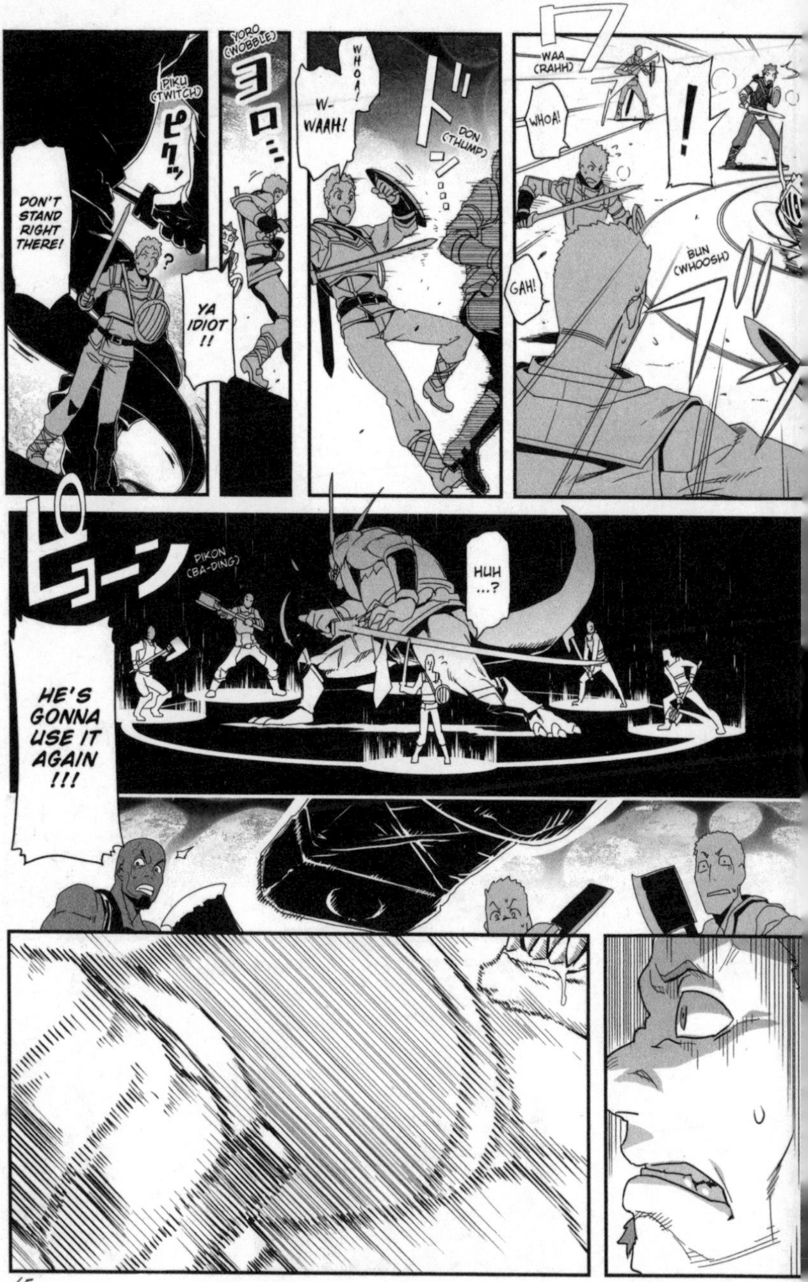
WAA (RAHH)
WHOA!
!
GAH!
BUN (WHOOSH)
WHOA!
W-WAAH!
DON (THUMP)
YORO (WOBBLE)
YA IDIOT!!
PIKU (TWITCH)
?
DON'T STAND RIGHT THERE!
HUH ...?
PIKON (BA-DING)
HE'S GONNA USE IT AGAIN!!!

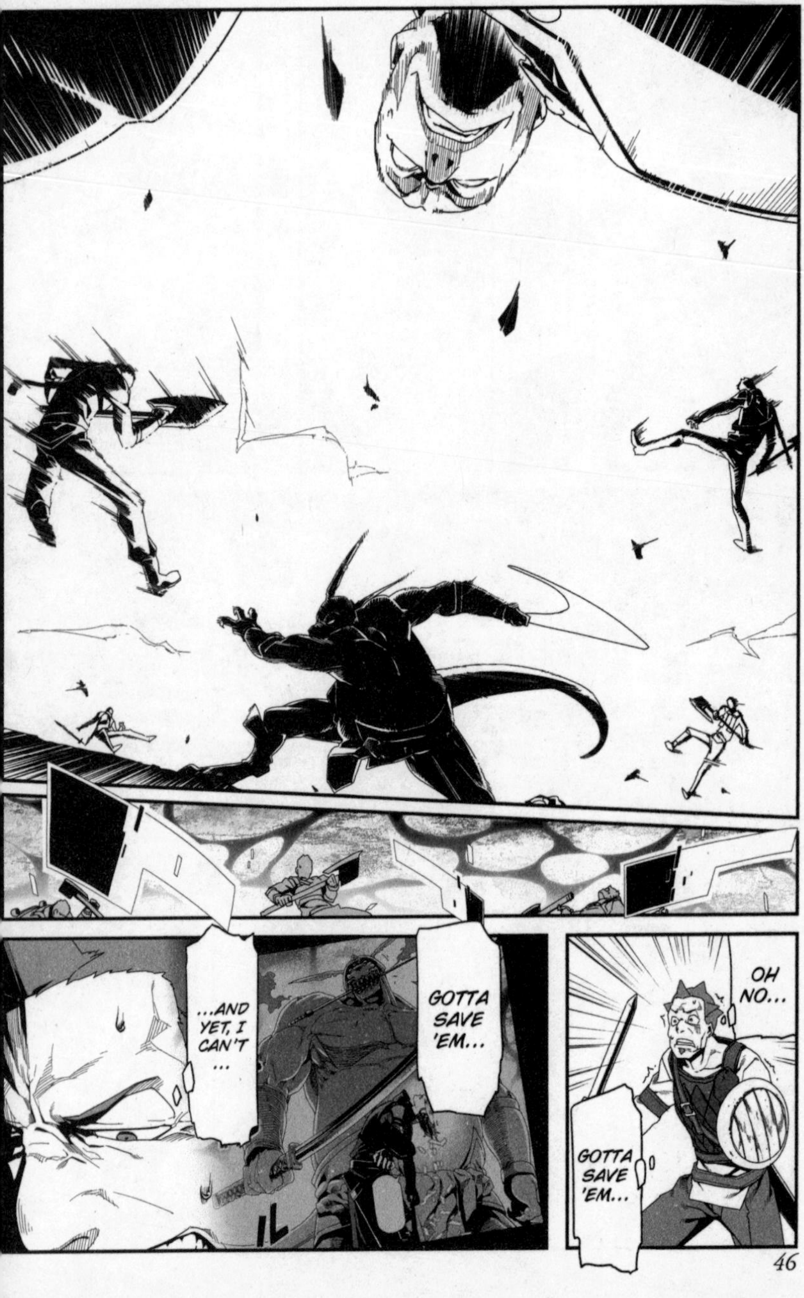
OH NO...
GOTTA SAVE 'EM...
GOTTA SAVE 'EM...
...AND YET, I CAN'T ...
IL

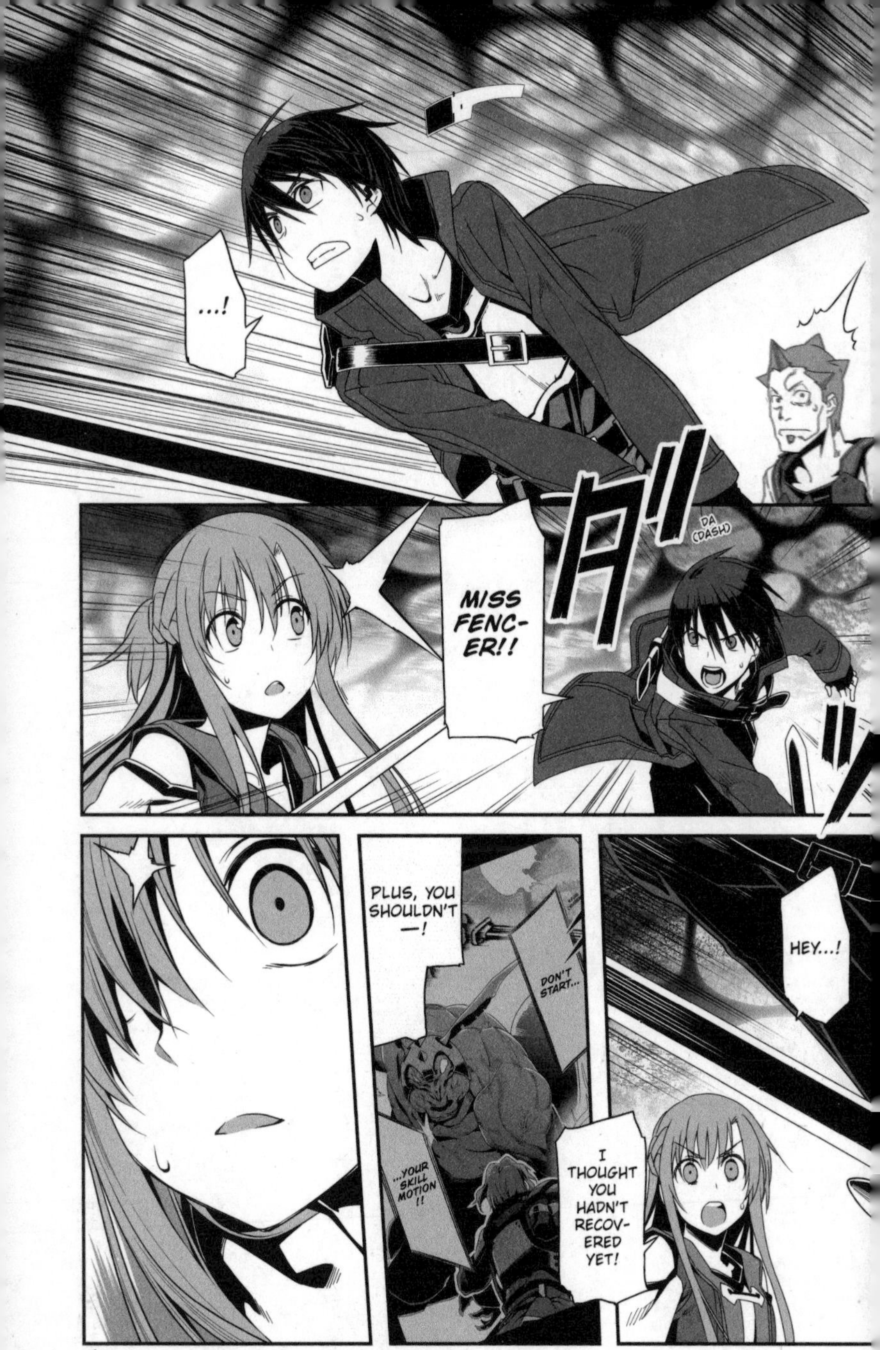
...!
DA
(DASH)
MISS FENCER!!
HEY...!
I THOUGHT YOU HADN'T RECOVERED YET!
PLUS, YOU SHOULDN'T—!
DON'T START...
...YOUR SKILL MOTION!!

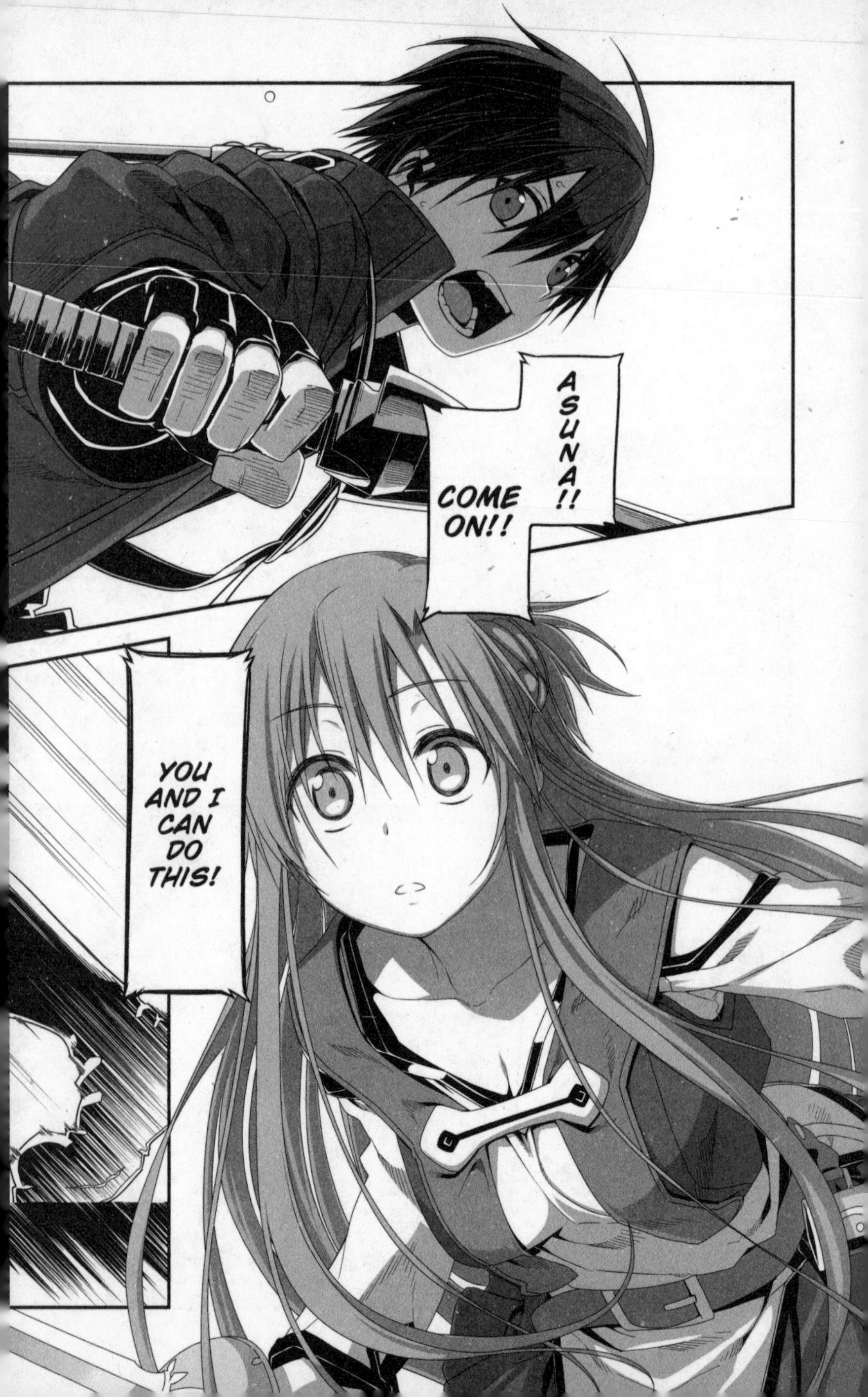
ASUNA!!
COME ON!!
YOU AND I CAN DO THIS!

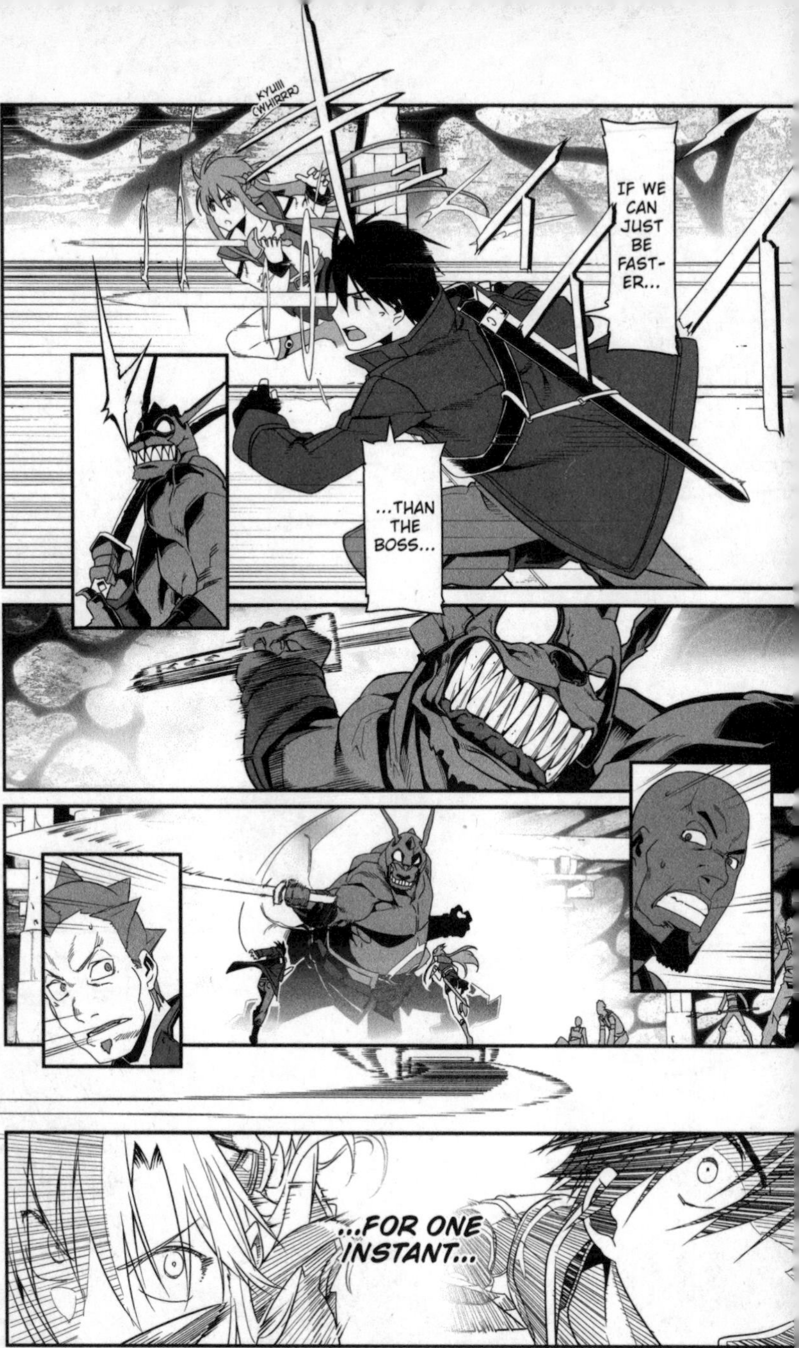
IF WE CAN JUST BE FASTER...
KYUIII (WHIRRR)
...THAN THE BOSS...
...FOR ONE INSTANT...

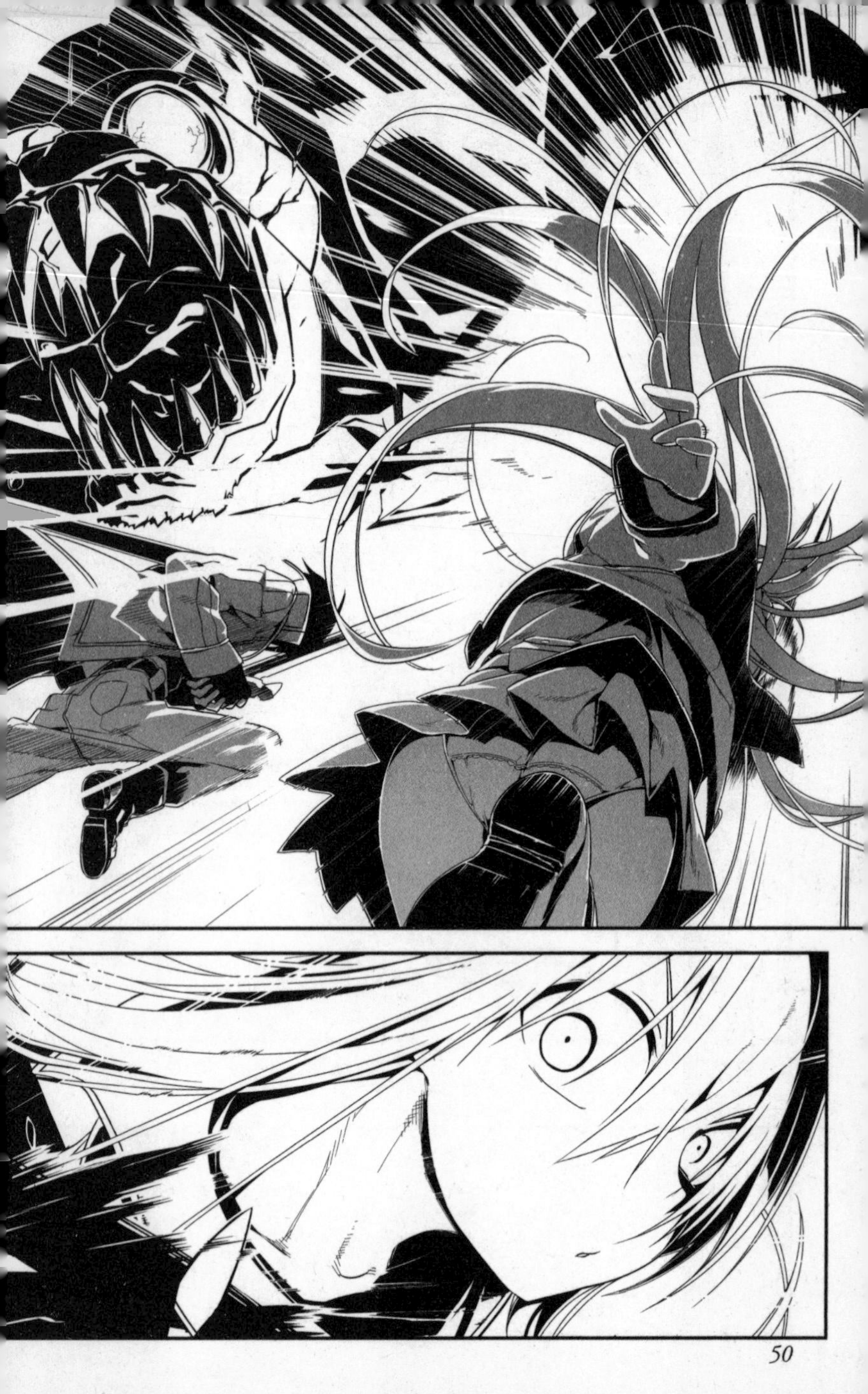

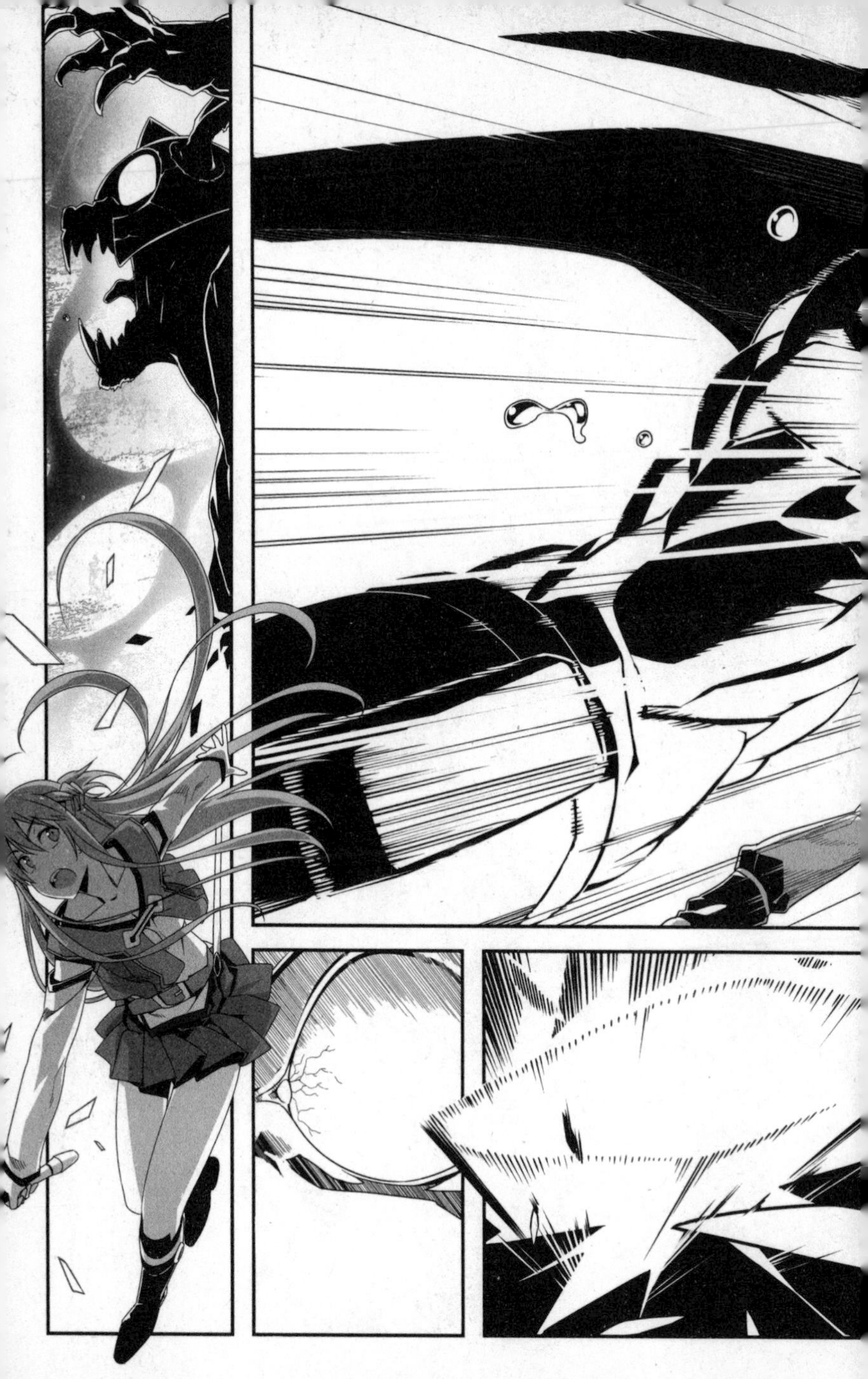

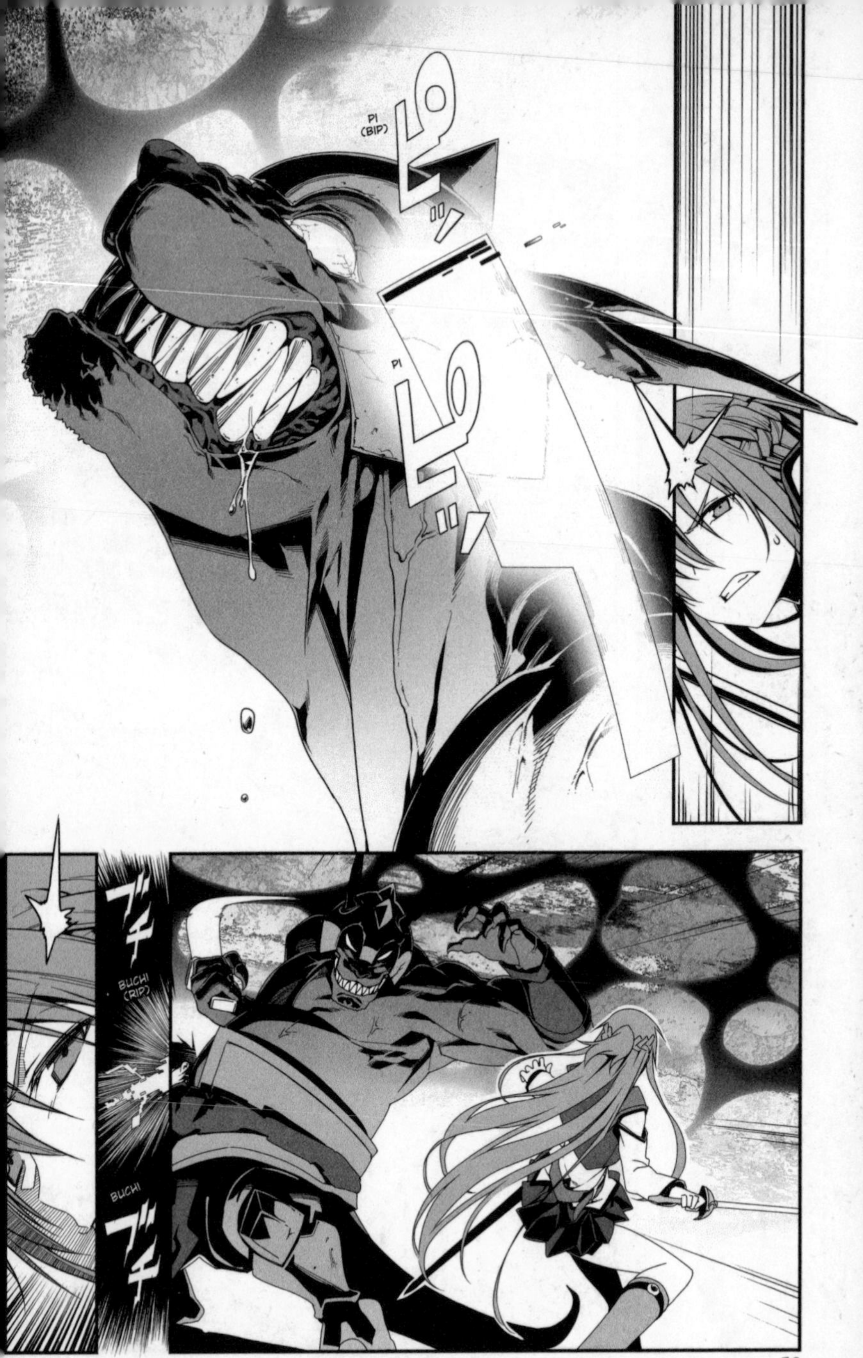
PI
(BIP)
PI
BUCHI
(RIP)
BUCHI

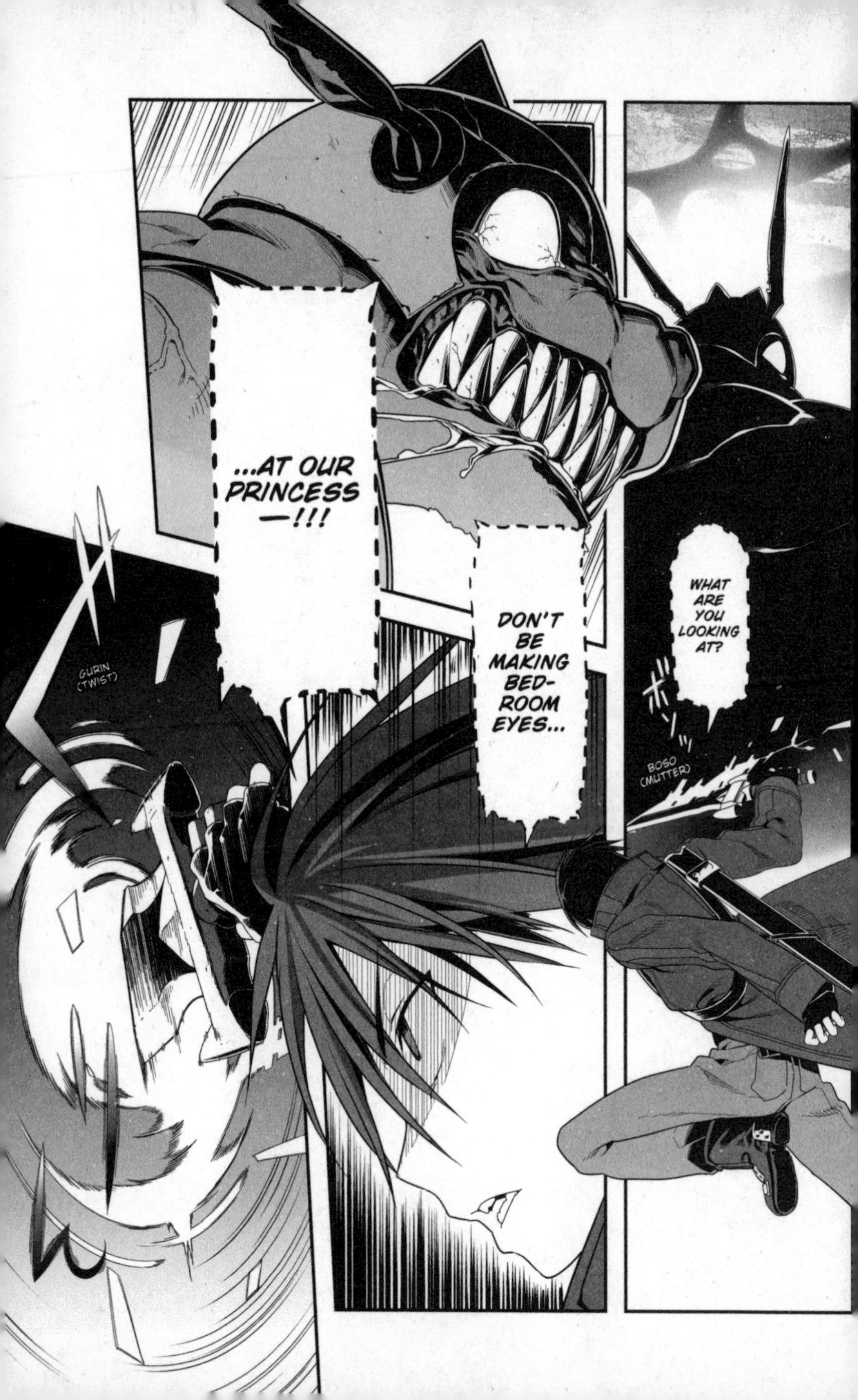
WHAT ARE YOU LOOKING AT?
BOSO (MUTTER)
DON'T BE MAKING BED-ROOM EYES...
...AT OUR PRINCESS—!!!
GURIN (TWIST)

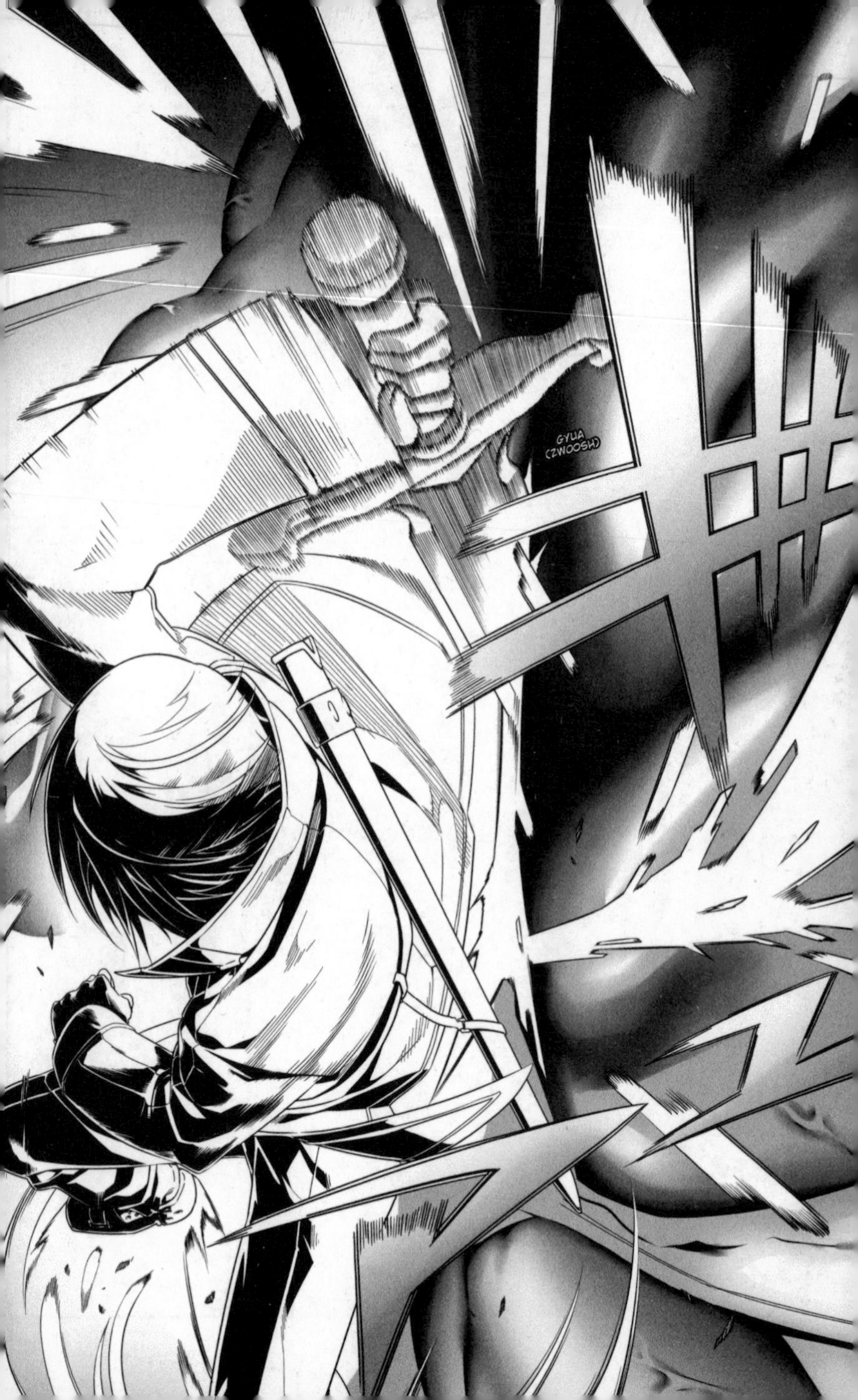
GYUA
(ZWOOSH)

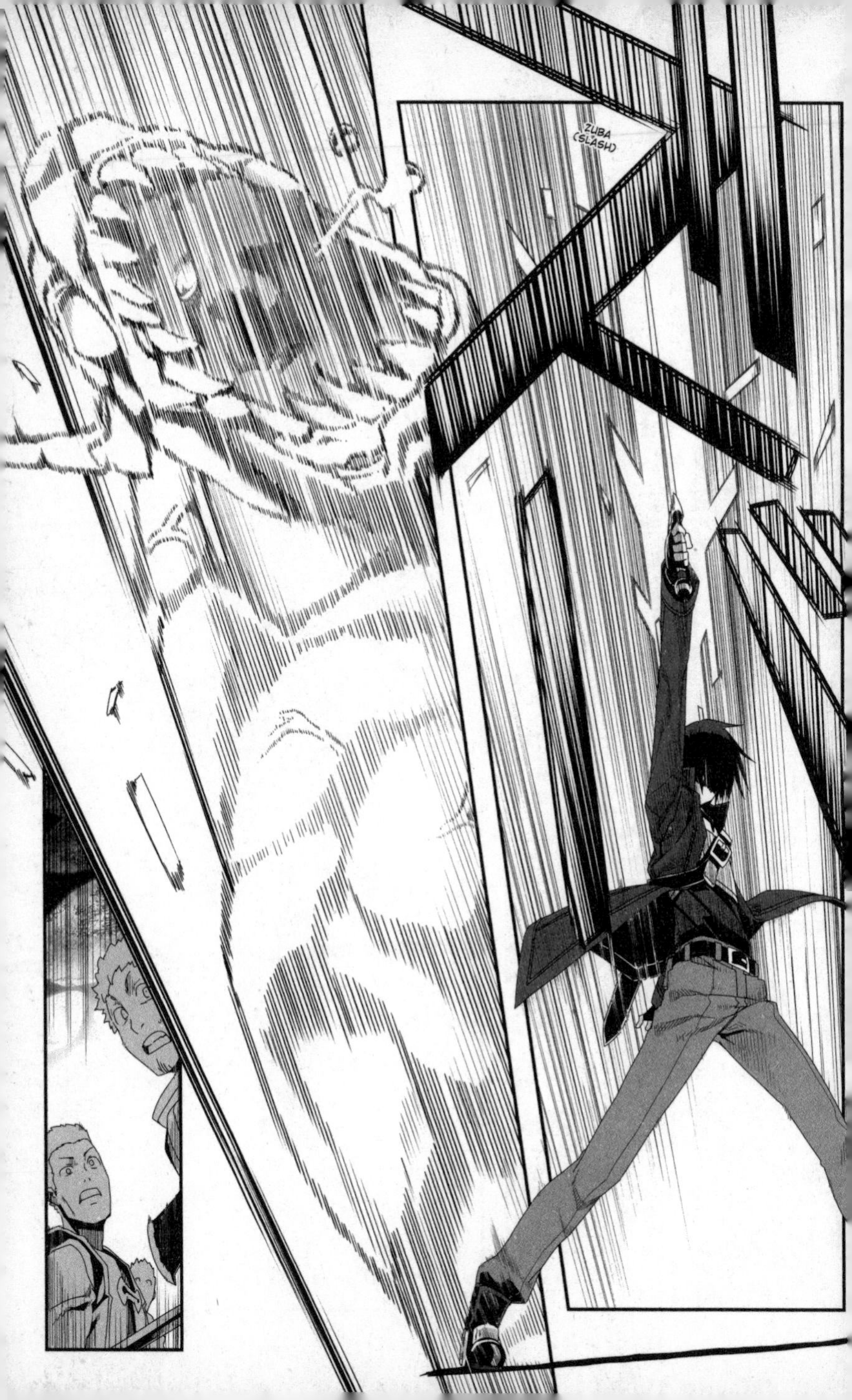
ZUBA (SLASH)

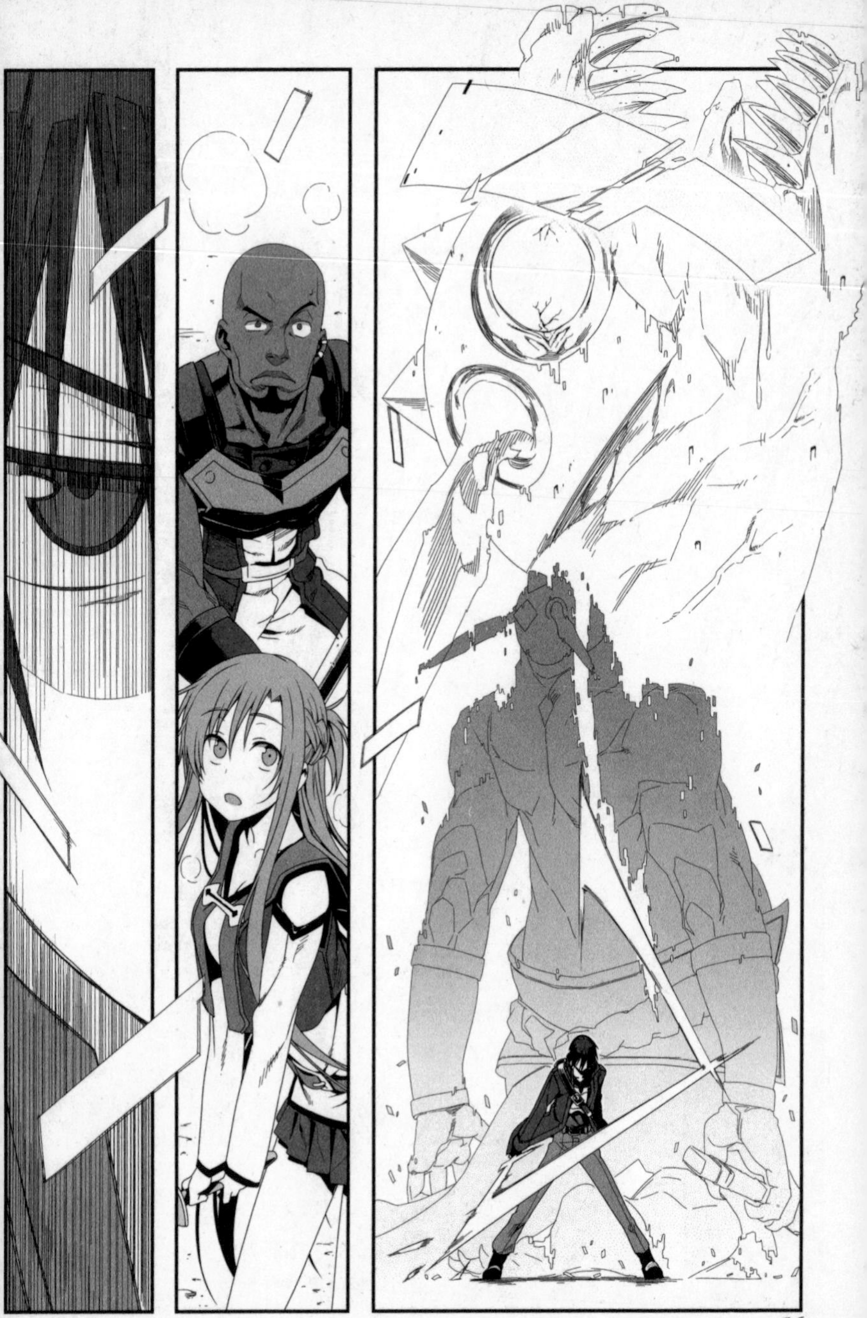

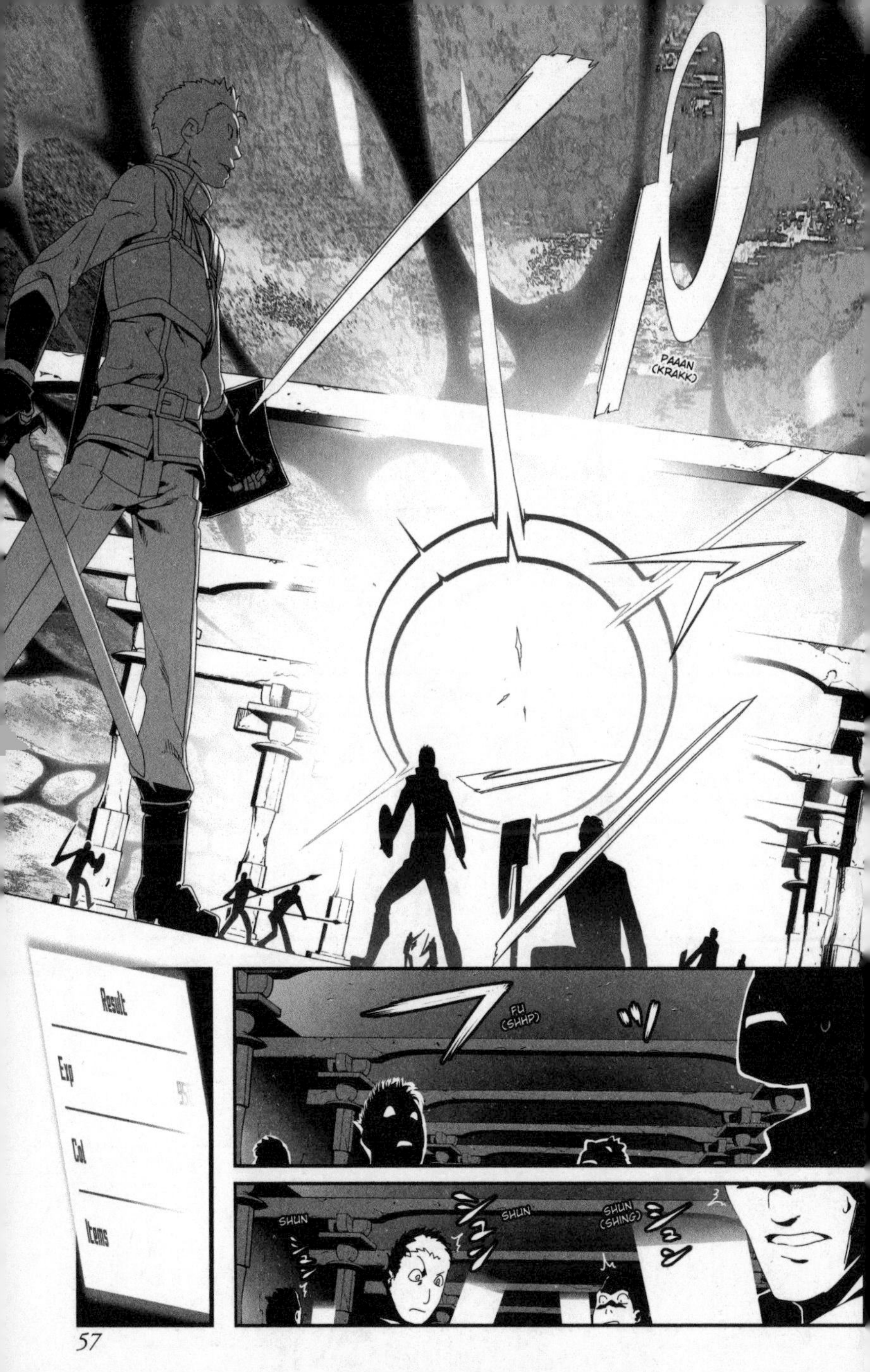
PAAAN
(KRAKK)
FU
(SHHP)
SHUN
(SHING)
SHUN
SHUN
Result
Exp
Col
Items

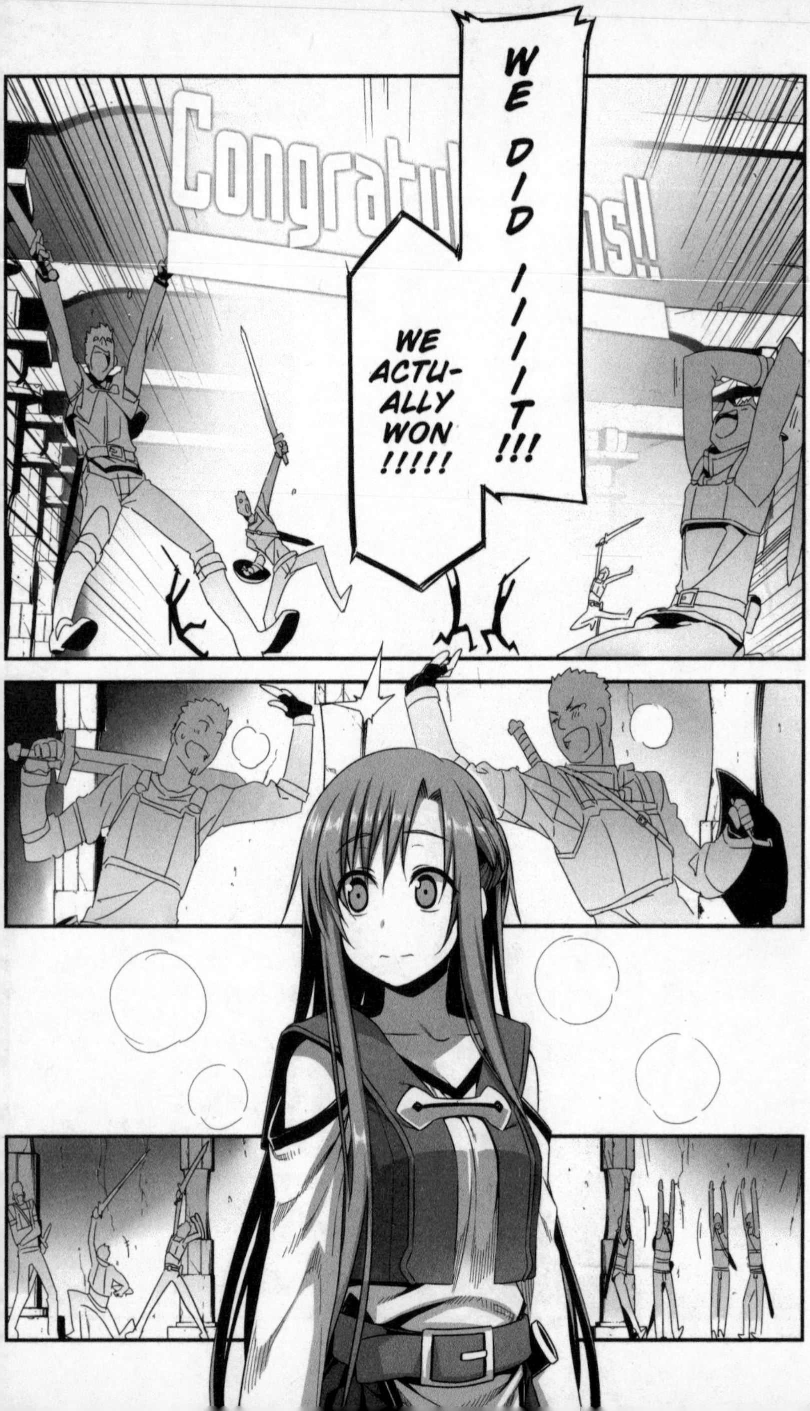
WE DID IIIIIT!!!
Congratul ns!!
WE ACTUALLY WON!!!!!

I DON'T BELIEVE IT...

THEY DID IT...

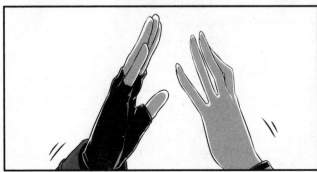

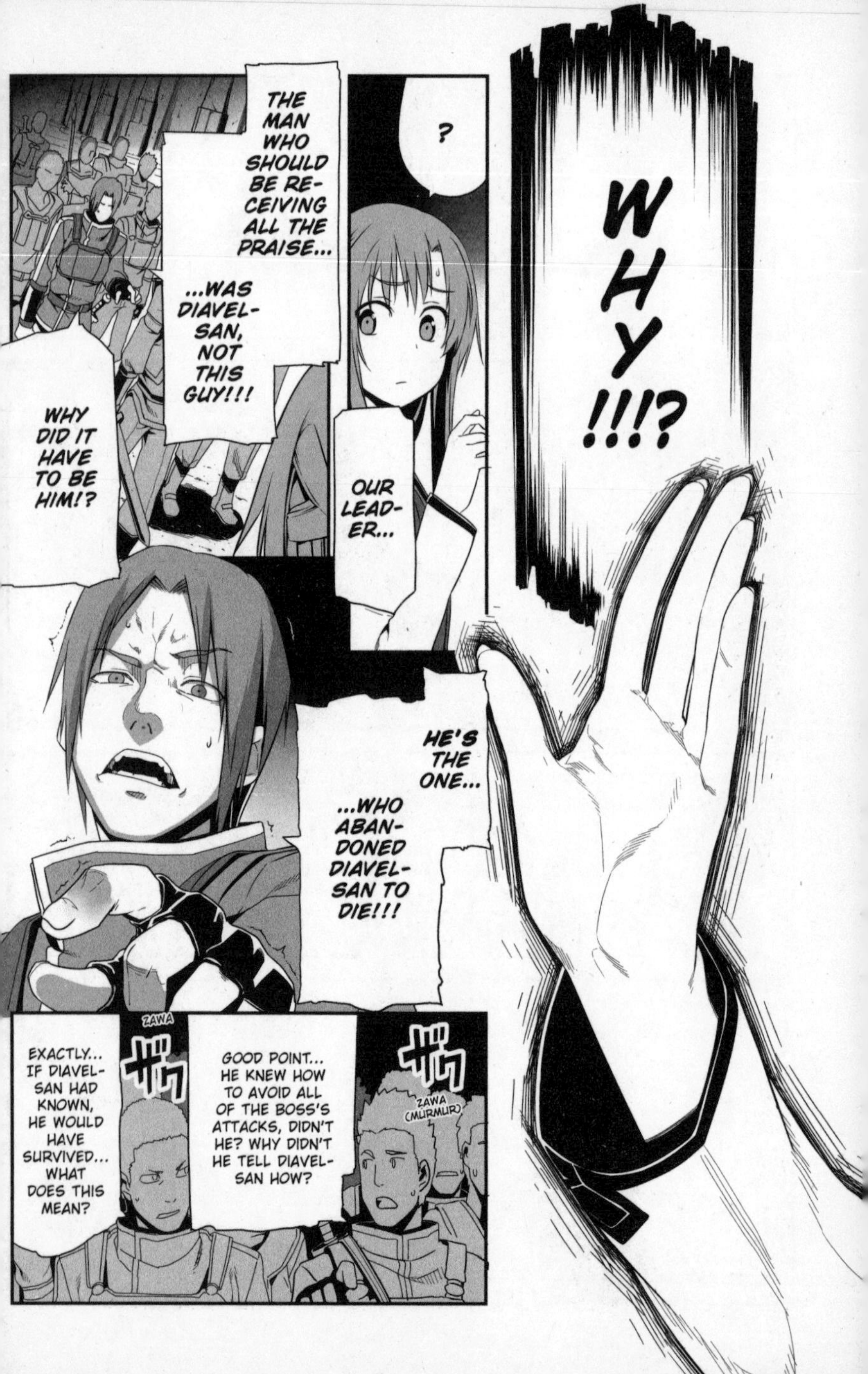
WHY!!!?
?
OUR LEADER...
THE MAN WHO SHOULD BE RECEIVING ALL THE PRAISE...
...WAS DIAVEL-SAN, NOT THIS GUY!!!
WHY DID IT HAVE TO BE HIM!?
HE'S THE ONE...
...WHO ABANDONED DIAVEL-SAN TO DIE!!!
ザワ
ZAWA (MURMUR)
GOOD POINT... HE KNEW HOW TO AVOID ALL OF THE BOSS'S ATTACKS, DIDN'T HE? WHY DIDN'T HE TELL DIAVEL-SAN HOW?
ザワ
ZAWA
EXACTLY... IF DIAVEL-SAN HAD KNOWN, HE WOULD HAVE SURVIVED... WHAT DOES THIS MEAN?

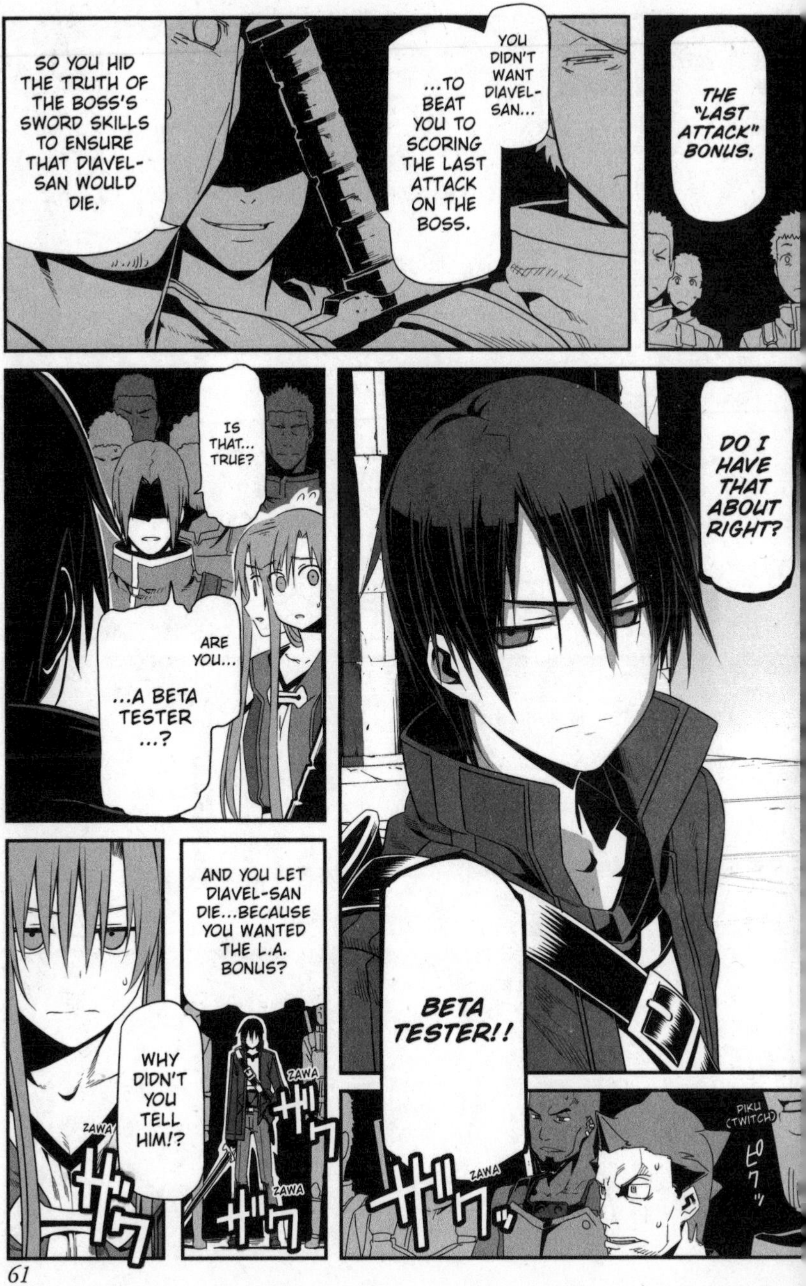
THE "LAST ATTACK" BONUS.
YOU DIDN'T WANT DIAVEL-SAN...
...TO BEAT YOU TO SCORING THE LAST ATTACK ON THE BOSS.
SO YOU HID THE TRUTH OF THE BOSS'S SWORD SKILLS TO ENSURE THAT DIAVEL-SAN WOULD DIE.
DO I HAVE THAT ABOUT RIGHT?
IS THAT... TRUE?
ARE YOU...
...A BETA TESTER ...?
BETA TESTER!!
PIKU (TWITCH)
ZAWA
AND YOU LET DIAVEL-SAN DIE...BECAUSE YOU WANTED THE L.A. BONUS?
WHY DIDN'T YOU TELL HIM!?
ZAWA
ZAWA
ZAWA

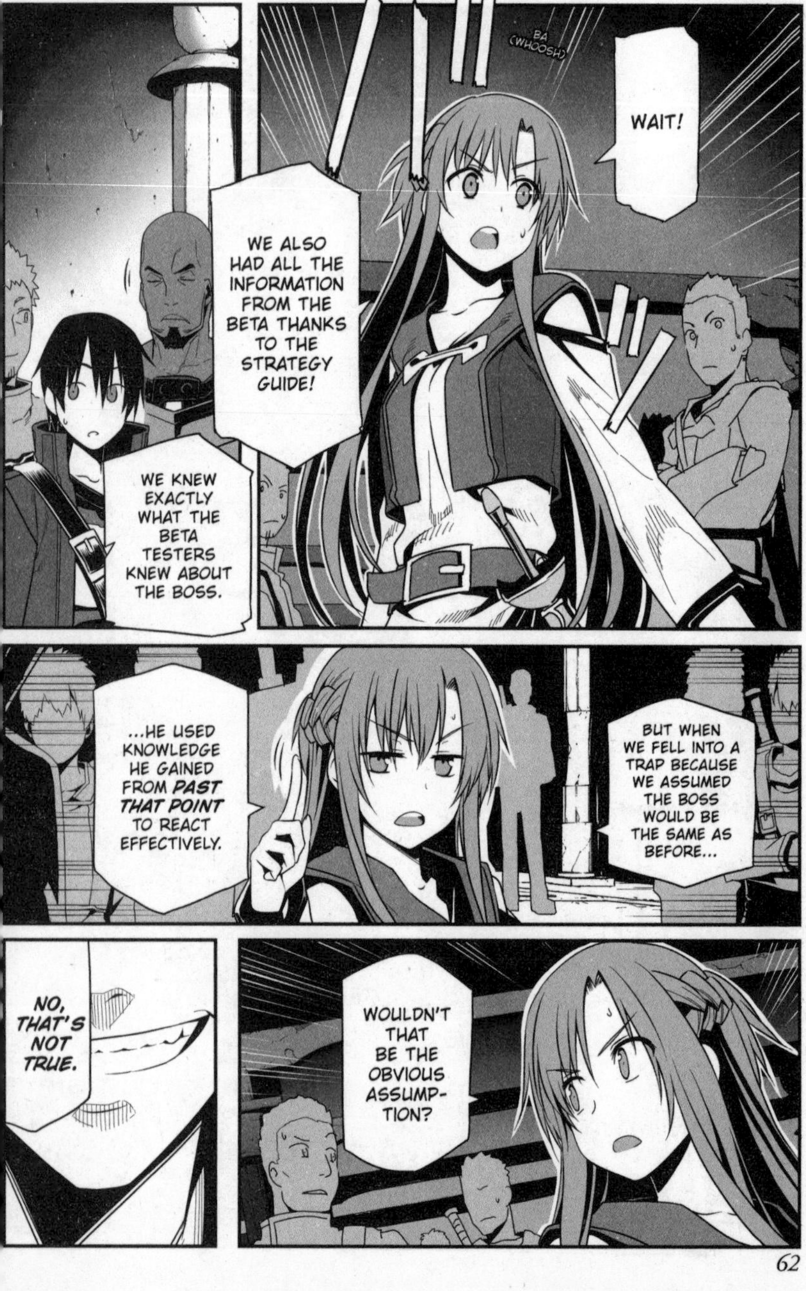
BA (WHOOSH)
WAIT!
WE ALSO HAD ALL THE INFORMATION FROM THE BETA THANKS TO THE STRATEGY GUIDE!
WE KNEW EXACTLY WHAT THE BETA TESTERS KNEW ABOUT THE BOSS.
BUT WHEN WE FELL INTO A TRAP BECAUSE WE ASSUMED THE BOSS WOULD BE THE SAME AS BEFORE...
...HE USED KNOWLEDGE HE GAINED FROM *PAST THAT POINT* TO REACT EFFECTIVELY.
WOULDN'T THAT BE THE OBVIOUS ASSUMP-TION?
NO, THAT'S NOT TRUE.

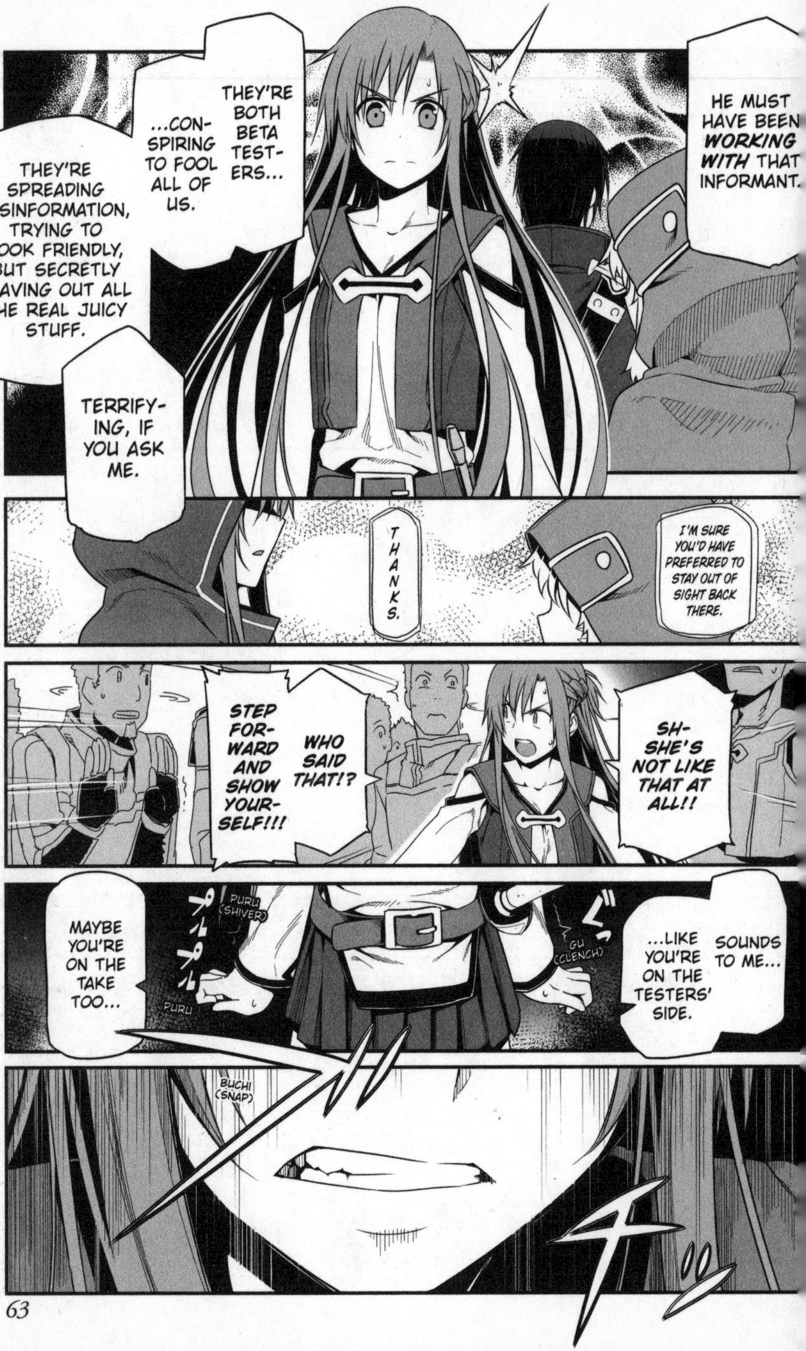
HE MUST HAVE BEEN *WORKING WITH* THAT INFORMANT.
THEY'RE BOTH BETA TEST- ERS...
...CON- SPIRING TO FOOL ALL OF US.
THEY'RE SPREADING MISINFORMATION, TRYING TO LOOK FRIENDLY, BUT SECRETLY LEAVING OUT ALL THE REAL JUICY STUFF.
TERRIFY- ING, IF YOU ASK ME.
I'M SURE YOU'D HAVE PREFERRED TO STAY OUT OF SIGHT BACK THERE.
THANKS.
SH- SHE'S NOT LIKE THAT AT ALL!!
WHO SAID THAT!?
STEP FOR- WARD AND SHOW YOUR- SELF!!!
SOUNDS TO ME...
...LIKE YOU'RE ON THE TESTERS' SIDE.
GU (CLENCH)
PURU (SHIVER)
PURU
MAYBE YOU'RE ON THE TAKE TOO...
BUCHI (SNAP)

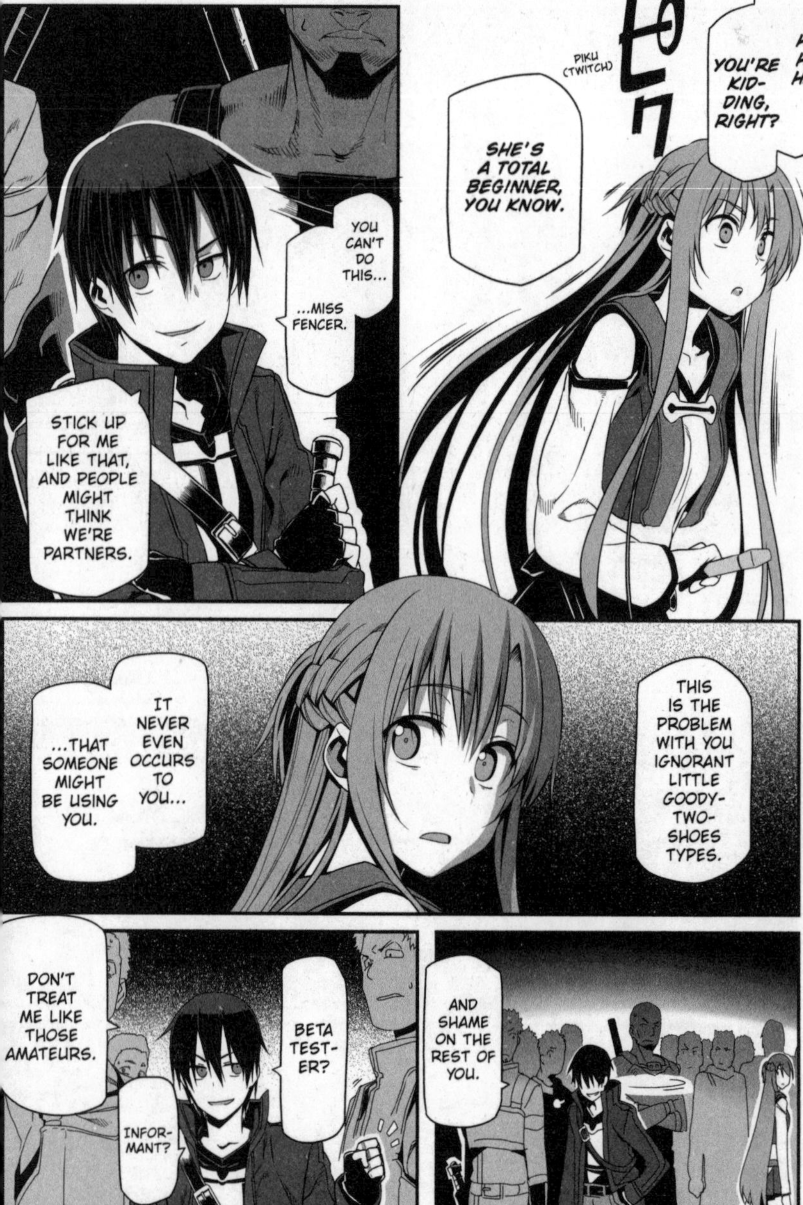
HA HA HA!
YOU'RE KID-DING, RIGHT?
ピク
PIKU (TWITCH)
SHE'S A TOTAL BEGINNER, YOU KNOW.
YOU CAN'T DO THIS...
...MISS FENCER.
STICK UP FOR ME LIKE THAT, AND PEOPLE MIGHT THINK WE'RE PARTNERS.
THIS IS THE PROBLEM WITH YOU IGNORANT LITTLE GOODY-TWO-SHOES TYPES.
IT NEVER EVEN OCCURS TO YOU...
...THAT SOMEONE MIGHT BE USING YOU.
AND SHAME ON THE REST OF YOU.
BETA TEST-ER?
INFOR-MANT?
DON'T TREAT ME LIKE THOSE AMATEURS.

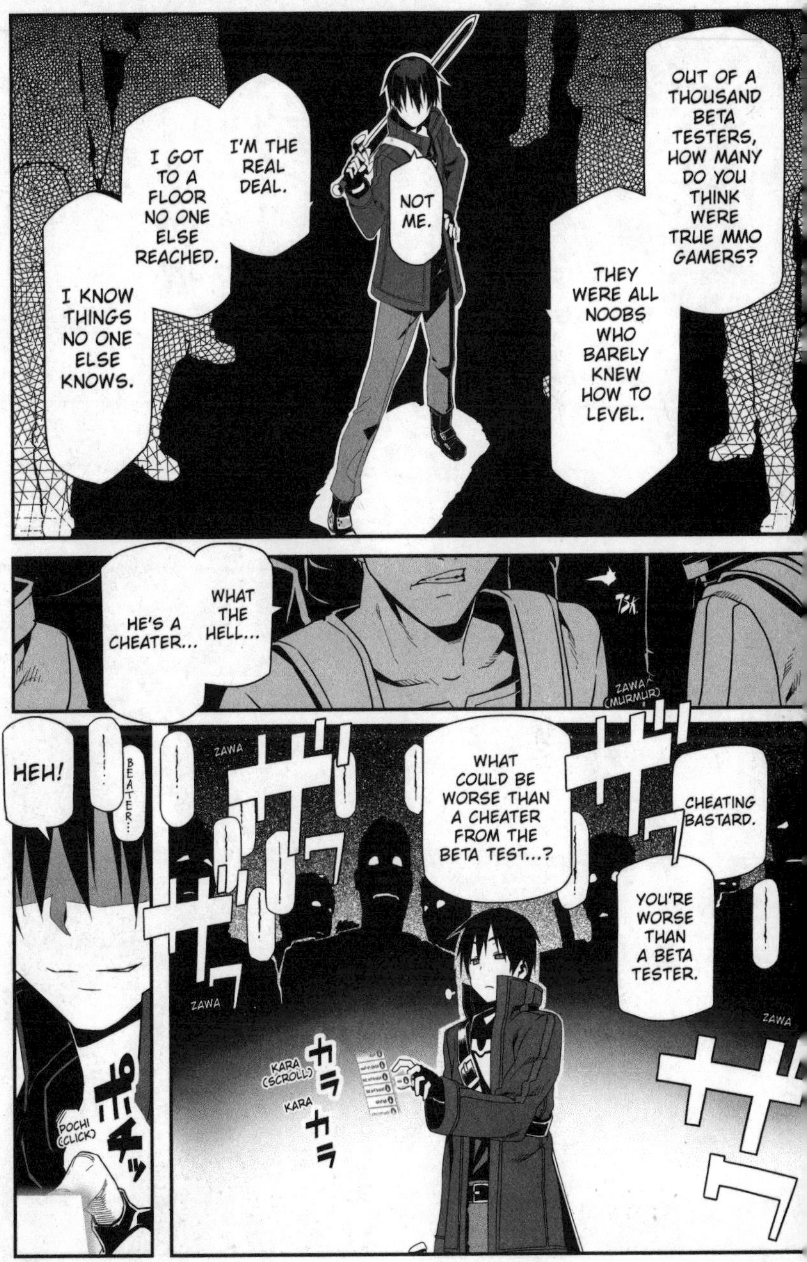
OUT OF A THOUSAND BETA TESTERS, HOW MANY DO YOU THINK WERE TRUE MMO GAMERS?
THEY WERE ALL NOOBS WHO BARELY KNEW HOW TO LEVEL.
NOT ME.
I'M THE REAL DEAL.
I GOT TO A FLOOR NO ONE ELSE REACHED.
I KNOW THINGS NO ONE ELSE KNOWS.
TSK.
WHAT THE HELL...
HE'S A CHEATER...
ZAWA (MURMUR)
CHEATING BASTARD.
YOU'RE WORSE THAN A BETA TESTER.
WHAT COULD BE WORSE THAN A CHEATER FROM THE BETA TEST...?
ZAWA
ZAWA
ZAWA
KARA (SCROLL)
KARA
BEATER...
HEH!
POCHI (CLICK)

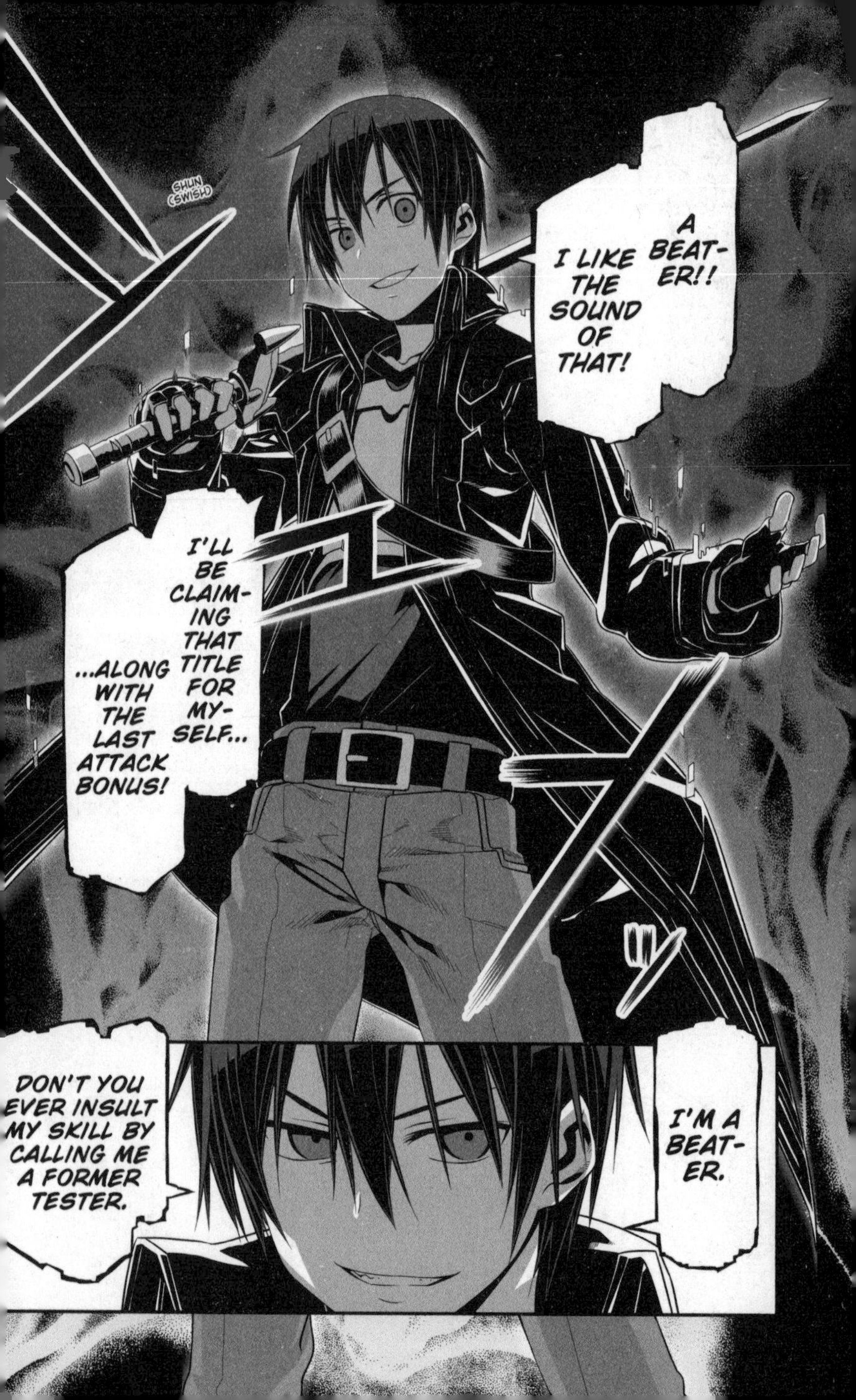
A BEATER!!
I LIKE THE SOUND OF THAT!
SHUN (SWISH)
I'LL BE CLAIMING THAT TITLE FOR MYSELF...
...ALONG WITH THE LAST ATTACK BONUS!
I'M A BEATER.
DON'T YOU EVER INSULT MY SKILL BY CALLING ME A FORMER TESTER.

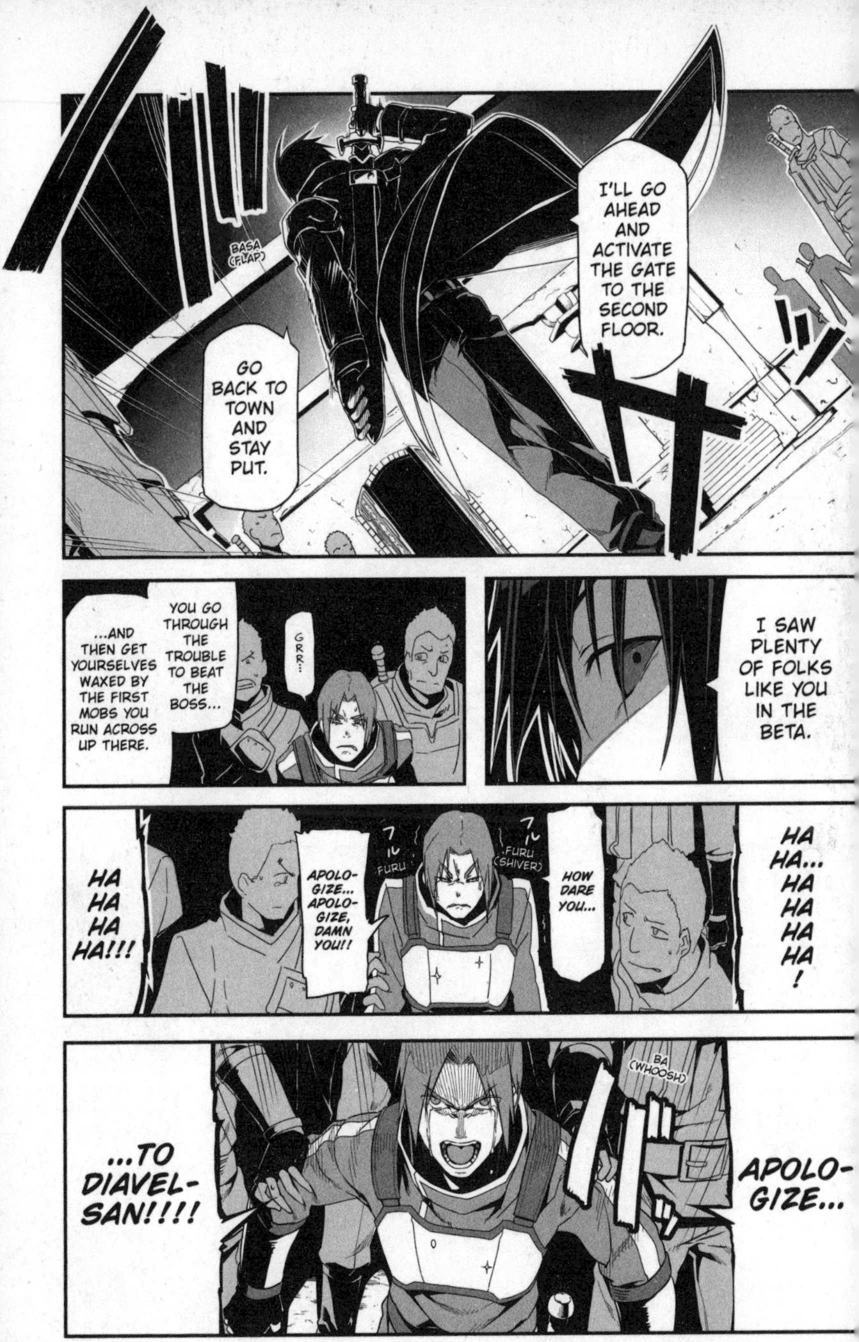
I'LL GO AHEAD AND ACTIVATE THE GATE TO THE SECOND FLOOR.
BASA (FLAP)
GO BACK TO TOWN AND STAY PUT.
I SAW PLENTY OF FOLKS LIKE YOU IN THE BETA.
GRR...
YOU GO THROUGH THE TROUBLE TO BEAT THE BOSS...
...AND THEN GET YOURSELVES WAXED BY THE FIRST MOBS YOU RUN ACROSS UP THERE.
HA HA... HA HA HA HA!
HOW DARE YOU...
フル FURU (SHIVER)
フル FURU
APOLOGIZE... APOLOGIZE, DAMN YOU!!
HA HA HA HA!!!
BA (WHOOSH)
APOLOGIZE...
...TO DIAVEL-SAN!!!!

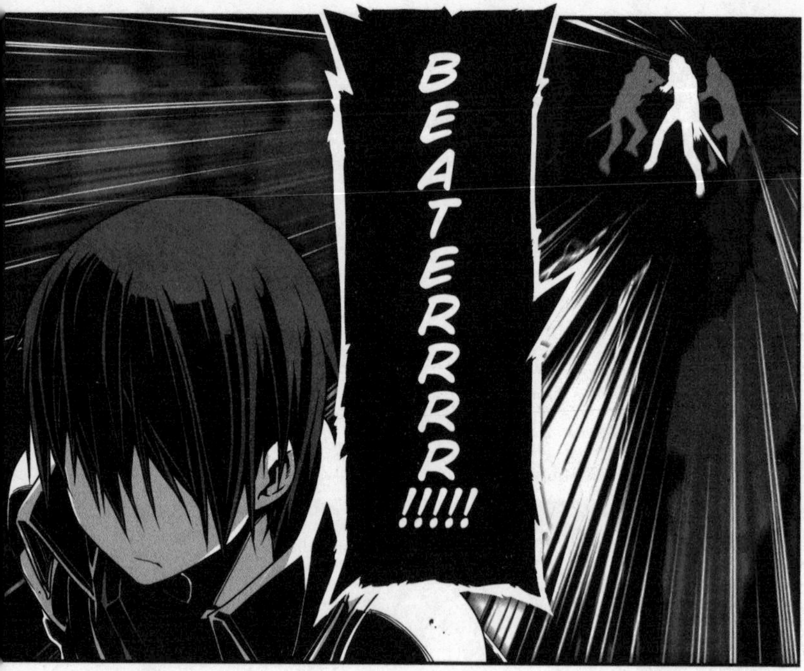
BEATERRRR!!!!!

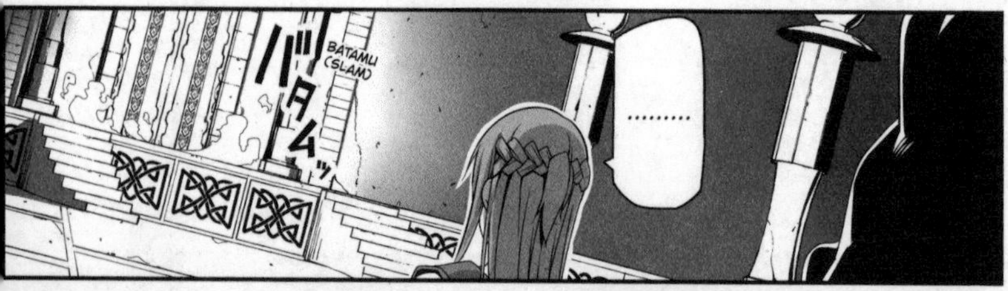
....
BATAMU (SLAM)

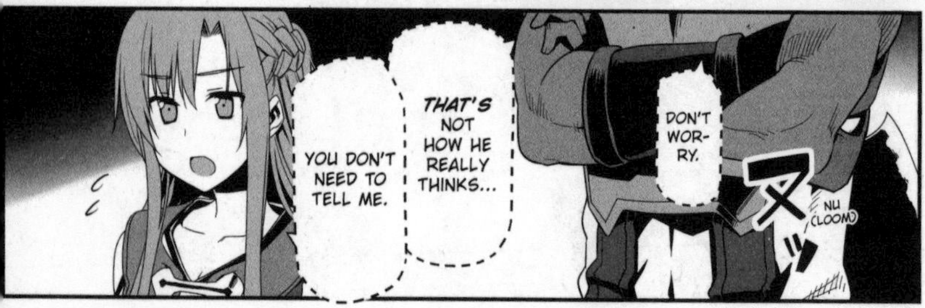
DON'T WOR-RY.
NU (LOOM)
THAT'S NOT HOW HE REALLY THINKS...
YOU DON'T NEED TO TELL ME.

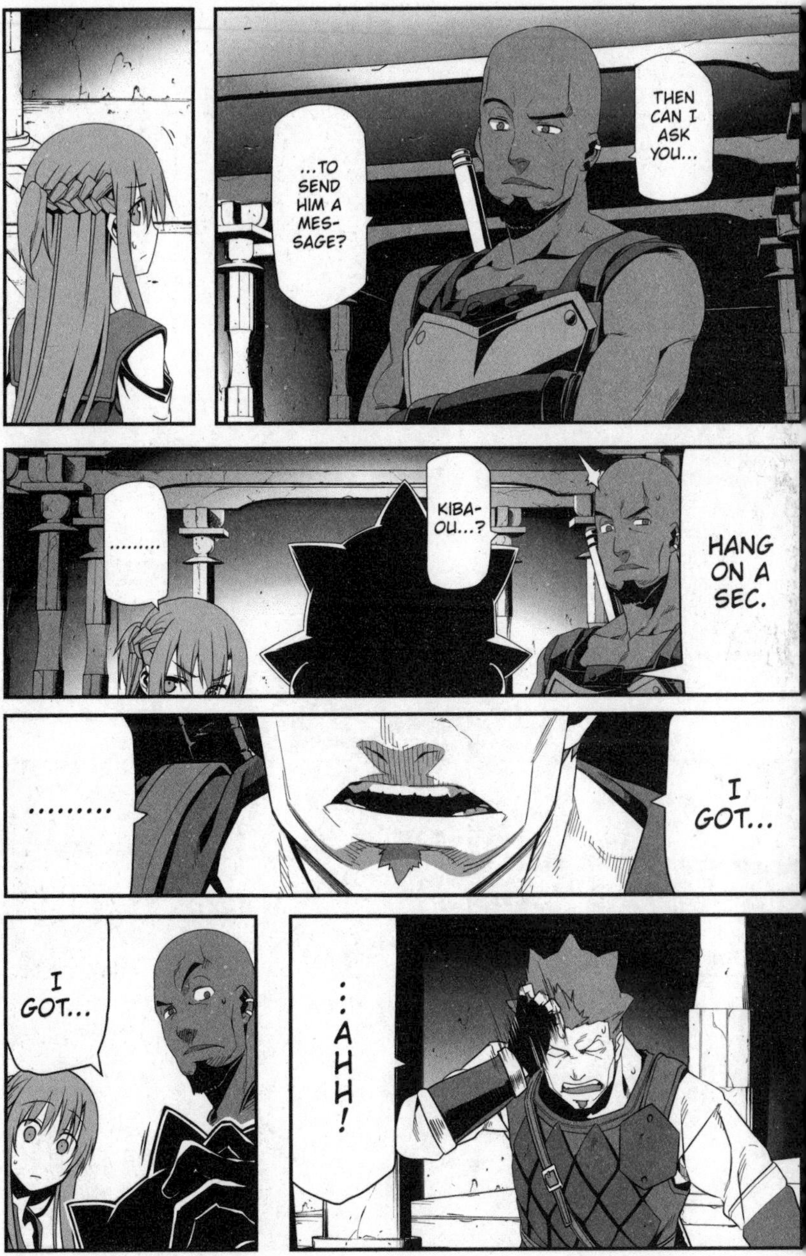
THEN CAN I ASK YOU...
...TO SEND HIM A MES-SAGE?
HANG ON A SEC.
KIBA-OU...?
....
I GOT...
....
...AHH!
I GOT...

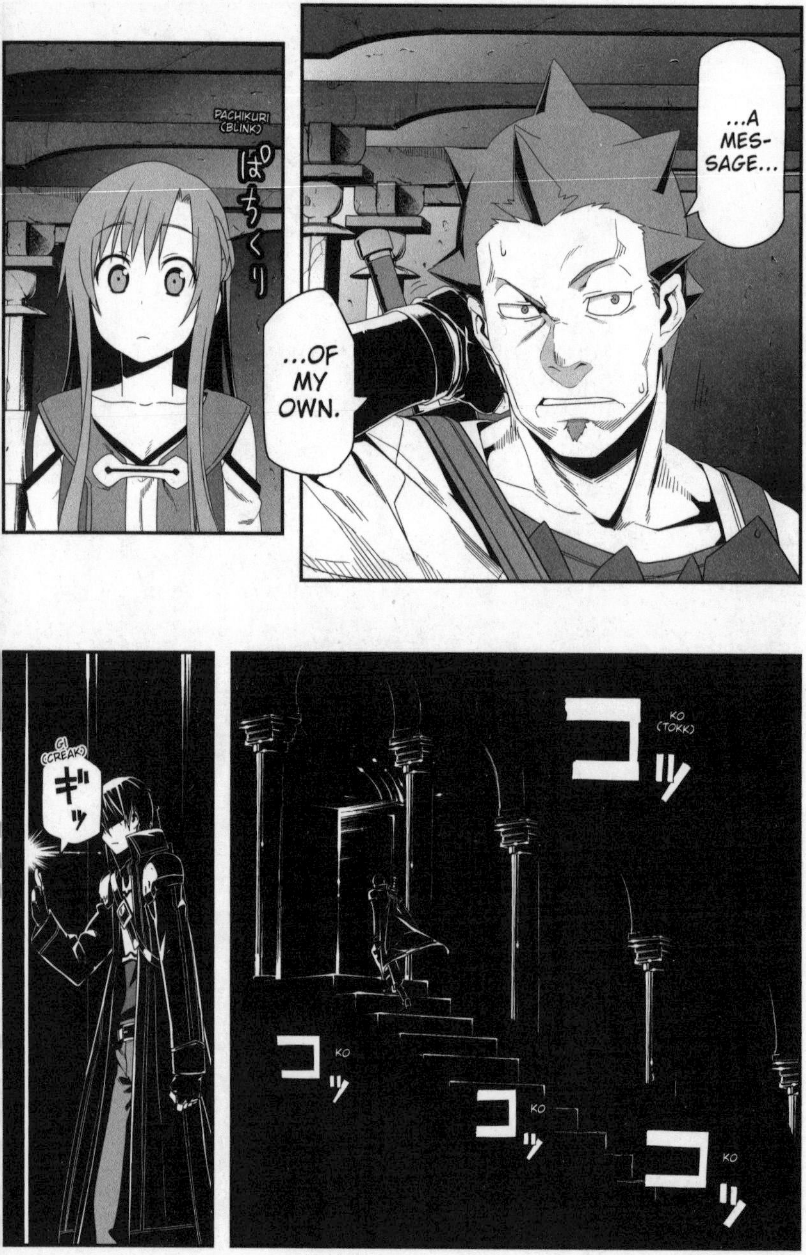
...A MES- SAGE...
...OF MY OWN.
PACHIKURI (BLINK)
ぱちくり
KO (TOKK)
コッ
KO
コッ
KO
コッ
KO
コッ
GI (CREAK)
ギッ

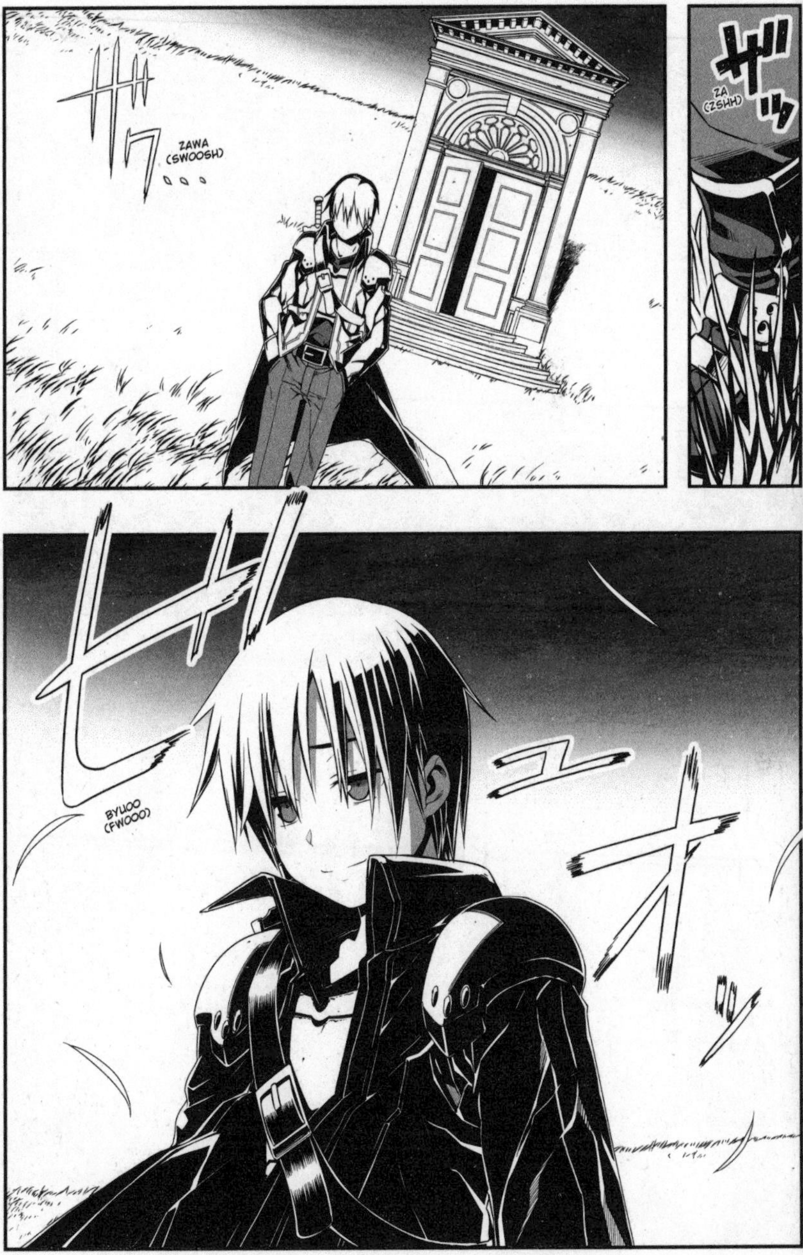
ZA (ZSHH)
ZAWA (SWOOSH)
BYUOO (FWOOO)

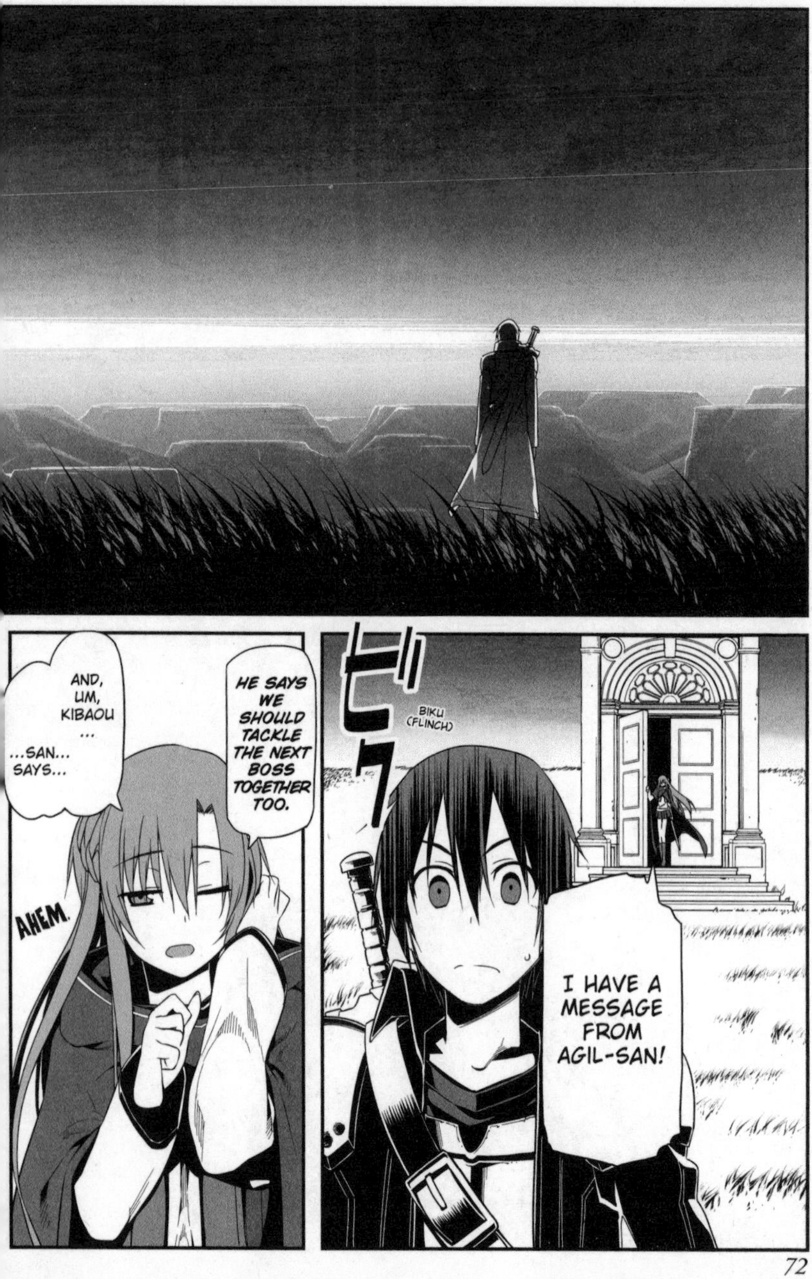
ビク
BIKU (FLINCH)
I HAVE A MESSAGE FROM AGIL-SAN!
HE SAYS WE SHOULD TACKLE THE NEXT BOSS TOGETHER TOO.
AND, UM, KIBAOU ...
...SAN... SAYS...
AHEM.

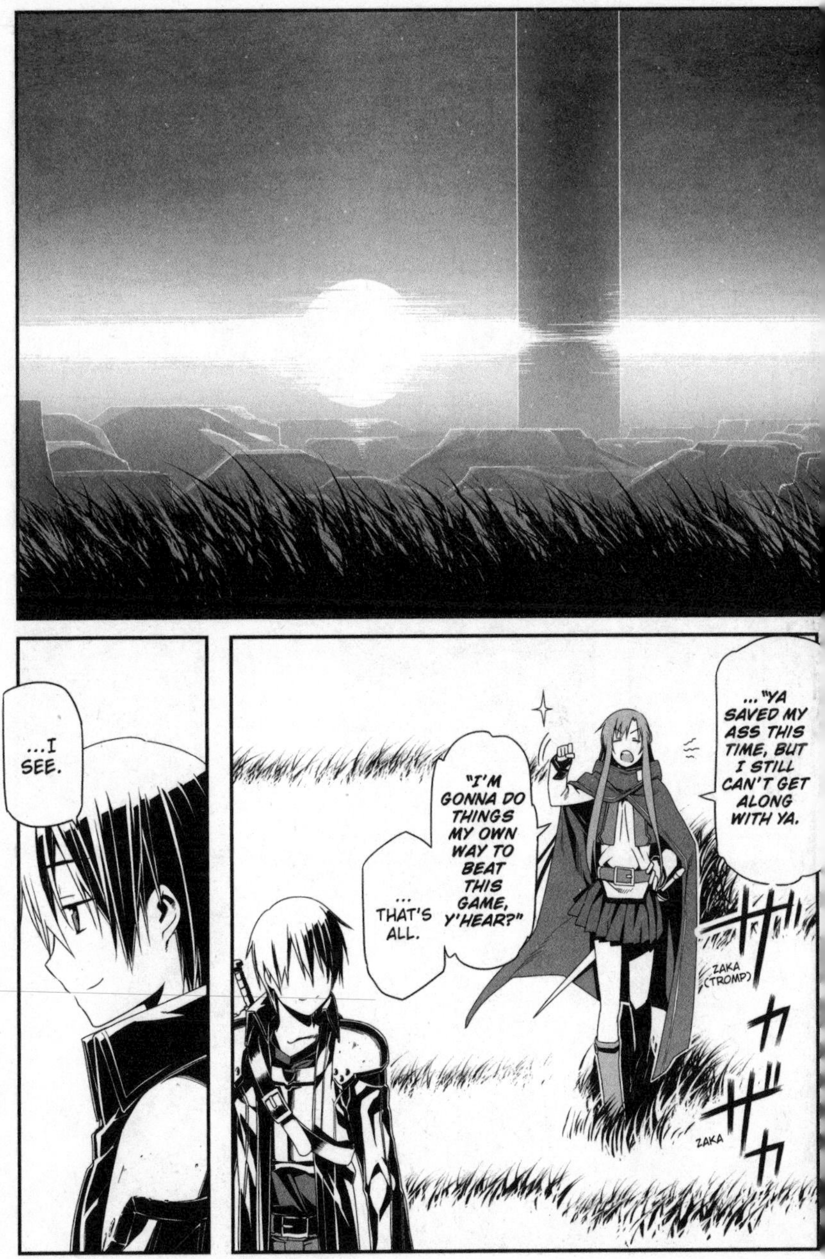
..."YA SAVED MY ASS THIS TIME, BUT I STILL CAN'T GET ALONG WITH YA.
"I'M GONNA DO THINGS MY OWN WAY TO BEAT THIS GAME, Y'HEAR?"
... THAT'S ALL.
ZAKA (TROMP)
ZAKA
...I SEE.

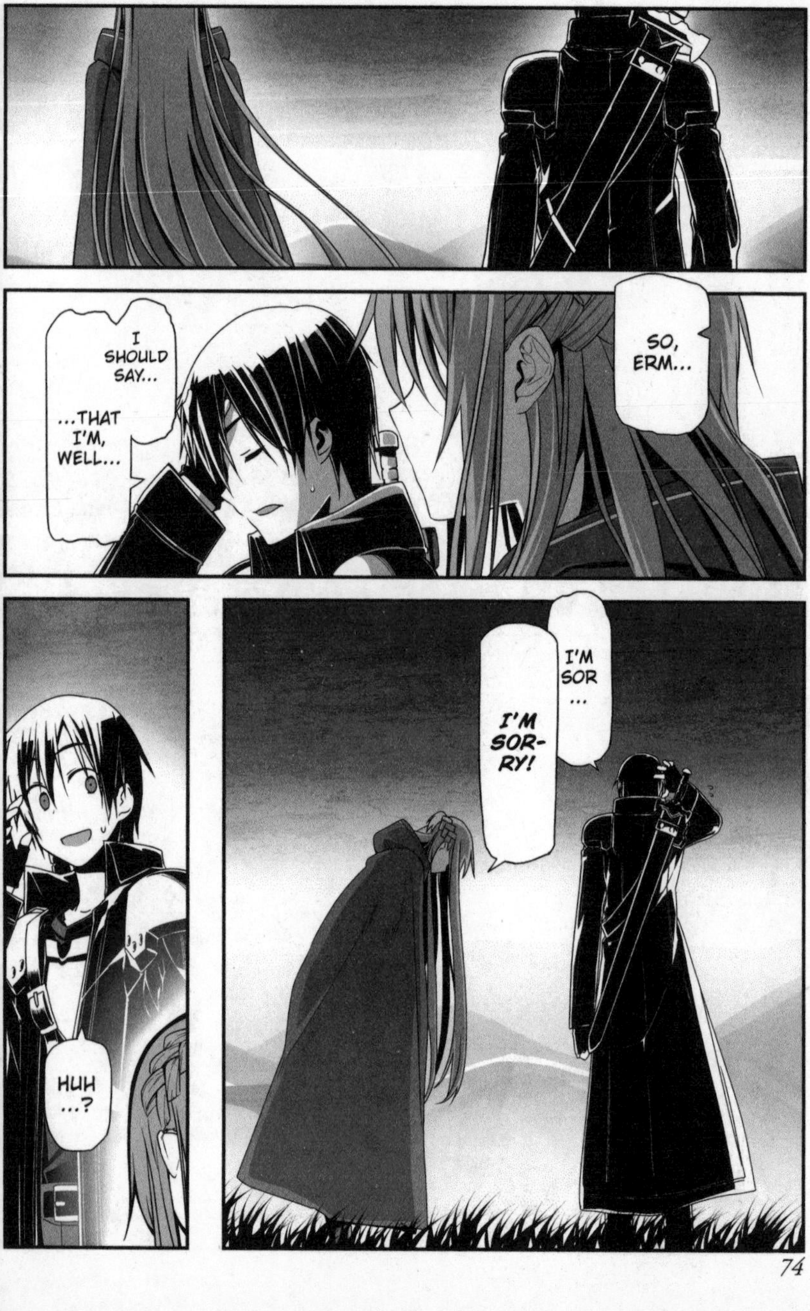
SO, ERM...
I SHOULD SAY...
...THAT I'M, WELL...
I'M SOR ...
I'M SORRY!
HUH ...?

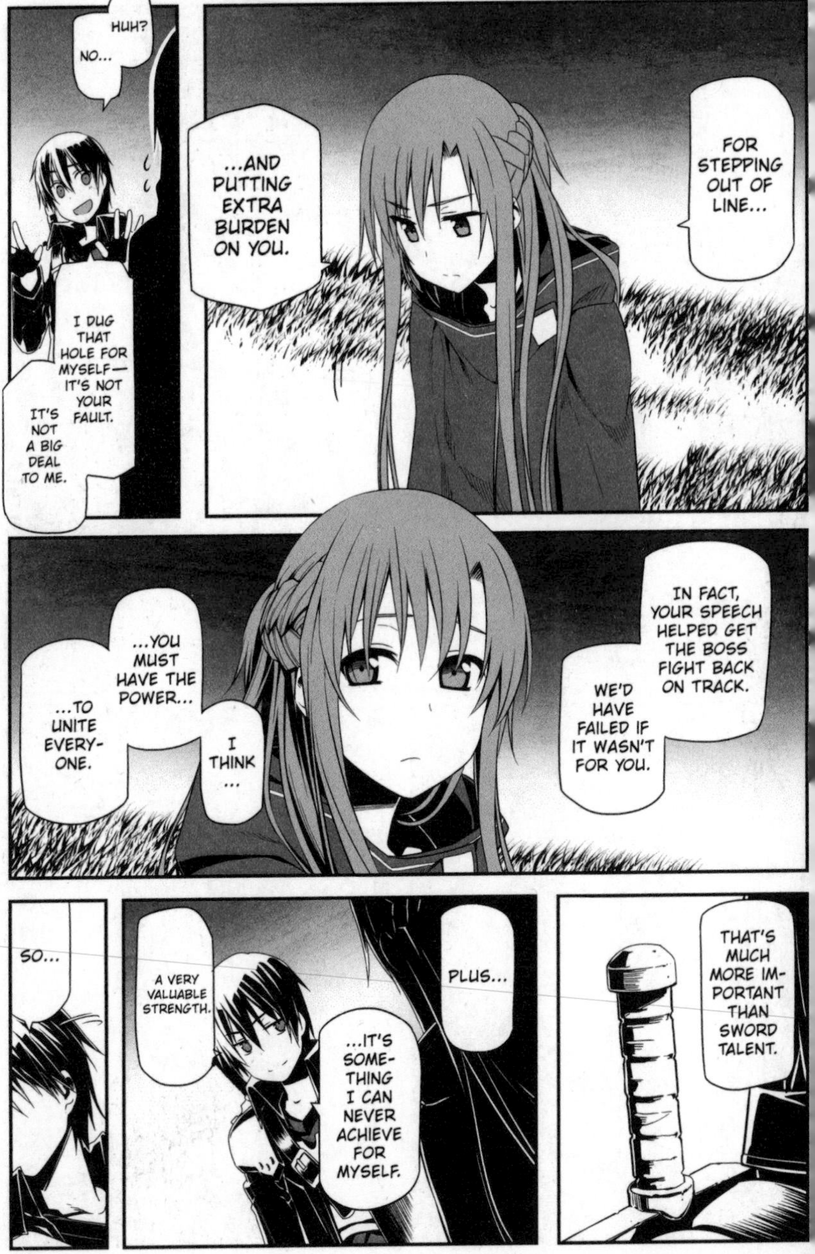
FOR STEPPING OUT OF LINE...
...AND PUTTING EXTRA BURDEN ON YOU.
HUH? NO...
I DUG THAT HOLE FOR MYSELF— IT'S NOT YOUR FAULT.
IT'S NOT A BIG DEAL TO ME.
IN FACT, YOUR SPEECH HELPED GET THE BOSS FIGHT BACK ON TRACK.
WE'D HAVE FAILED IF IT WASN'T FOR YOU.
I THINK...
...YOU MUST HAVE THE POWER...
...TO UNITE EVERY-ONE.
THAT'S MUCH MORE IM-PORTANT THAN SWORD TALENT.
PLUS...
...IT'S SOME-THING I CAN NEVER ACHIEVE FOR MYSELF.
A VERY VALUABLE STRENGTH.
SO...

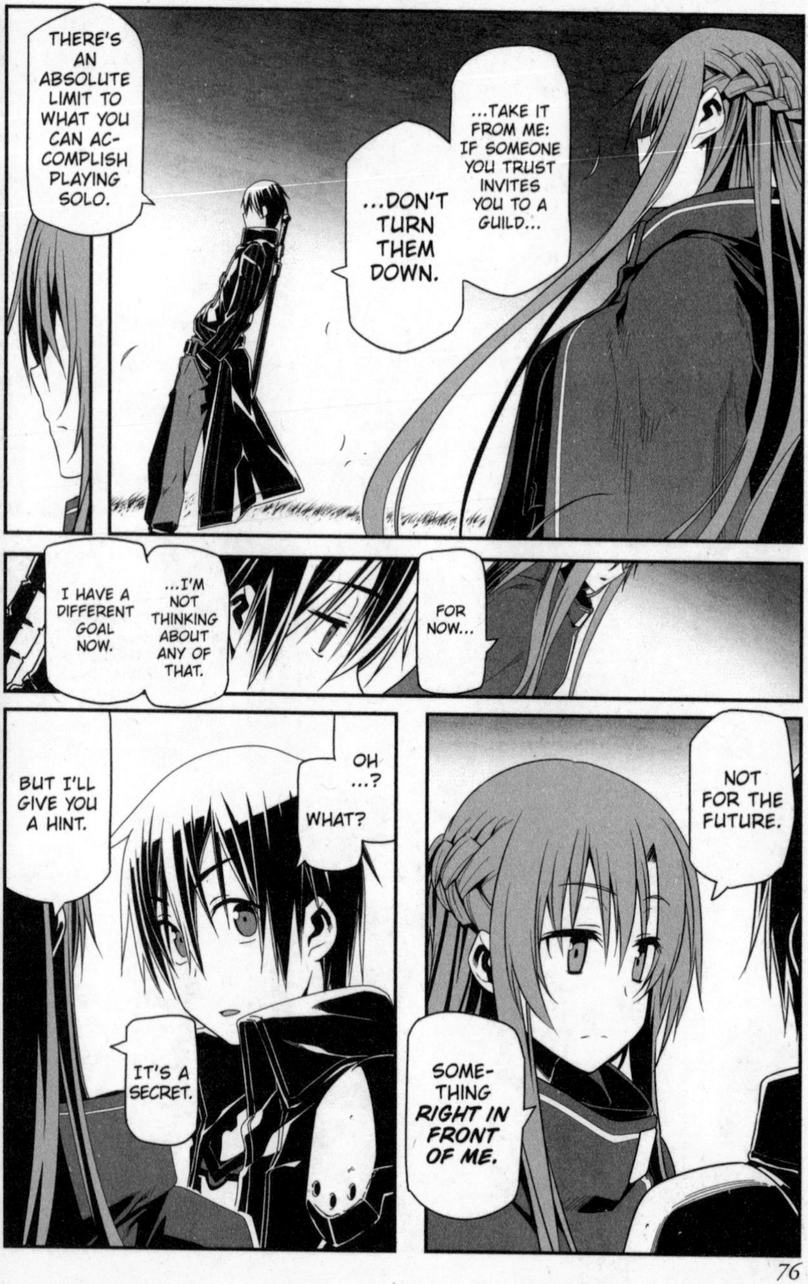
...TAKE IT FROM ME: IF SOMEONE YOU TRUST INVITES YOU TO A GUILD...
...DON'T TURN THEM DOWN.
THERE'S AN ABSOLUTE LIMIT TO WHAT YOU CAN AC-COMPLISH PLAYING SOLO.
FOR NOW...
...I'M NOT THINKING ABOUT ANY OF THAT.
I HAVE A DIFFERENT GOAL NOW.
NOT FOR THE FUTURE.
SOME-THING ***RIGHT IN FRONT*** OF ME.
OH ...? WHAT?
BUT I'LL GIVE YOU A HINT.
IT'S A SECRET.

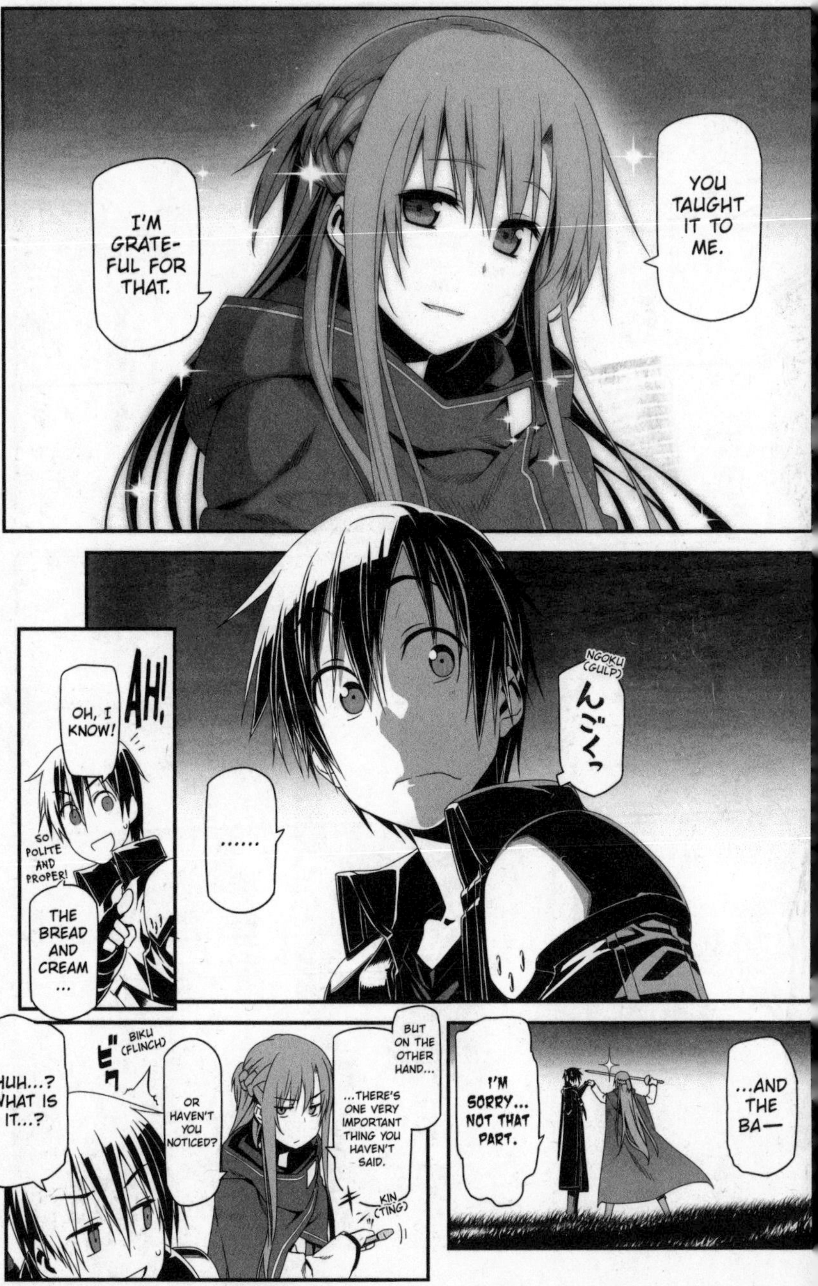
YOU TAUGHT IT TO ME.
I'M GRATEFUL FOR THAT.
NGOKU (GULP)
んごくっ
......
AH!
OH, I KNOW!
SO POLITE AND PROPER!
THE BREAD AND CREAM...
...AND THE BA—
I'M SORRY... NOT THAT PART.
BUT ON THE OTHER HAND...
...THERE'S ONE VERY IMPORTANT THING YOU HAVEN'T SAID.
KIN (TING)
OR HAVEN'T YOU NOTICED?
BIKU (FLINCH)
HUH...? WHAT IS IT...?

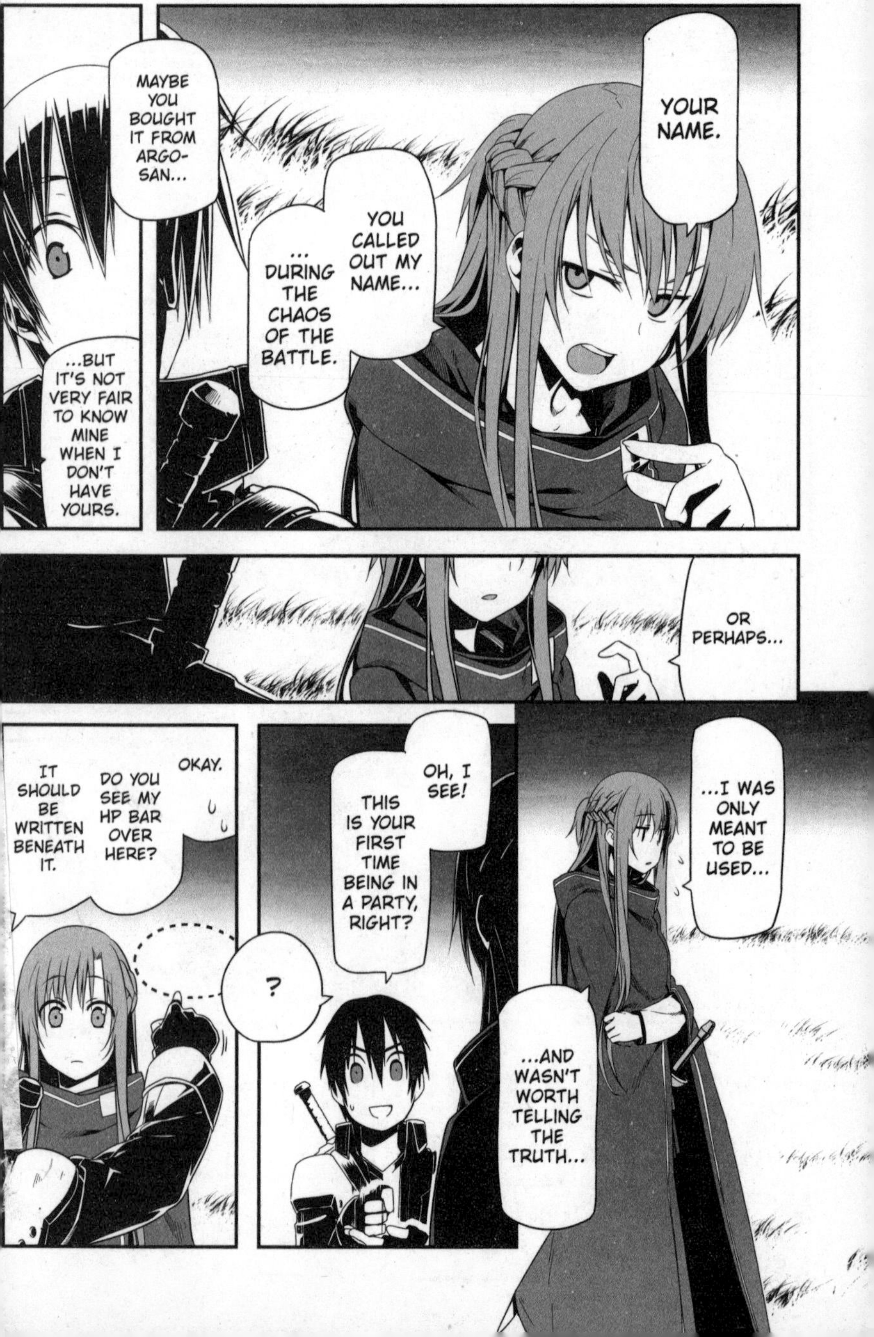
YOUR NAME.
YOU CALLED OUT MY NAME...
...DURING THE CHAOS OF THE BATTLE.
MAYBE YOU BOUGHT IT FROM ARGO-SAN...
...BUT IT'S NOT VERY FAIR TO KNOW MINE WHEN I DON'T HAVE YOURS.
OR PERHAPS...
...I WAS ONLY MEANT TO BE USED...
...AND WASN'T WORTH TELLING THE TRUTH...
OH, I SEE!
THIS IS YOUR FIRST TIME BEING IN A PARTY, RIGHT?
?
OKAY.
DO YOU SEE MY HP BAR OVER HERE?
IT SHOULD BE WRITTEN BENEATH IT.

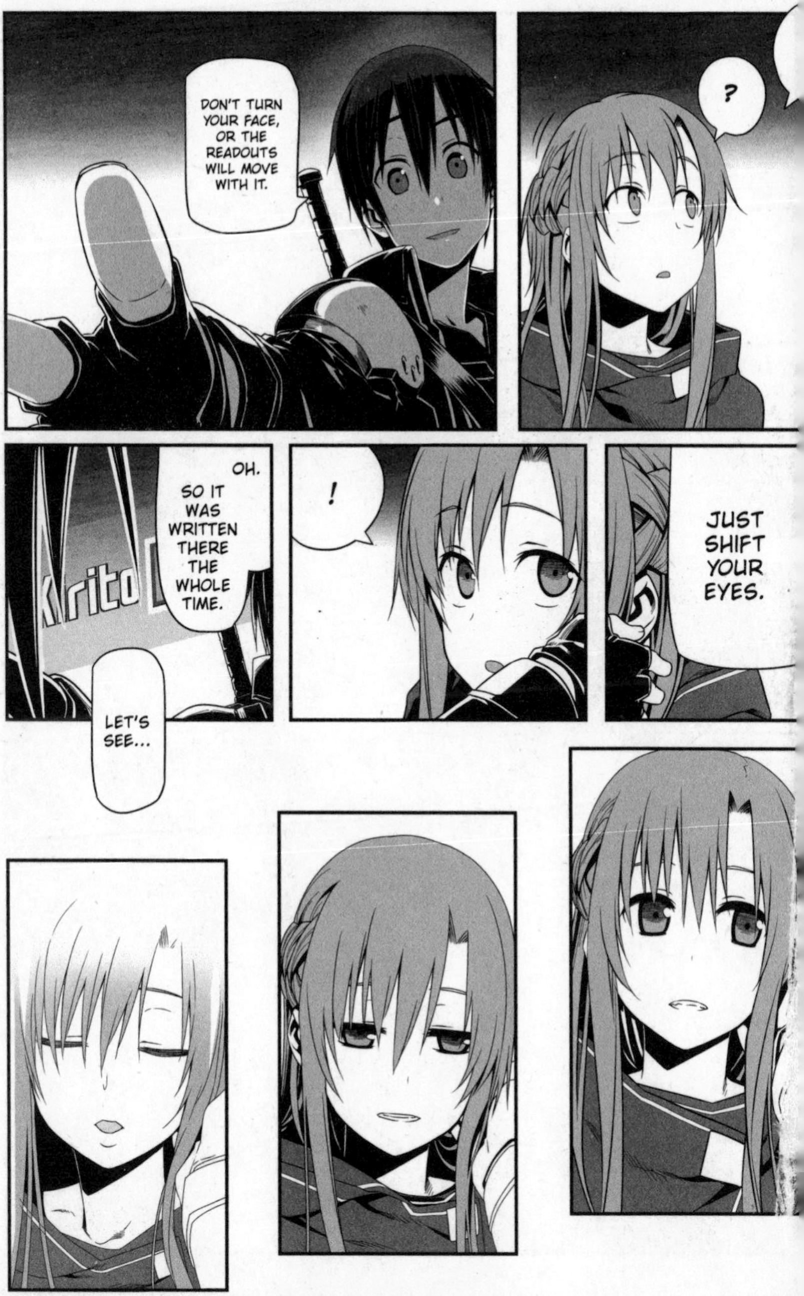
?
DON'T TURN YOUR FACE, OR THE READOUTS WILL MOVE WITH IT.
JUST SHIFT YOUR EYES.
!
OH.
SO IT WAS WRITTEN THERE THE WHOLE TIME.
Kirito
LET'S SEE...

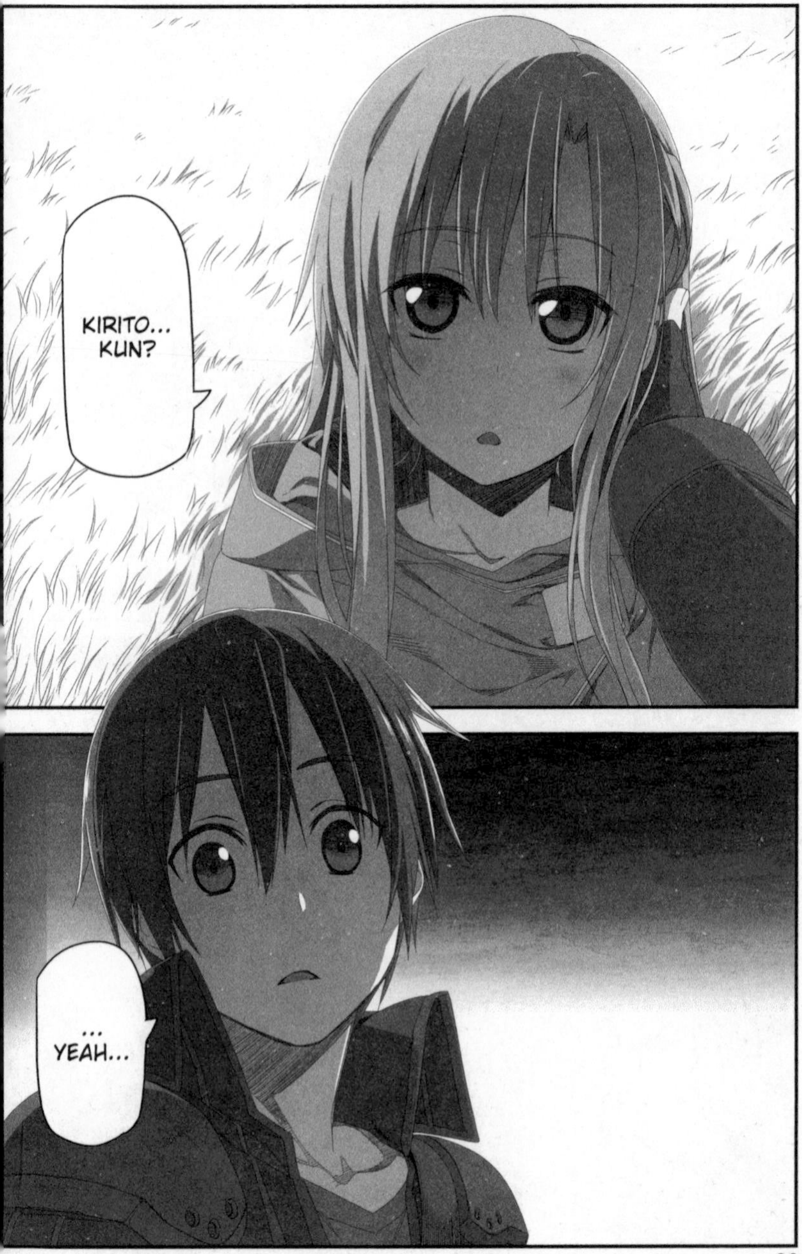
KIRITO... KUN?
... YEAH...

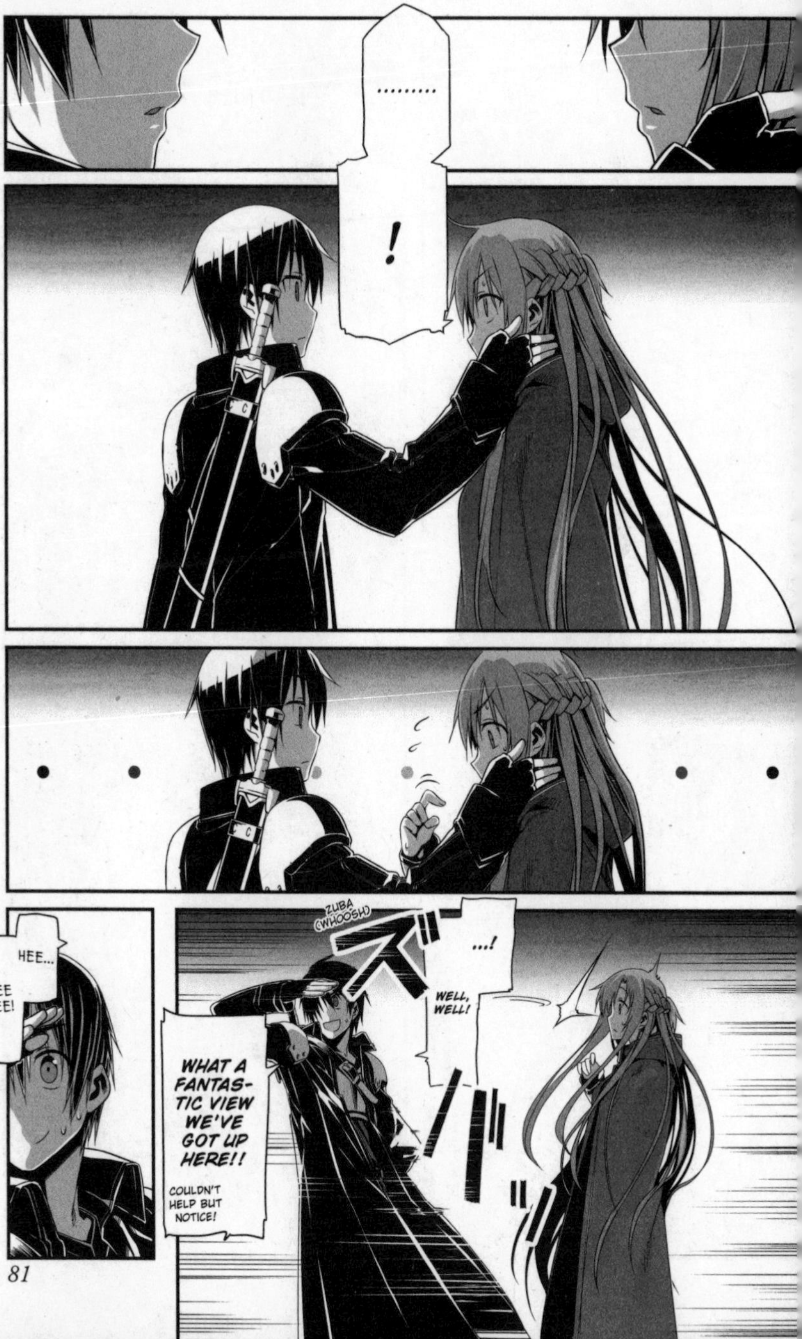

....
!
...!
ZUBA (WHOOSH)
WELL, WELL!
WHAT A FANTAS-TIC VIEW WE'VE GOT UP HERE!!
COULDN'T HELP BUT NOTICE!
HEE...
HEE HEE!

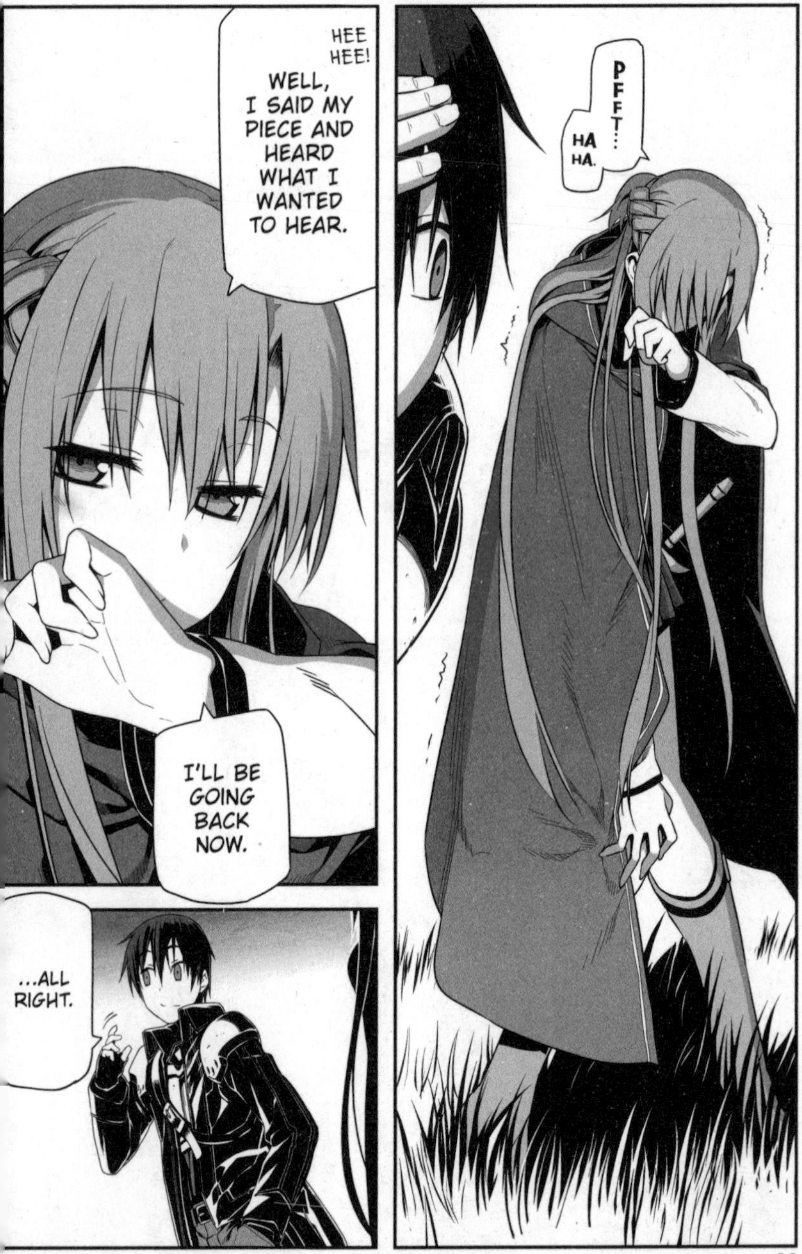
PFFT...
HA HA.
HEE HEE!
WELL, I SAID MY PIECE AND HEARD WHAT I WANTED TO HEAR.
I'LL BE GOING BACK NOW.
...ALL RIGHT.

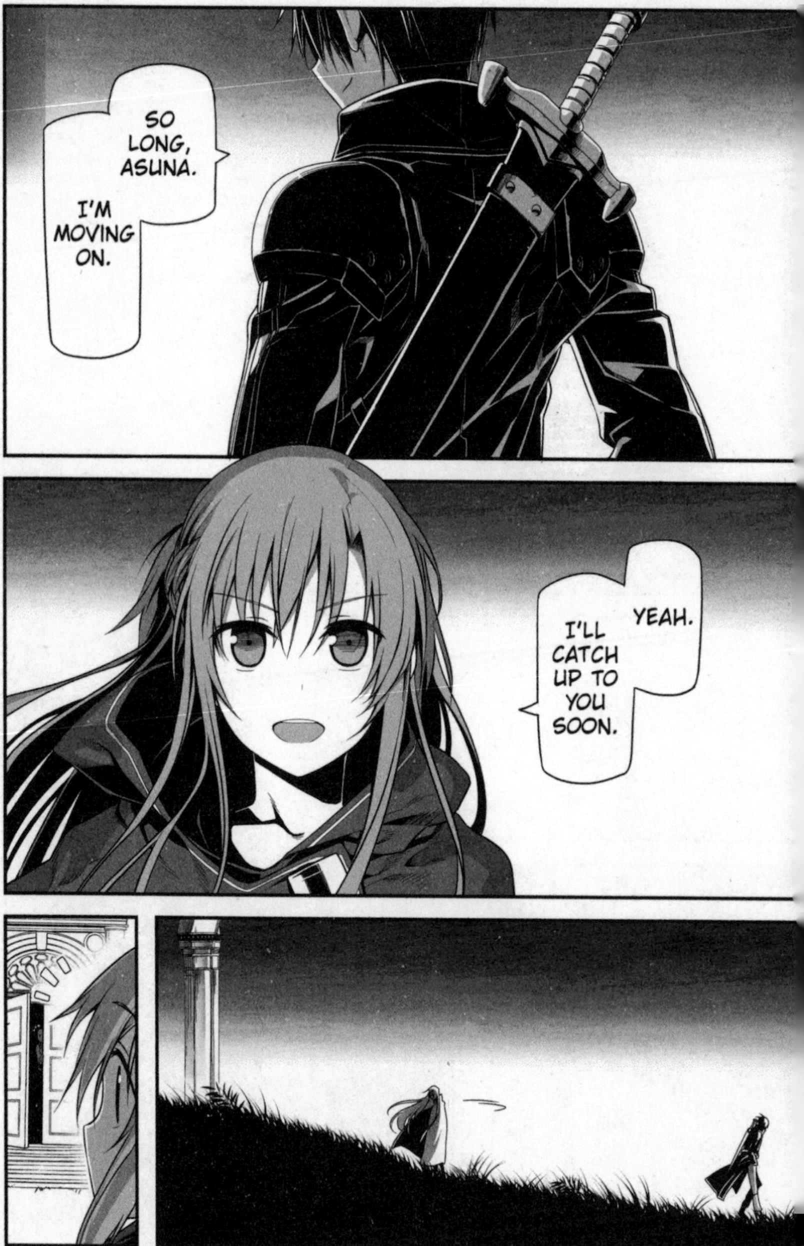
SO LONG, ASUNA.
I'M MOVING ON.
YEAH.
I'LL CATCH UP TO YOU SOON.

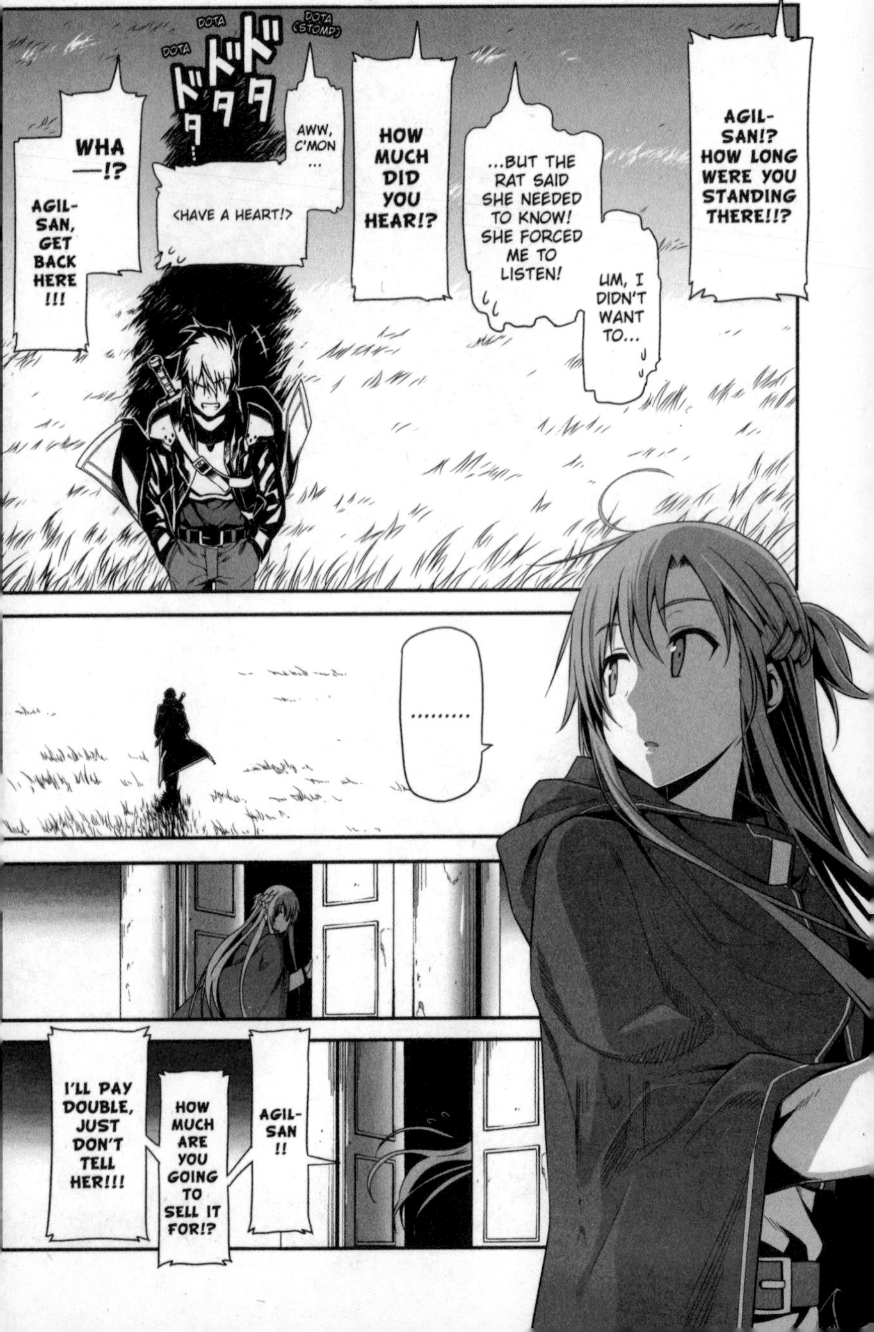
AGIL-SAN!? HOW LONG WERE YOU STANDING THERE!!?
UM, I DIDN'T WANT TO...
...BUT THE RAT SAID SHE NEEDED TO KNOW! SHE FORCED ME TO LISTEN!
HOW MUCH DID YOU HEAR!?
AWW, C'MON...
DOTA (STOMP)
DOTA
DOTA
<HAVE A HEART!>
WHA—!?
AGIL-SAN, GET BACK HERE!!!
....
AGIL-SAN!!
HOW MUCH ARE YOU GOING TO SELL IT FOR!?
I'LL PAY DOUBLE, JUST DON'T TELL HER!!!

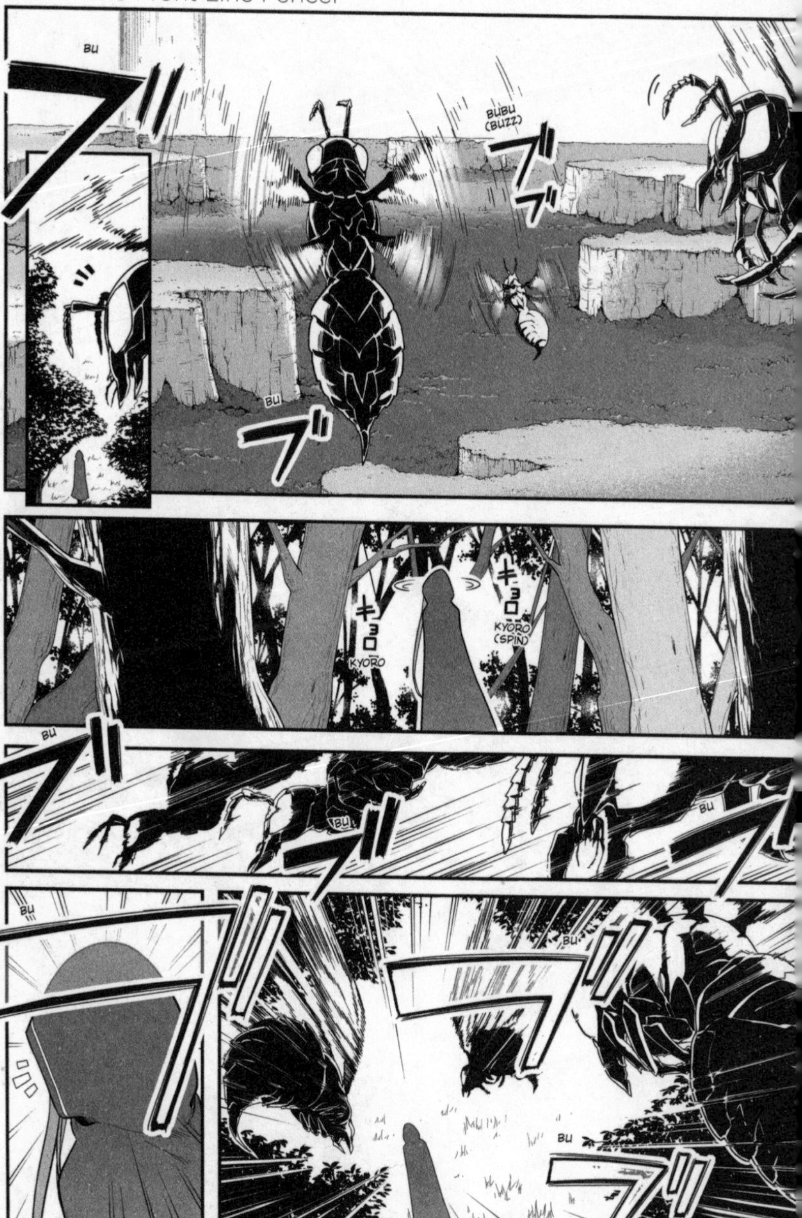
BUBU (BUZZ)
BU
BU
KYORO (SPIN)
KYORO
BU
BU
BU
BU
BU
BU

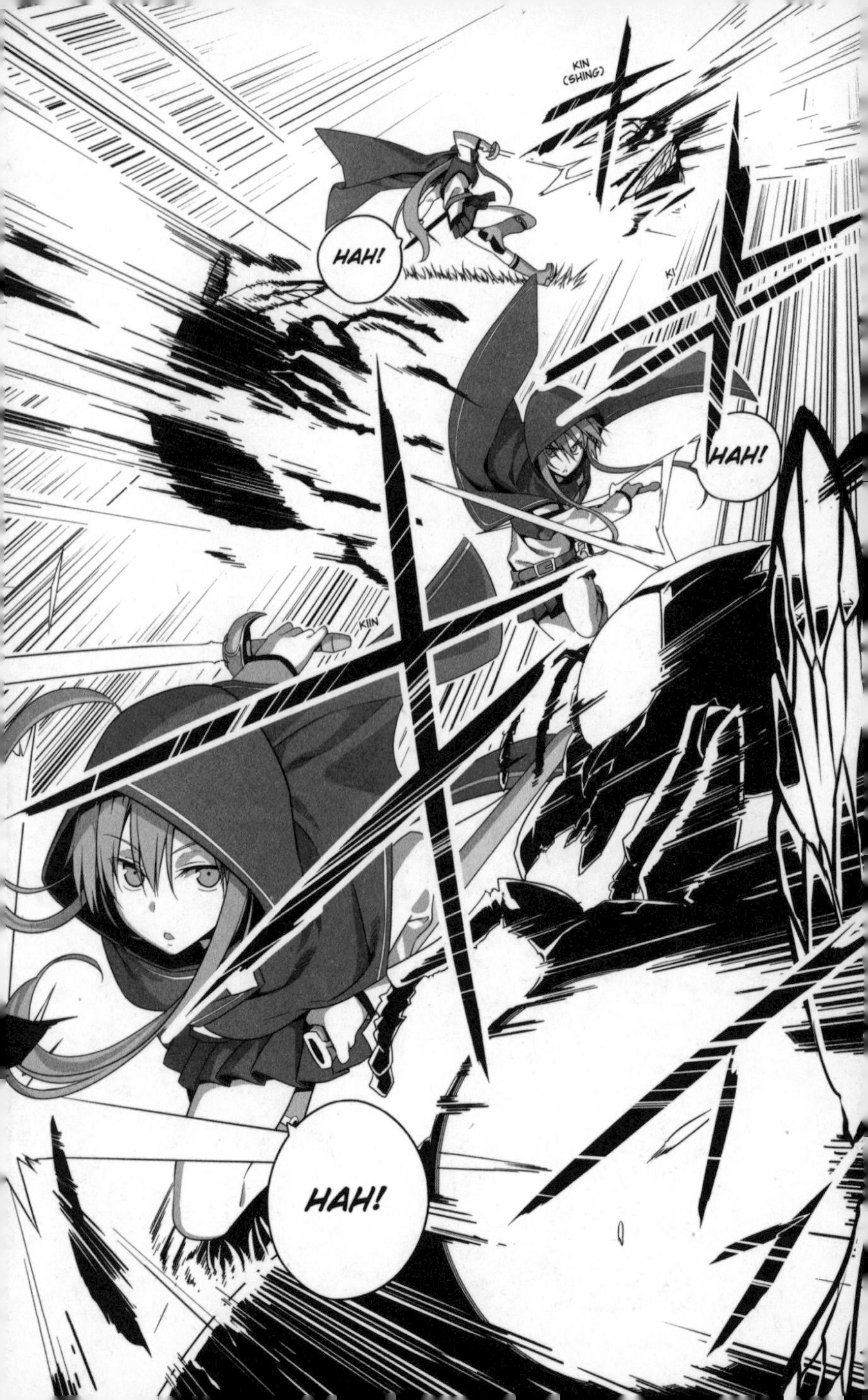
KIN
(SHING)
HAH!
KI
HAH!
KIIN
HAH!

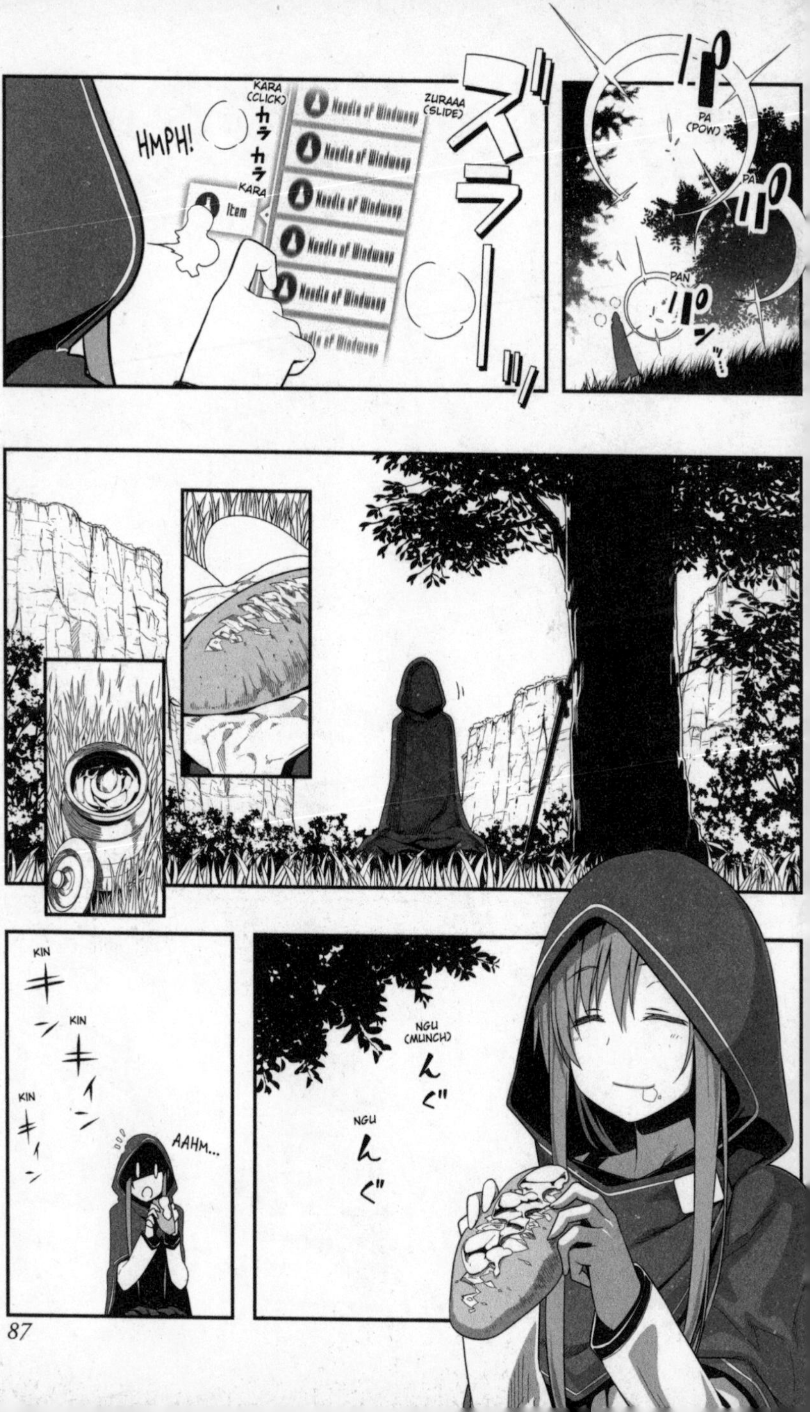
PA (POW)
パ
PA
パ
PAN
パン…
ZURAAA (SLIDE)
ズラーーッ
KARA (CLICK)
カラ
カラ
KARA
Needle of Windwasp
Needle of Windwasp
Needle of Windwasp
Needle of Windwasp
Needle of Windwasp
Item
HMPH!
NGU (MUNCH)
んぐ
NGU
んぐ
KIN
キーン
KIN
キイーン
KIN
キイン
AAHM...

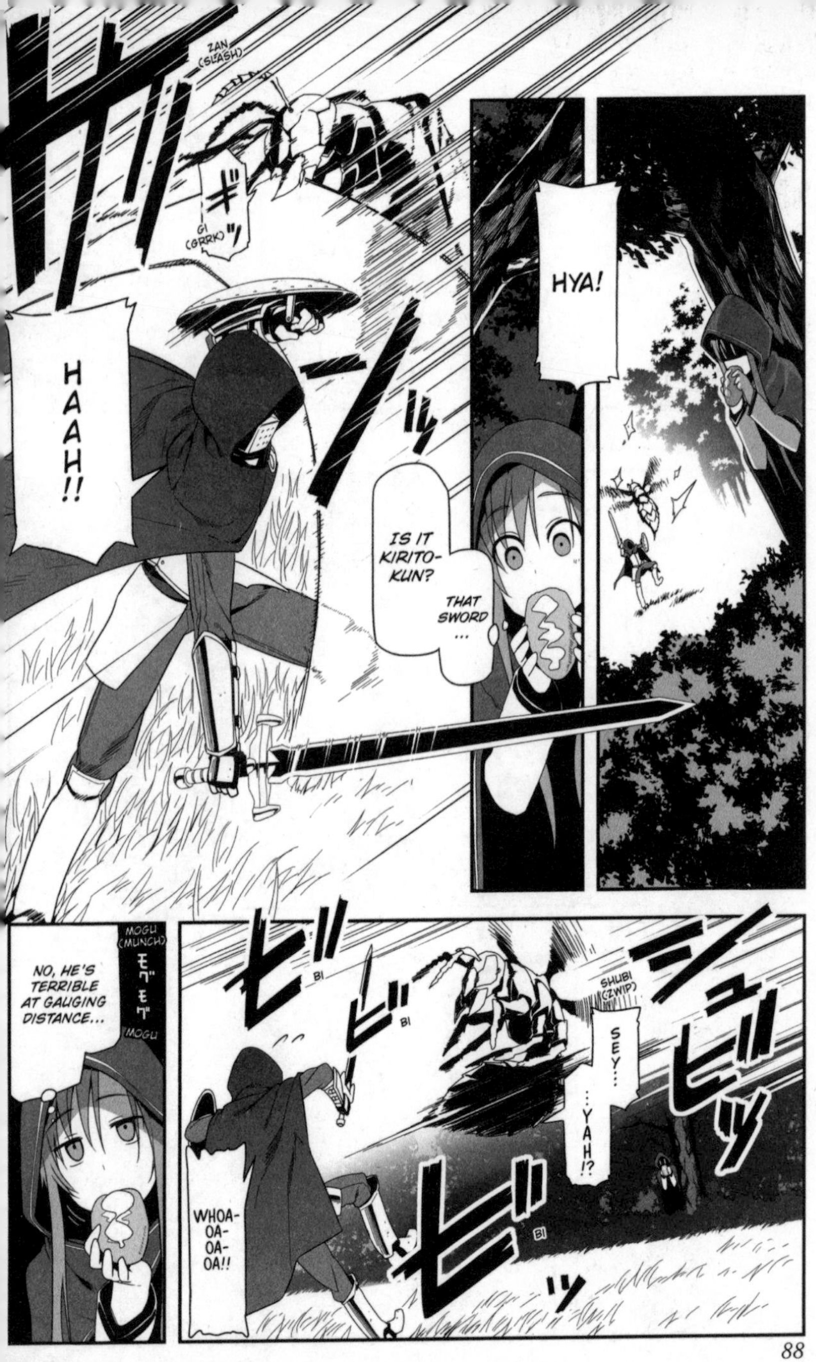
HYA!
IS IT KIRITO-KUN?
THAT SWORD ...
ZAN (SLASH)
GI (GRRK)
HAAAH!!
SHUBI (ZWIP)
SEY...
...YAH!?
BI
BI
BI
WHOA-OA-OA-OA!!
MOGU (MUNCH) MOGU
NO, HE'S TERRIBLE AT GAUGING DISTANCE...

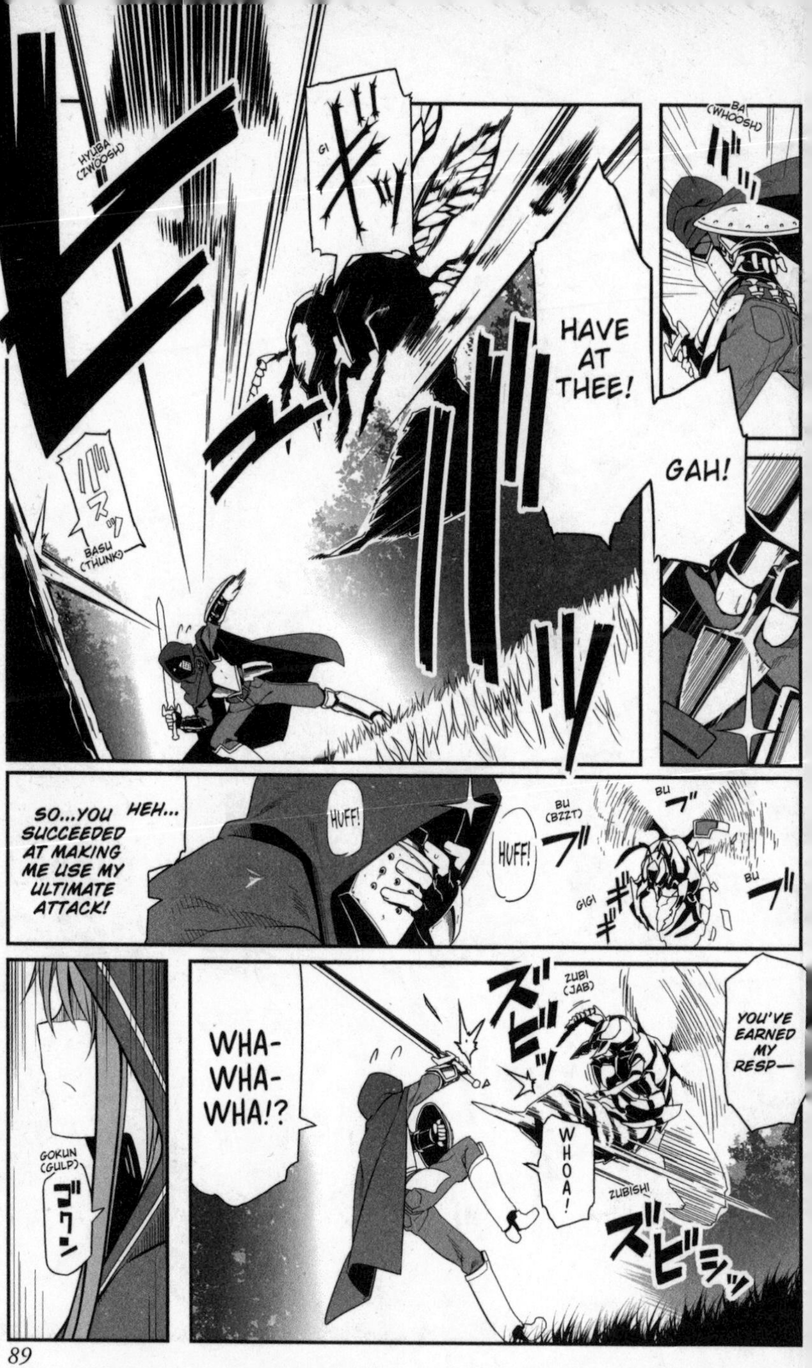
BA (WHOOSH)
バッ
HAVE AT THEE!
GAH!
GI
ギギッ
HYUBA (ZWOOSH)
BASU (THUNK)
バスッ
BU (BZZT)
ブ
BU
ブ
BU
ブ
GIGI
ギギ
HUFF!
HUFF!
HEH...
SO...YOU SUCCEEDED AT MAKING ME USE MY ULTIMATE ATTACK!
YOU'VE EARNED MY RESP—
ZUBI (JAB)
ズビッ
WHOA!
ZUBISHI
ズビシッ
WHA-WHA-WHA!?
GOKUN (GULP)
ゴクン

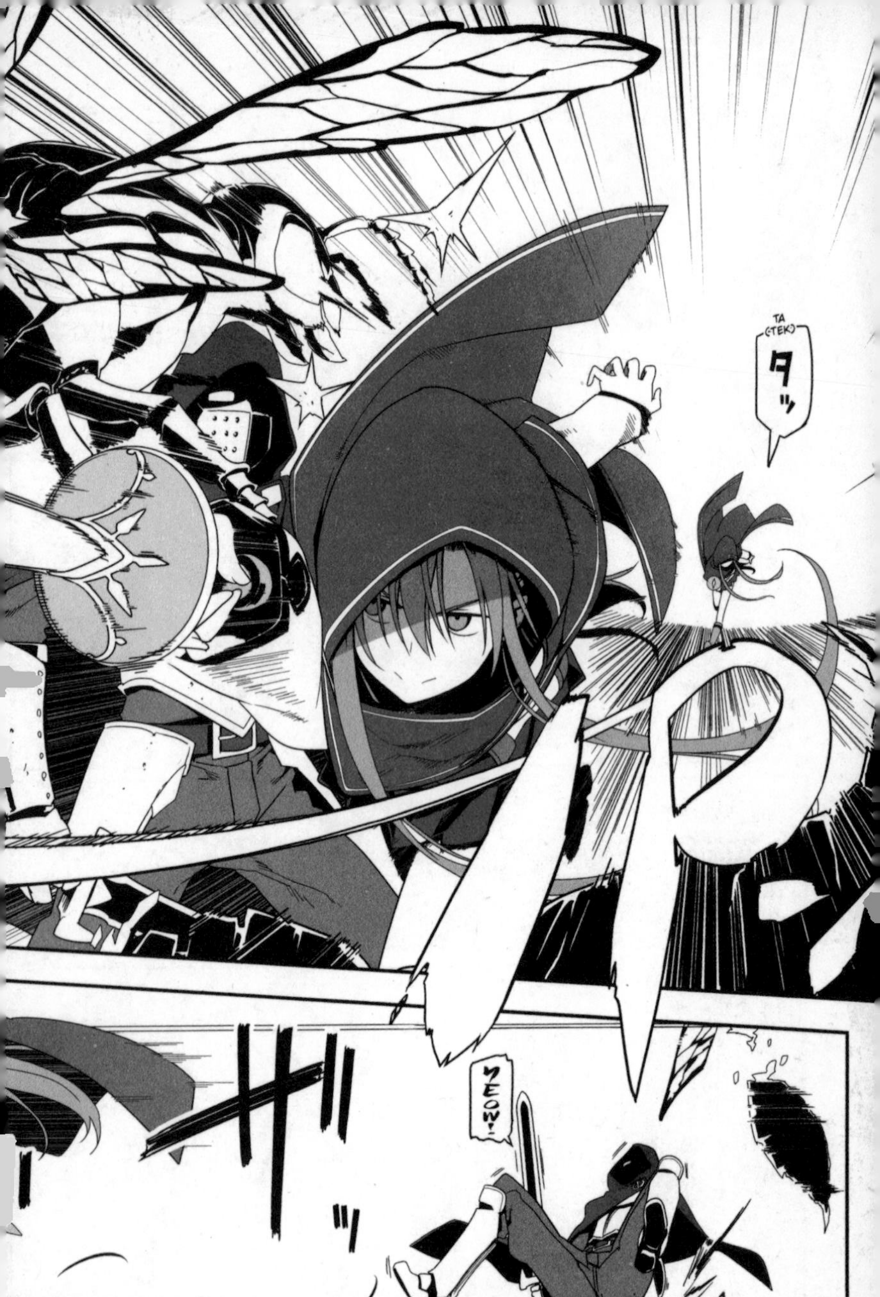
TA (TEK)
タッ
MYEOW!

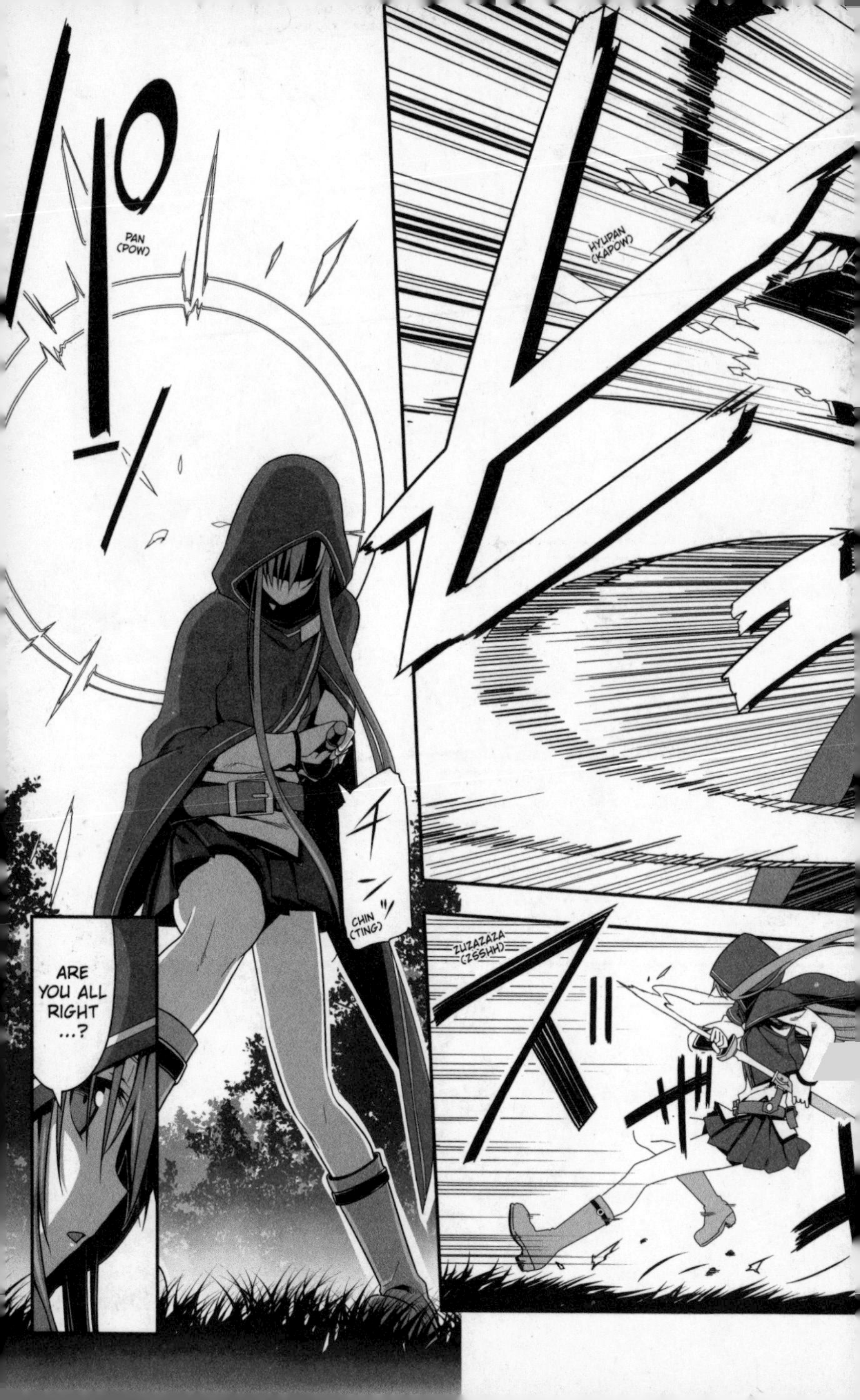
HYUPAN (KAPOW)
ZUZAZAZA (ZSSHH)
PAN (POW)
CHIN (TING)
ARE YOU ALL RIGHT ...?

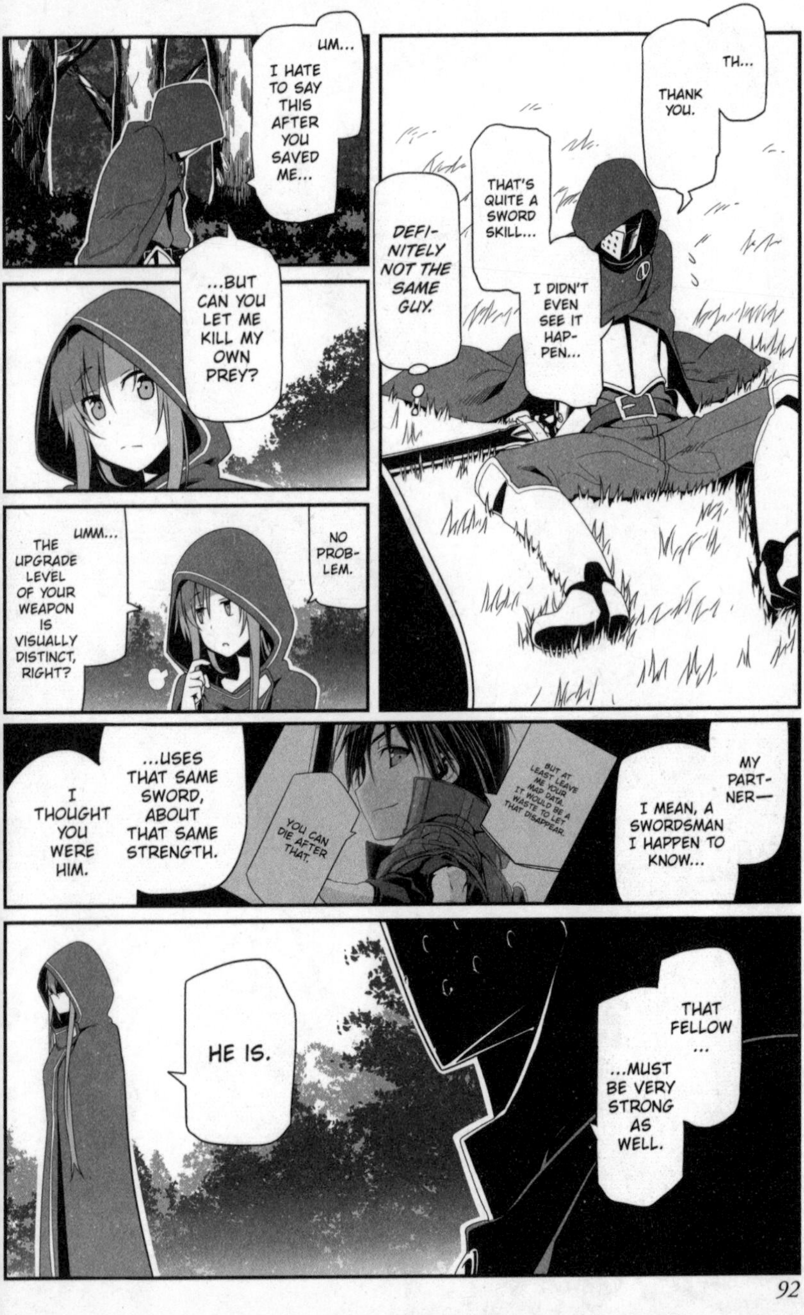
TH...
THANK YOU.
THAT'S QUITE A SWORD SKILL...
I DIDN'T EVEN SEE IT HAPPEN...
DEFINITELY NOT THE SAME GUY.
UM...
I HATE TO SAY THIS AFTER YOU SAVED ME...
...BUT CAN YOU LET ME KILL MY OWN PREY?
NO PROBLEM.
UMM...
THE UPGRADE LEVEL OF YOUR WEAPON IS VISUALLY DISTINCT, RIGHT?
MY PARTNER—
I MEAN, A SWORDSMAN I HAPPEN TO KNOW...
BUT AT LEAST LEAVE ME YOUR MAP DATA. IT WOULD BE A WASTE TO LET THAT DISAPPEAR.
YOU CAN DIE AFTER THAT.
...USES THAT SAME SWORD, ABOUT THAT SAME STRENGTH.
I THOUGHT YOU WERE HIM.
THAT FELLOW...
...MUST BE VERY STRONG AS WELL.
HE IS.

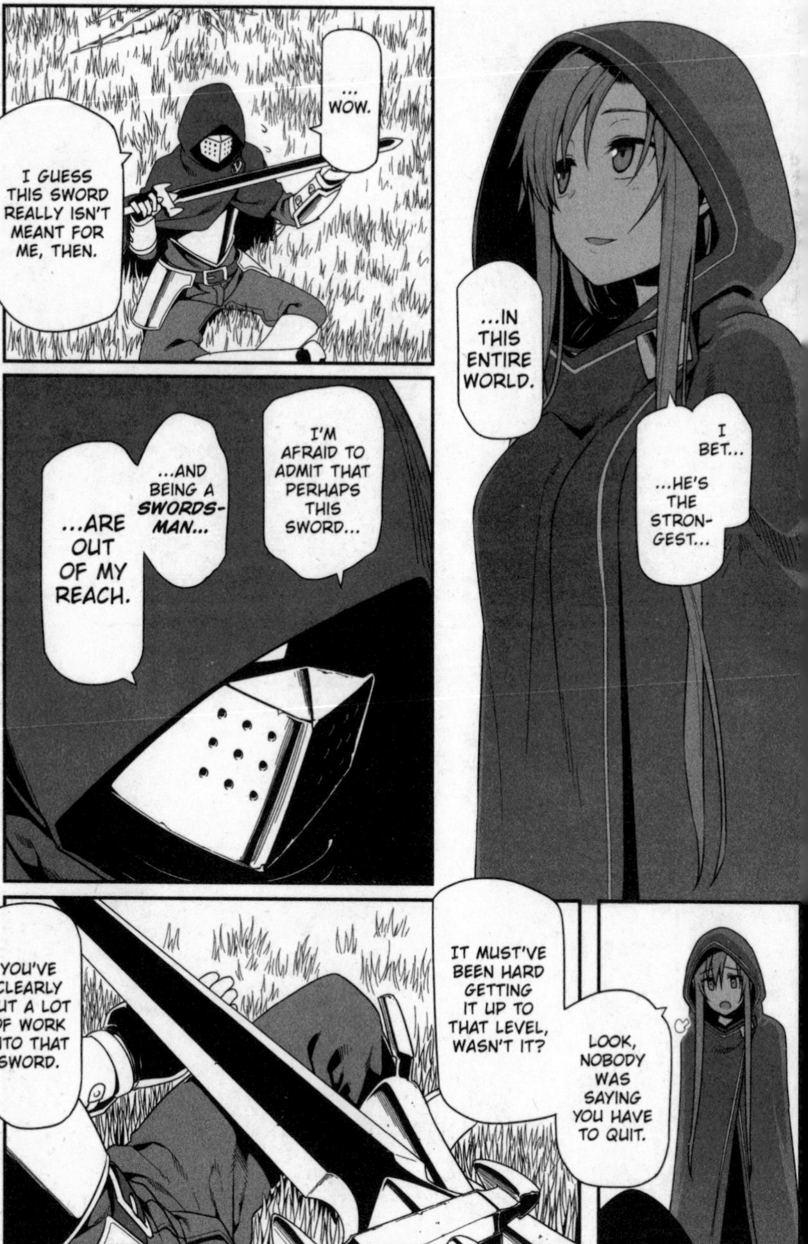
I BET...
...HE'S THE STRONGEST...
...IN THIS ENTIRE WORLD.
...WOW.
I GUESS THIS SWORD REALLY ISN'T MEANT FOR ME, THEN.
I'M AFRAID TO ADMIT THAT PERHAPS THIS SWORD...
...AND BEING A ***SWORDSMAN...***
...ARE OUT OF MY REACH.
LOOK, NOBODY WAS SAYING YOU HAVE TO QUIT.
IT MUST'VE BEEN HARD GETTING IT UP TO THAT LEVEL, WASN'T IT?
YOU'VE CLEARLY PUT A LOT OF WORK INTO THAT SWORD.

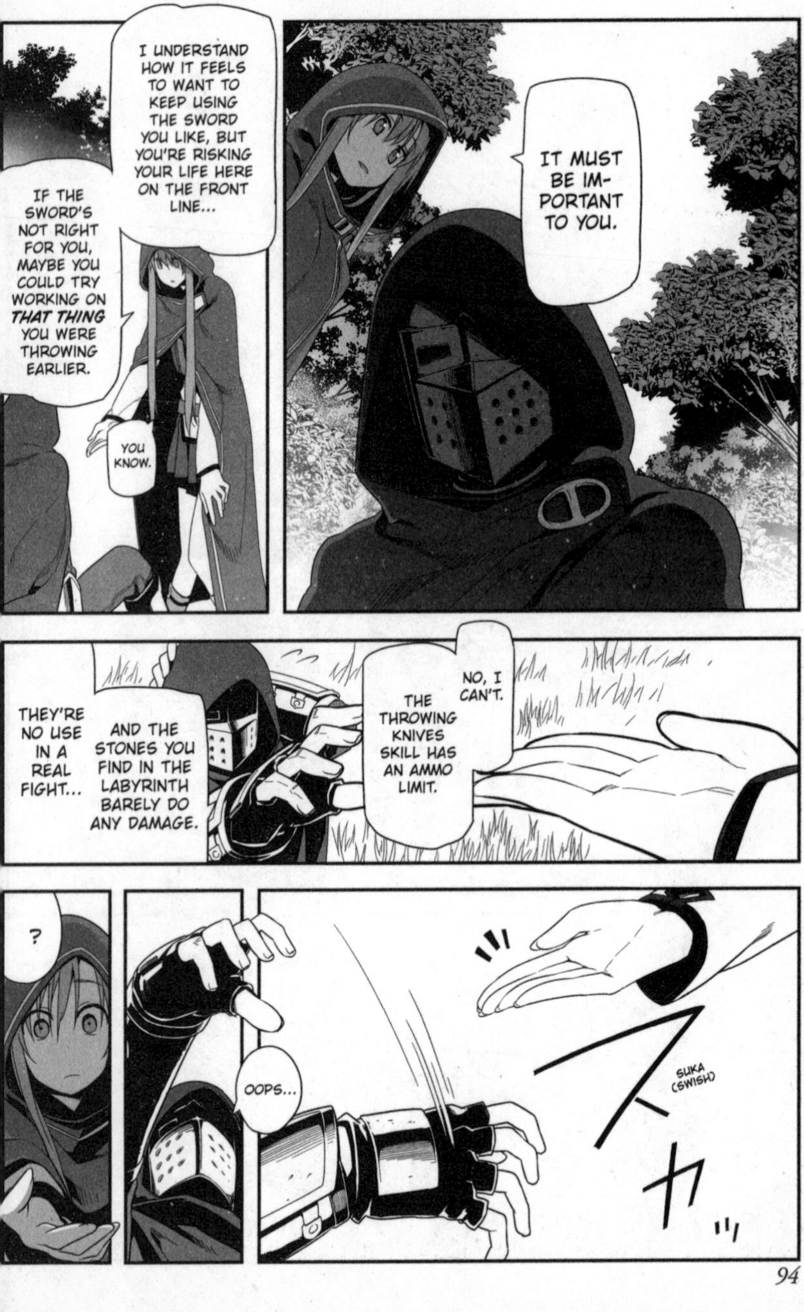
IT MUST BE IMPORTANT TO YOU.
I UNDERSTAND HOW IT FEELS TO WANT TO KEEP USING THE SWORD YOU LIKE, BUT YOU'RE RISKING YOUR LIFE HERE ON THE FRONT LINE...
IF THE SWORD'S NOT RIGHT FOR YOU, MAYBE YOU COULD TRY WORKING ON ***THAT THING*** YOU WERE THROWING EARLIER.
YOU KNOW.
NO, I CAN'T.
THE THROWING KNIVES SKILL HAS AN AMMO LIMIT.
AND THE STONES YOU FIND IN THE LABYRINTH BARELY DO ANY DAMAGE.
THEY'RE NO USE IN A REAL FIGHT...
SUKA (SWISH)
OOPS...
?

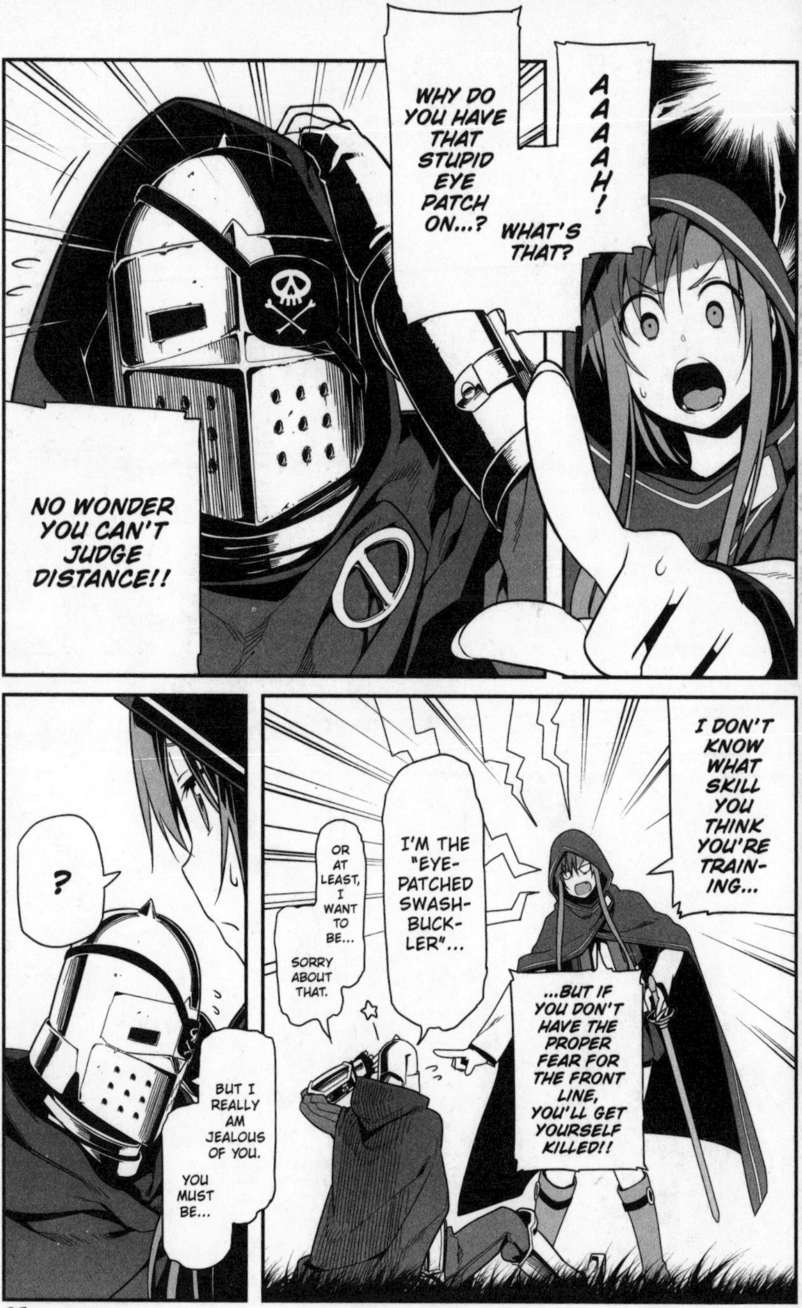
AAAAH!
WHAT'S THAT?
WHY DO YOU HAVE THAT STUPID EYE PATCH ON...?
NO WONDER YOU CAN'T JUDGE DISTANCE!!
I DON'T KNOW WHAT SKILL YOU THINK YOU'RE TRAINING...
...BUT IF YOU DON'T HAVE THE PROPER FEAR FOR THE FRONT LINE, YOU'LL GET YOURSELF KILLED!!
I'M THE "EYE-PATCHED SWASHBUCKLER"...
OR AT LEAST, I WANT TO BE... SORRY ABOUT THAT.
?
BUT I REALLY AM JEALOUS OF YOU. YOU MUST BE...

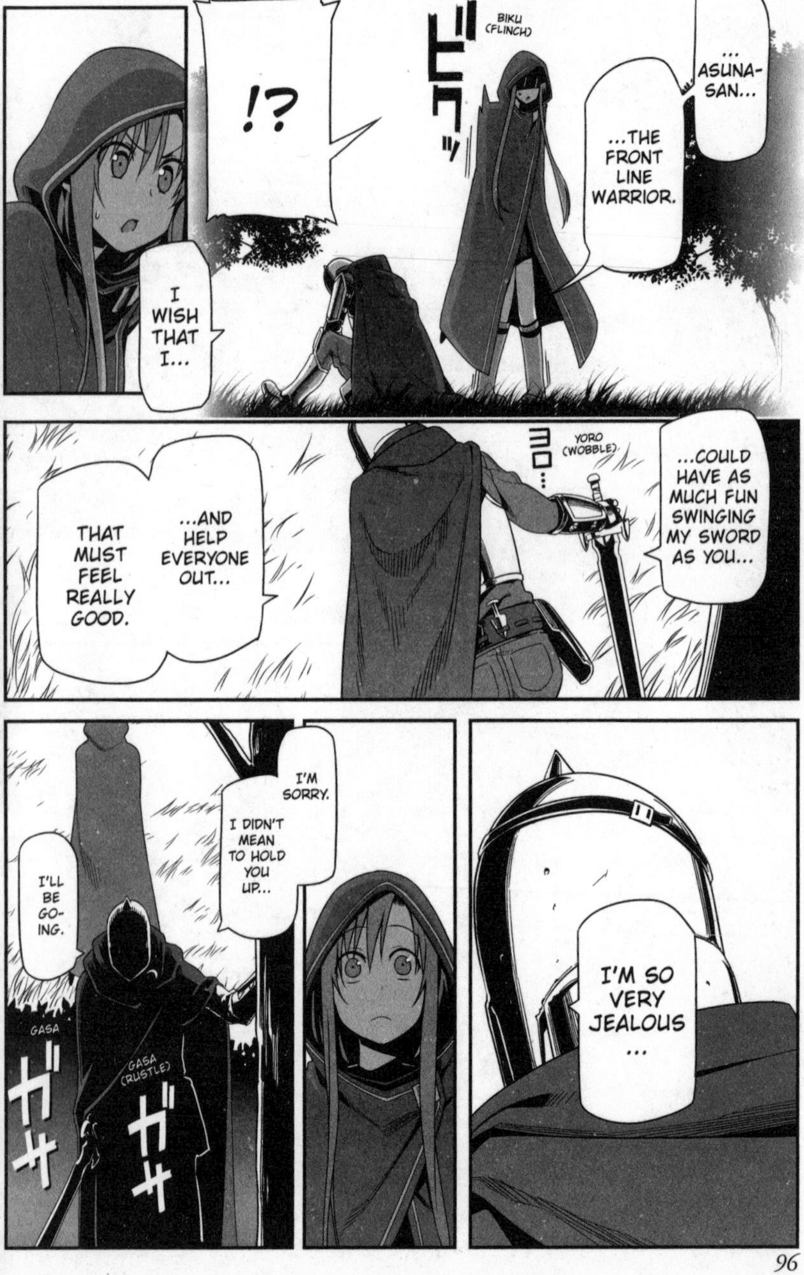
...ASUNA-SAN...
...THE FRONT LINE WARRIOR.
ビクッ
BIKU (FLINCH)
!?
I WISH THAT I...
...COULD HAVE AS MUCH FUN SWINGING MY SWORD AS YOU...
ヨロ…
YORO (WOBBLE)
...AND HELP EVERYONE OUT...
THAT MUST FEEL REALLY GOOD.
I'M SO VERY JEALOUS ...
I'M SORRY.
I DIDN'T MEAN TO HOLD YOU UP...
I'LL BE GO-ING.
ガサ
GASA (RUSTLE)
ガサ
GASA

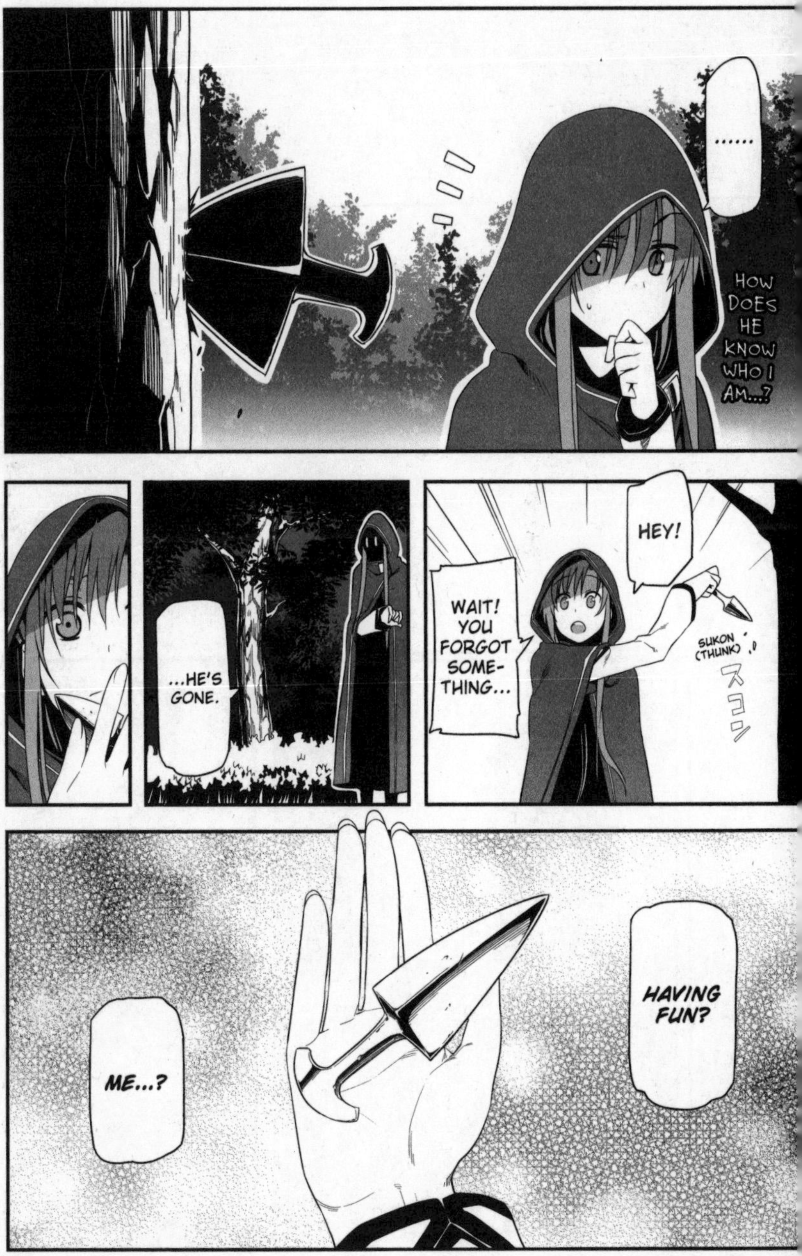
......
HOW DOES HE KNOW WHO I AM...?
HEY!
WAIT! YOU FORGOT SOME-THING...
SUKON (THUNK)
スコン
...HE'S GONE.
HAVING FUN?
ME...?

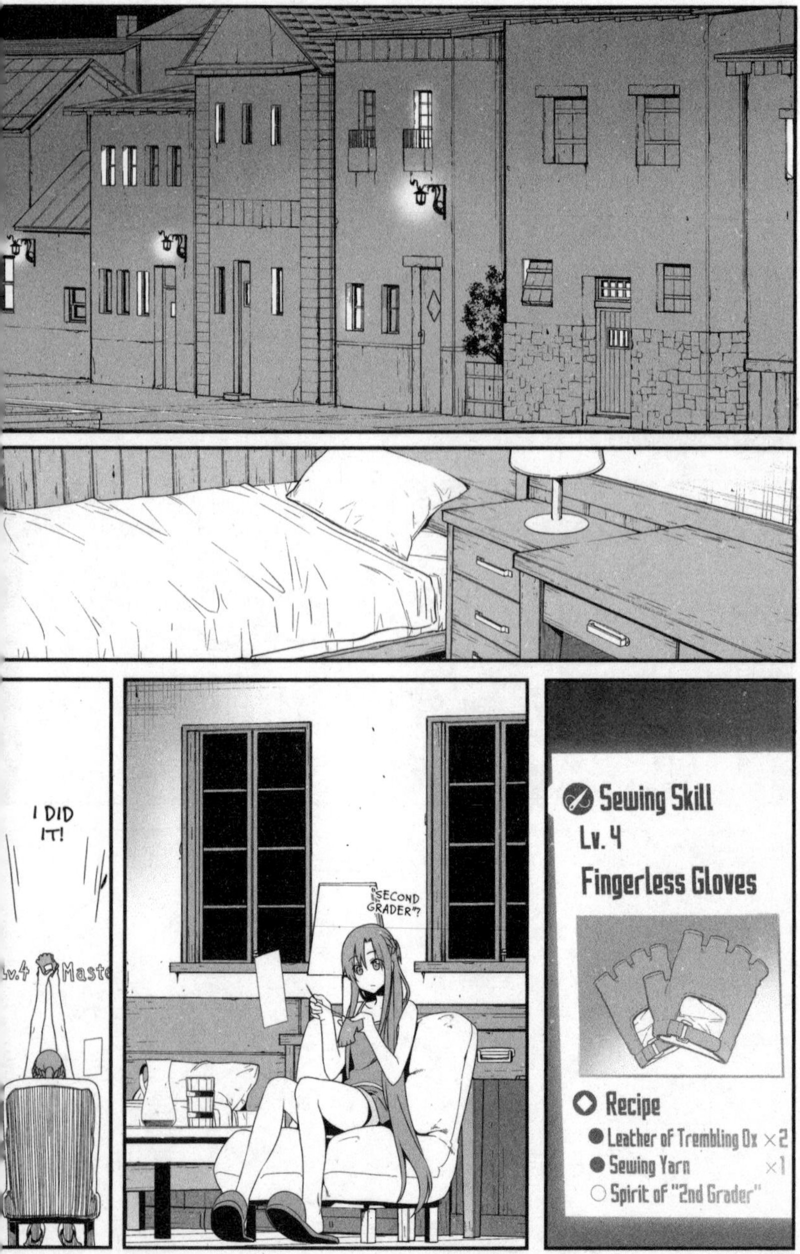
Sewing Skill
Lv. 4
Fingerless Gloves
Recipe
Leather of Trembling Ox ×2
Sewing Yarn ×1
Spirit of "2nd Grader"
"SECOND GRADER"?
I DID IT!

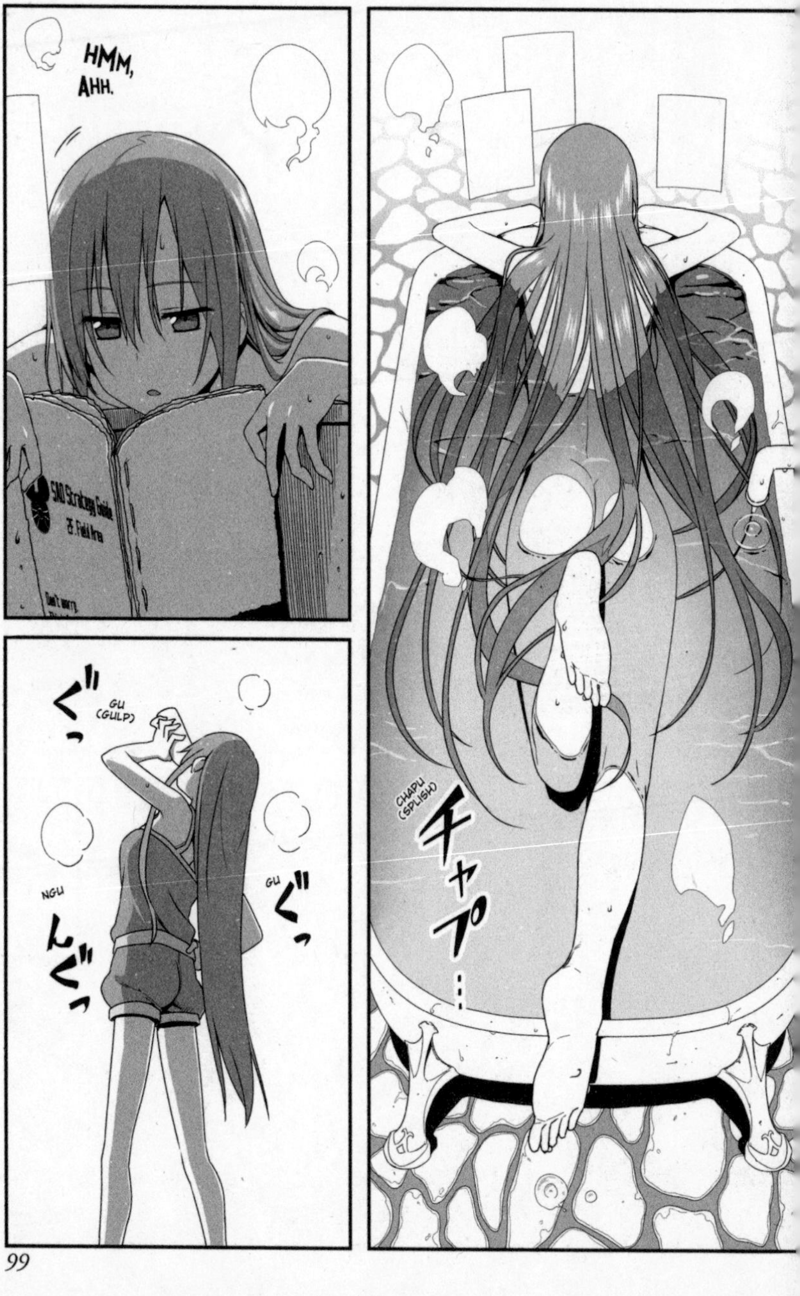
CHAPU (SPLISH)
チャプ…
HMM, AHH.
SAO Strategy Guide
25. Field Area
Don't worry.
ぐっ
GU (GULP)
ぐっ
GU
んぐっ
NGU

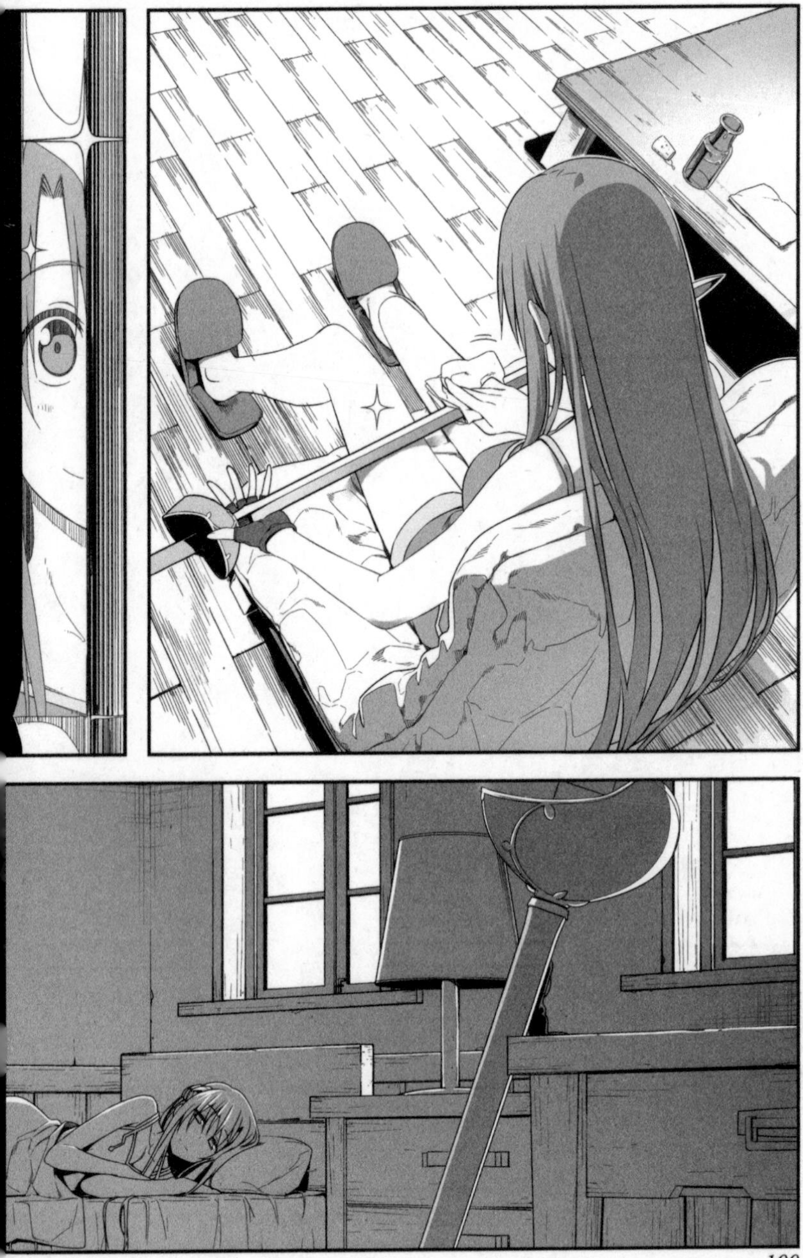

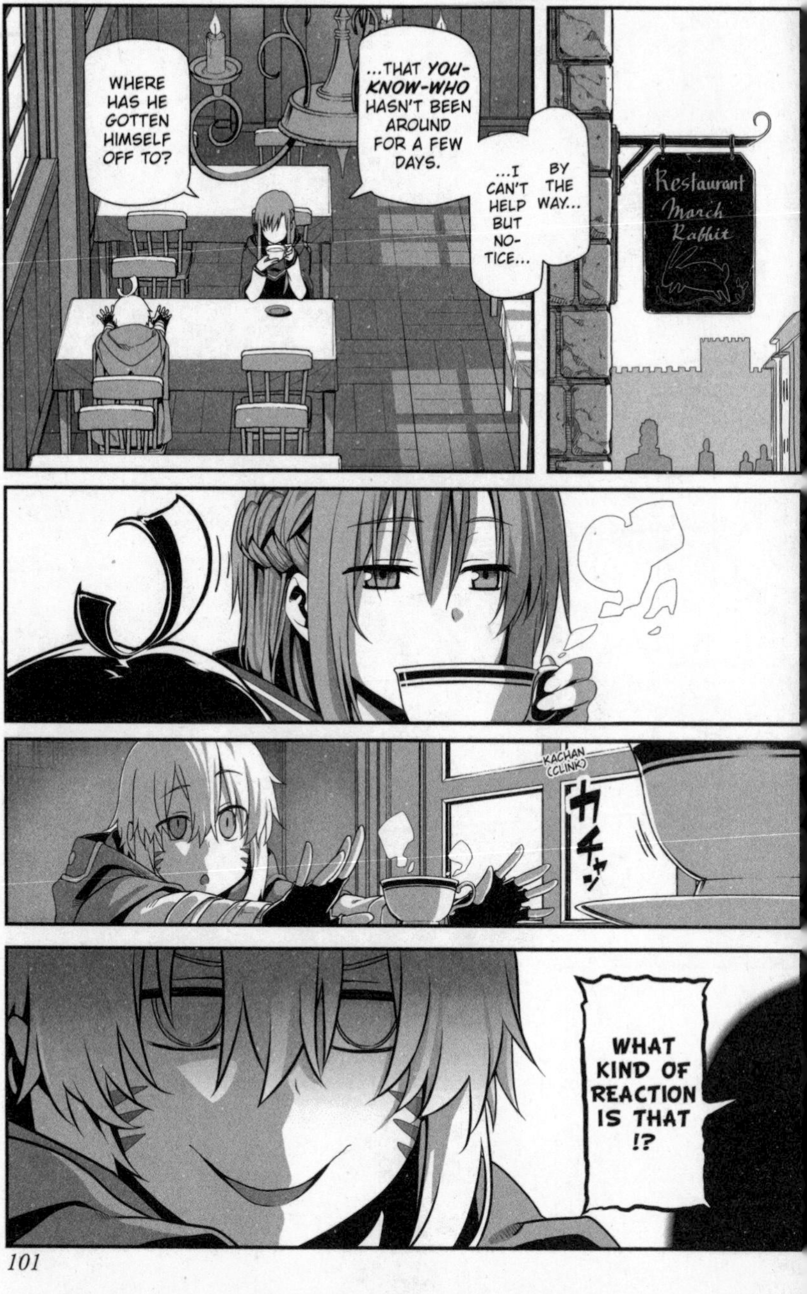
Restaurant March Rabbit
BY THE WAY... ...I CAN'T HELP BUT NOTICE...
...THAT YOU-KNOW-WHO HASN'T BEEN AROUND FOR A FEW DAYS.
WHERE HAS HE GOTTEN HIMSELF OFF TO?
カチャン
KACHAN (CLINK)
WHAT KIND OF REACTION IS THAT!?

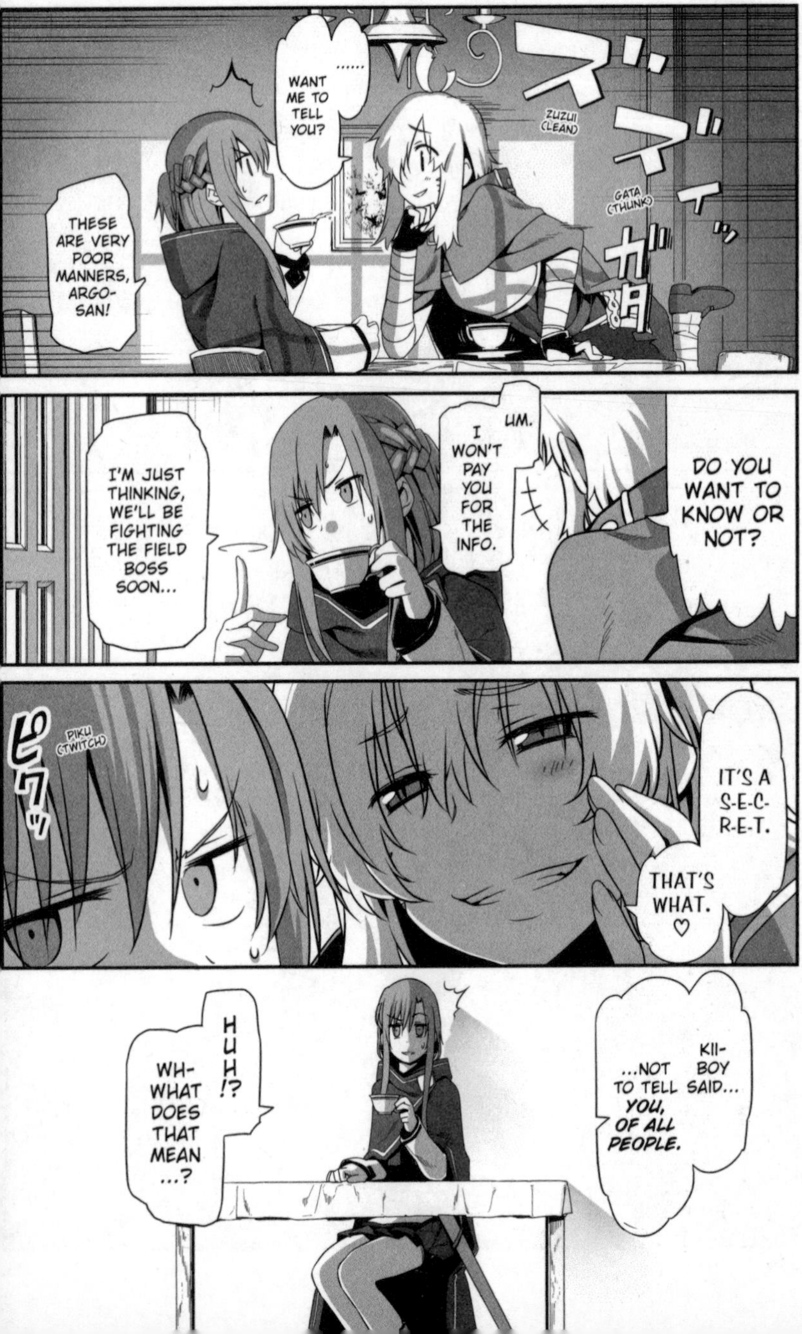
ZUZUII (CLEAN)
GATA (THUNK)
...... WANT ME TO TELL YOU?
THESE ARE VERY POOR MANNERS, ARGO-SAN!
DO YOU WANT TO KNOW OR NOT?
UM. I WON'T PAY YOU FOR THE INFO.
I'M JUST THINKING, WE'LL BE FIGHTING THE FIELD BOSS SOON...
IT'S A S-E-C-R-E-T.
THAT'S WHAT. ♡
PIKU (TWITCH)
KII-BOY SAID...
...NOT TO TELL YOU, OF ALL PEOPLE.
HUH!?
WH-WHAT DOES THAT MEAN...?

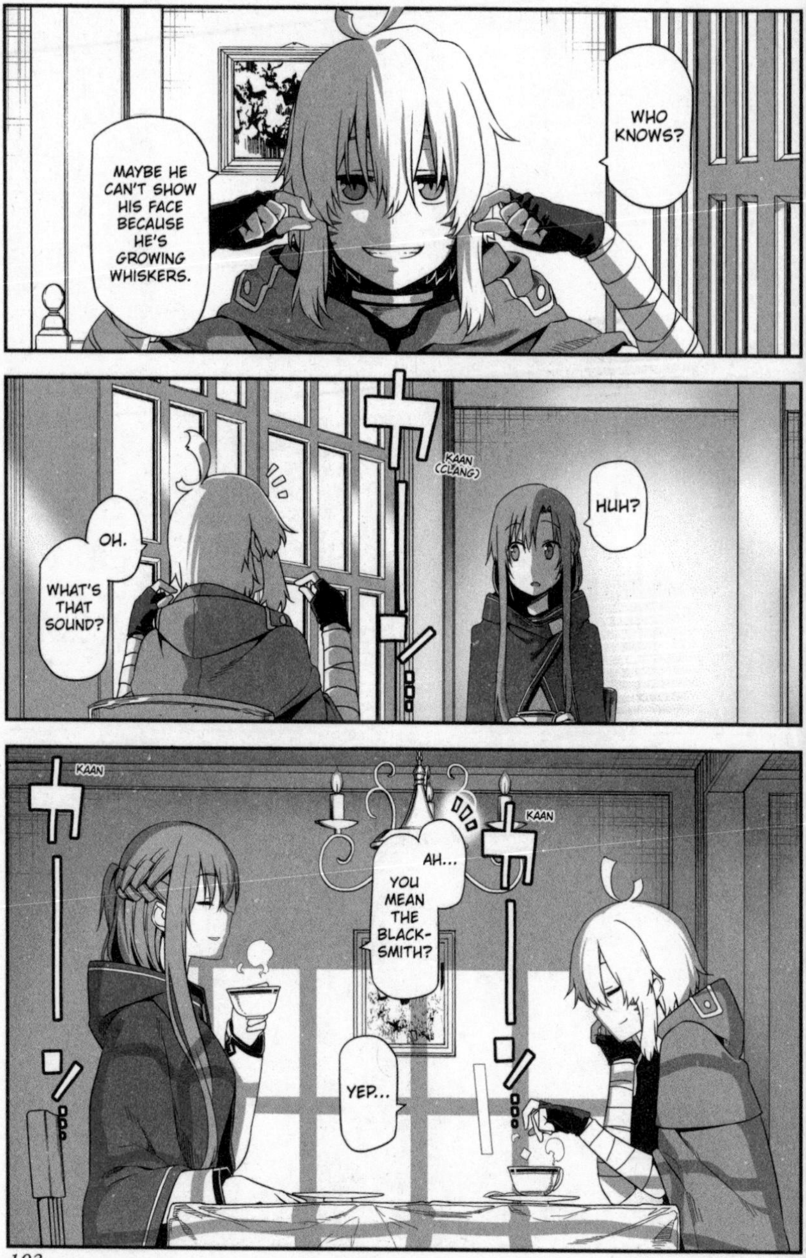
WHO KNOWS?
MAYBE HE CAN'T SHOW HIS FACE BECAUSE HE'S GROWING WHISKERS.
KAAN (CLANG)
HUH?
OH.
WHAT'S THAT SOUND?
KAAN
KAAN
AH... YOU MEAN THE BLACK-SMITH?
YEP...

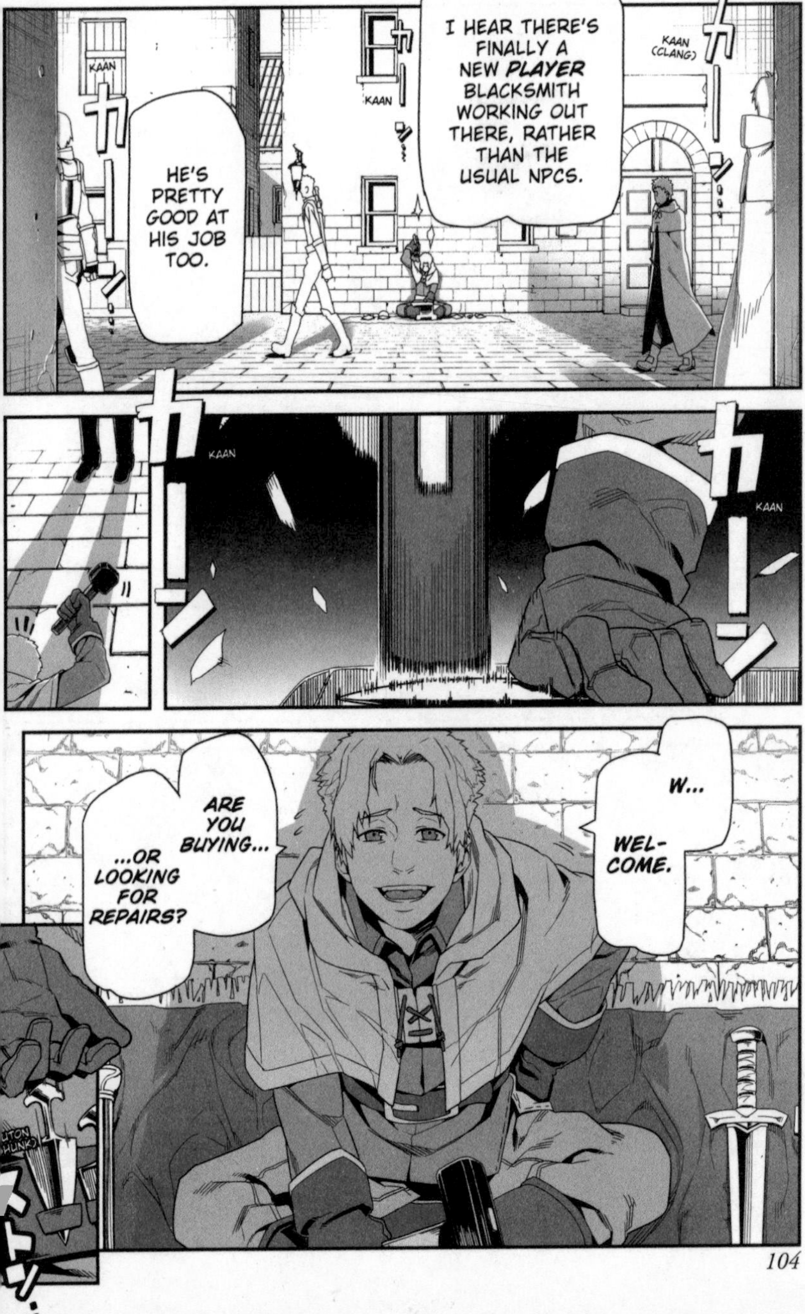
KAAN (CLANG)
I HEAR THERE'S FINALLY A NEW PLAYER BLACKSMITH WORKING OUT THERE, RATHER THAN THE USUAL NPCS.
KAAN
KAAN
HE'S PRETTY GOOD AT HIS JOB TOO.
KAAN
KAAN
W...
WEL-COME.
ARE YOU BUYING...
...OR LOOKING FOR REPAIRS?

#009: Reunion

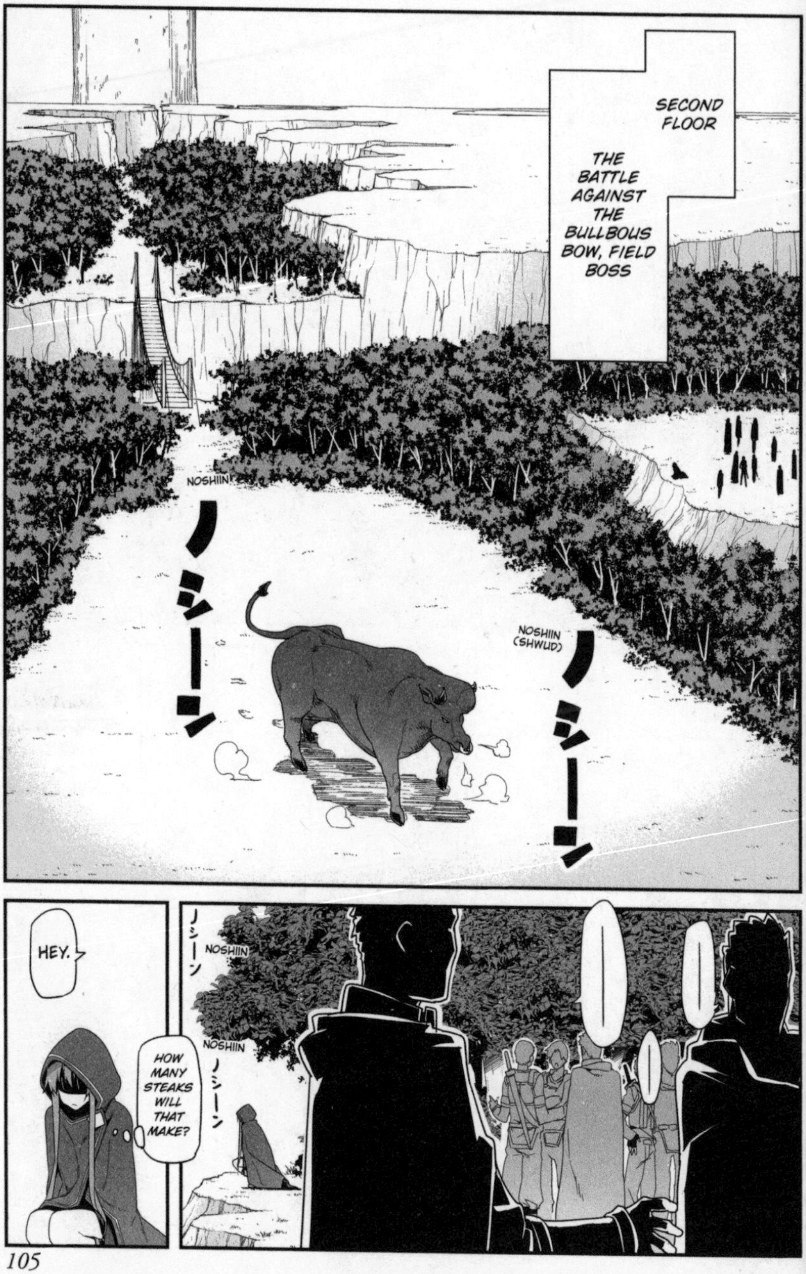
SECOND FLOOR
THE BATTLE AGAINST THE BULLBOUS BOW, FIELD BOSS
NOSHIIN (SHWUD)
ノシーン
NOSHIIN
ノシーン
ノシーン
NOSHIIN
ノシーン
NOSHIIN
HEY.
HOW MANY STEAKS WILL THAT MAKE?

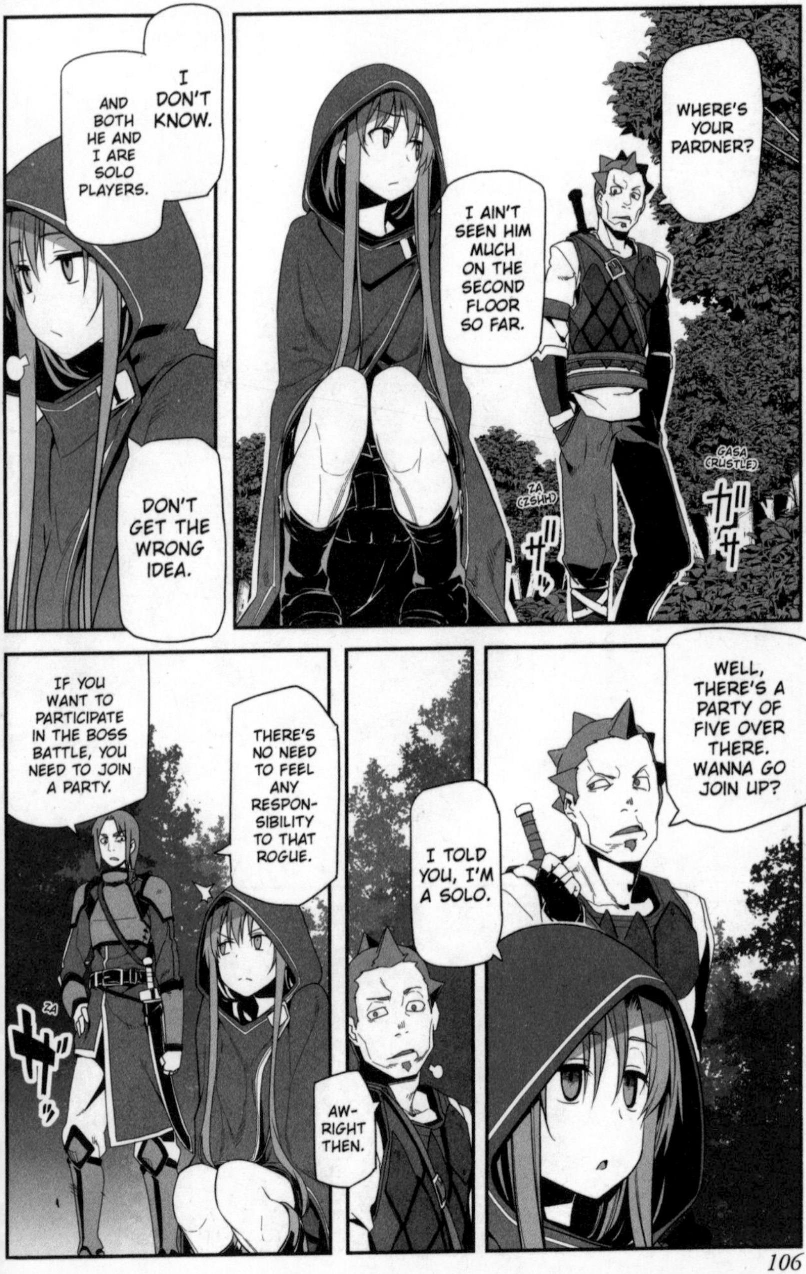
WHERE'S YOUR PARDNER?
I AIN'T SEEN HIM MUCH ON THE SECOND FLOOR SO FAR.
GASA (RUSTLE)
ZA (ZSHH)
I DON'T KNOW.
AND BOTH HE AND I ARE SOLO PLAYERS.
DON'T GET THE WRONG IDEA.
WELL, THERE'S A PARTY OF FIVE OVER THERE. WANNA GO JOIN UP?
I TOLD YOU, I'M A SOLO.
AW-RIGHT THEN.
THERE'S NO NEED TO FEEL ANY RESPON-SIBILITY TO THAT ROGUE.
IF YOU WANT TO PARTICIPATE IN THE BOSS BATTLE, YOU NEED TO JOIN A PARTY.
ZA

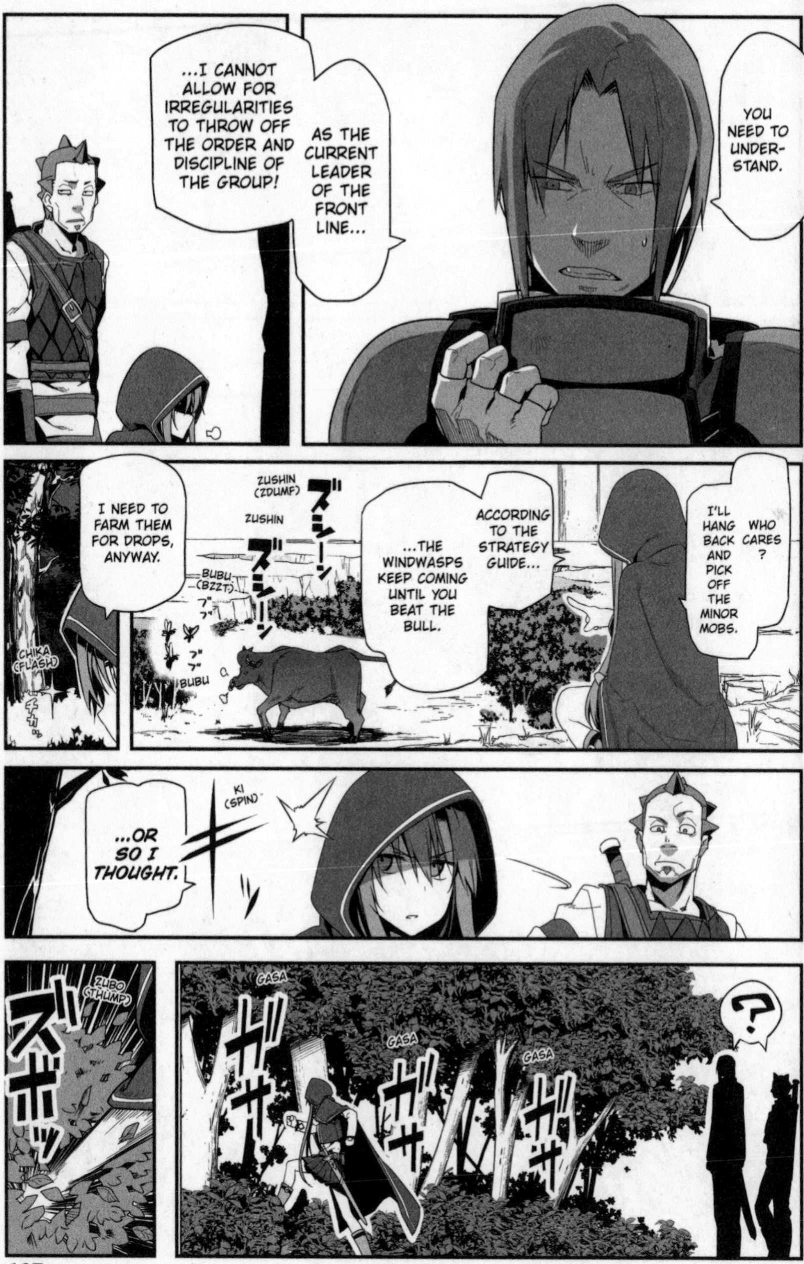
YOU NEED TO UNDER-STAND.
AS THE CURRENT LEADER OF THE FRONT LINE...
...I CANNOT ALLOW FOR IRREGULARITIES TO THROW OFF THE ORDER AND DISCIPLINE OF THE GROUP!
WHO CARES?
I'LL HANG BACK AND PICK OFF THE MINOR MOBS.
ACCORDING TO THE STRATEGY GUIDE...
...THE WINDWASPS KEEP COMING UNTIL YOU BEAT THE BULL.
ZUSHIN (ZDUMF)
ZUSHIN
BUBU (BZZT)
BUBU
I NEED TO FARM THEM FOR DROPS, ANYWAY.
CHIKA (FLASH)
KI (SPIN)
...OR SO I THOUGHT.
?
GASA
GASA
GASA
ZUBO (THUMP)

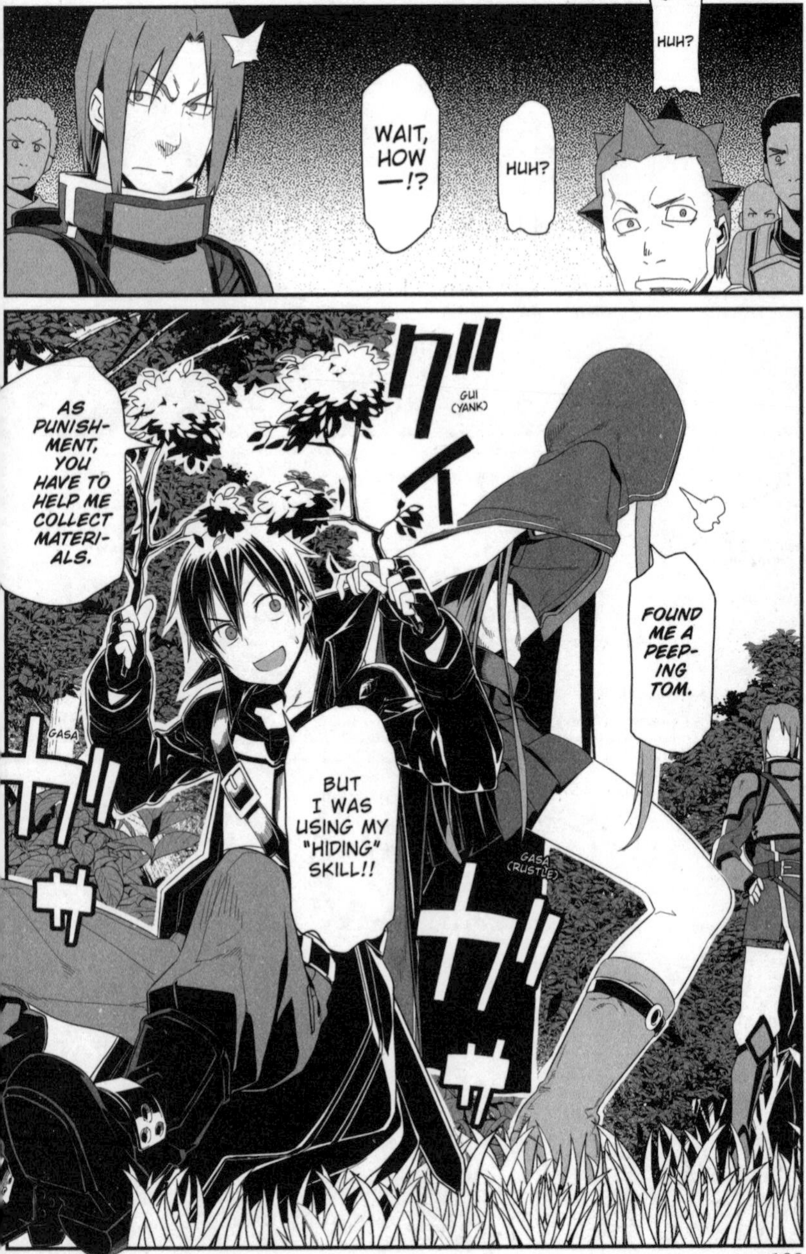
HUH?
HUH?
WAIT, HOW—!?
グイ
GUI (YANK)
FOUND ME A PEEPING TOM.
AS PUNISHMENT, YOU HAVE TO HELP ME COLLECT MATERIALS.
ガサ
GASA (RUSTLE)
BUT I WAS USING MY "HIDING" SKILL!!
ガサ
GASA

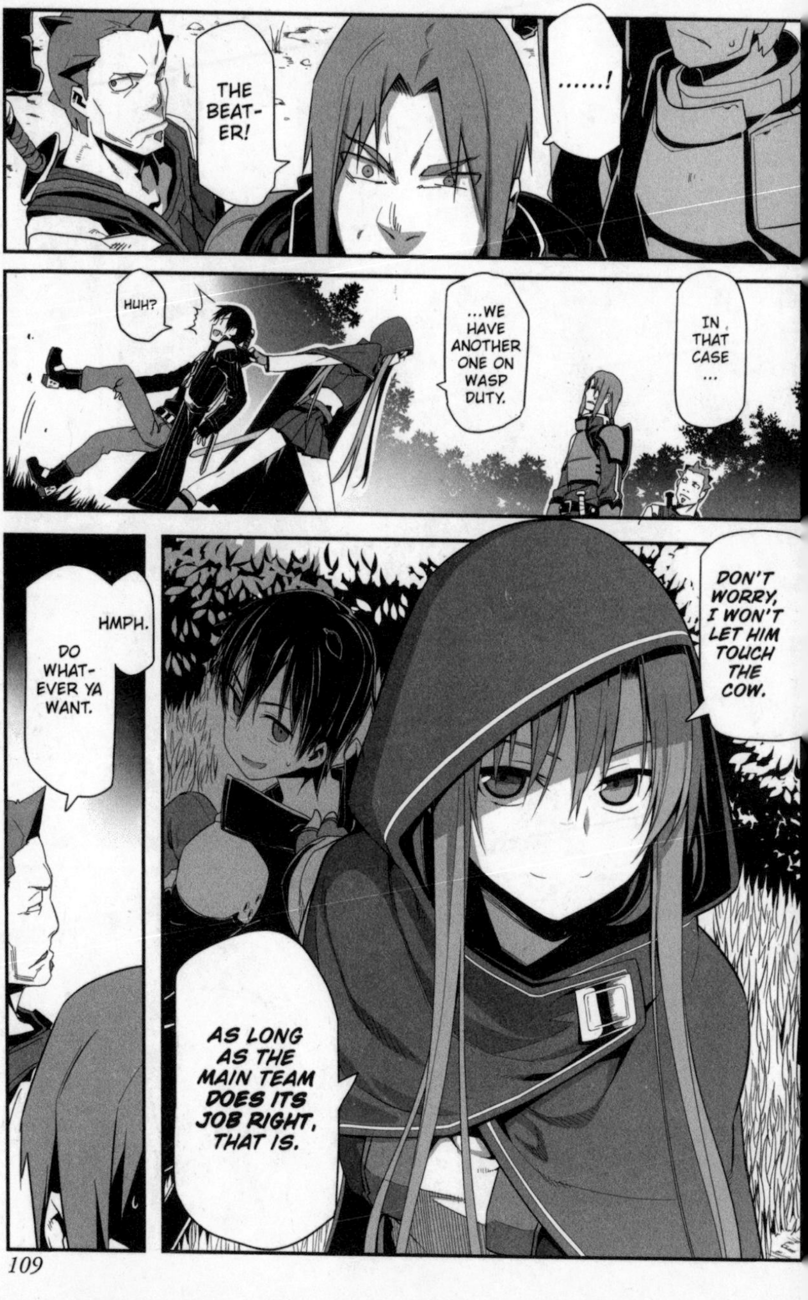
......!
THE BEAT-ER!
IN THAT CASE ...
...WE HAVE ANOTHER ONE ON WASP DUTY.
HUH?
DON'T WORRY, I WON'T LET HIM TOUCH THE COW.
HMPH.
DO WHAT-EVER YA WANT.
AS LONG AS THE MAIN TEAM DOES ITS JOB RIGHT, THAT IS.

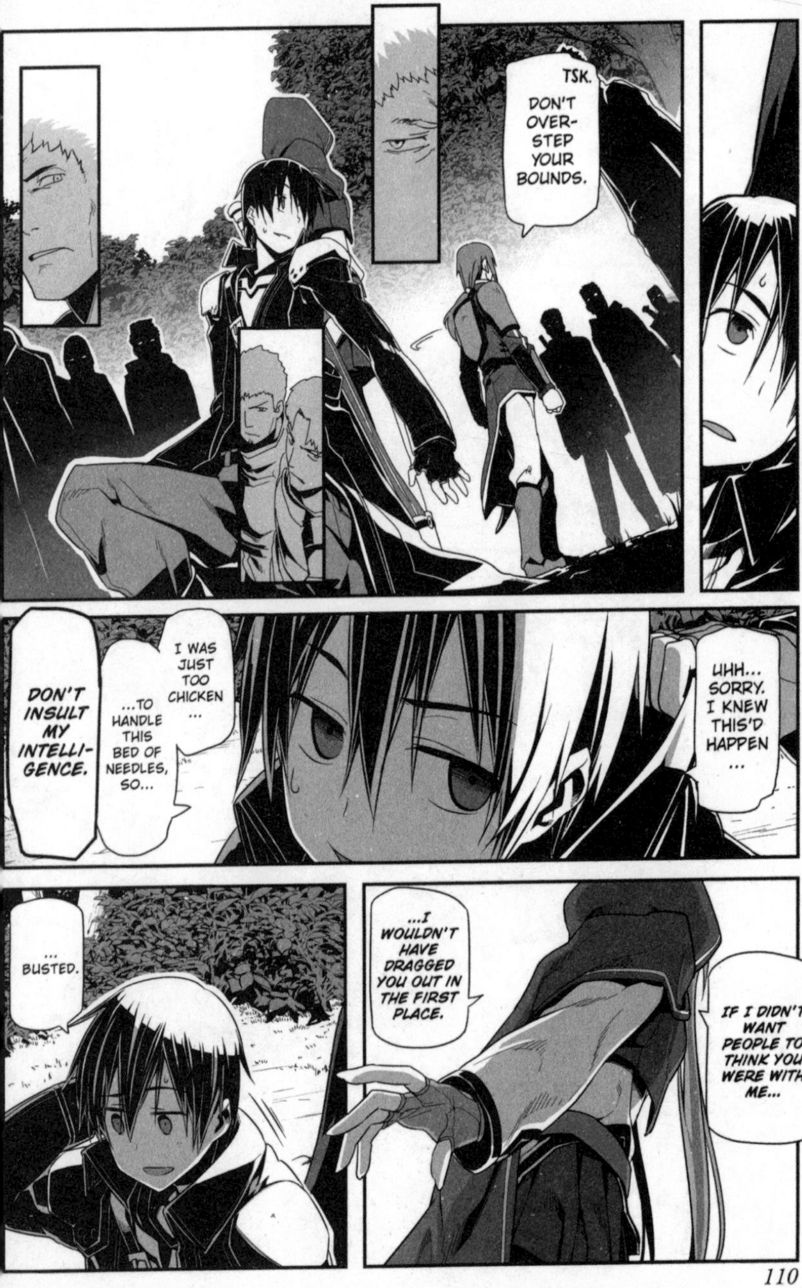
TSK.
DON'T OVER-STEP YOUR BOUNDS.
UHH... SORRY. I KNEW THIS'D HAPPEN...
I WAS JUST TOO CHICKEN...
...TO HANDLE THIS BED OF NEEDLES, SO...
DON'T INSULT MY INTELLI-GENCE.
IF I DIDN'T WANT PEOPLE TO THINK YOU WERE WITH ME...
...I WOULDN'T HAVE DRAGGED YOU OUT IN THE FIRST PLACE.
...BUSTED.

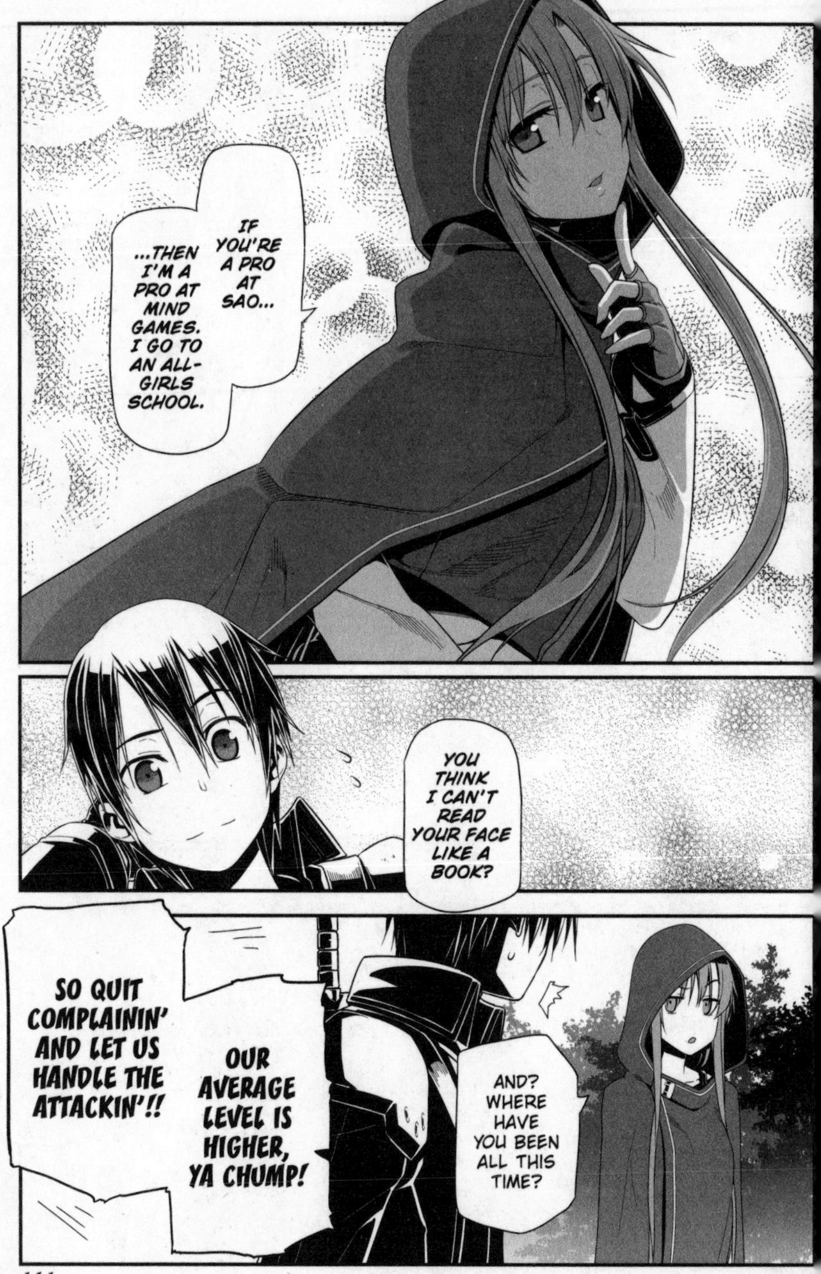
IF YOU'RE A PRO AT SAO...
...THEN I'M A PRO AT MIND GAMES. I GO TO AN ALL-GIRLS SCHOOL.
YOU THINK I CAN'T READ YOUR FACE LIKE A BOOK?
AND? WHERE HAVE YOU BEEN ALL THIS TIME?
OUR AVERAGE LEVEL IS HIGHER, YA CHUMP!
SO QUIT COMPLAININ' AND LET US HANDLE THE ATTACKIN'!!

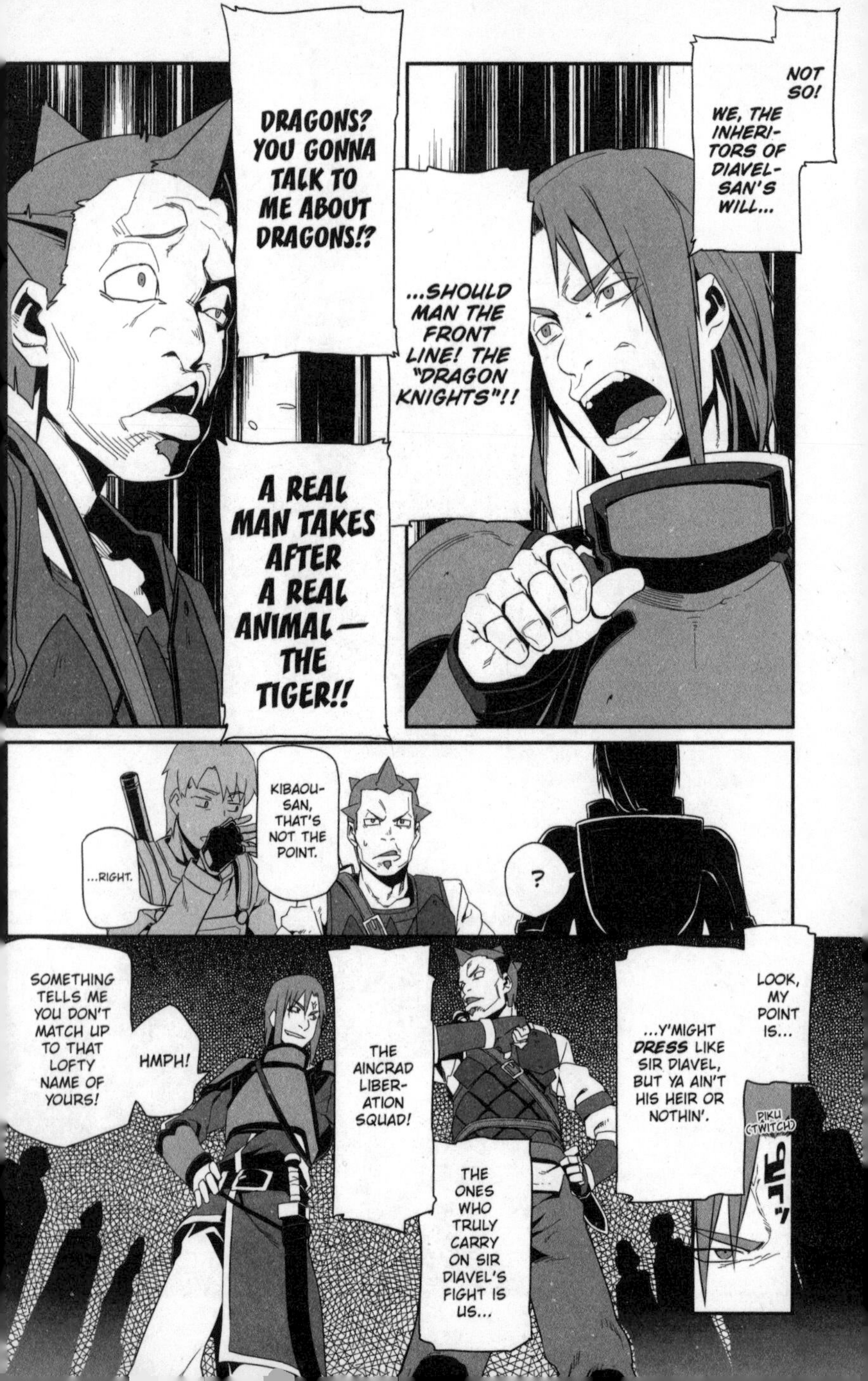
NOT SO!
WE, THE INHERITORS OF DIAVEL-SAN'S WILL...
...SHOULD MAN THE FRONT LINE! THE "DRAGON KNIGHTS"!!
DRAGONS? YOU GONNA TALK TO ME ABOUT DRAGONS!?
A REAL MAN TAKES AFTER A REAL ANIMAL—THE TIGER!!
?
KIBAOU-SAN, THAT'S NOT THE POINT.
...RIGHT.
LOOK, MY POINT IS...
...Y'MIGHT DRESS LIKE SIR DIAVEL, BUT YA AIN'T HIS HEIR OR NOTHIN'.
PIKU (TWITCH)
THE AINCRAD LIBERATION SQUAD!
THE ONES WHO TRULY CARRY ON SIR DIAVEL'S FIGHT IS US...
HMPH!
SOMETHING TELLS ME YOU DON'T MATCH UP TO THAT LOFTY NAME OF YOURS!

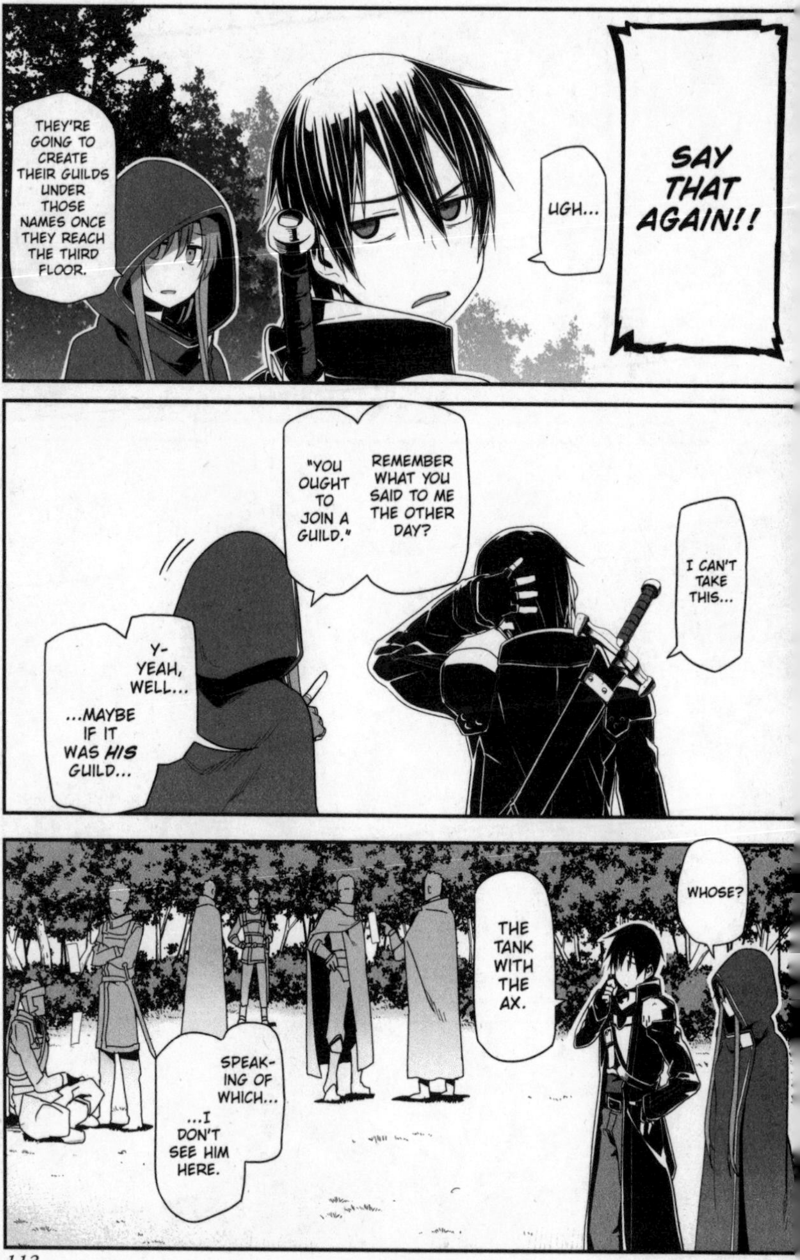
SAY THAT AGAIN!!
UGH...
THEY'RE GOING TO CREATE THEIR GUILDS UNDER THOSE NAMES ONCE THEY REACH THE THIRD FLOOR.
I CAN'T TAKE THIS...
REMEMBER WHAT YOU SAID TO ME THE OTHER DAY?
"YOU OUGHT TO JOIN A GUILD."
Y-YEAH, WELL...
...MAYBE IF IT WAS *HIS* GUILD...
WHOSE?
THE TANK WITH THE AX.
SPEAK-ING OF WHICH...
...I DON'T SEE HIM HERE.

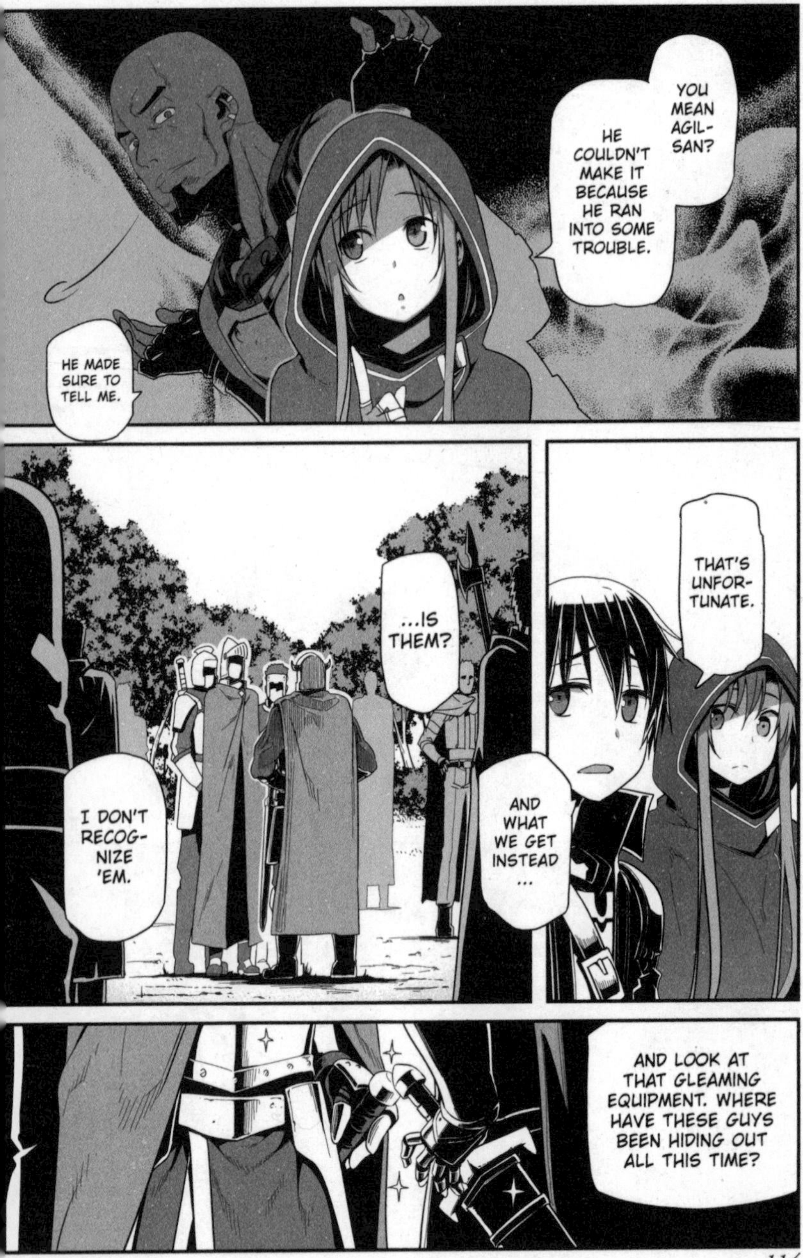
YOU MEAN AGIL-SAN?
HE COULDN'T MAKE IT BECAUSE HE RAN INTO SOME TROUBLE.
HE MADE SURE TO TELL ME.
THAT'S UNFOR-TUNATE.
AND WHAT WE GET INSTEAD ...
...IS THEM?
I DON'T RECOG-NIZE 'EM.
AND LOOK AT THAT GLEAMING EQUIPMENT. WHERE HAVE THESE GUYS BEEN HIDING OUT ALL THIS TIME?

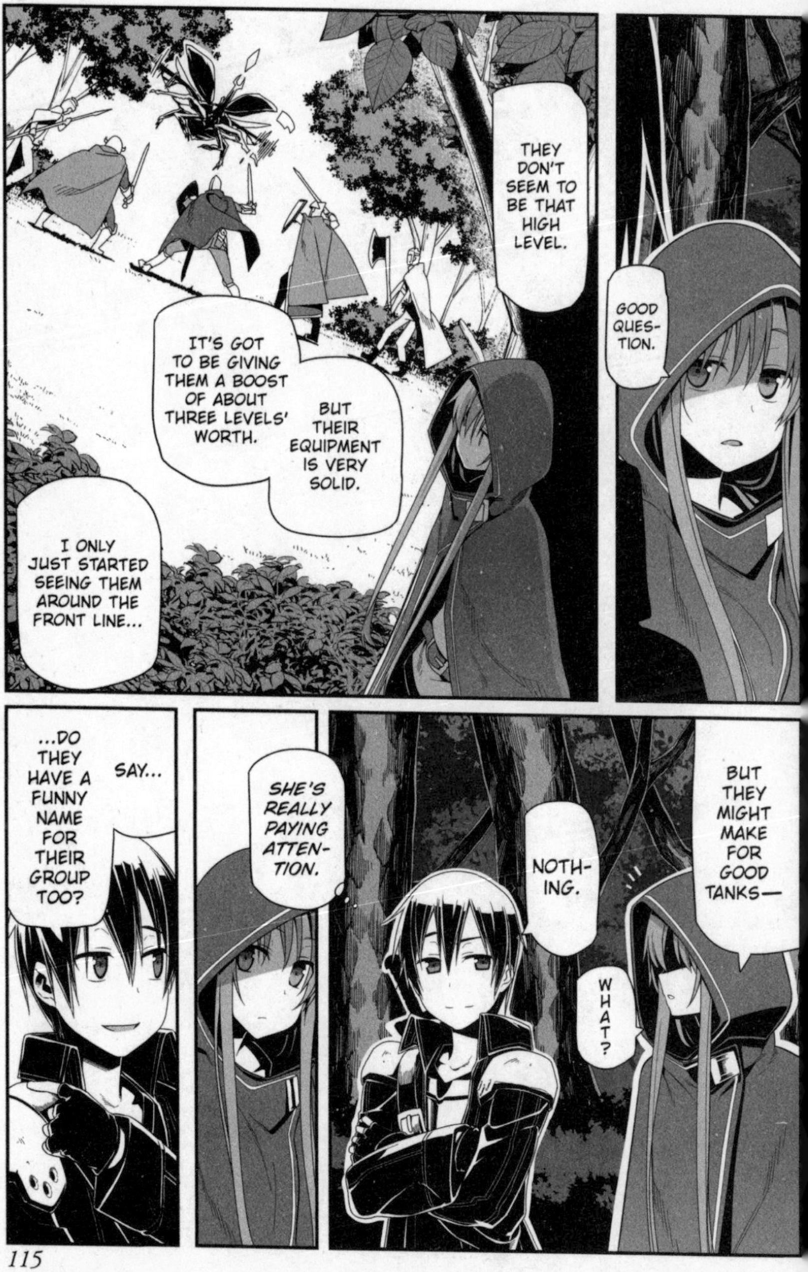
GOOD QUES-TION.
THEY DON'T SEEM TO BE THAT HIGH LEVEL.
BUT THEIR EQUIPMENT IS VERY SOLID.
IT'S GOT TO BE GIVING THEM A BOOST OF ABOUT THREE LEVELS' WORTH.
I ONLY JUST STARTED SEEING THEM AROUND THE FRONT LINE...
BUT THEY MIGHT MAKE FOR GOOD TANKS—
WHAT?
NOTH-ING.
SHE'S REALLY PAYING ATTEN-TION.
SAY...
...DO THEY HAVE A FUNNY NAME FOR THEIR GROUP TOO?

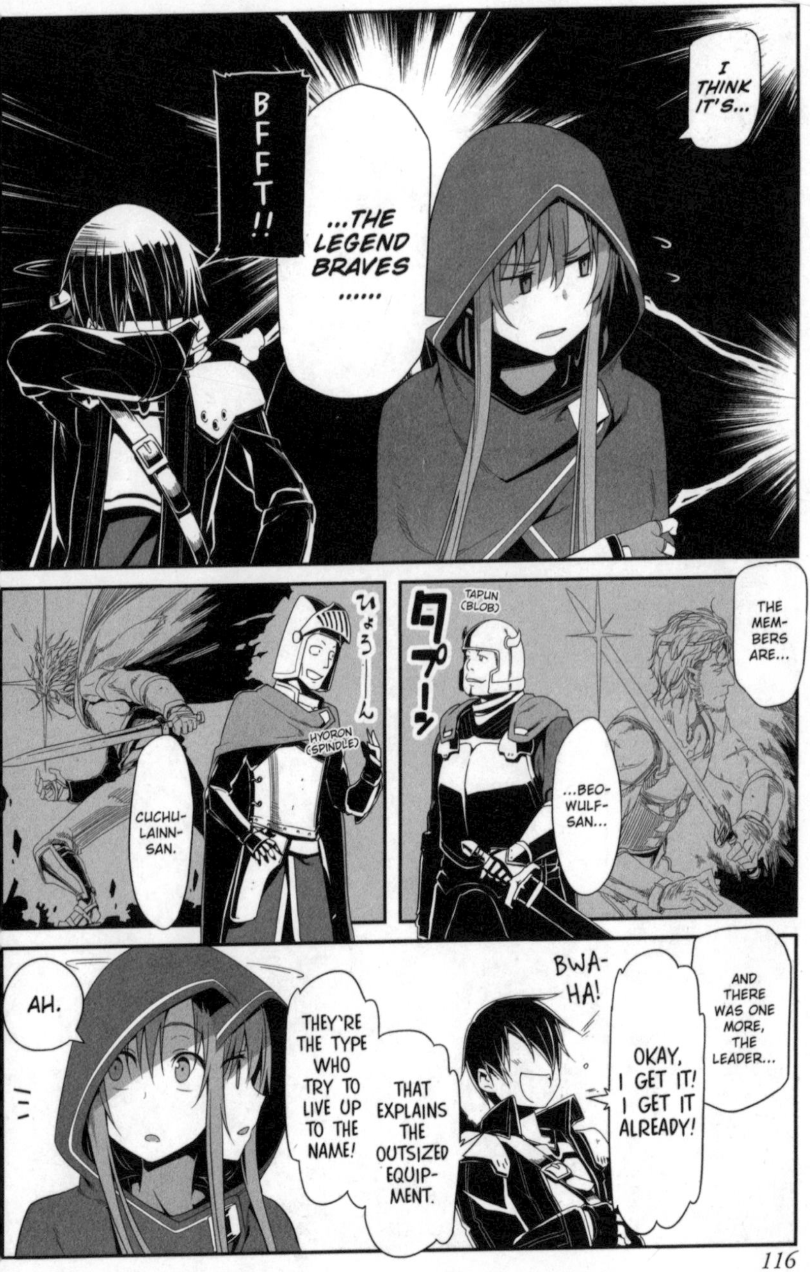
I THINK IT'S...
...THE LEGEND BRAVES ......
BFFT!!
THE MEMBERS ARE...
タプーッ
TAPUN (BLOB)
...BEO-WULF-SAN...
ひょろーん
HYORON (SPINDLE)
CUCHULAINN-SAN.
AND THERE WAS ONE MORE, THE LEADER...
BWA-HA!
OKAY, I GET IT! I GET IT ALREADY!
THAT EXPLAINS THE OUTSIZED EQUIPMENT.
THEY'RE THE TYPE WHO TRY TO LIVE UP TO THE NAME!
AH.

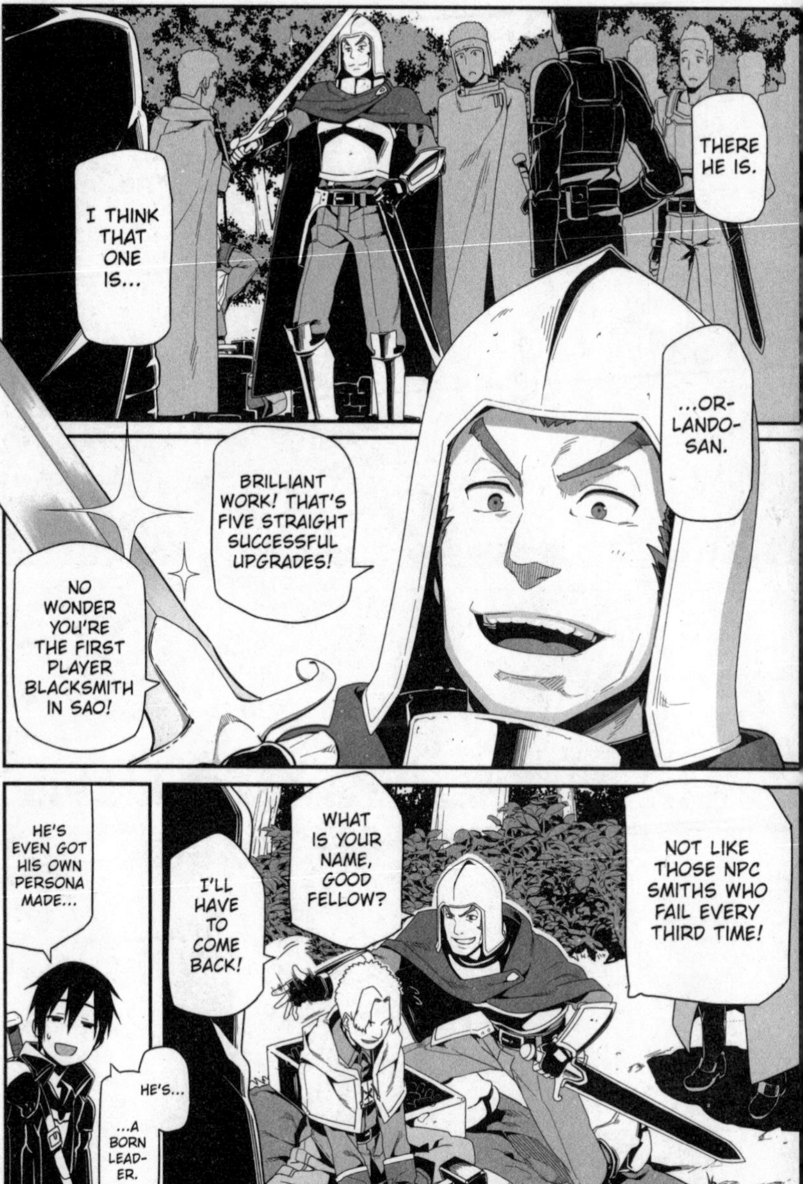
THERE HE IS.
I THINK THAT ONE IS...
...OR-LANDO-SAN.
BRILLIANT WORK! THAT'S FIVE STRAIGHT SUCCESSFUL UPGRADES!
NO WONDER YOU'RE THE FIRST PLAYER BLACKSMITH IN SAO!
NOT LIKE THOSE NPC SMITHS WHO FAIL EVERY THIRD TIME!
WHAT IS YOUR NAME, GOOD FELLOW?
I'LL HAVE TO COME BACK!
HE'S EVEN GOT HIS OWN PERSONA MADE...
HE'S...
...A BORN LEADER.

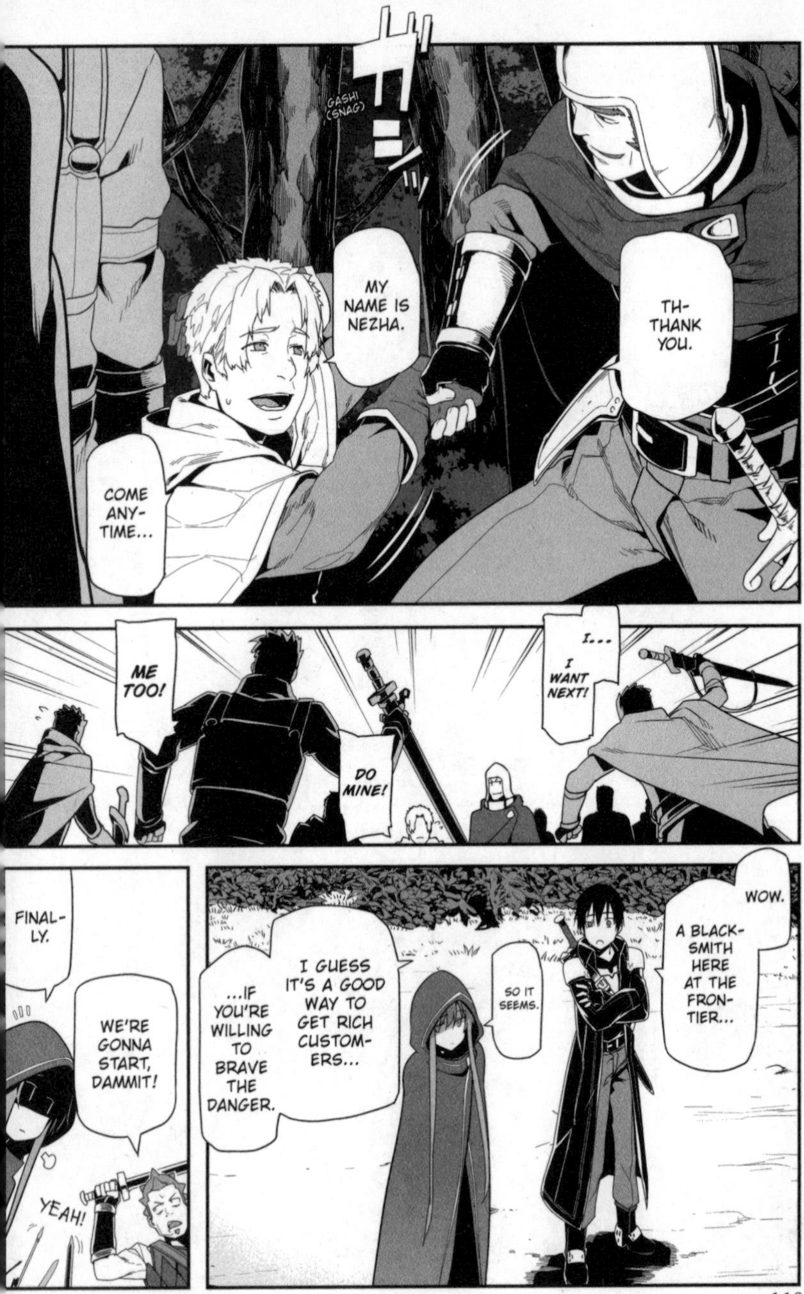
GASHI (SNAG)
TH-THANK YOU.
MY NAME IS NEZHA.
COME ANYTIME...
I... I WANT NEXT!
ME TOO!
DO MINE!
WOW. A BLACKSMITH HERE AT THE FRONTIER...
SO IT SEEMS.
I GUESS IT'S A GOOD WAY TO GET RICH CUSTOMERS...
...IF YOU'RE WILLING TO BRAVE THE DANGER.
FINALLY.
WE'RE GONNA START, DAMMIT!
YEAH!

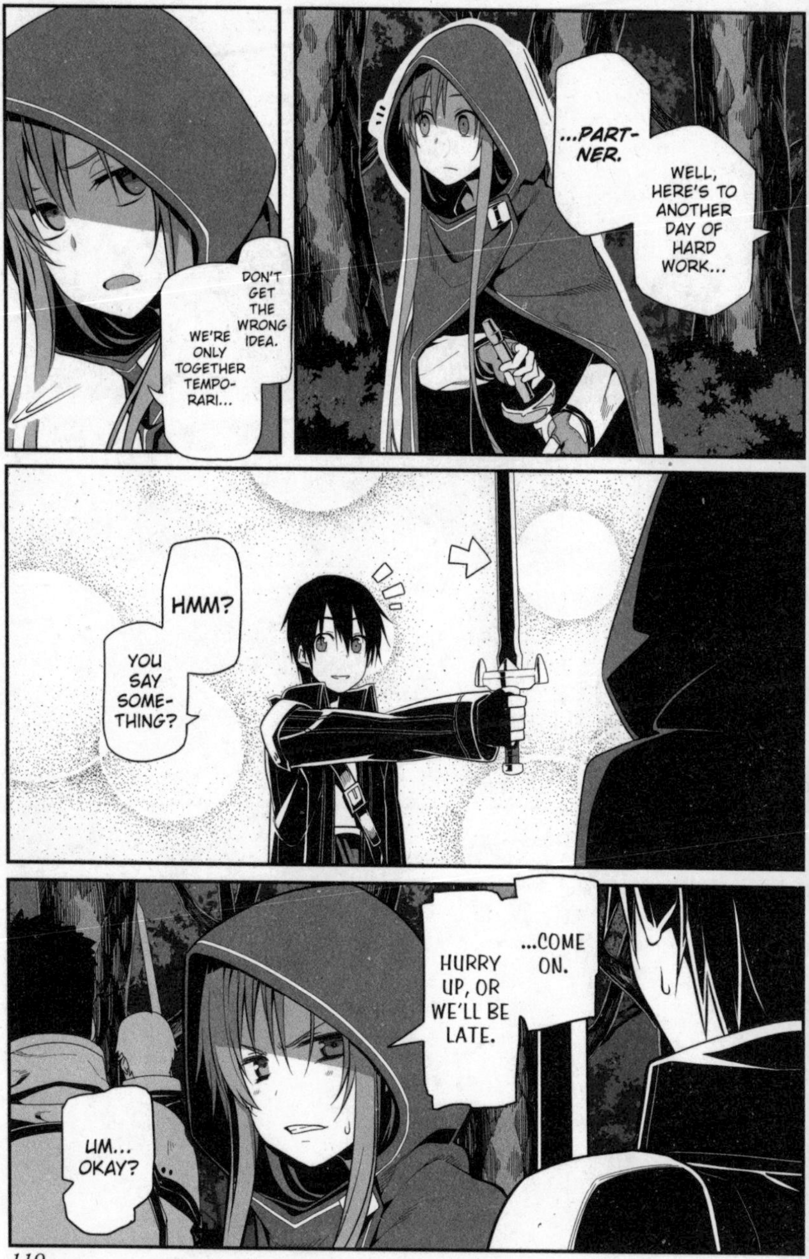
...PART-NER.
WELL, HERE'S TO ANOTHER DAY OF HARD WORK...
DON'T GET THE WRONG IDEA.
WE'RE ONLY TOGETHER TEMPO-RARI...
HMM?
YOU SAY SOME-THING?
...COME ON.
HURRY UP, OR WE'LL BE LATE.
UM... OKAY?

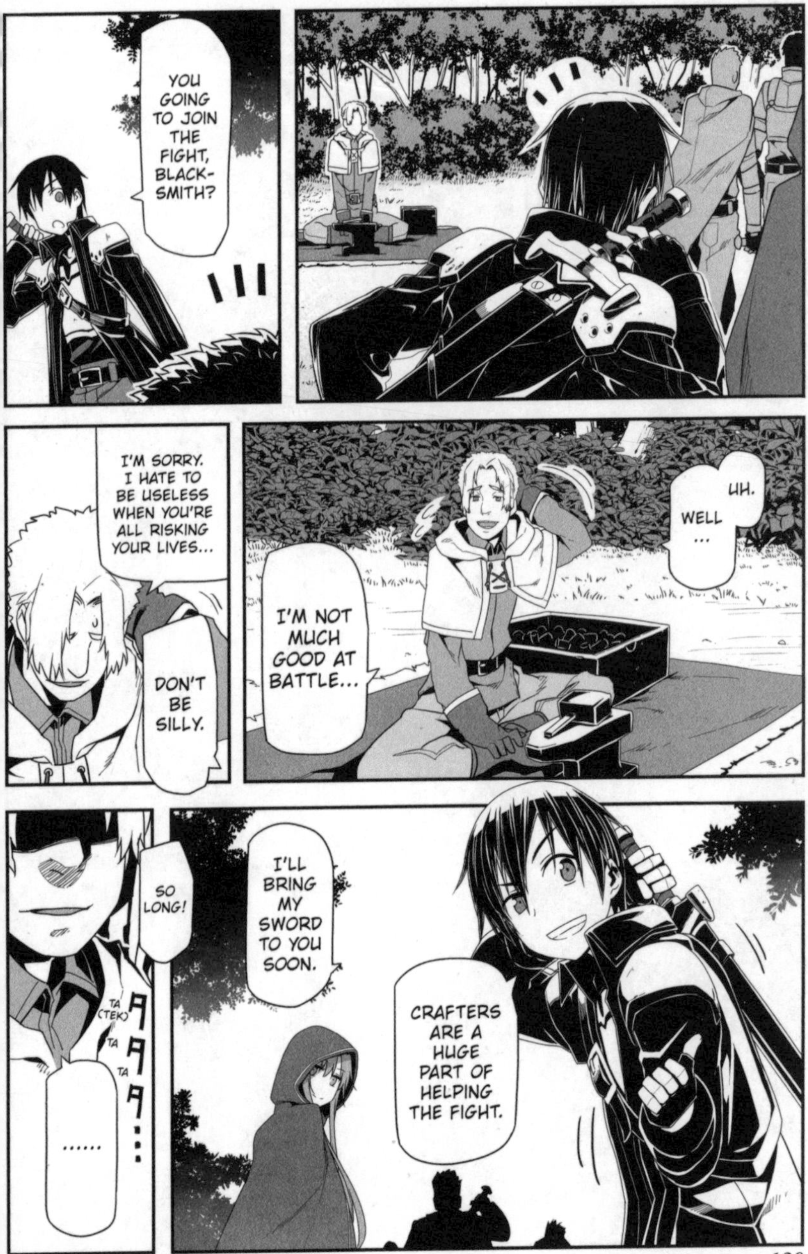
YOU GOING TO JOIN THE FIGHT, BLACKSMITH?
UH. WELL ...
I'M NOT MUCH GOOD AT BATTLE...
I'M SORRY. I HATE TO BE USELESS WHEN YOU'RE ALL RISKING YOUR LIVES...
DON'T BE SILLY.
I'LL BRING MY SWORD TO YOU SOON.
CRAFTERS ARE A HUGE PART OF HELPING THE FIGHT.
SO LONG!
TA (TEK) TA TA
......

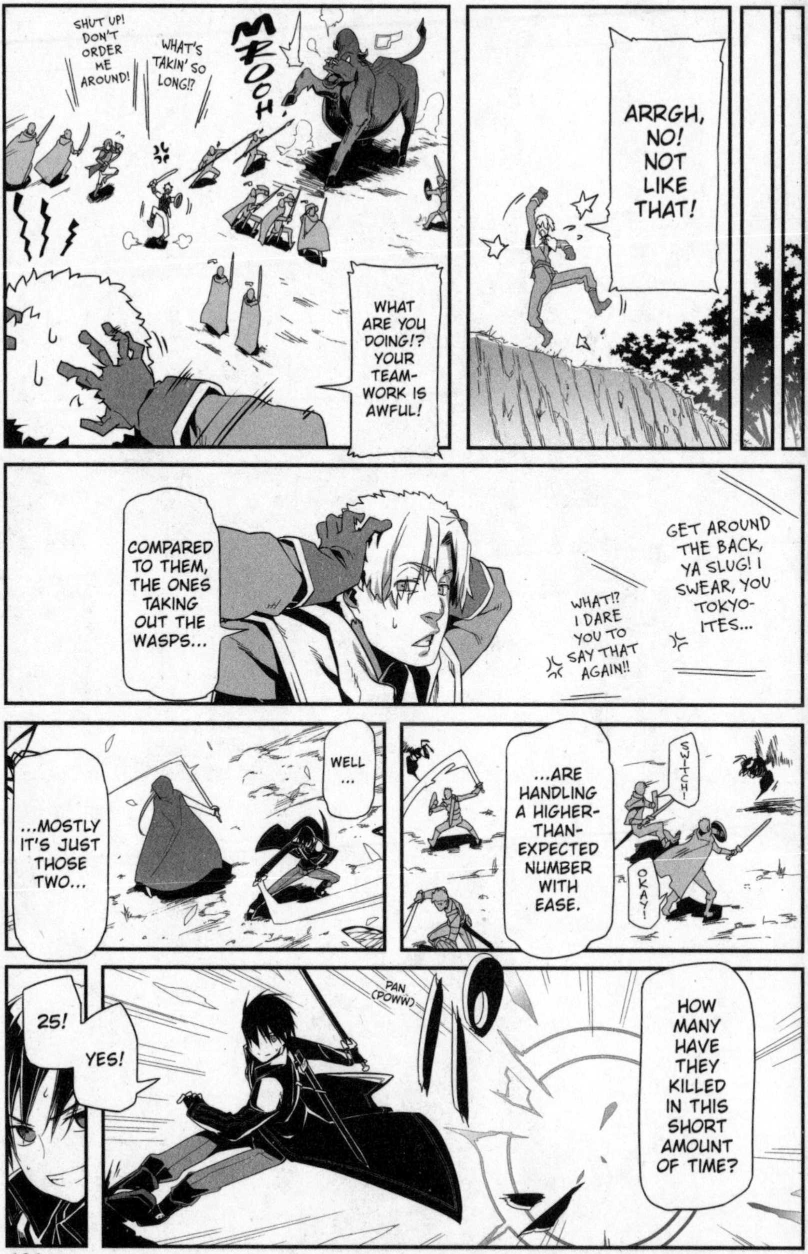
ARRGH, NO! NOT LIKE THAT!
MROOOH
WHAT'S TAKIN' SO LONG!?
SHUT UP! DON'T ORDER ME AROUND!
WHAT ARE YOU DOING!? YOUR TEAM-WORK IS AWFUL!
GET AROUND THE BACK, YA SLUG! I SWEAR, YOU TOKYO-ITES...
WHAT!? I DARE YOU TO SAY THAT AGAIN!!
COMPARED TO THEM, THE ONES TAKING OUT THE WASPS...
SWITCH!
...ARE HANDLING A HIGHER-THAN-EXPECTED NUMBER WITH EASE.
OKAY!
WELL...
...MOSTLY IT'S JUST THOSE TWO...
HOW MANY HAVE THEY KILLED IN THIS SHORT AMOUNT OF TIME?
PAN (POWW)
25!
YES!

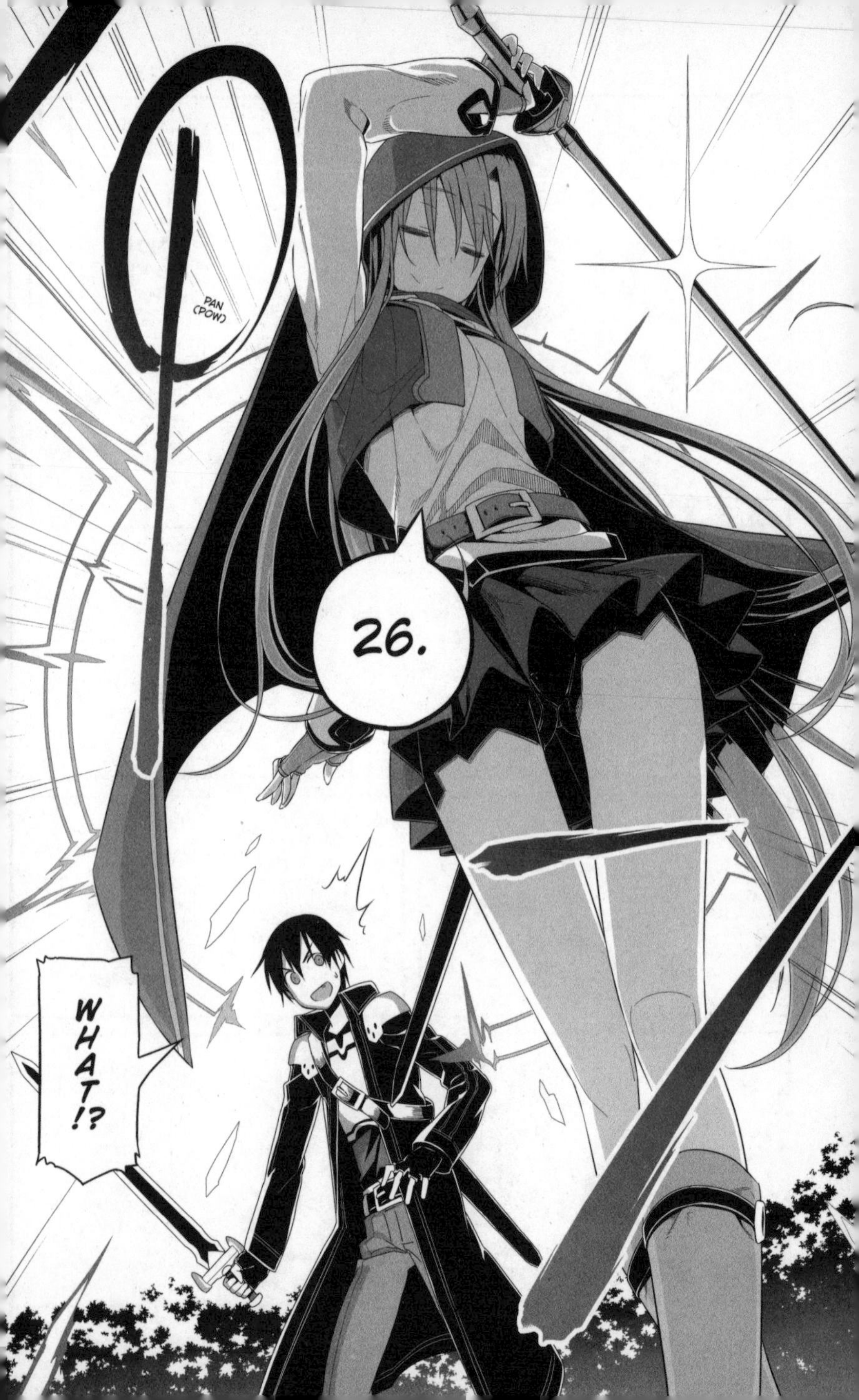
PAN (POW)
26.
WHAT!?

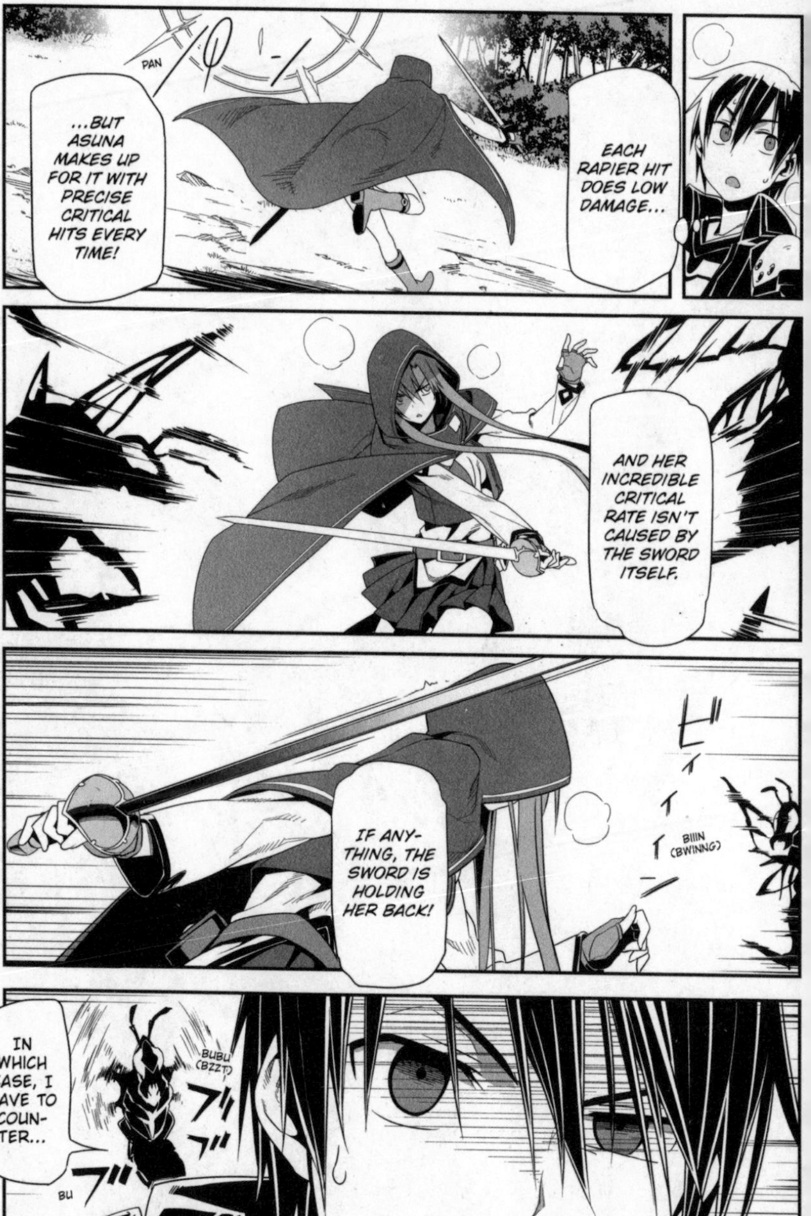
EACH RAPIER HIT DOES LOW DAMAGE...
PAN
...BUT ASUNA MAKES UP FOR IT WITH PRECISE CRITICAL HITS EVERY TIME!
AND HER INCREDIBLE CRITICAL RATE ISN'T CAUSED BY THE SWORD ITSELF.
BIIIN (BWINNG)
IF ANY-THING, THE SWORD IS HOLDING HER BACK!
BUBU (BZZT)
IN WHICH CASE, I HAVE TO COUN-TER...
BU

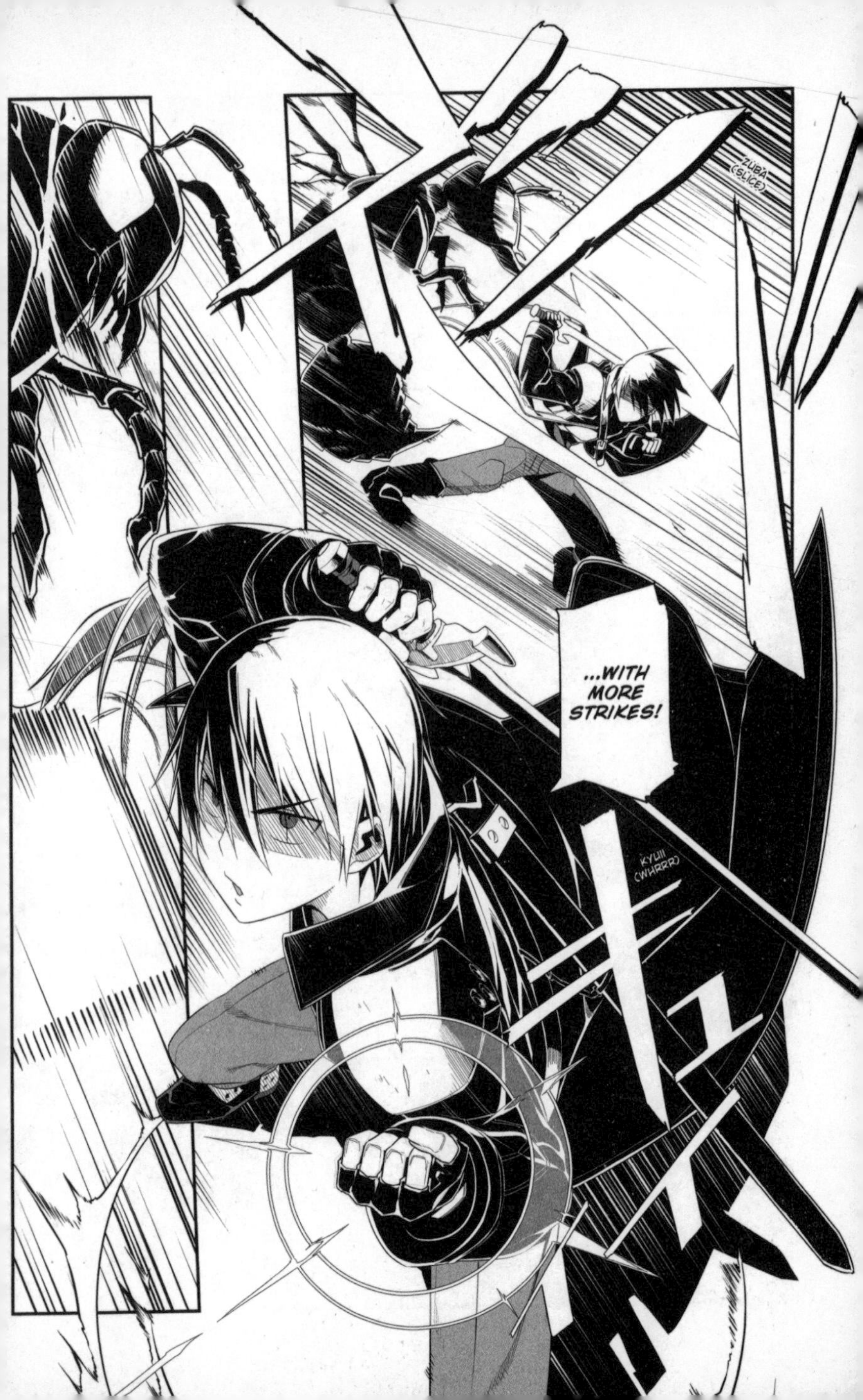
ZUBA (SLICE)
...WITH MORE STRIKES!
KYUII (WHRRR)

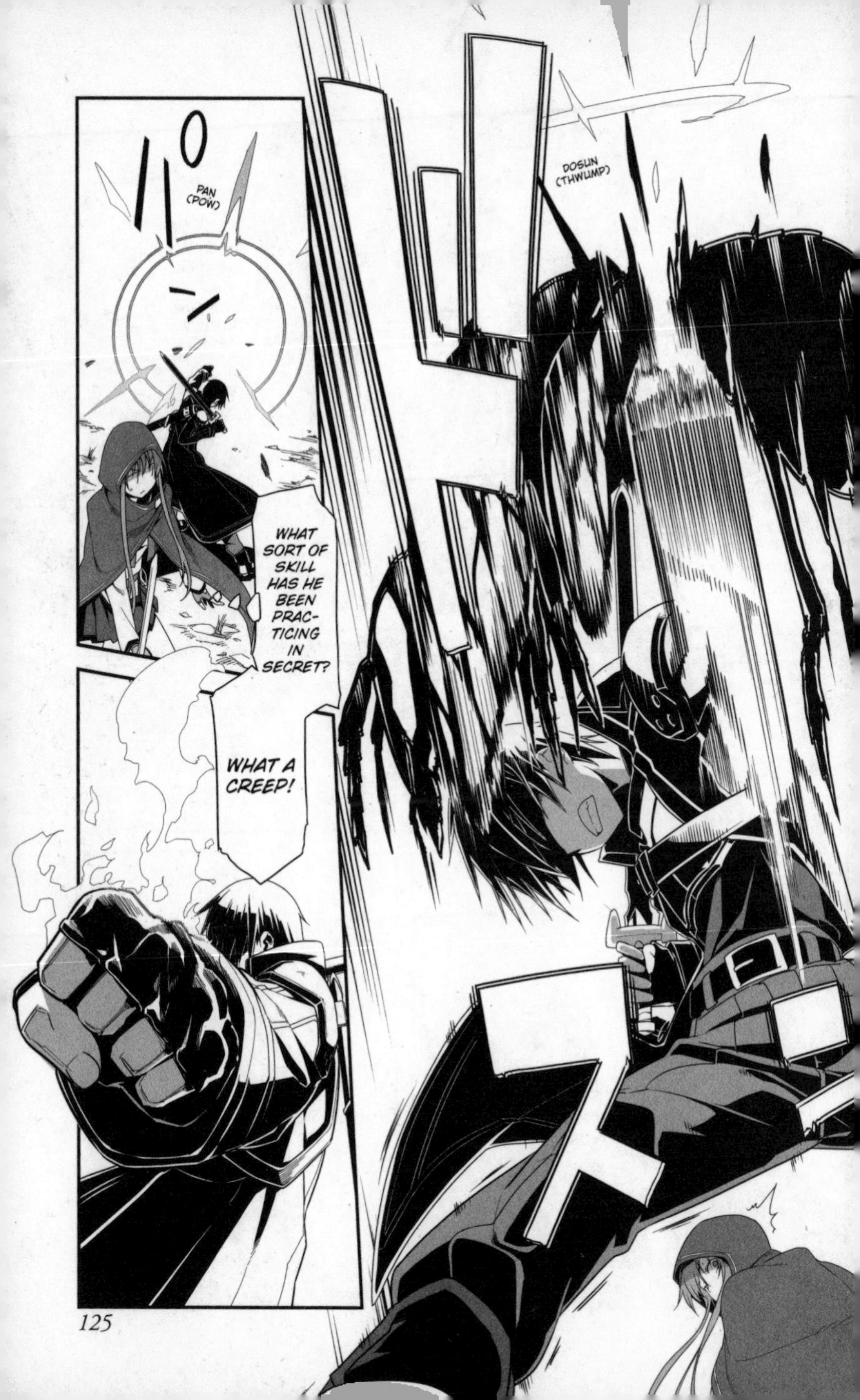
DOSUN (THWUMP)
PAN (POW)
WHAT SORT OF SKILL HAS HE BEEN PRACTICING IN SECRET?
WHAT A CREEP!

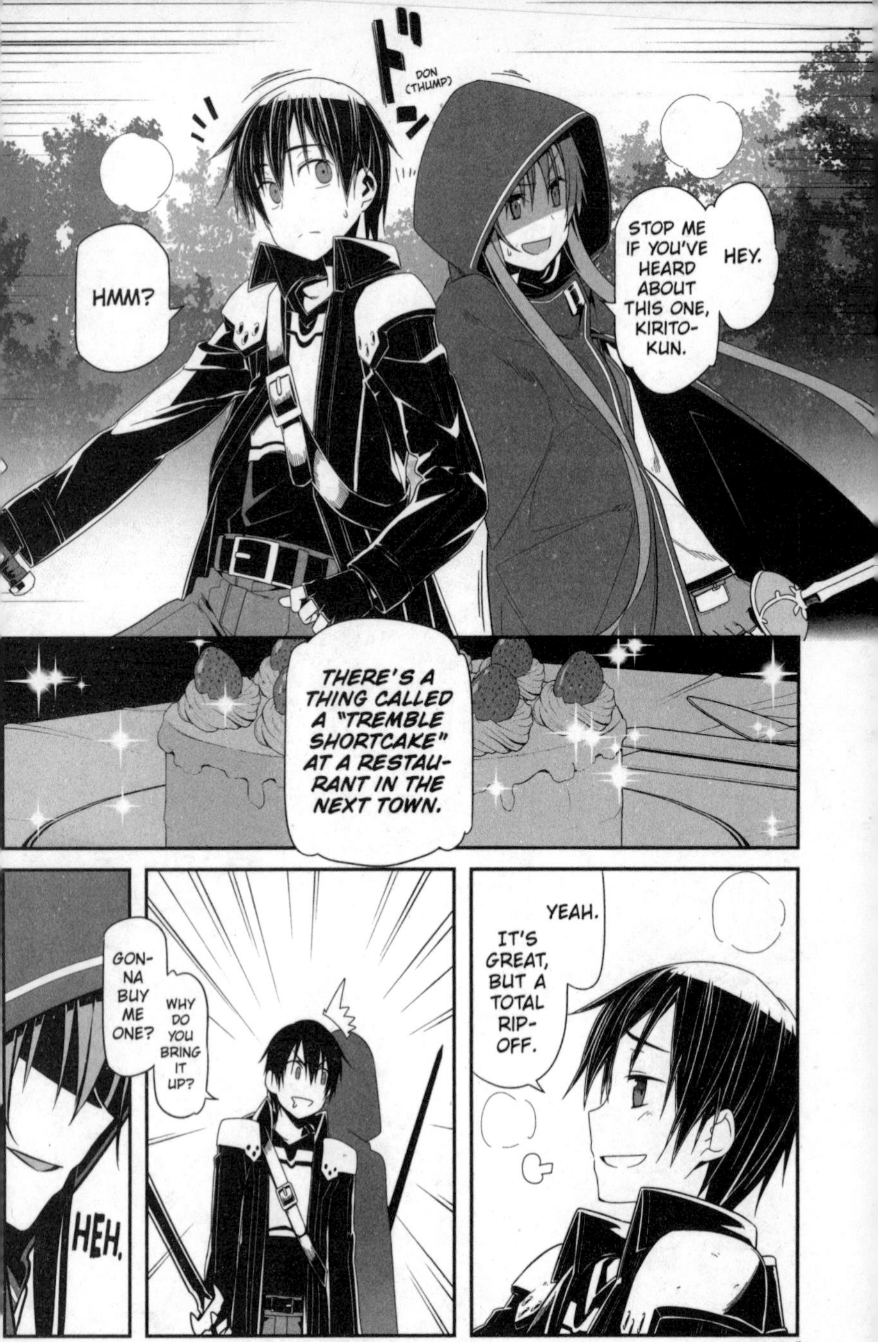
ドン
DON (THUMP)
HEY.
STOP ME IF YOU'VE HEARD ABOUT THIS ONE, KIRITO-KUN.
HMM?
THERE'S A THING CALLED A "TREMBLE SHORTCAKE" AT A RESTAURANT IN THE NEXT TOWN.
YEAH.
IT'S GREAT, BUT A TOTAL RIP-OFF.
WHY DO YOU BRING IT UP?
GON-NA BUY ME ONE?
HEH.

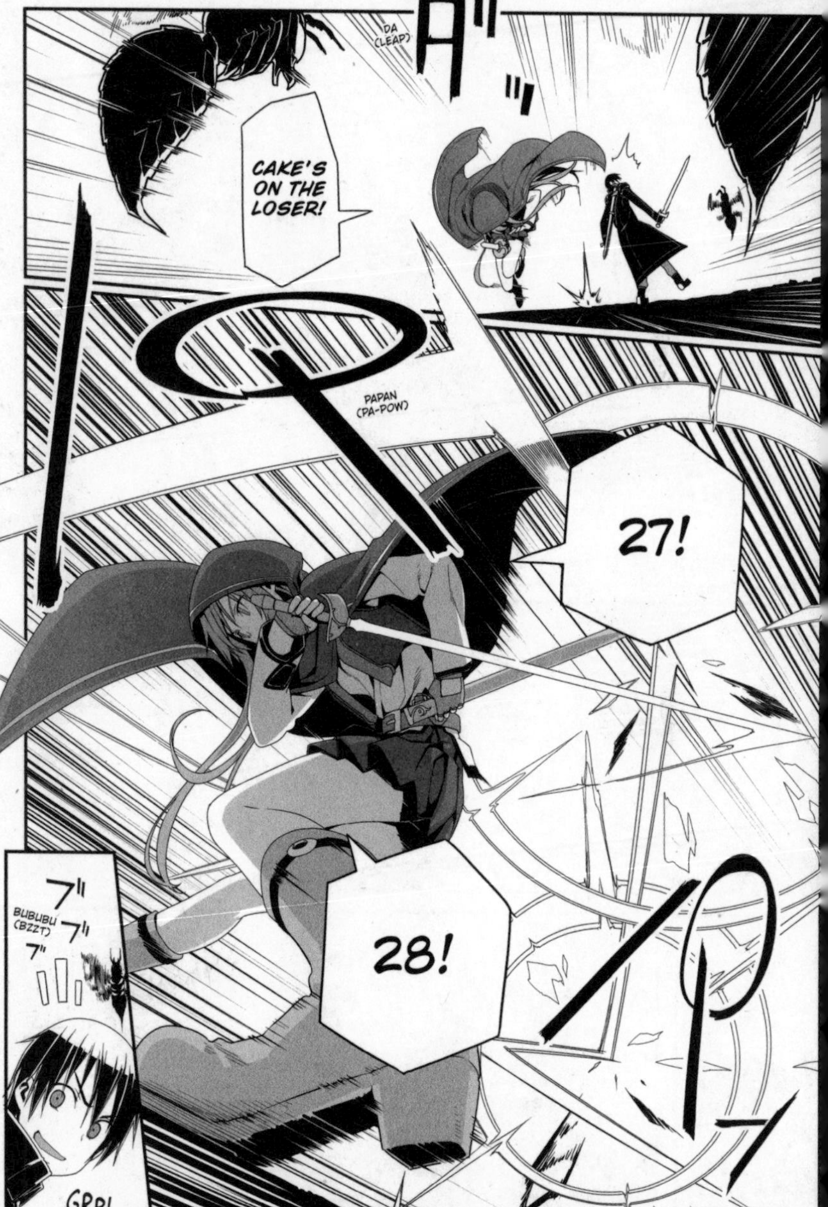
DA (LEAP)
CAKE'S ON THE LOSER!
PAPAN (PA-POW)
27!
28!
BUBUBU (BZZT)
GRR!

BUBU
(BZZT)

HUH?

WHY'S THAT MOB JUST PASSING BY EVERY-ONE...?

BU

KEEP GOING! WE'RE ALMOST THERE!!

MROOH!!

YEAH!

BU'IN
(BZZ)

29!

KUI
(ZINK)

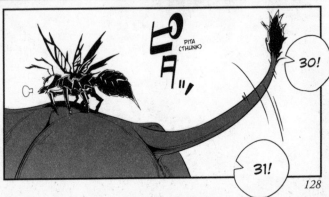

PITA
(THUNK)

30!

31!

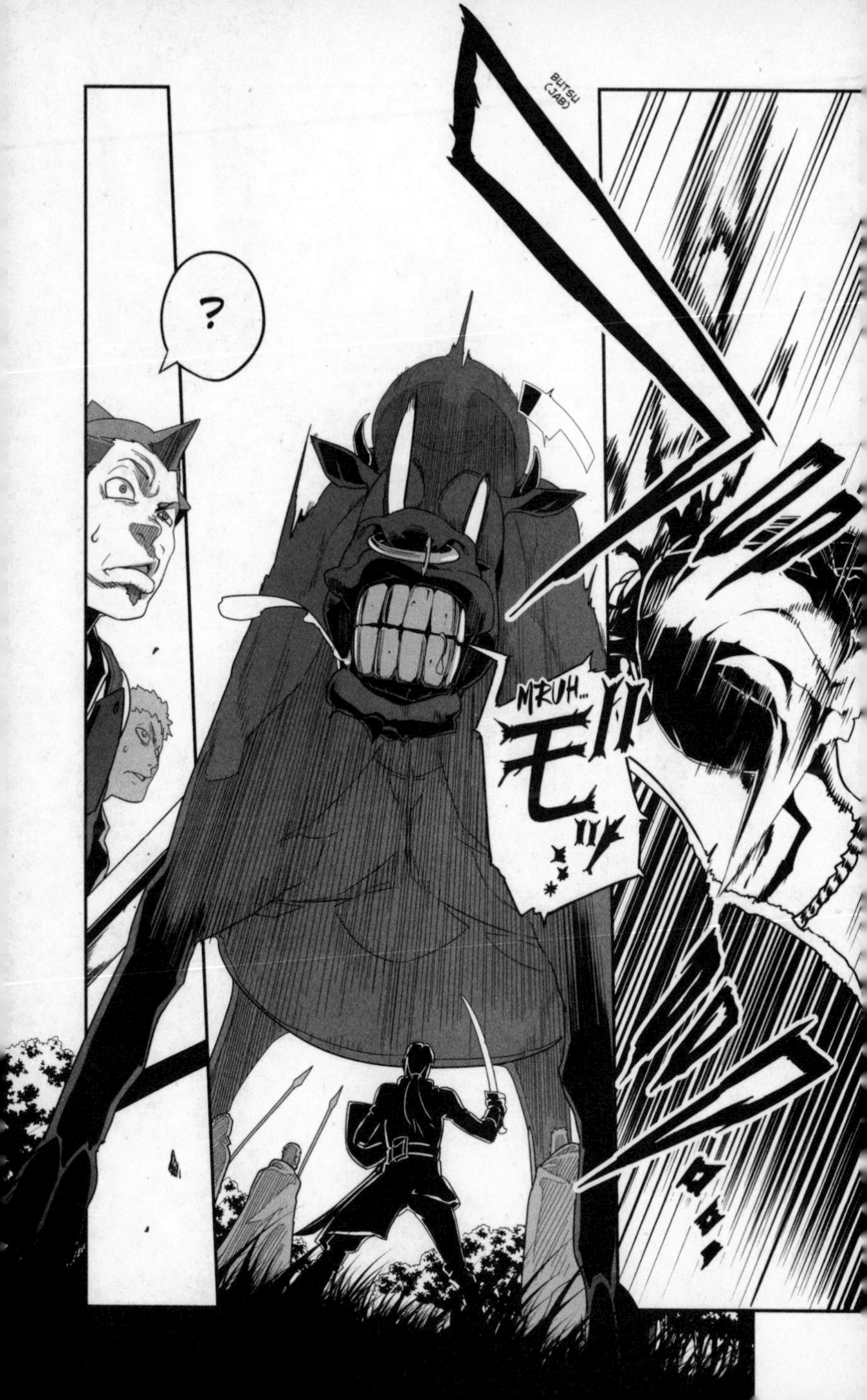
BUTSU (JAB)
MRUH...
モー!!
?

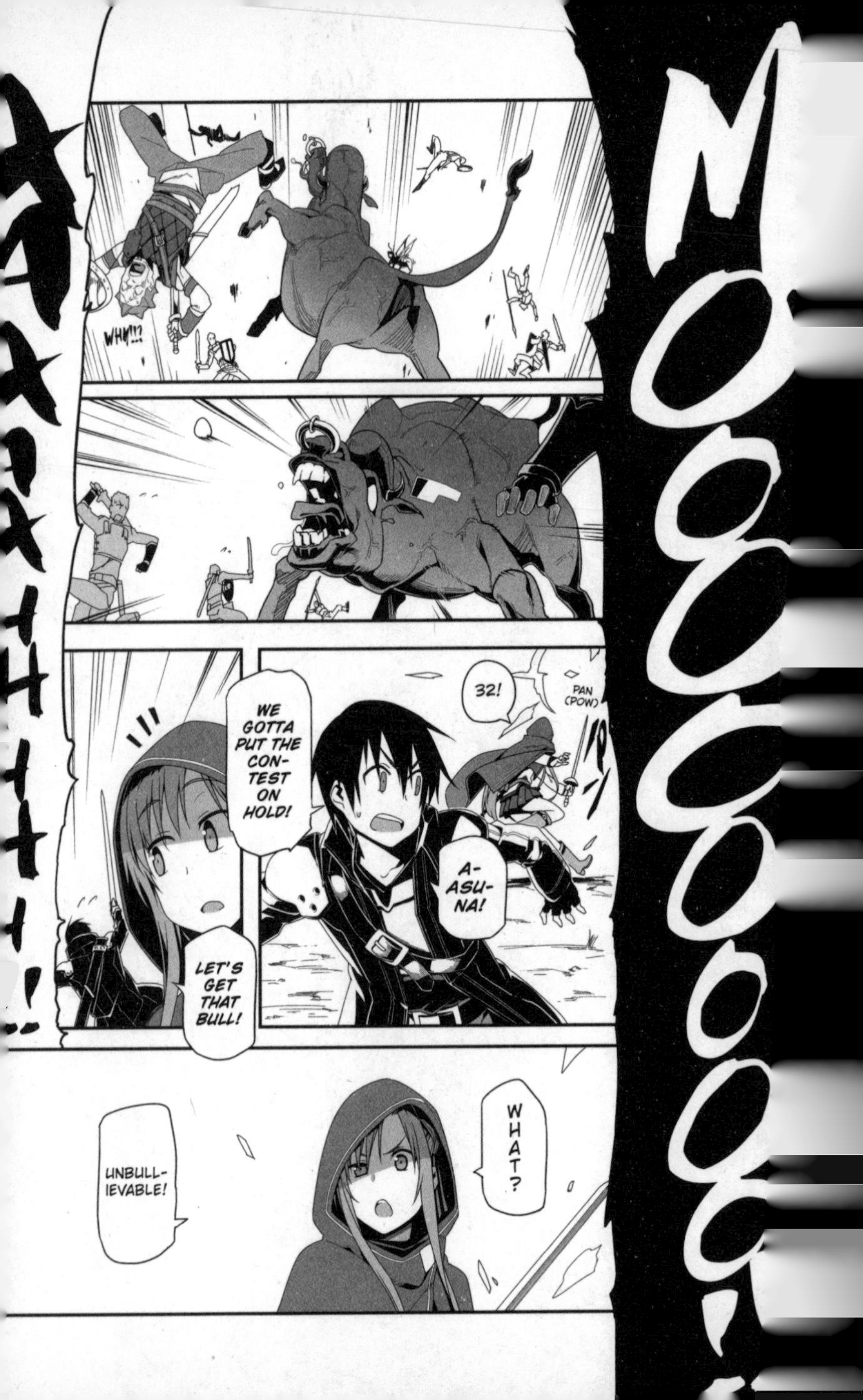
MOOOOOOOO
WHY!!?
32!
PAN (POW)
WE GOTTA PUT THE CON-TEST ON HOLD!
A-ASUNA!
LET'S GET THAT BULL!
WHAT?
UNBULL-IEVABLE!

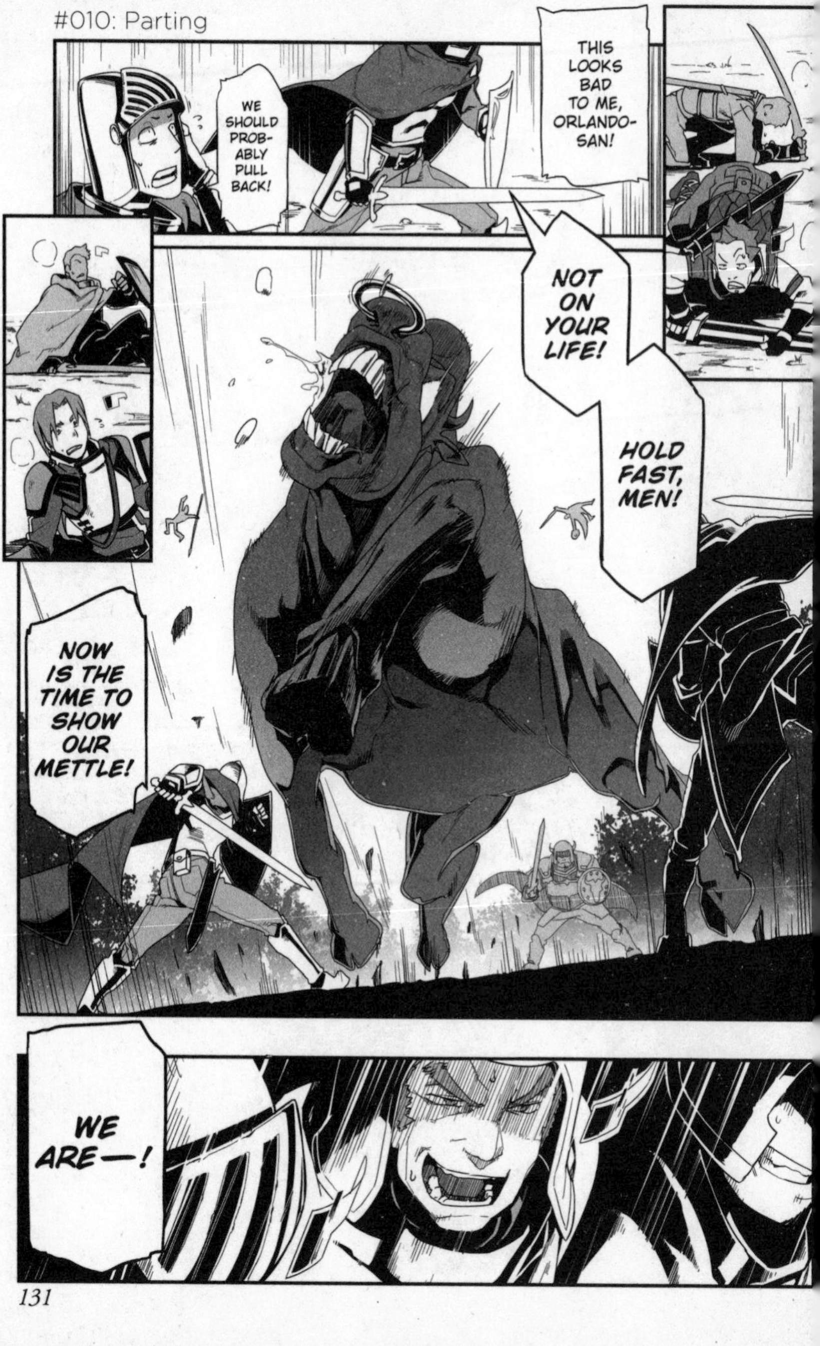
THIS LOOKS BAD TO ME, ORLANDO-SAN!
WE SHOULD PROBABLY PULL BACK!
NOT ON YOUR LIFE!
HOLD FAST, MEN!
NOW IS THE TIME TO SHOW OUR METTLE!
WE ARE—!

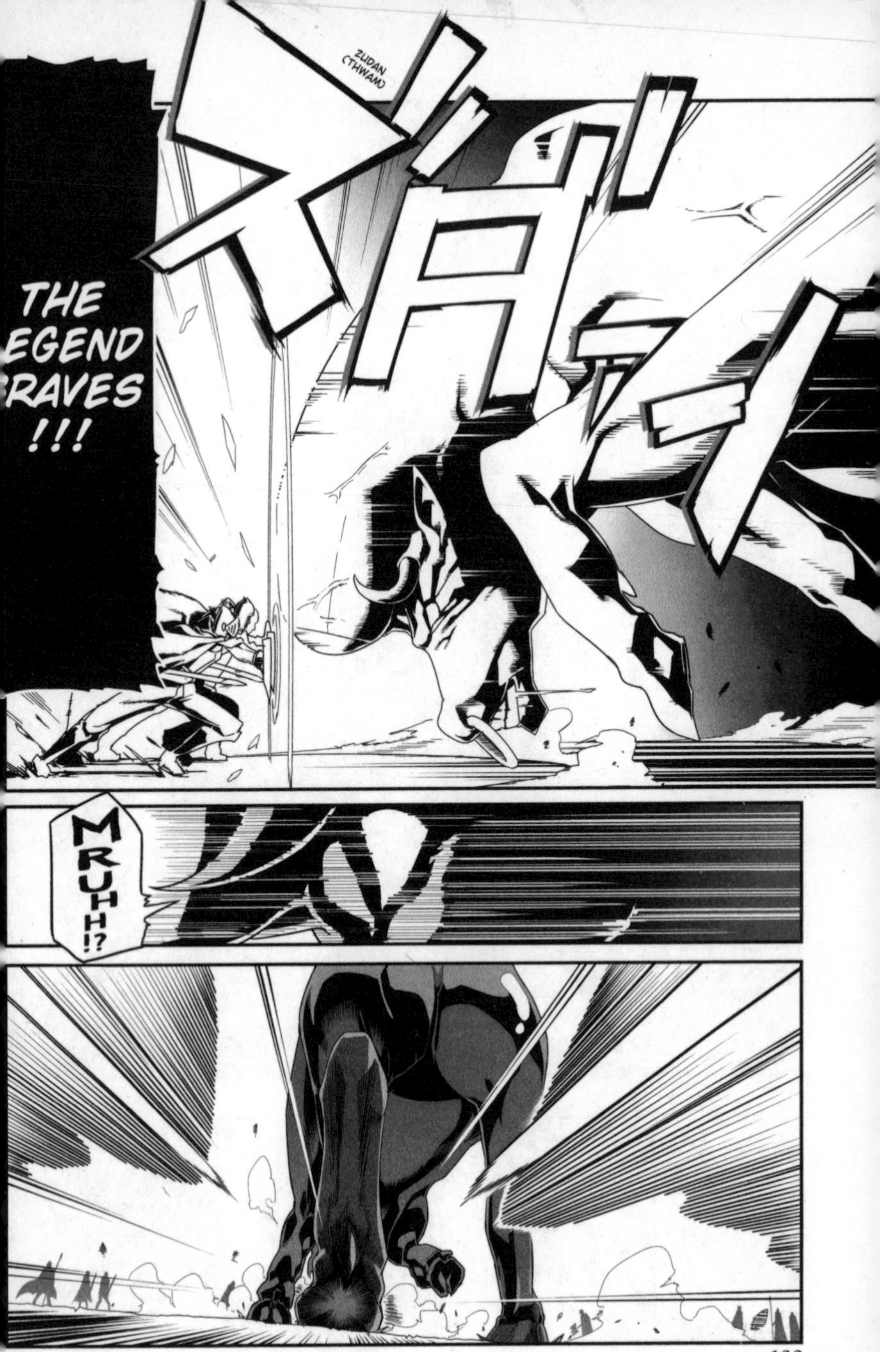
ZUDAN (THWAM)
THE EGEND RAVES !!!
MRUHH!?

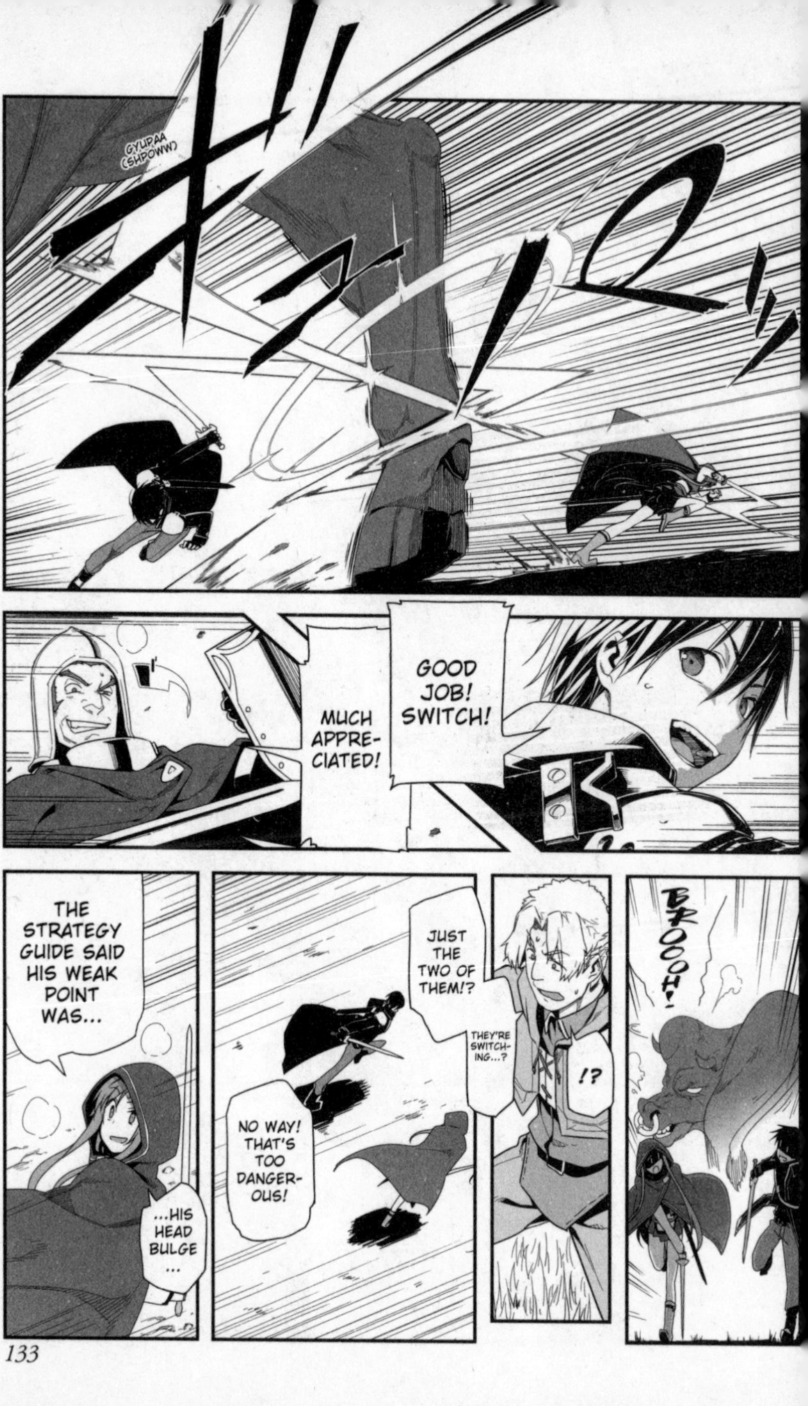
GYUPAA (SHPOWW)
GOOD JOB! SWITCH!
MUCH APPRECIATED!
BROOOOH!
JUST THE TWO OF THEM!?
THEY'RE SWITCHING...?
!?
NO WAY! THAT'S TOO DANGEROUS!
THE STRATEGY GUIDE SAID HIS WEAK POINT WAS...
...HIS HEAD BULGE...

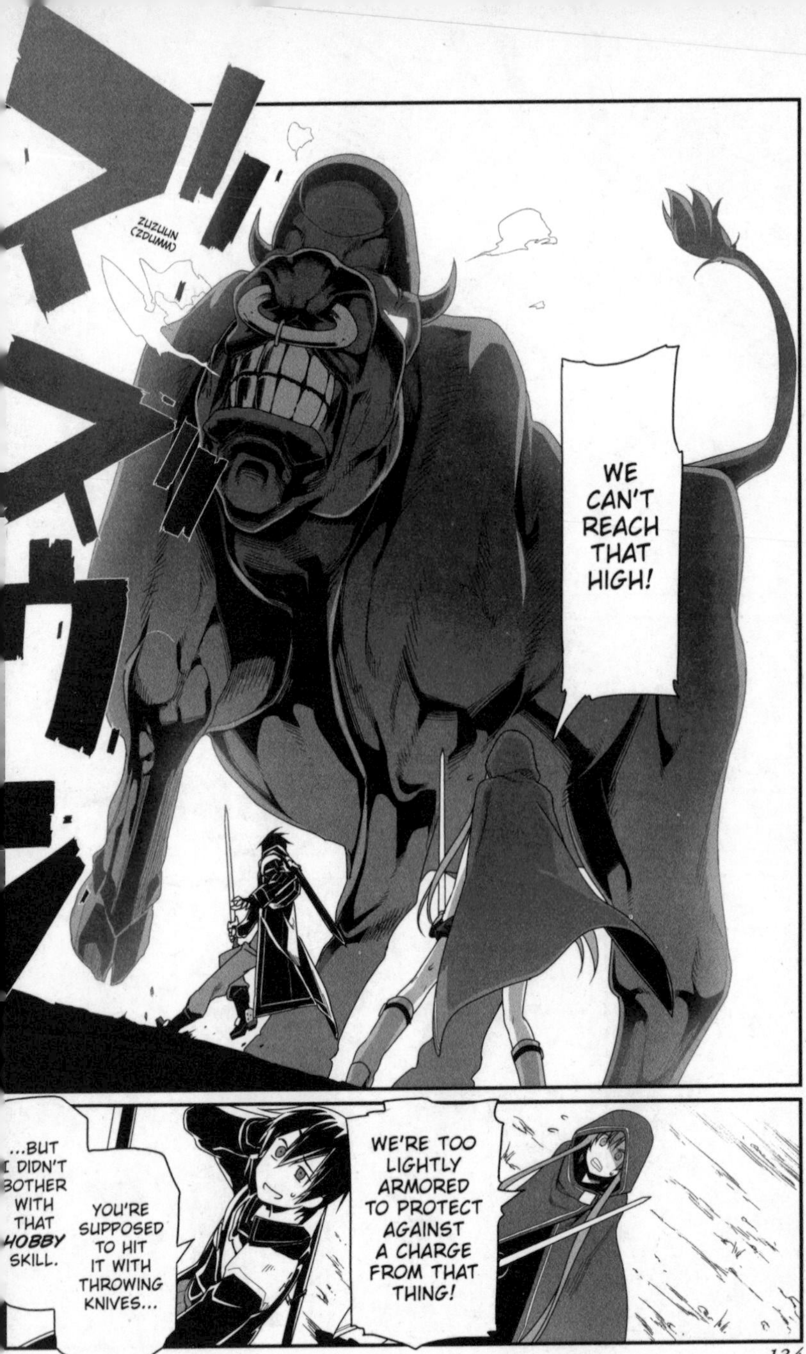
ZUZULIN (ZDUMM)
WE CAN'T REACH THAT HIGH!
WE'RE TOO LIGHTLY ARMORED TO PROTECT AGAINST A CHARGE FROM THAT THING!
YOU'RE SUPPOSED TO HIT IT WITH THROWING KNIVES...
...BUT I DIDN'T BOTHER WITH THAT *HOBBY* SKILL.

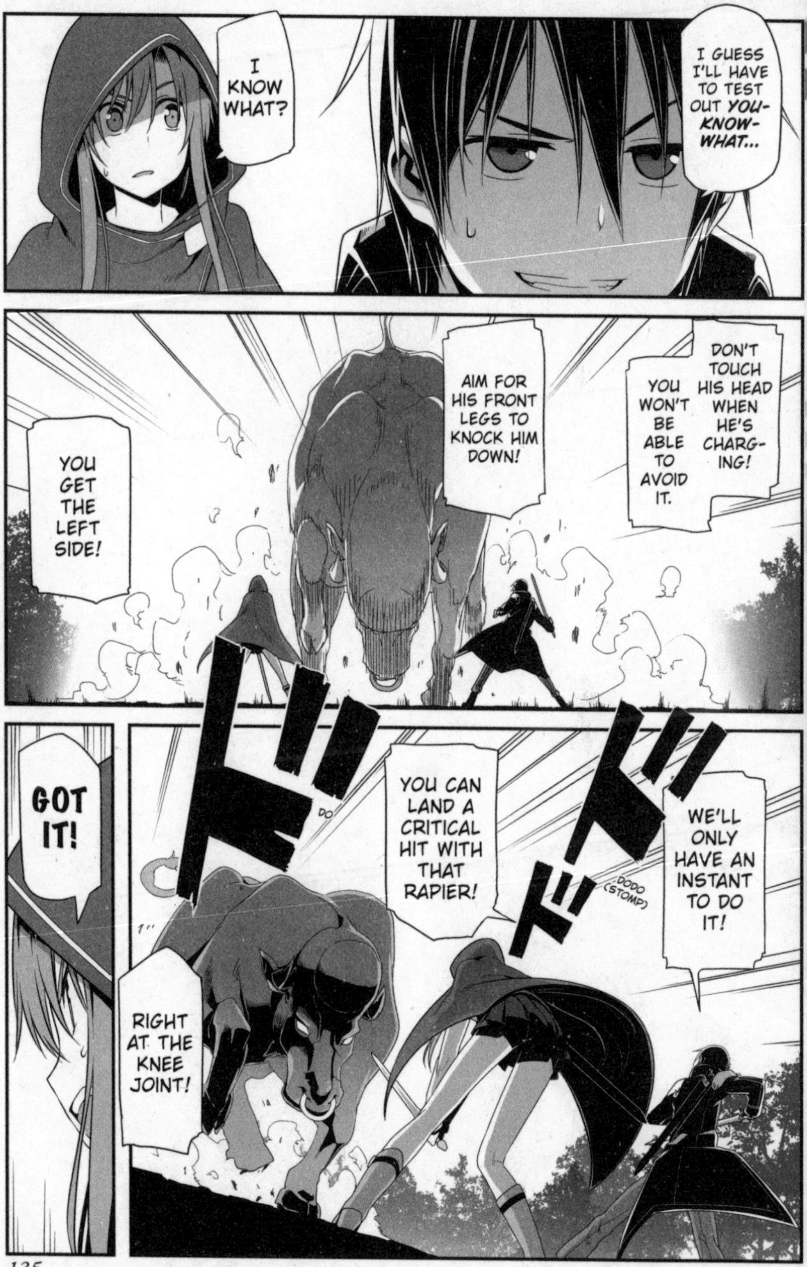
I GUESS I'LL HAVE TO TEST OUT *YOU-KNOW-WHAT...*
I KNOW WHAT?
DON'T TOUCH HIS HEAD WHEN HE'S CHARGING!
YOU WON'T BE ABLE TO AVOID IT.
AIM FOR HIS FRONT LEGS TO KNOCK HIM DOWN!
YOU GET THE LEFT SIDE!
WE'LL ONLY HAVE AN INSTANT TO DO IT!
DODO (STOMP)
YOU CAN LAND A CRITICAL HIT WITH THAT RAPIER!
DO
RIGHT AT THE KNEE JOINT!
GOT IT!

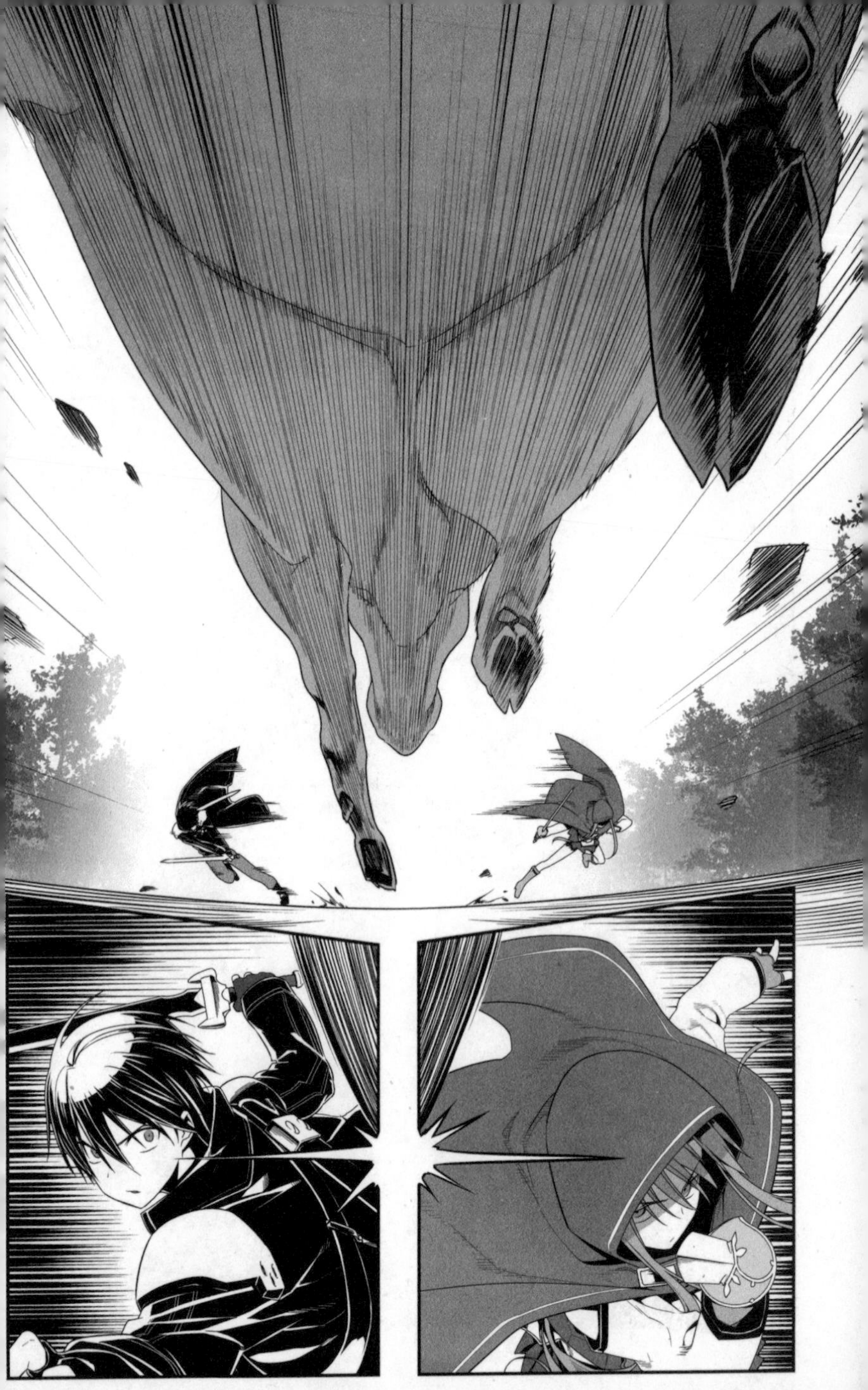

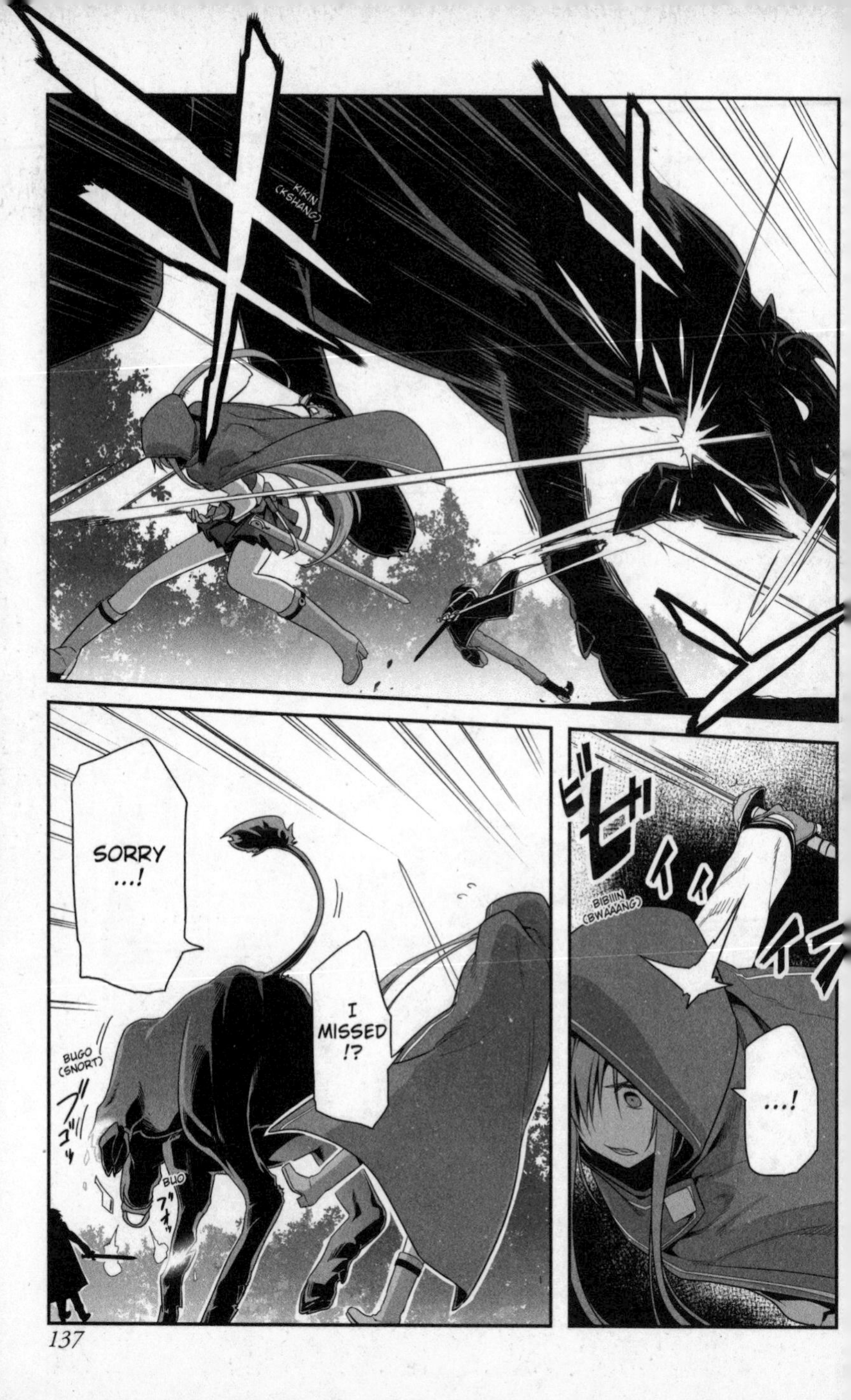
KIKIN
(KSHANG)
BIBIIIN
(BWAAANG)
...!
I MISSED !?
SORRY ...!
BUGO
(SNORT)
BUO

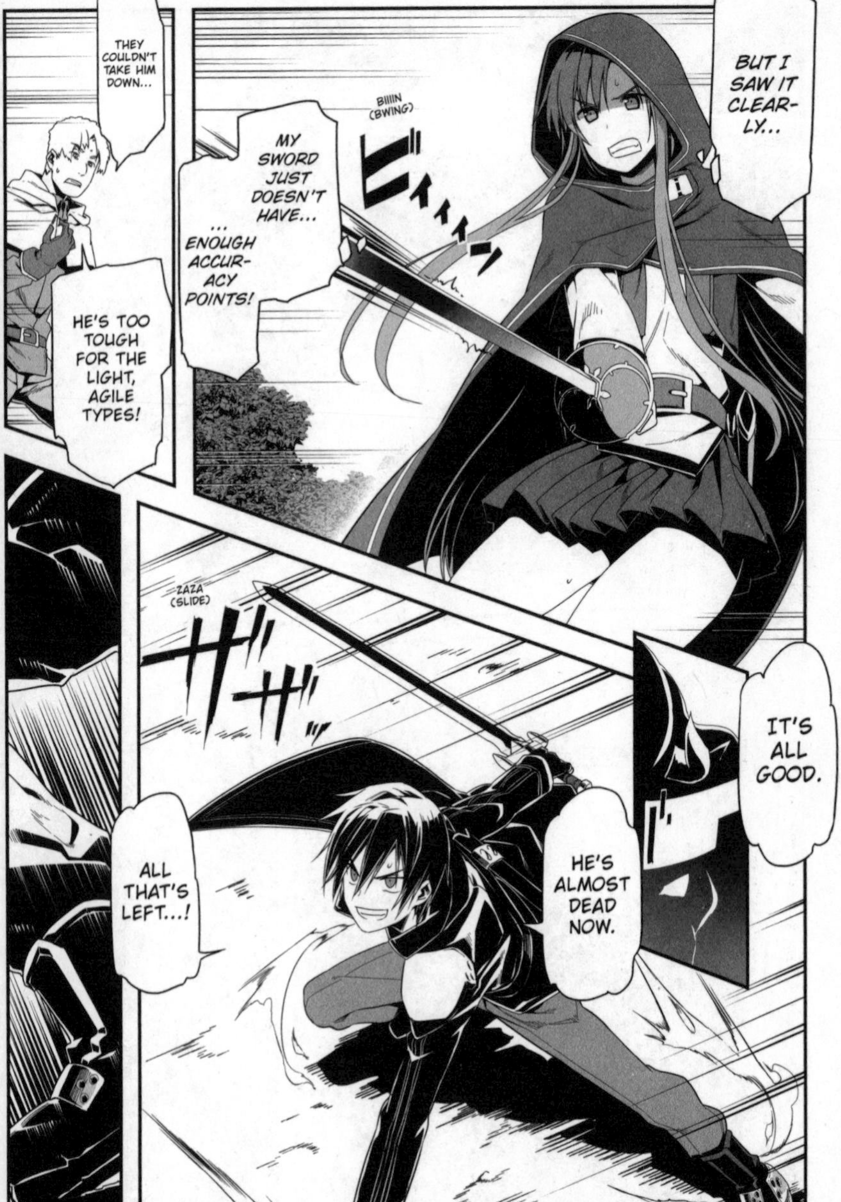
BUT I SAW IT CLEAR-LY...
BIIIN (BWING)
MY SWORD JUST DOESN'T HAVE...
...ENOUGH ACCUR-ACY POINTS!
THEY COULDN'T TAKE HIM DOWN...
HE'S TOO TOUGH FOR THE LIGHT, AGILE TYPES!
ZAZA (SLIDE)
IT'S ALL GOOD.
HE'S ALMOST DEAD NOW.
ALL THAT'S LEFT...!

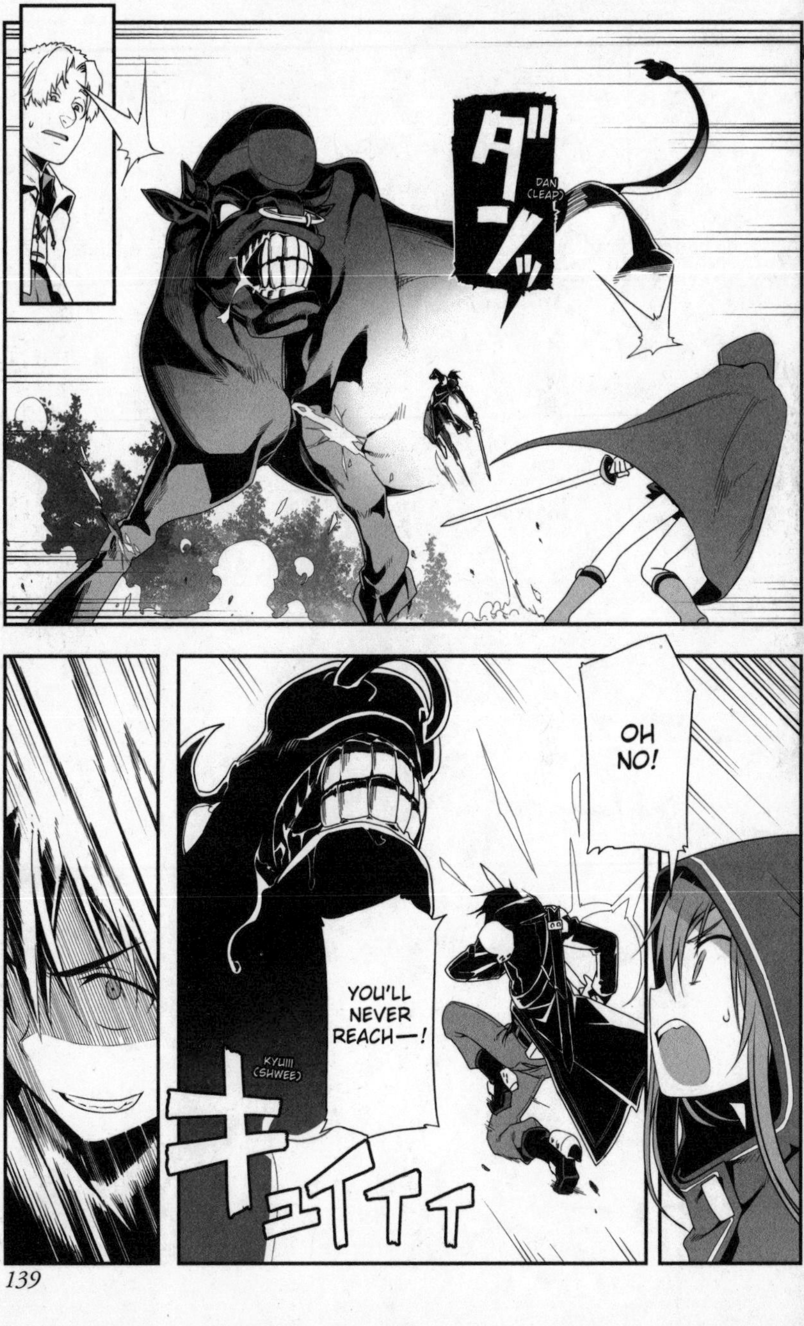
ダーンッ
DAN (LEAP)
OH NO!
YOU'LL NEVER REACH—!
キュイイイ
KYUIII (SHWEE)

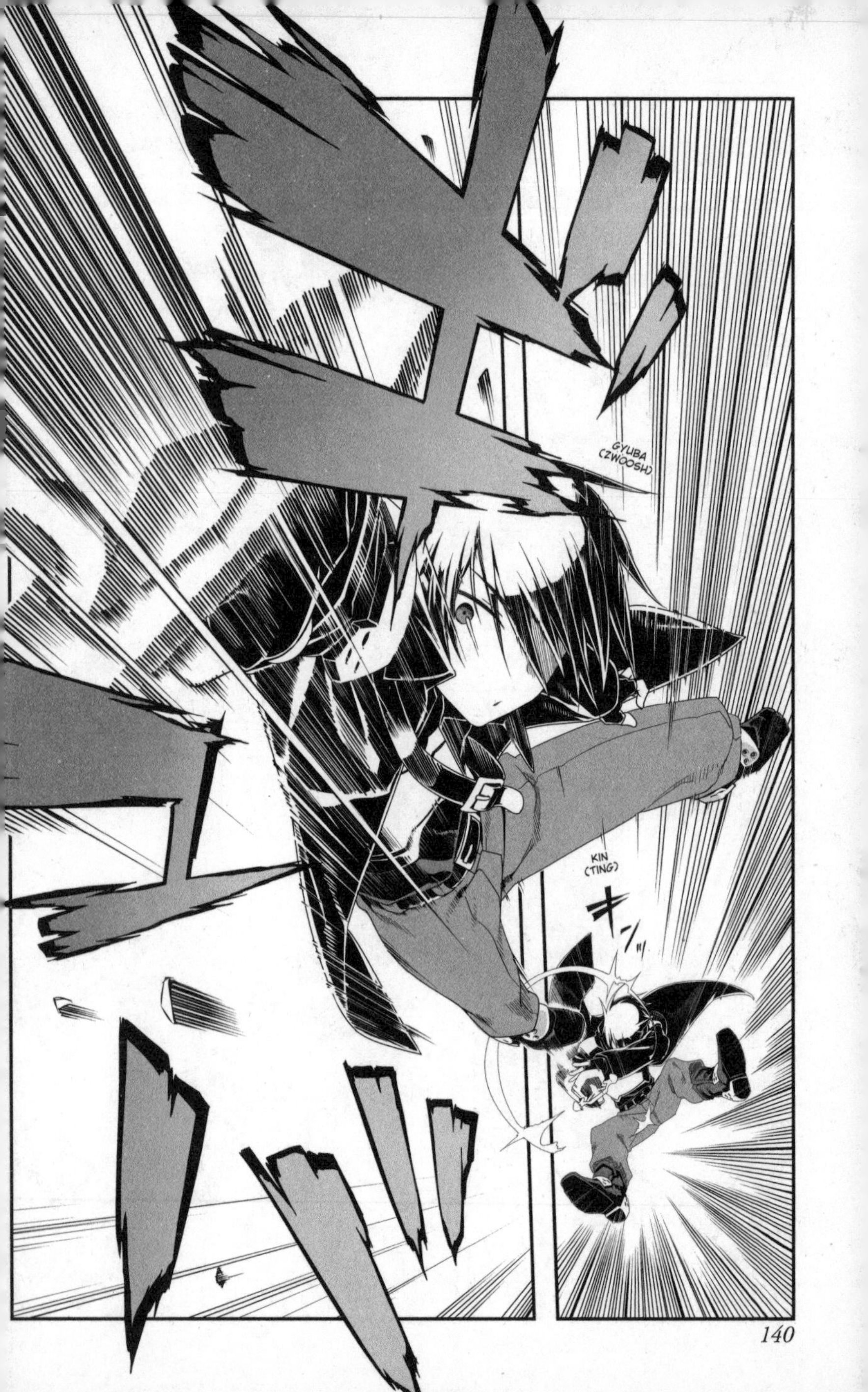
GYUBA
(ZWOOSH)
KIN
(TING)

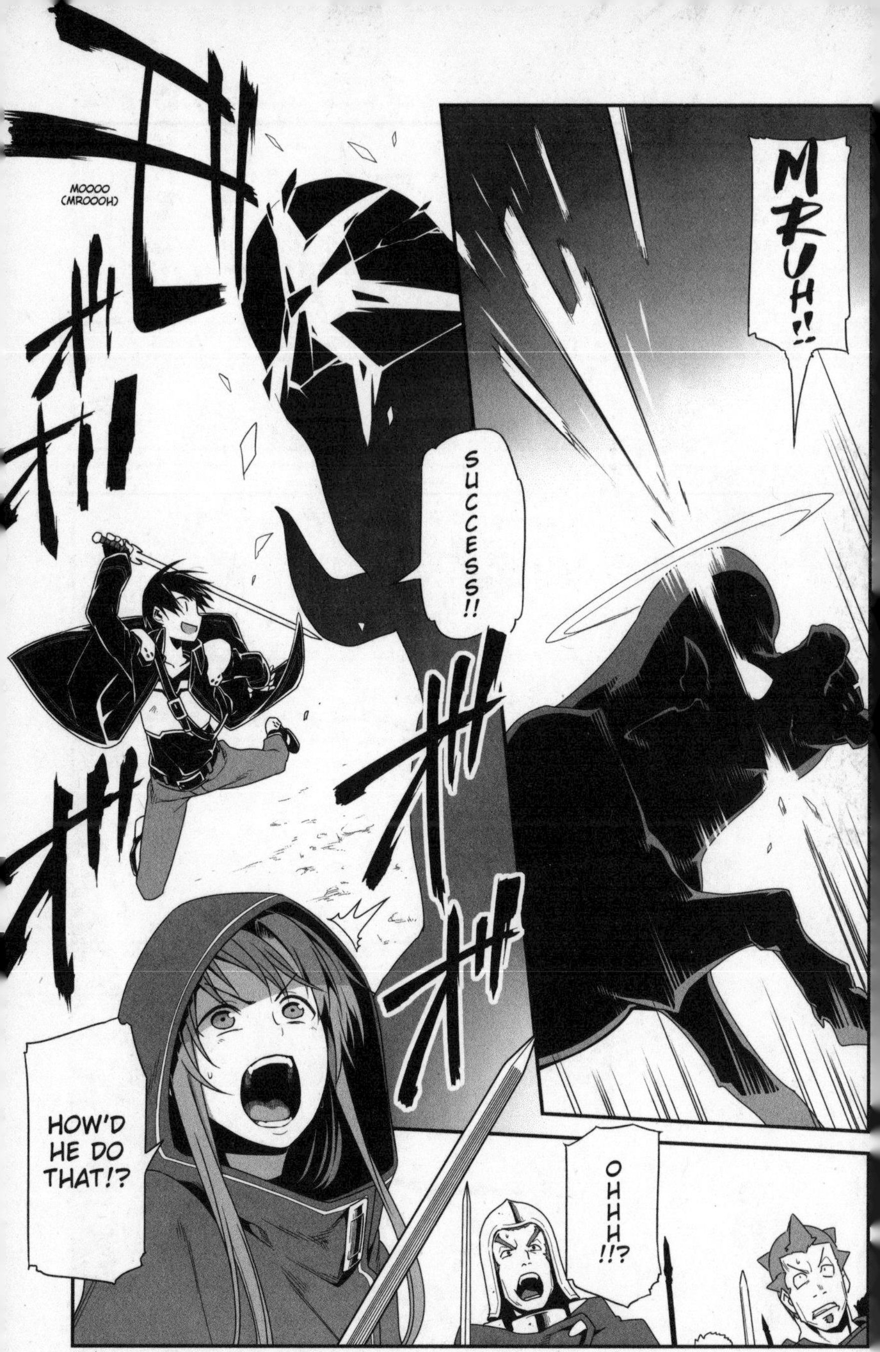
MRUH!!
SUCCESS!!
MOOOO (MROOOH)
OHHHH!!?
HOW'D HE DO THAT!?

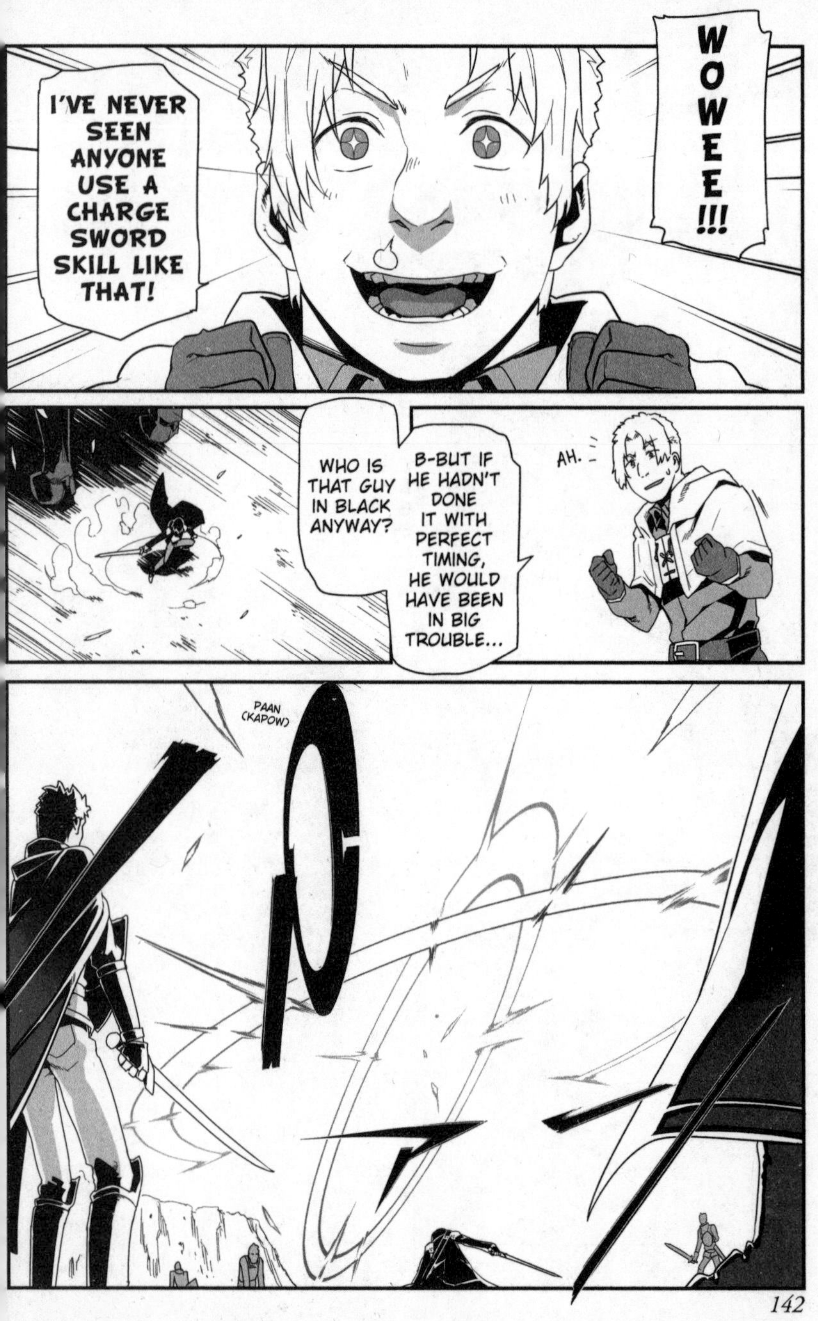
WOWEE!!!
I'VE NEVER SEEN ANYONE USE A CHARGE SWORD SKILL LIKE THAT!
AH.
B-BUT IF HE HADN'T DONE IT WITH PERFECT TIMING, HE WOULD HAVE BEEN IN BIG TROUBLE...
WHO IS THAT GUY IN BLACK ANYWAY?
PAAN (KAPOW)

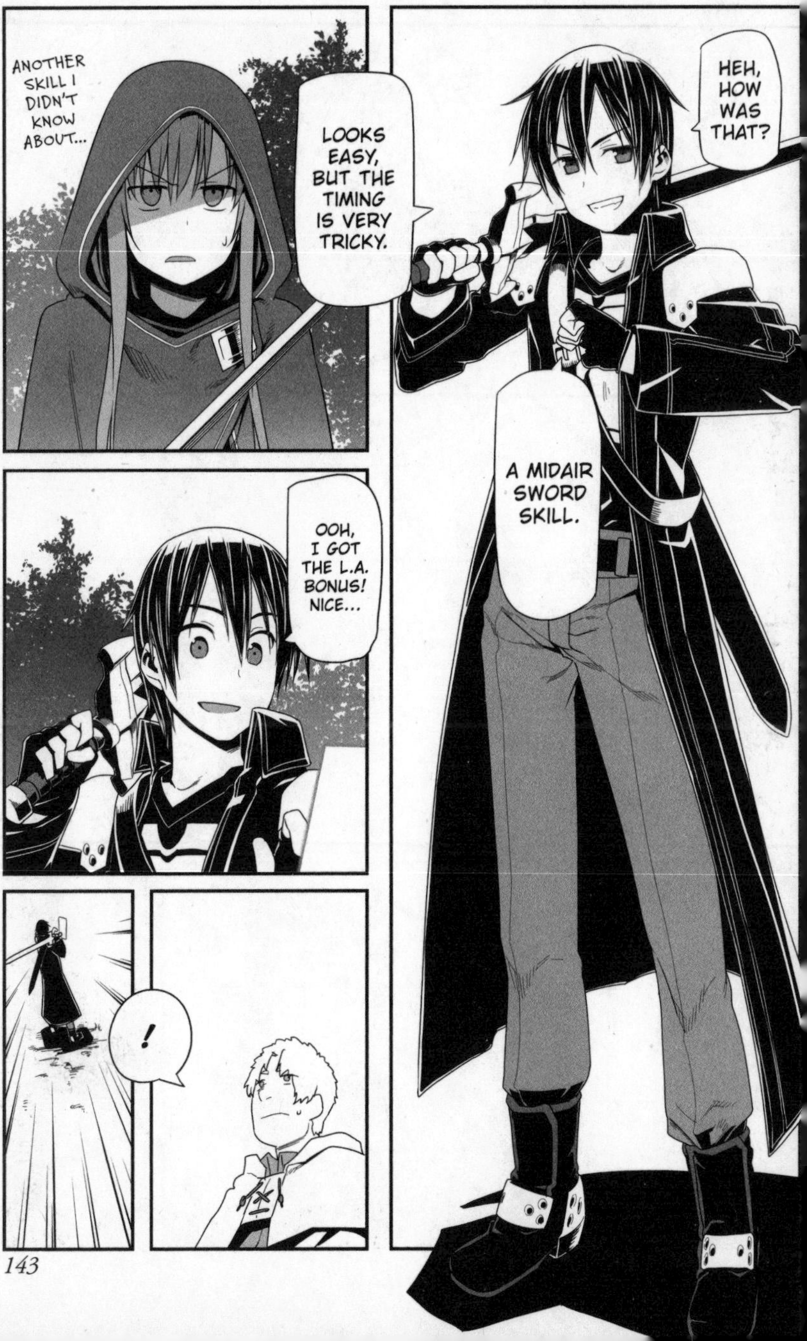
HEH, HOW WAS THAT?
A MIDAIR SWORD SKILL.
LOOKS EASY, BUT THE TIMING IS VERY TRICKY.
ANOTHER SKILL I DIDN'T KNOW ABOUT...
OOH, I GOT THE L.A. BONUS! NICE...
!

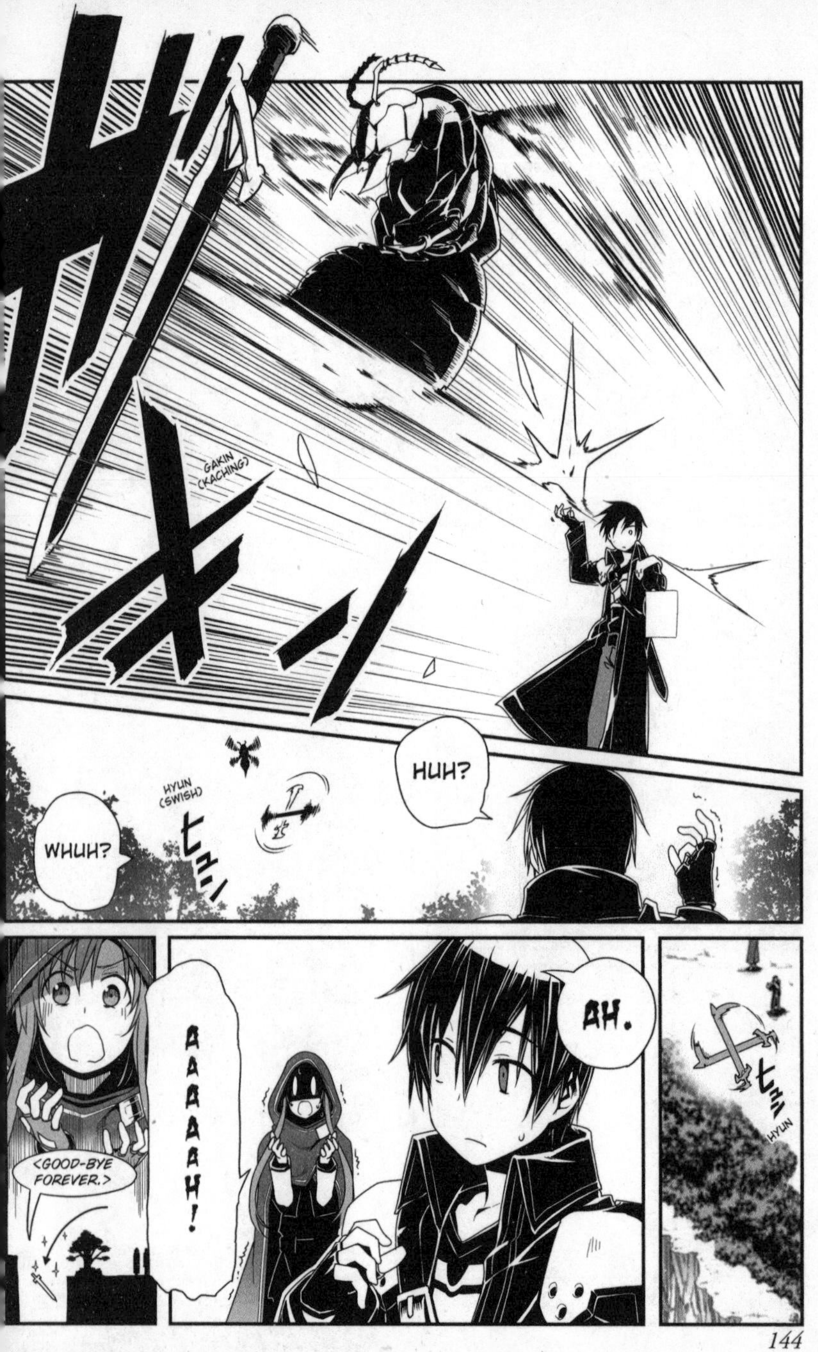
GAKIN (KACHING)
HUH?
HYUN (SWISH)
WHUH?
HYUN
AH.
AAAAAAH!
<GOOD-BYE FOREVER.>

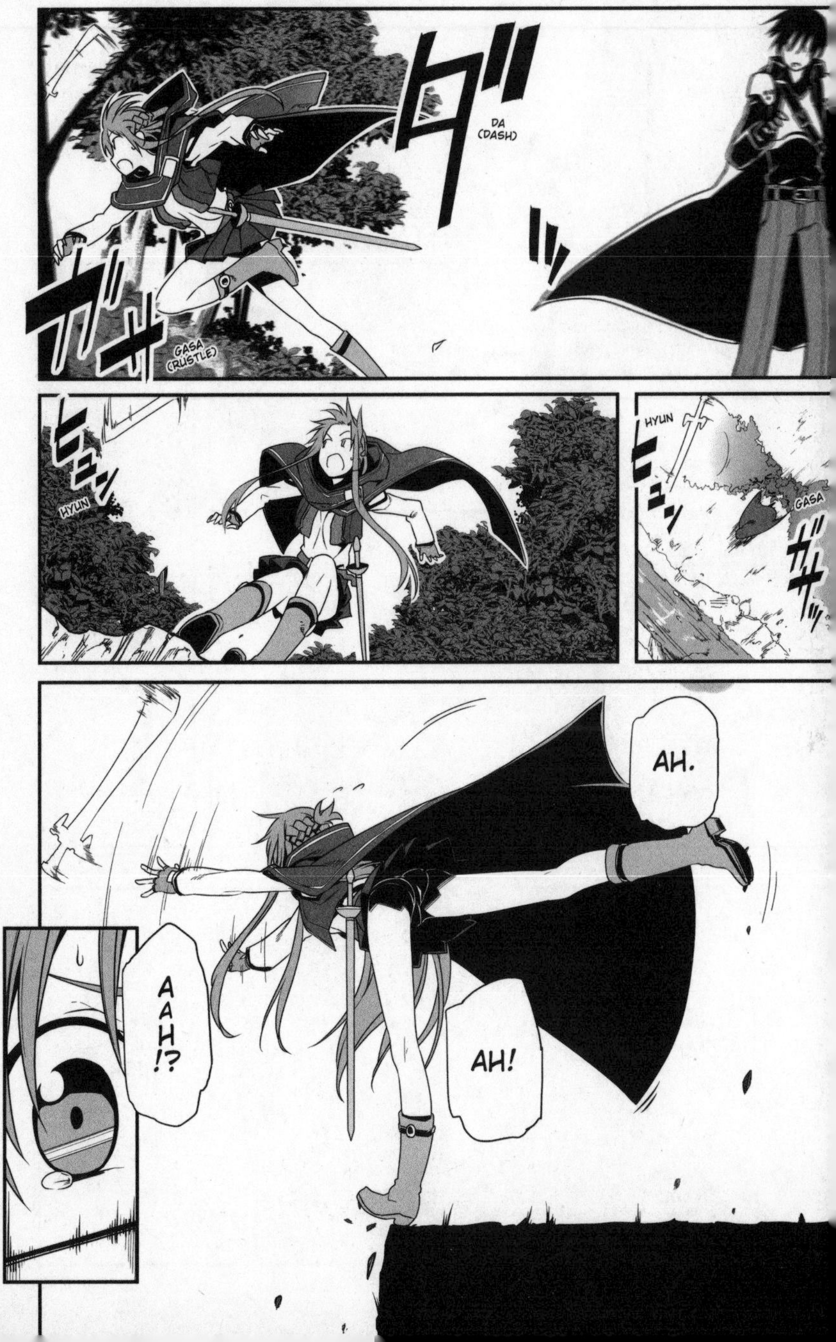
DA (DASH)
GASA (RUSTLE)
HYUN
GASA
HYUN
AH.
AH!
AAH!?

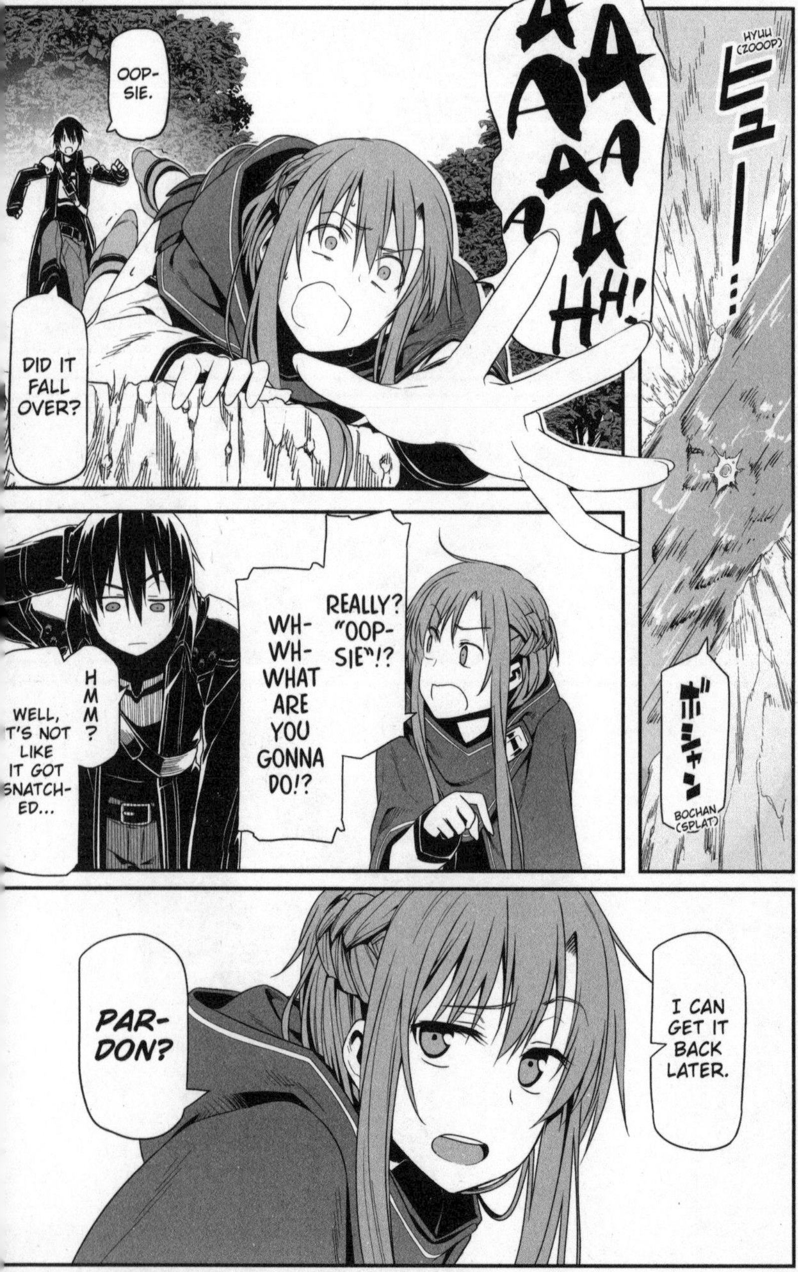
ヒュー…
HYUU (ZOOOP)
ボシャン
BOCHAN (SPLAT)
AAAAAAAHH!
OOP-SIE.
DID IT FALL OVER?
REALLY? "OOP-SIE"!?
WH-WH-WHAT ARE YOU GONNA DO!?
HMM?
WELL, IT'S NOT LIKE IT GOT SNATCHED...
I CAN GET IT BACK LATER.
PAR-DON?

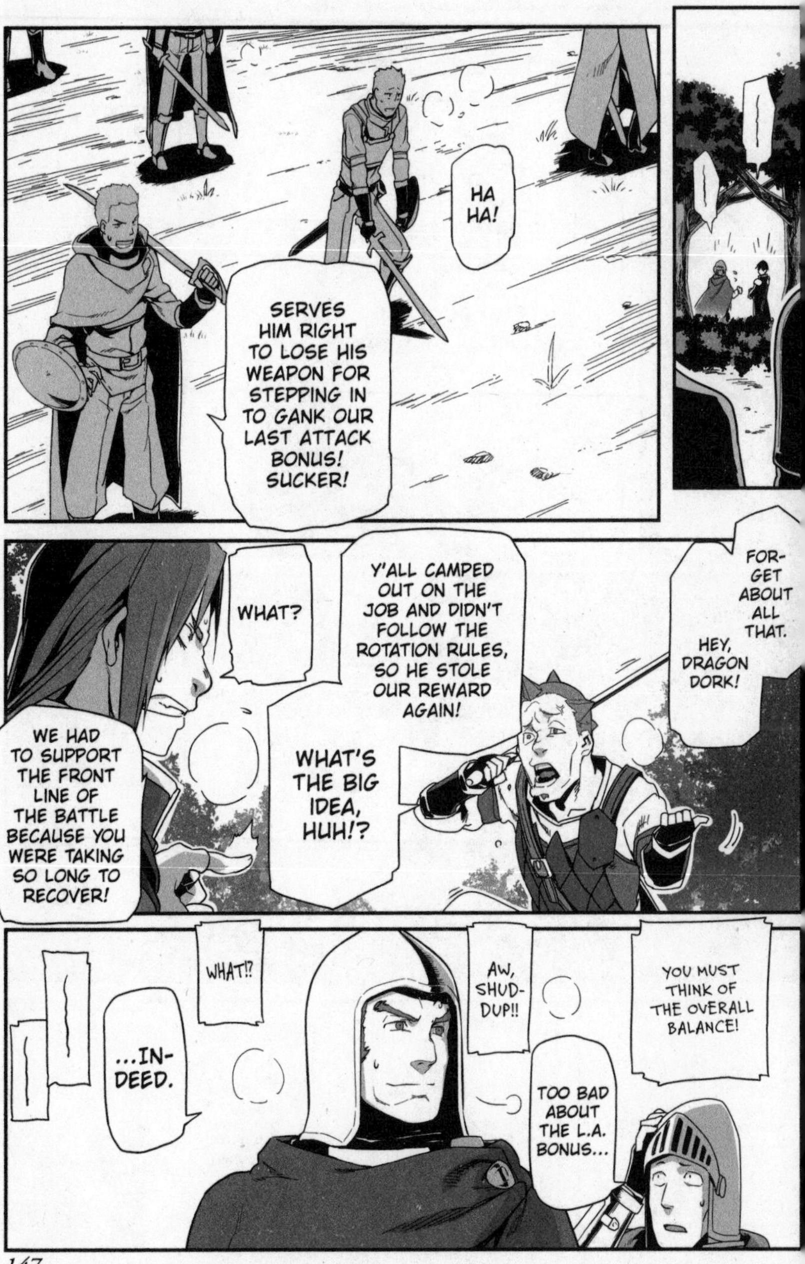
HA HA!
SERVES HIM RIGHT TO LOSE HIS WEAPON FOR STEPPING IN TO GANK OUR LAST ATTACK BONUS! SUCKER!
FOR-GET ABOUT ALL THAT.
HEY, DRAGON DORK!
Y'ALL CAMPED OUT ON THE JOB AND DIDN'T FOLLOW THE ROTATION RULES, SO HE STOLE OUR REWARD AGAIN!
WHAT'S THE BIG IDEA, HUH!?
WHAT?
WE HAD TO SUPPORT THE FRONT LINE OF THE BATTLE BECAUSE YOU WERE TAKING SO LONG TO RECOVER!
YOU MUST THINK OF THE OVERALL BALANCE!
AW, SHUD-DUP!!
TOO BAD ABOUT THE L.A. BONUS...
WHAT!?
...IN-DEED.

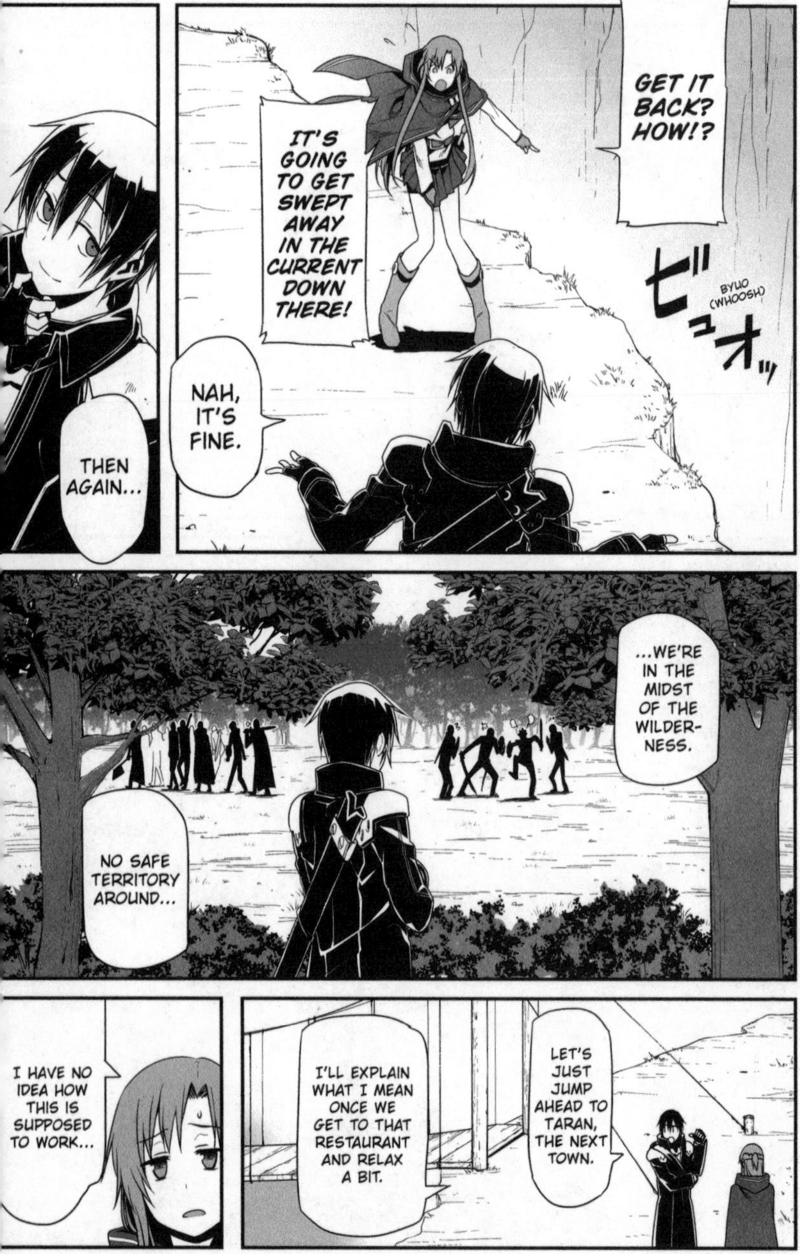
GET IT BACK? HOW!?
IT'S GOING TO GET SWEPT AWAY IN THE CURRENT DOWN THERE!
ビュオッ
BYUO (WHOOSH)
NAH, IT'S FINE.
THEN AGAIN...
...WE'RE IN THE MIDST OF THE WILDERNESS.
NO SAFE TERRITORY AROUND...
LET'S JUST JUMP AHEAD TO TARAN, THE NEXT TOWN.
I'LL EXPLAIN WHAT I MEAN ONCE WE GET TO THAT RESTAURANT AND RELAX A BIT.
I HAVE NO IDEA HOW THIS IS SUPPOSED TO WORK...

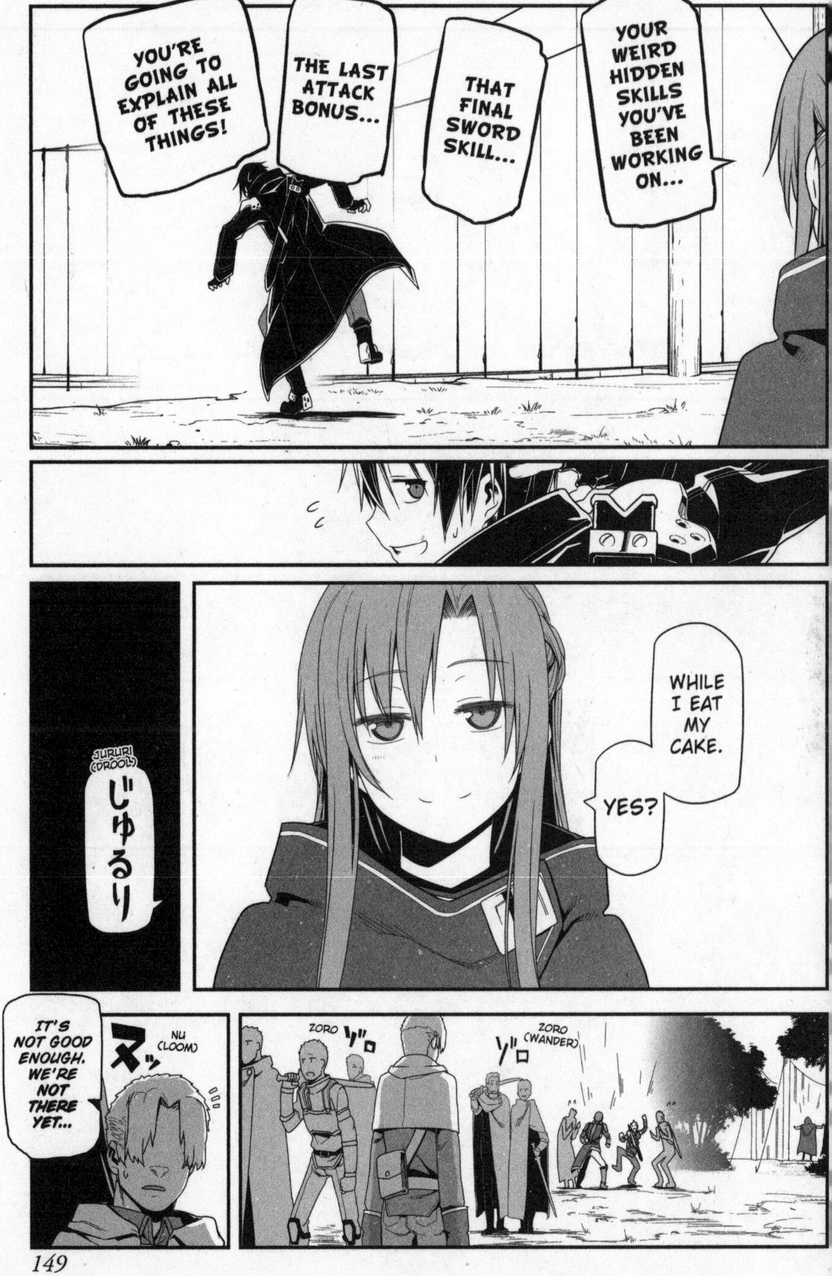
YOUR WEIRD HIDDEN SKILLS YOU'VE BEEN WORKING ON...
THAT FINAL SWORD SKILL...
THE LAST ATTACK BONUS...
YOU'RE GOING TO EXPLAIN ALL OF THESE THINGS!
WHILE I EAT MY CAKE.
YES?
じゅるり
JURURI (DROOL)
ゾロ
ZORO (WANDER)
ゾロ
ZORO
ヌッ
NU (LOOM)
IT'S NOT GOOD ENOUGH. WE'RE NOT THERE YET...

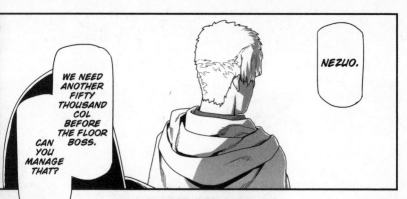

NEZUO.

WE NEED ANOTHER FIFTY THOUSAND COL BEFORE THE FLOOR BOSS. CAN YOU MANAGE THAT?

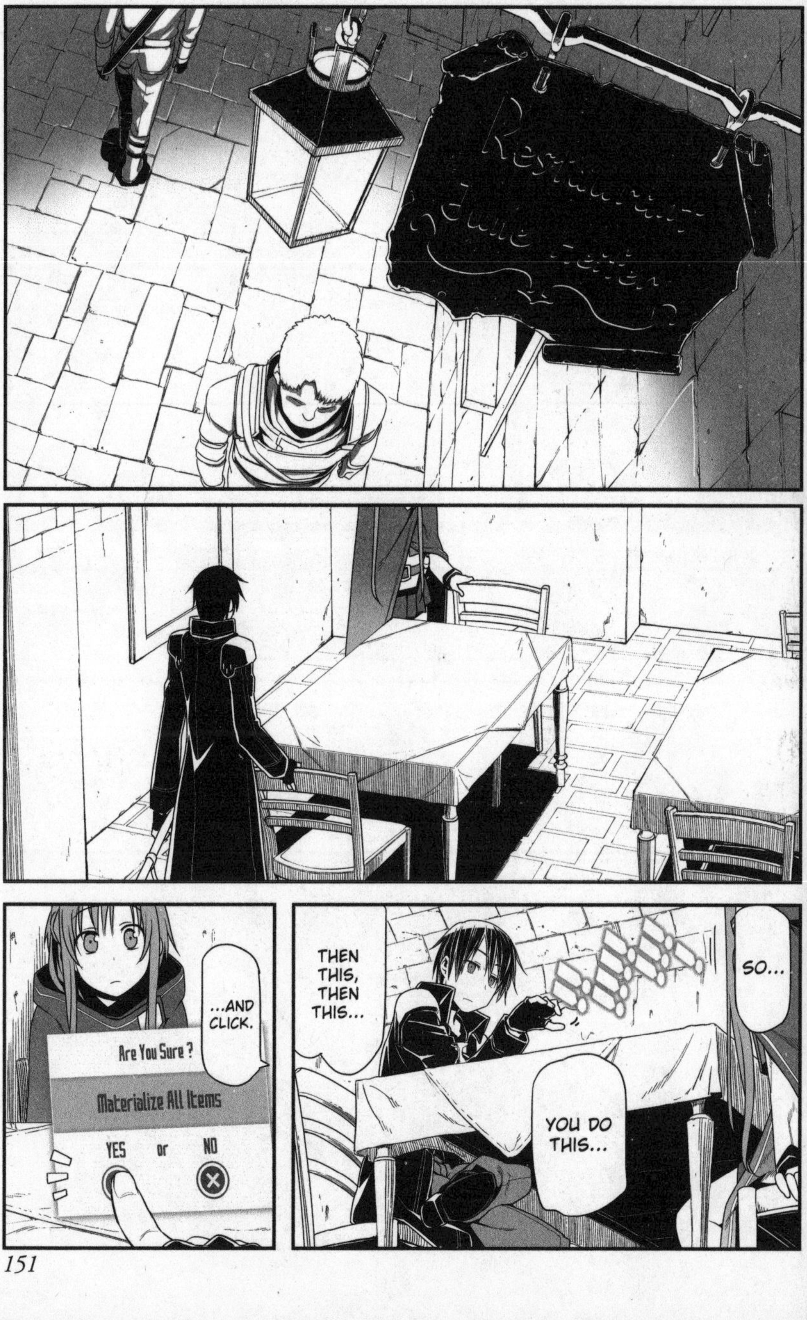
SO...
THEN THIS, THEN THIS...
YOU DO THIS...
...AND CLICK.
Are You Sure ?
Materialize All Items
YES or NO

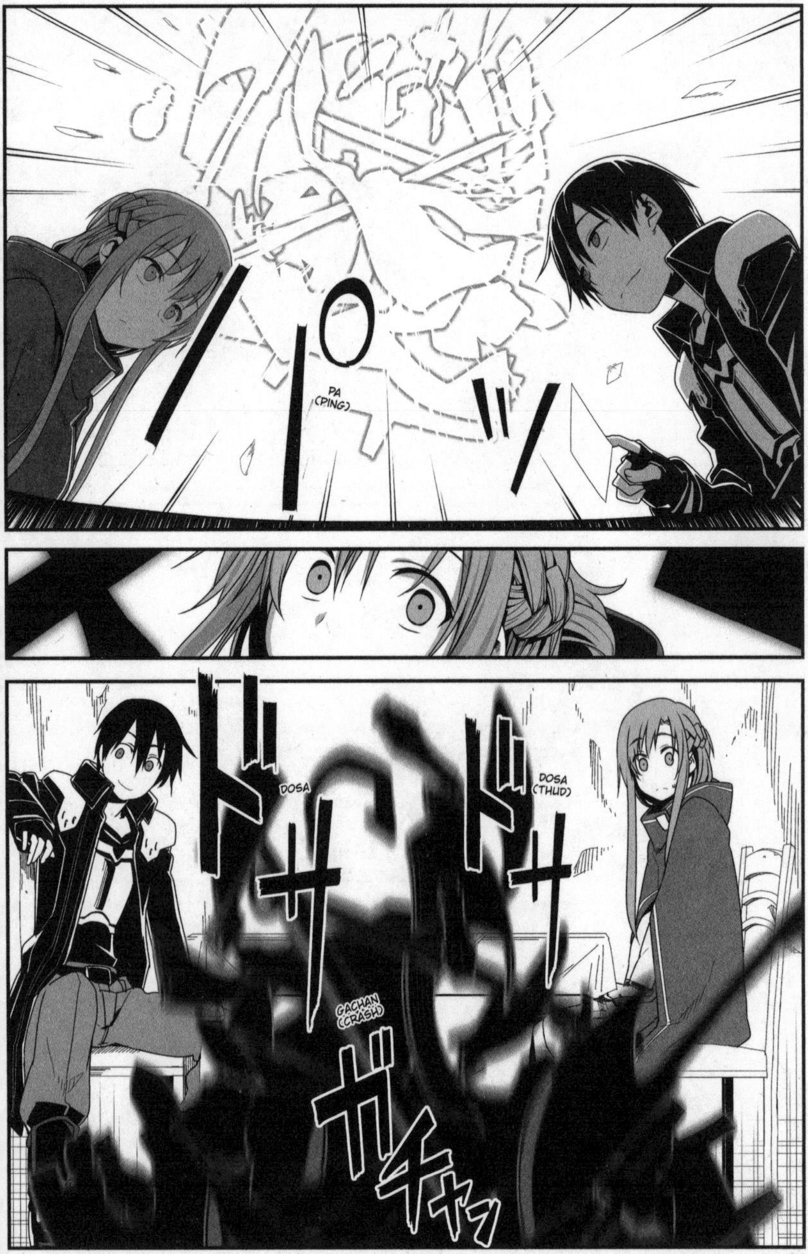
PA
(PING)
DOSA
(THUD)
DOSA
GACHAN
(CRASH)

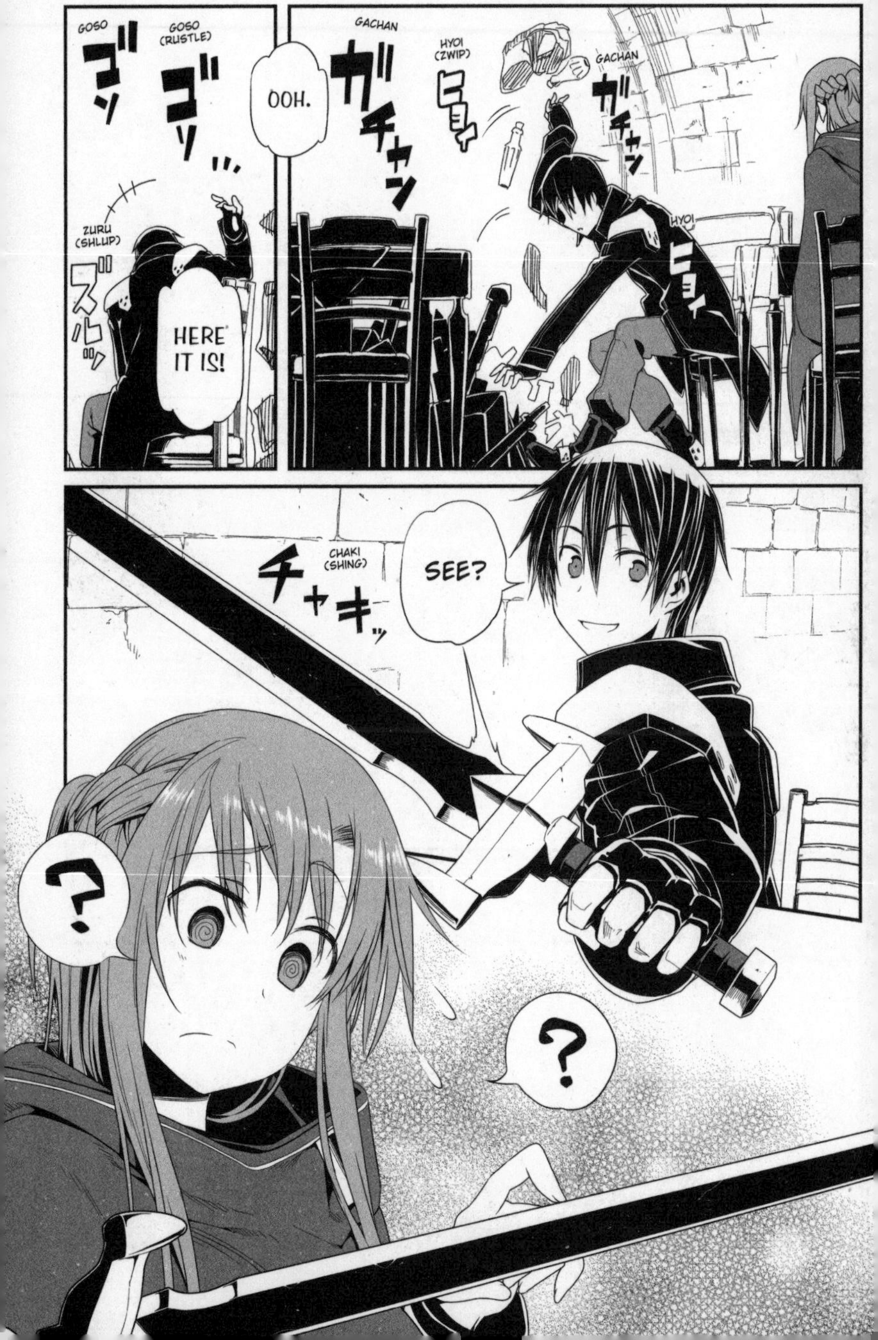

GACHAN
ガチャン
HYOI
ヒョイ
HYOI (ZWIP)
ヒョイ
GACHAN
ガチャン
OOH.
GOSO (RUSTLE)
ゴソッ
GOSO
ゴソッ
HERE IT IS!
ZURU (SHLUP)
ズルッ
SEE?
CHAKI (SHING)
チャキッ
?
?

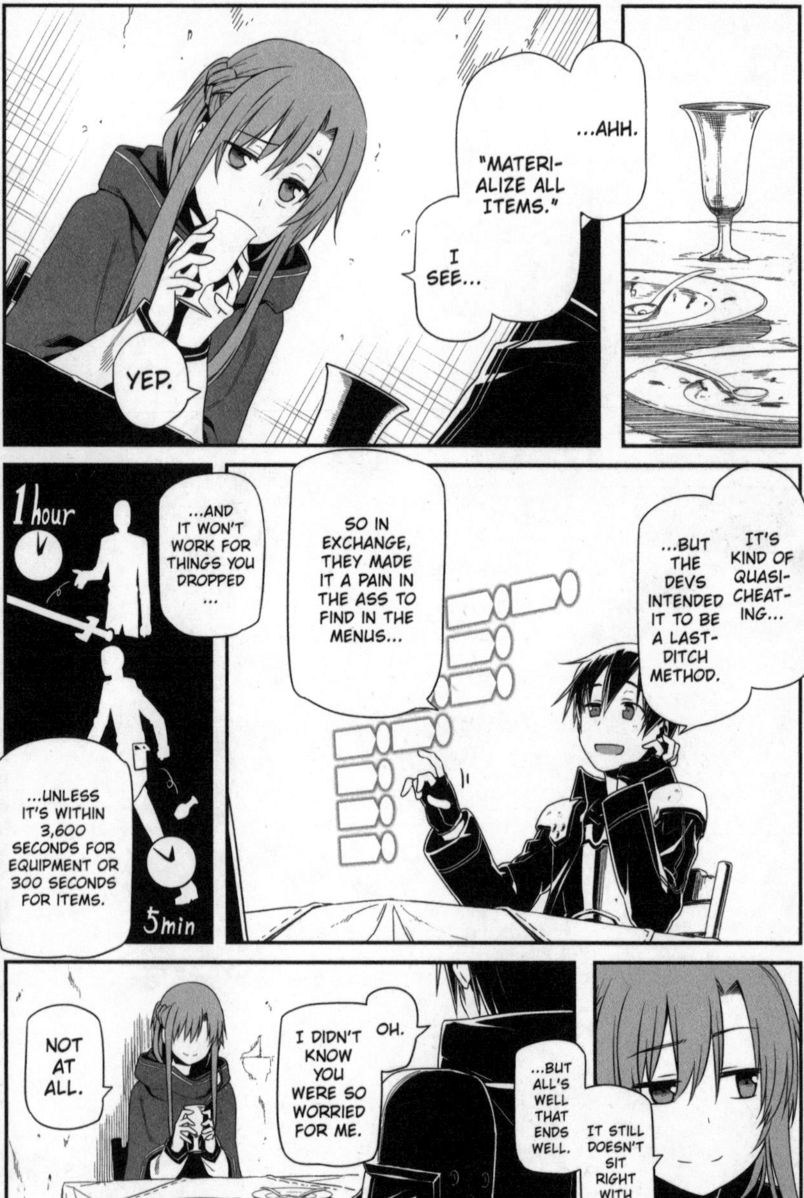
...AHH.
"MATERIALIZE ALL ITEMS."
I SEE...
YEP.
IT'S KIND OF QUASI-CHEATING...
...BUT THE DEVS INTENDED IT TO BE A LAST-DITCH METHOD.
SO IN EXCHANGE, THEY MADE IT A PAIN IN THE ASS TO FIND IN THE MENUS...
...AND IT WON'T WORK FOR THINGS YOU DROPPED ...
1 hour
...UNLESS IT'S WITHIN 3,600 SECONDS FOR EQUIPMENT OR 300 SECONDS FOR ITEMS.
5min
IT STILL DOESN'T SIT RIGHT WITH ME...
...BUT ALL'S WELL THAT ENDS WELL.
OH.
I DIDN'T KNOW YOU WERE SO WORRIED FOR ME.
NOT AT ALL.

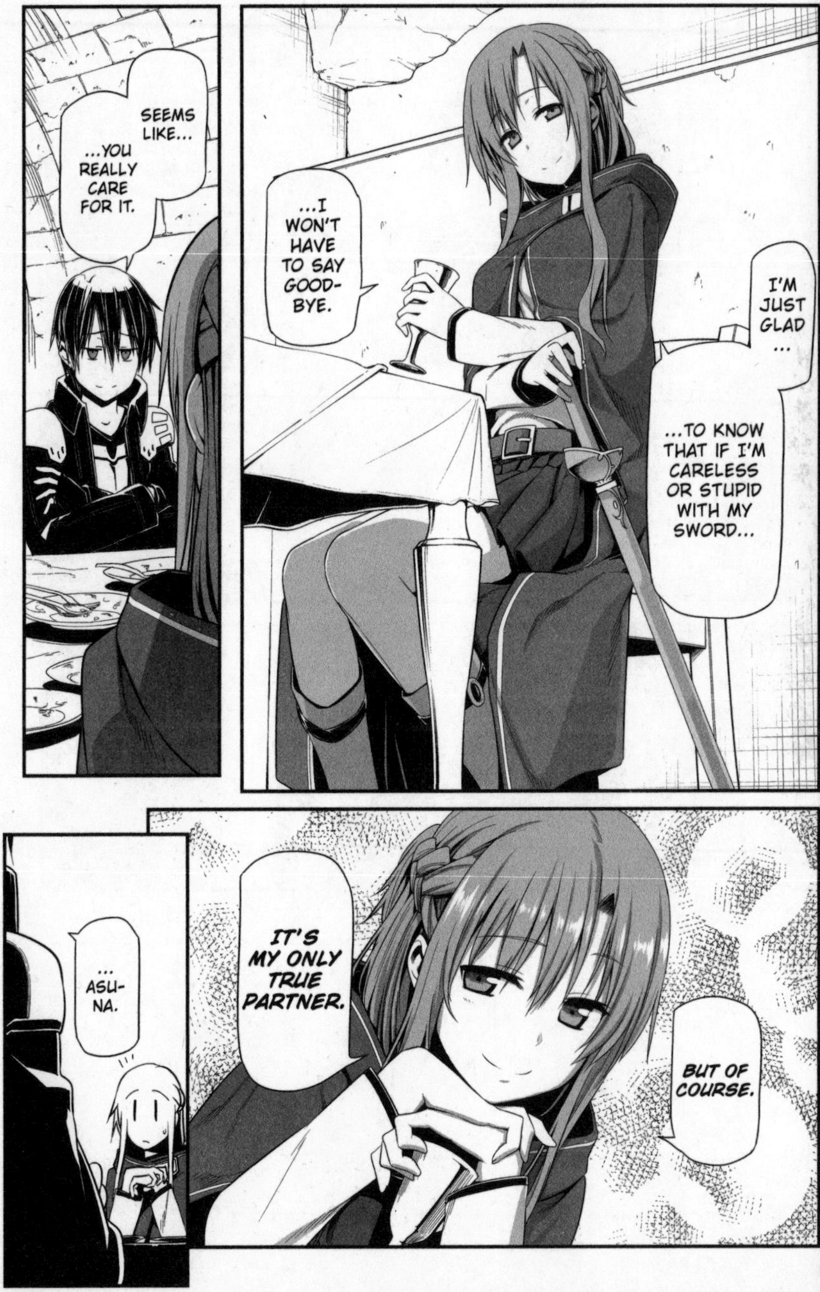
I'M JUST GLAD ...
...TO KNOW THAT IF I'M CARELESS OR STUPID WITH MY SWORD...
...I WON'T HAVE TO SAY GOOD-BYE.
SEEMS LIKE...
...YOU REALLY CARE FOR IT.
BUT OF COURSE.
IT'S MY ONLY TRUE PARTNER.
... ASU-NA.

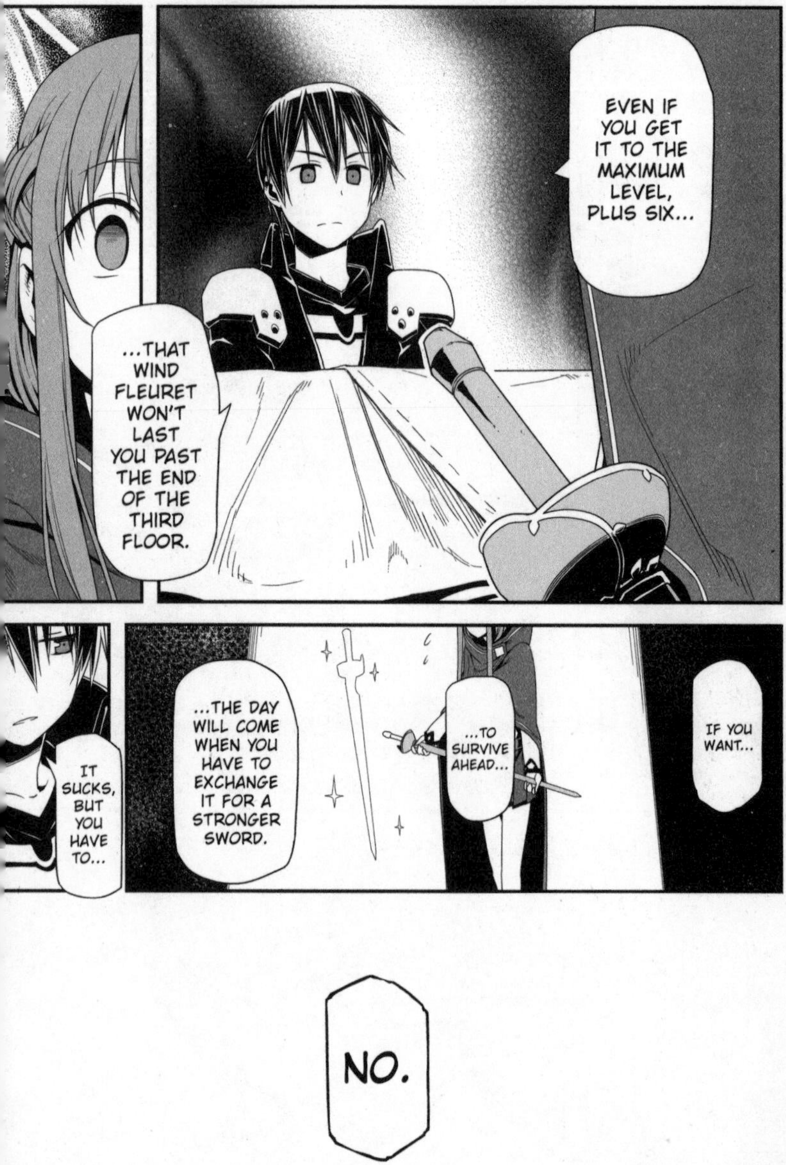
EVEN IF YOU GET IT TO THE MAXIMUM LEVEL, PLUS SIX...
...THAT WIND FLEURET WON'T LAST YOU PAST THE END OF THE THIRD FLOOR.
IF YOU WANT...
...TO SURVIVE AHEAD...
...THE DAY WILL COME WHEN YOU HAVE TO EXCHANGE IT FOR A STRONGER SWORD.
IT SUCKS, BUT YOU HAVE TO...
NO.

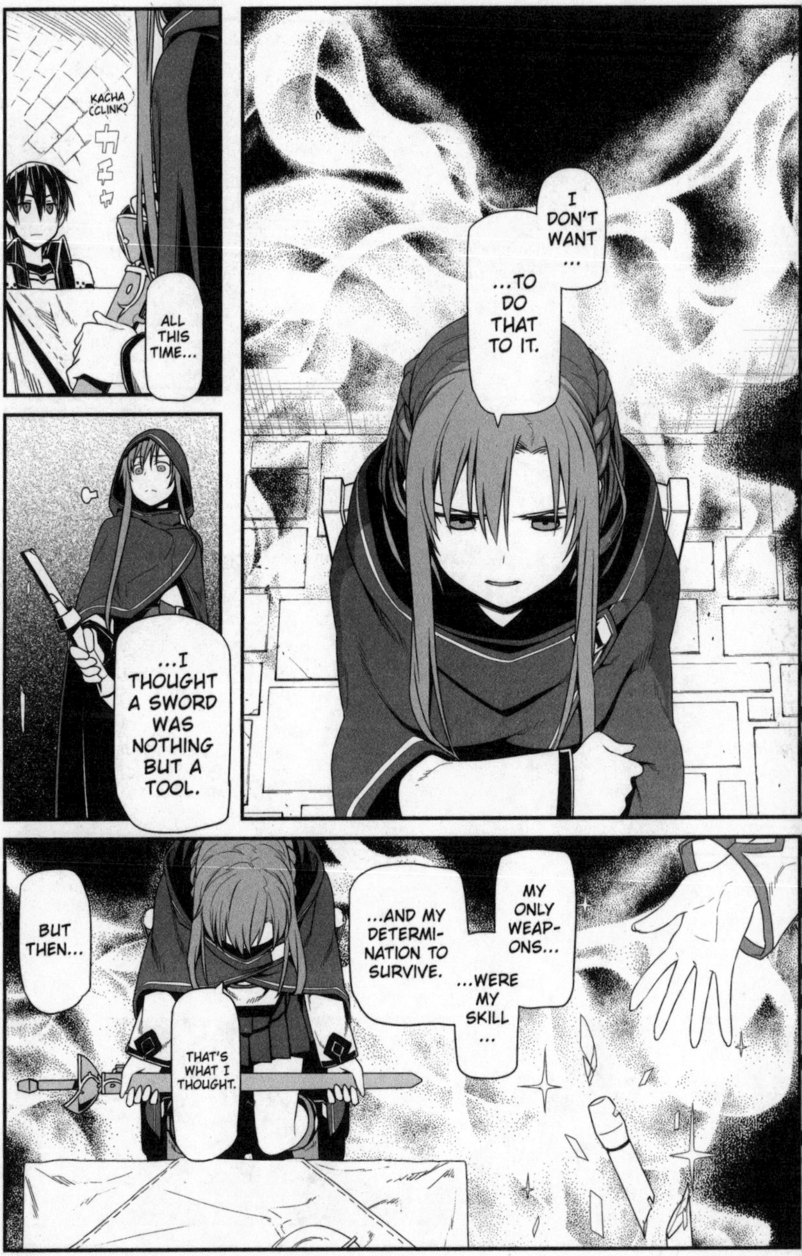
I DON'T WANT ...
...TO DO THAT TO IT.
KACHA (CLINK)
カチャ
ALL THIS TIME...
...I THOUGHT A SWORD WAS NOTHING BUT A TOOL.
MY ONLY WEAPONS...
...WERE MY SKILL ...
...AND MY DETERMINATION TO SURVIVE.
BUT THEN...
THAT'S WHAT I THOUGHT.

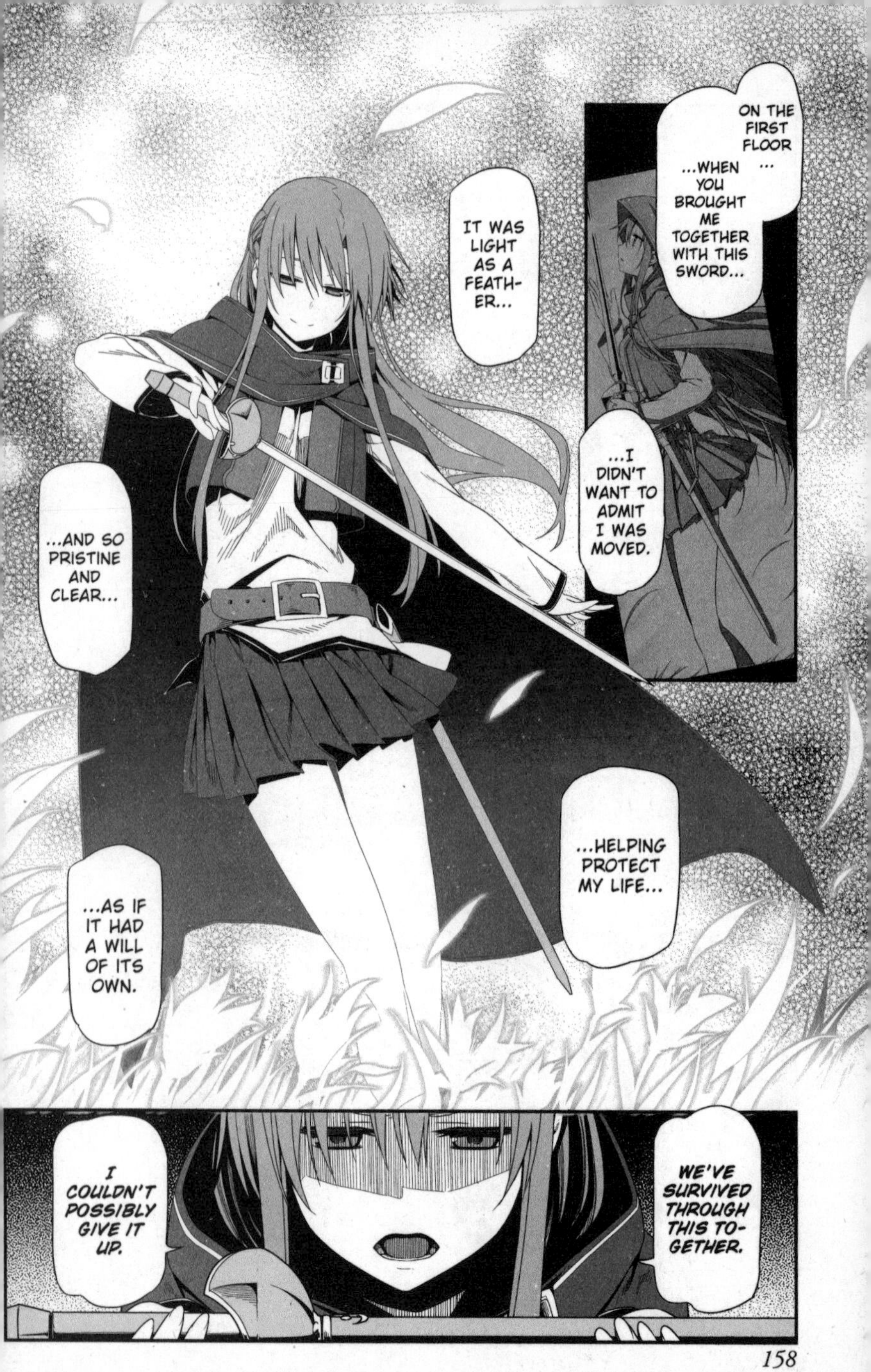
ON THE FIRST FLOOR...
...WHEN YOU BROUGHT ME TOGETHER WITH THIS SWORD...
...I DIDN'T WANT TO ADMIT I WAS MOVED.
IT WAS LIGHT AS A FEATH-ER...
...AND SO PRISTINE AND CLEAR...
...HELPING PROTECT MY LIFE...
...AS IF IT HAD A WILL OF ITS OWN.
WE'VE SURVIVED THROUGH THIS TO-GETHER.
I COULDN'T POSSIBLY GIVE IT UP.

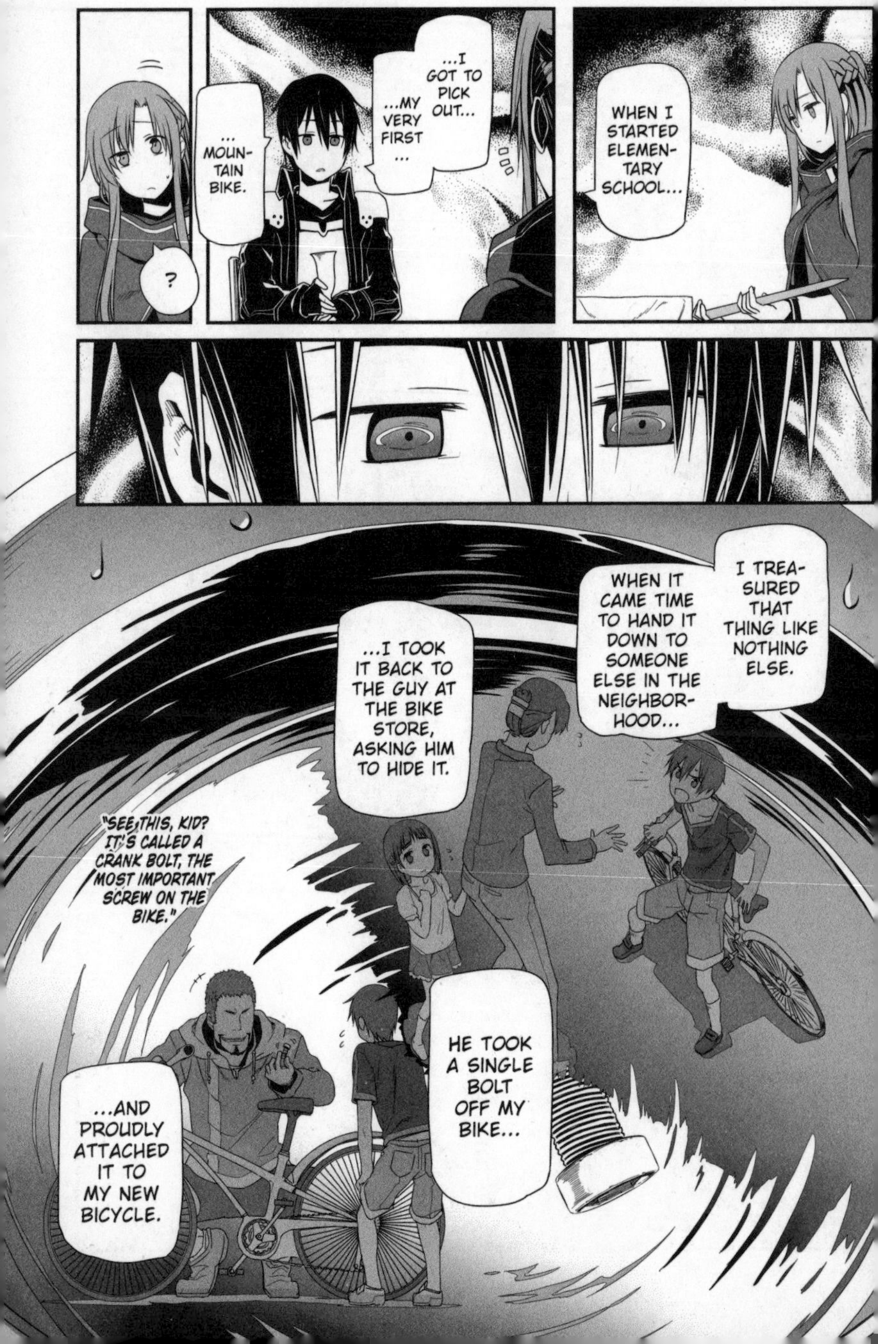
WHEN I STARTED ELEMENTARY SCHOOL...
...I GOT TO PICK OUT...
...MY VERY FIRST ...
... MOUNTAIN BIKE.
?
I TREASURED THAT THING LIKE NOTHING ELSE.
WHEN IT CAME TIME TO HAND IT DOWN TO SOMEONE ELSE IN THE NEIGHBORHOOD...
...I TOOK IT BACK TO THE GUY AT THE BIKE STORE, ASKING HIM TO HIDE IT.
"SEE THIS, KID? IT'S CALLED A CRANK BOLT, THE MOST IMPORTANT SCREW ON THE BIKE."
HE TOOK A SINGLE BOLT OFF MY BIKE...
...AND PROUDLY ATTACHED IT TO MY NEW BICYCLE.

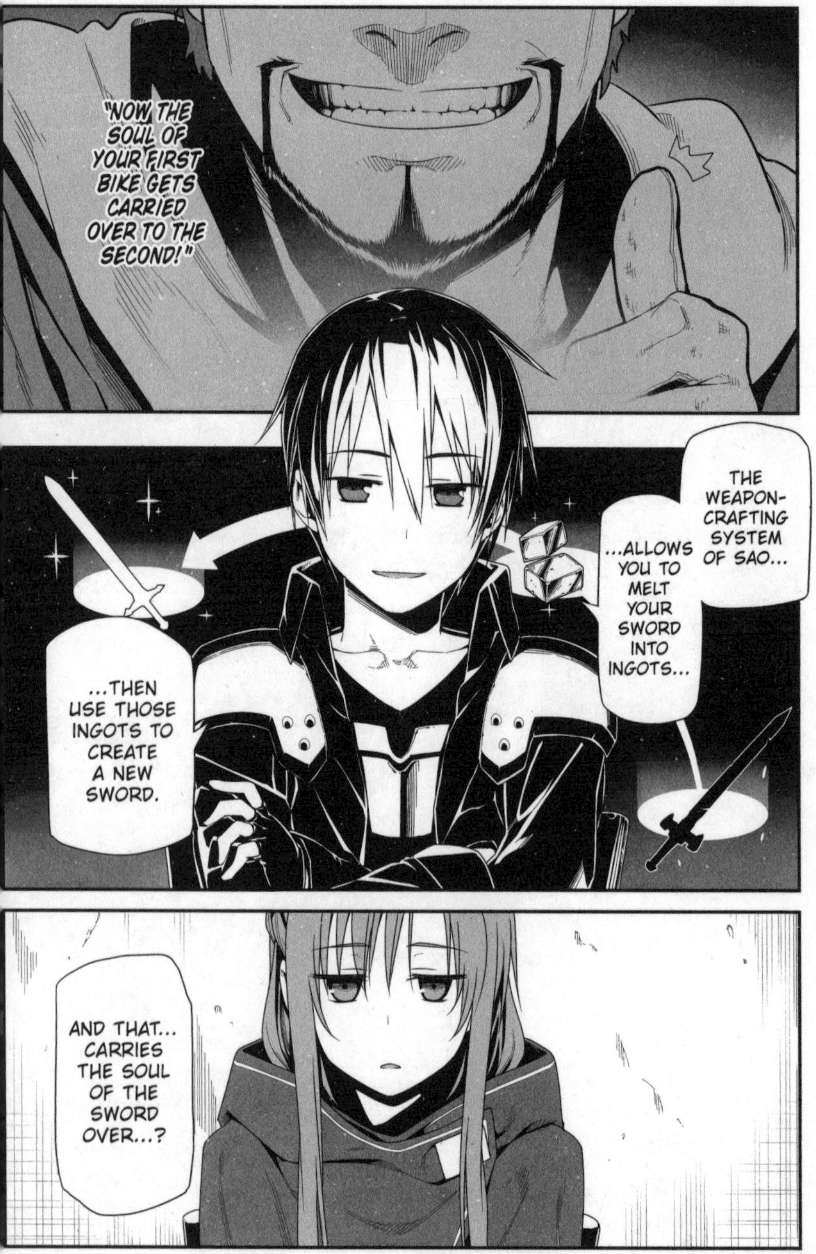
"NOW THE SOUL OF YOUR FIRST BIKE GETS CARRIED OVER TO THE SECOND!"
THE WEAPON-CRAFTING SYSTEM OF SAO...
...ALLOWS YOU TO MELT YOUR SWORD INTO INGOTS...
...THEN USE THOSE INGOTS TO CREATE A NEW SWORD.
AND THAT... CARRIES THE SOUL OF THE SWORD OVER...?

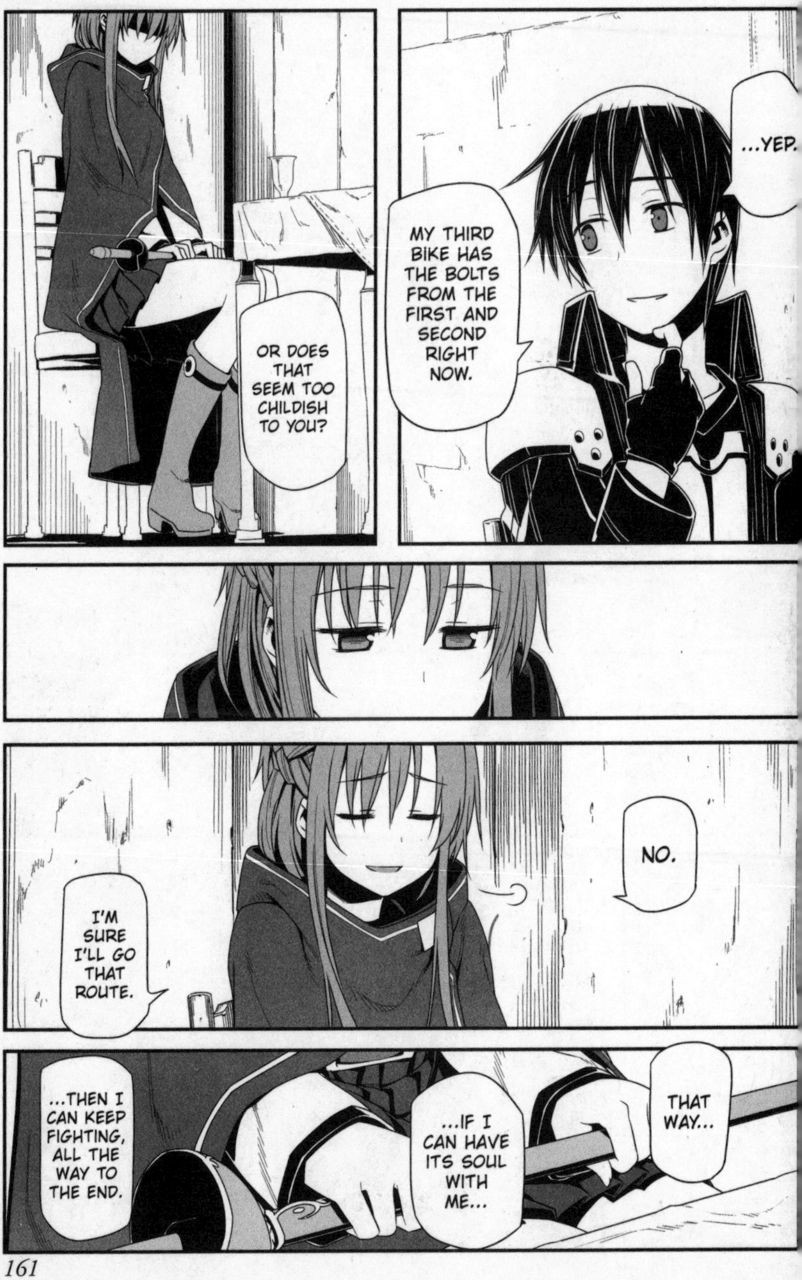
...YEP.
MY THIRD BIKE HAS THE BOLTS FROM THE FIRST AND SECOND RIGHT NOW.
OR DOES THAT SEEM TOO CHILDISH TO YOU?
NO.
I'M SURE I'LL GO THAT ROUTE.
THAT WAY...
...IF I CAN HAVE ITS SOUL WITH ME...
...THEN I CAN KEEP FIGHTING, ALL THE WAY TO THE END.

THAT'S THE FEEL-ING...

...I GET.

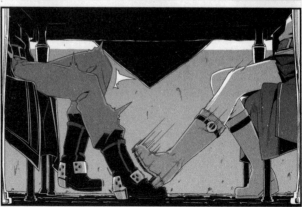

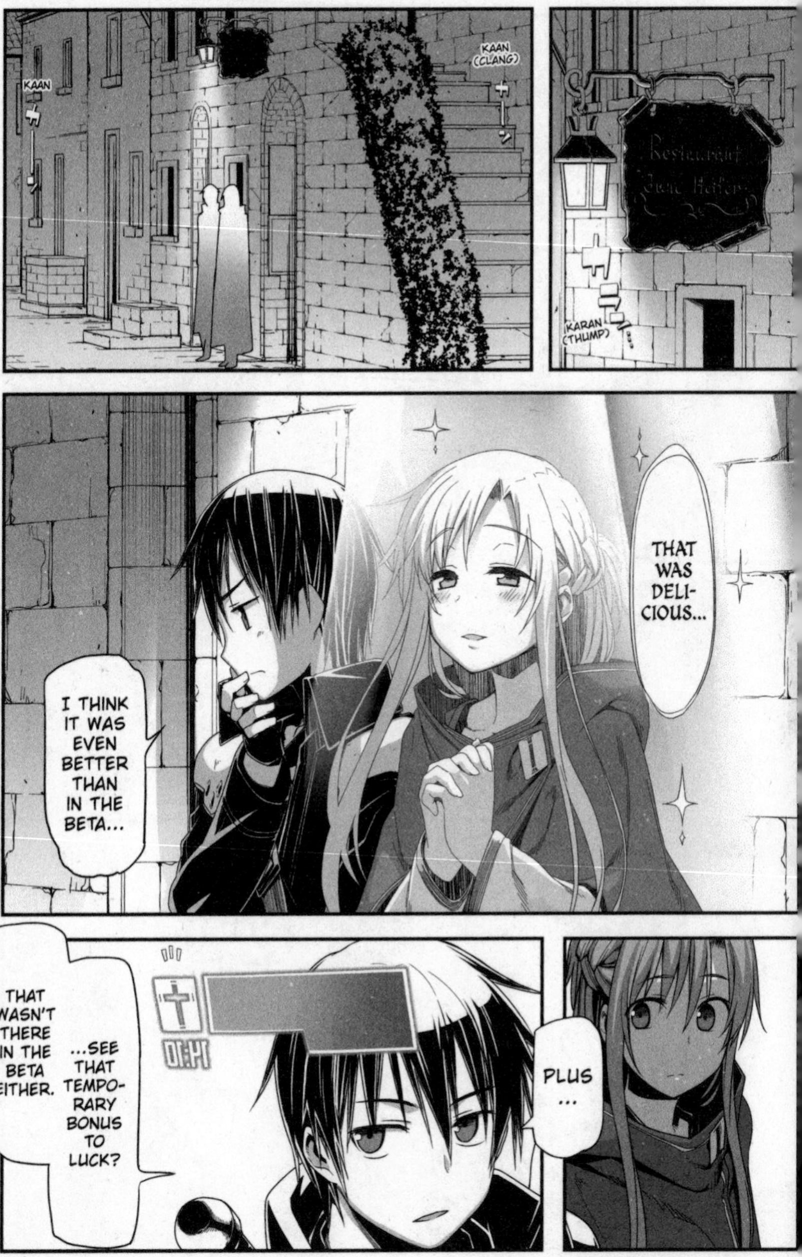
KARAN (THUMP)
KAAN (CLANG)
KAAN
THAT WAS DELICIOUS...
I THINK IT WAS EVEN BETTER THAN IN THE BETA...
PLUS ...
...SEE THAT TEMPORARY BONUS TO LUCK?
THAT WASN'T THERE IN THE BETA EITHER.

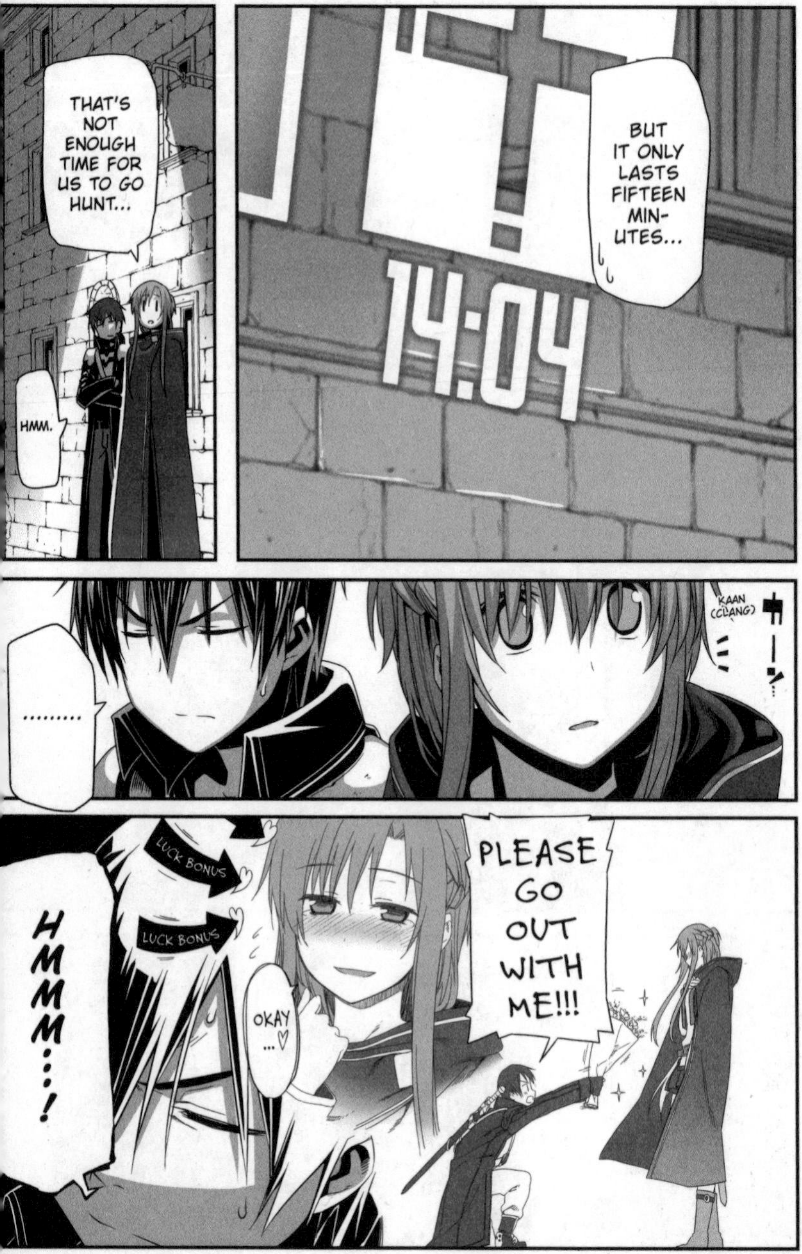
14:04
BUT IT ONLY LASTS FIFTEEN MIN-UTES...
THAT'S NOT ENOUGH TIME FOR US TO GO HUNT...
HMM.
KAAN (CLANG)
....
PLEASE GO OUT WITH ME!!!
OKAY ...♡
LUCK BONUS
LUCK BONUS
HMMM...!

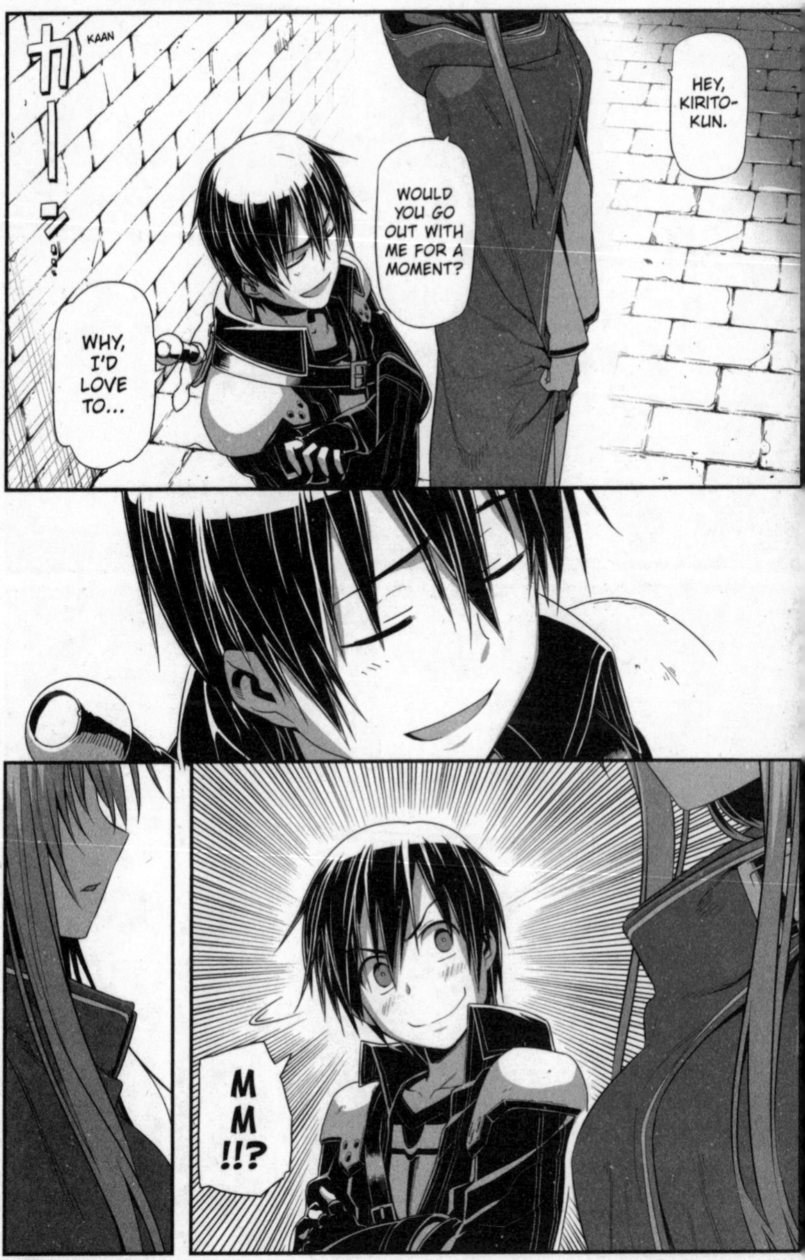
HEY, KIRITO-KUN.
WOULD YOU GO OUT WITH ME FOR A MOMENT?
カーン
KAAN
WHY, I'D LOVE TO...
MM!!?

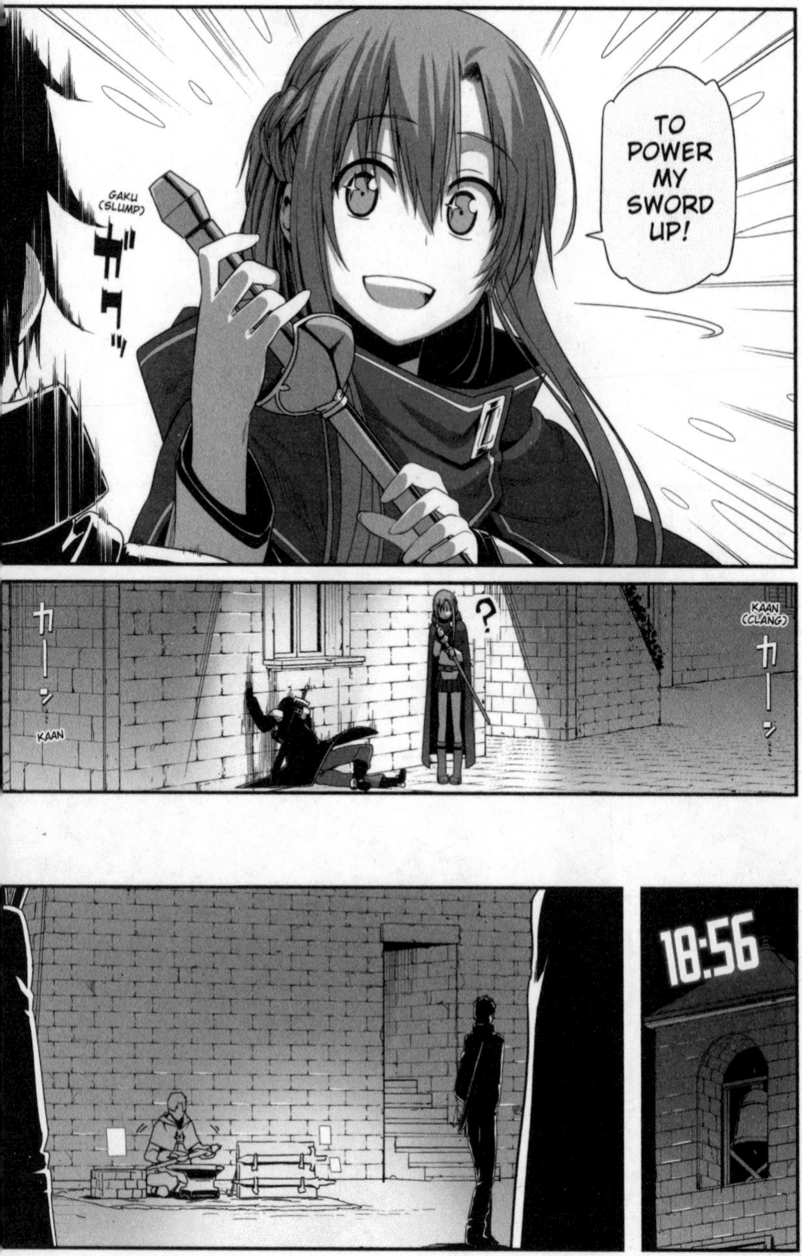
TO POWER MY SWORD UP!
GAKU (SLUMP)
ガクッ
KAAN (CLANG)
カーン
?
カーン
KAAN
18:56

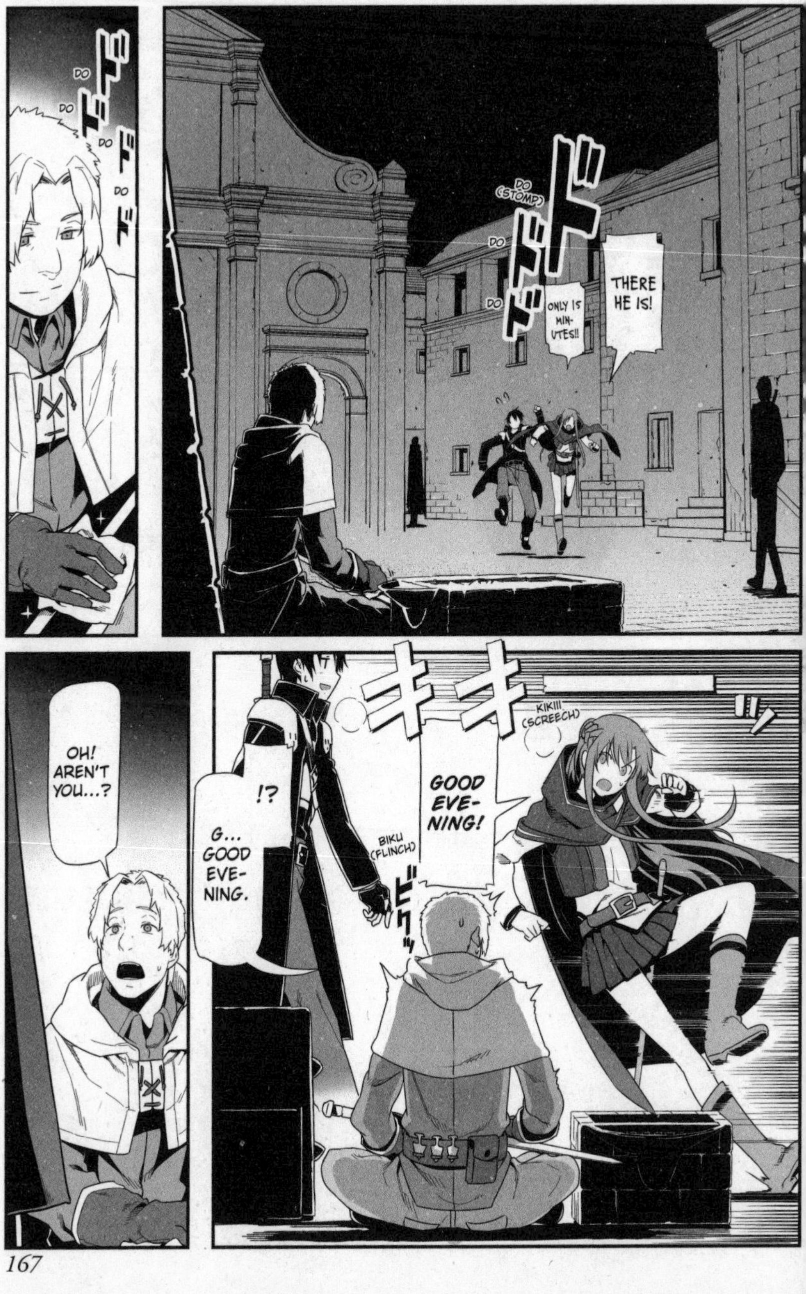
THERE HE IS!
DO (STOMP)
DO
ONLY 15 MIN-UTES!!
DO
DO
DO
DO
DO
KIKIII (SCREECH)
GOOD EVE-NING!
BIKU (FLINCH)
!?
G... GOOD EVE-NING.
OH! AREN'T YOU...?

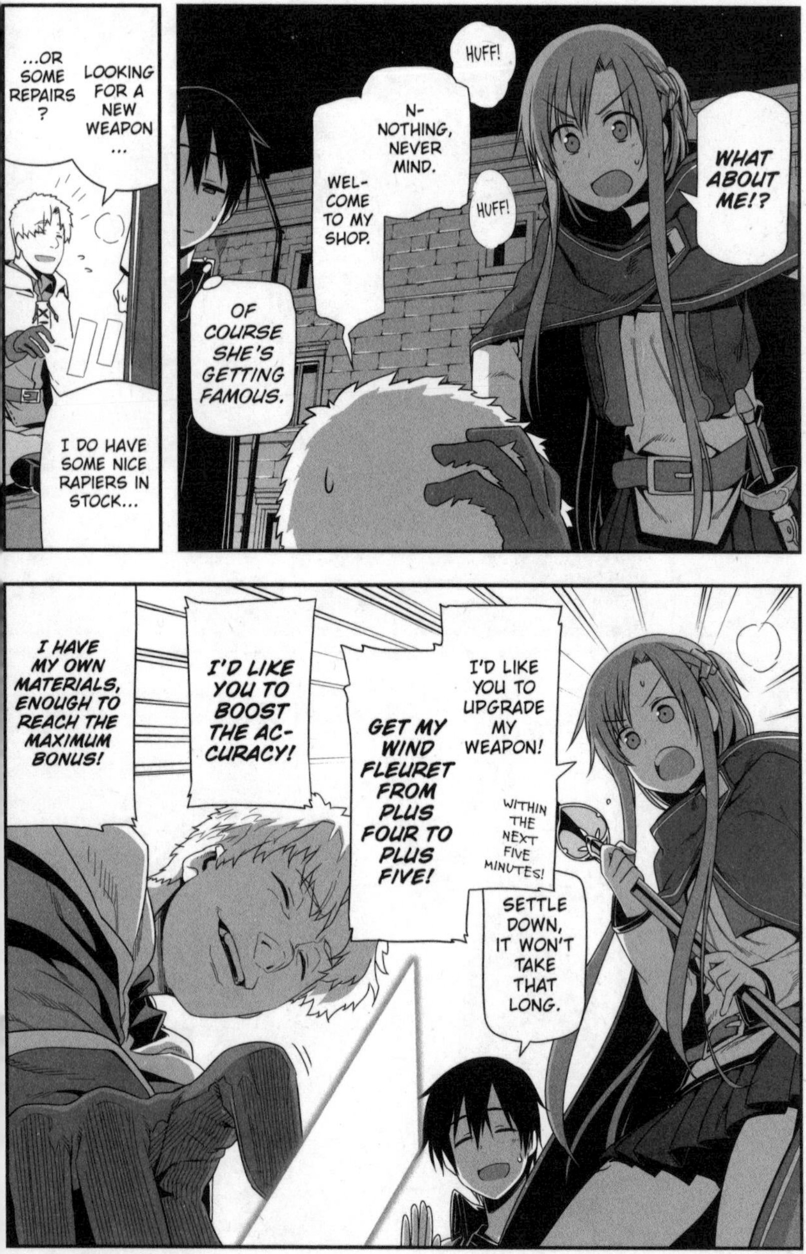
WHAT ABOUT ME!?
HUFF!
HUFF!
N-NOTHING, NEVER MIND.
WEL-COME TO MY SHOP.
OF COURSE SHE'S GETTING FAMOUS.
LOOKING FOR A NEW WEAPON...
...OR SOME REPAIRS?
I DO HAVE SOME NICE RAPIERS IN STOCK...
I'D LIKE YOU TO UPGRADE MY WEAPON!
WITHIN THE NEXT FIVE MINUTES!
GET MY WIND FLEURET FROM PLUS FOUR TO PLUS FIVE!
I'D LIKE YOU TO BOOST THE AC-CURACY!
I HAVE MY OWN MATERIALS, ENOUGH TO REACH THE MAXIMUM BONUS!
SETTLE DOWN, IT WON'T TAKE THAT LONG.

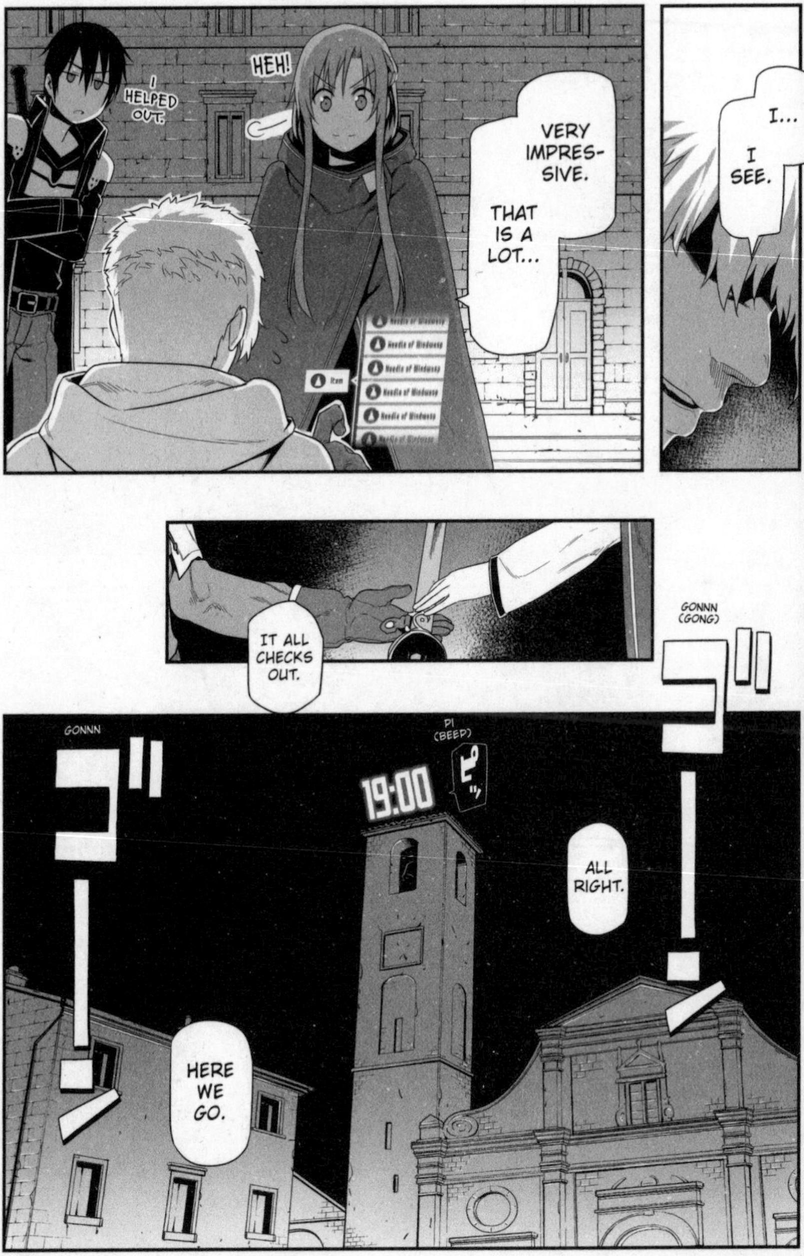
I...
I SEE.
VERY IMPRESSIVE.
THAT IS A LOT...
HEH!
I HELPED OUT.
GONNN (GONG)
IT ALL CHECKS OUT.
PI (BEEP)
19:00
ALL RIGHT.
GONNN
HERE WE GO.

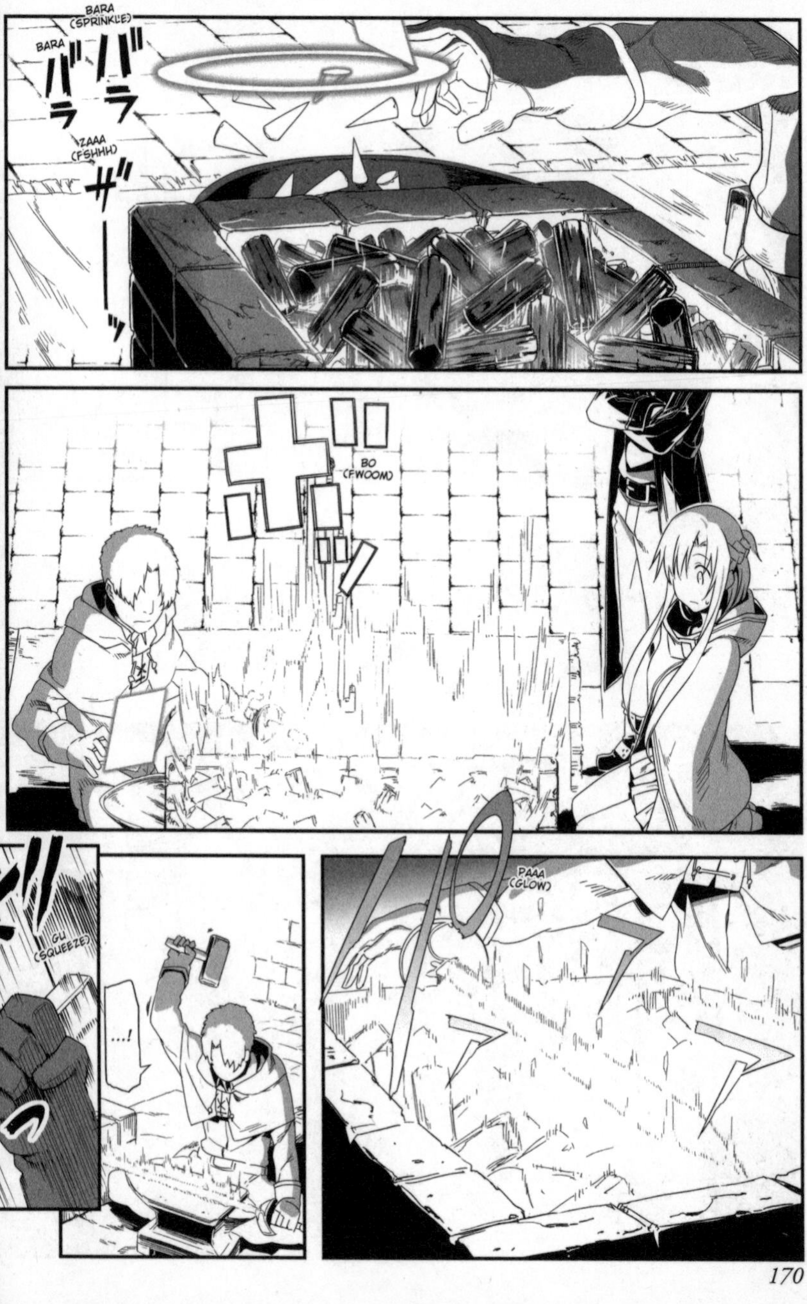
BARA (SPRINKLE)
BARA
ZAAA (FSHHH)
BO (FWOOM)
PAAA (GLOW)
GU (SQUEEZE)
...!

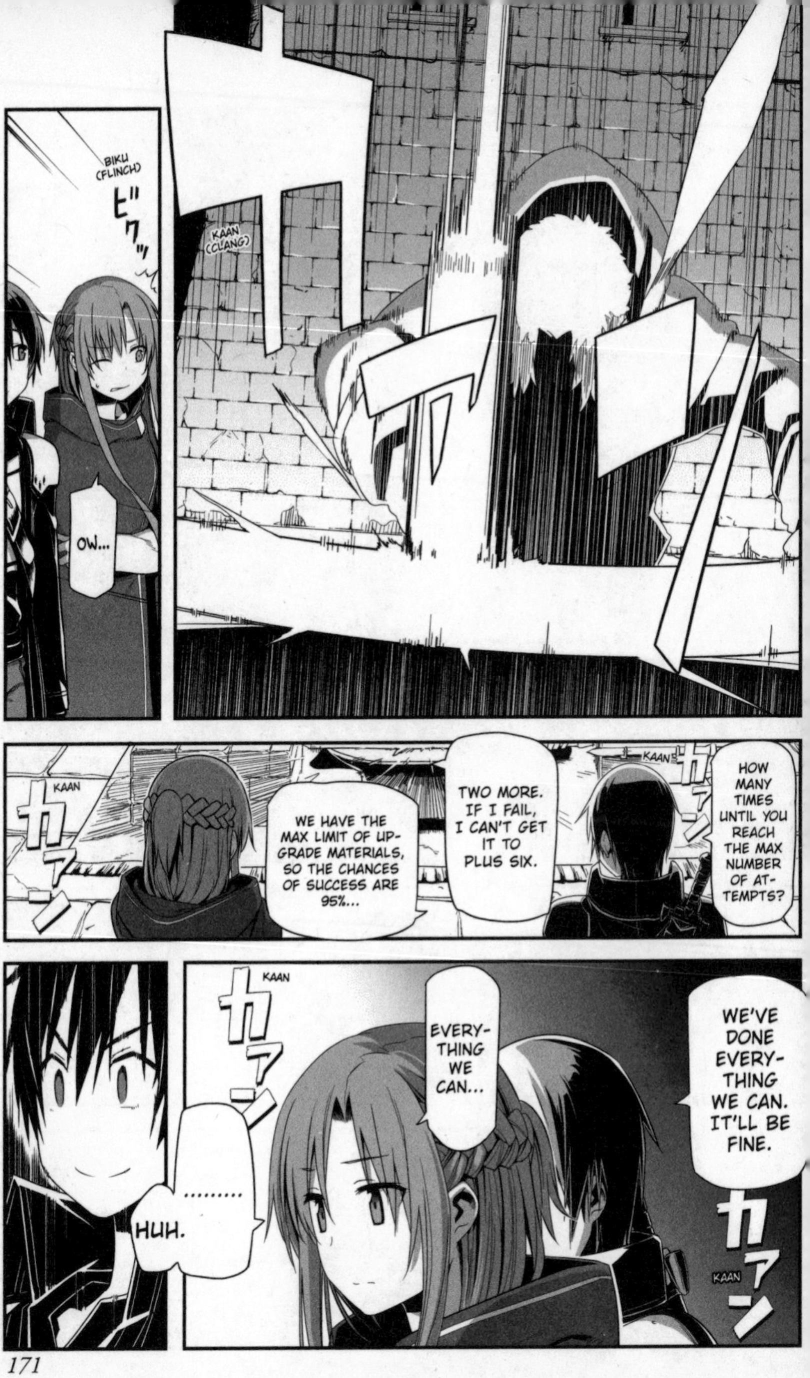
KAAN (CLANG)
BIKU (FLINCH)
OW...
HOW MANY TIMES UNTIL YOU REACH THE MAX NUMBER OF ATTEMPTS?
KAAN
TWO MORE. IF I FAIL, I CAN'T GET IT TO PLUS SIX.
WE HAVE THE MAX LIMIT OF UPGRADE MATERIALS, SO THE CHANCES OF SUCCESS ARE 95%...
KAAN
WE'VE DONE EVERYTHING WE CAN. IT'LL BE FINE.
KAAN
EVERYTHING WE CAN...
KAAN
....
HUH.

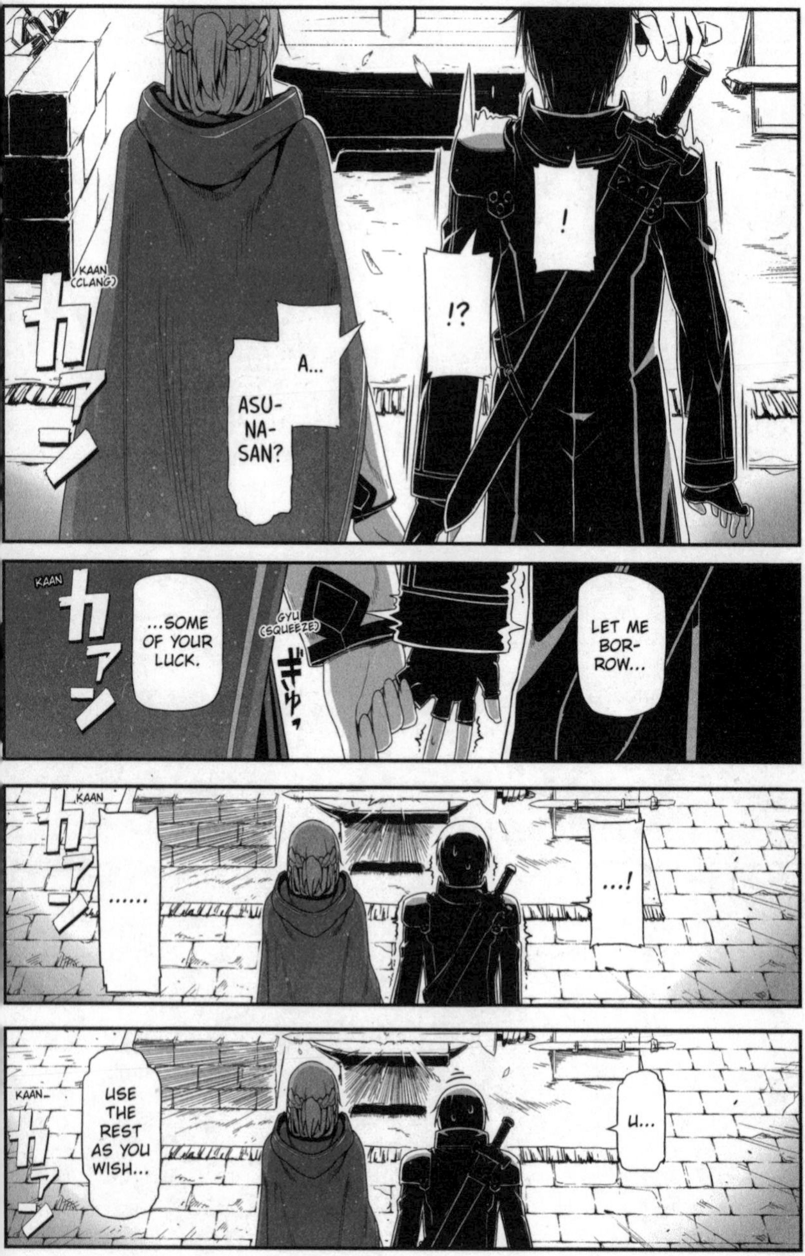
!
!?
A... ASUNA-SAN?
KAAN (CLANG)
LET ME BORROW...
GYU (SQUEEZE)
...SOME OF YOUR LUCK.
KAAN
...!
......
KAAN
U...
USE THE REST AS YOU WISH...
KAAN-

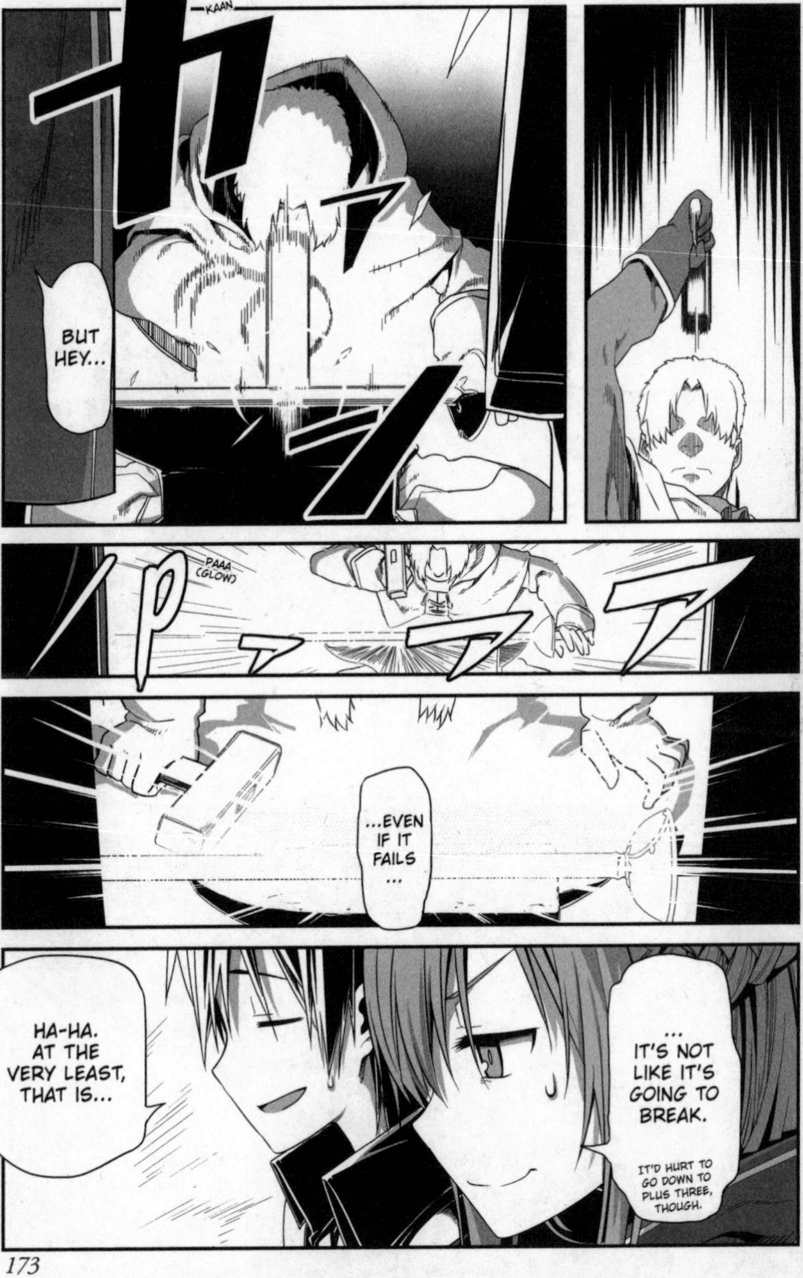
KAAN
BUT HEY...
PAAA (GLOW)
...EVEN IF IT FAILS...
...IT'S NOT LIKE IT'S GOING TO BREAK.
IT'D HURT TO GO DOWN TO PLUS THREE, THOUGH.
HA-HA. AT THE VERY LEAST, THAT IS...

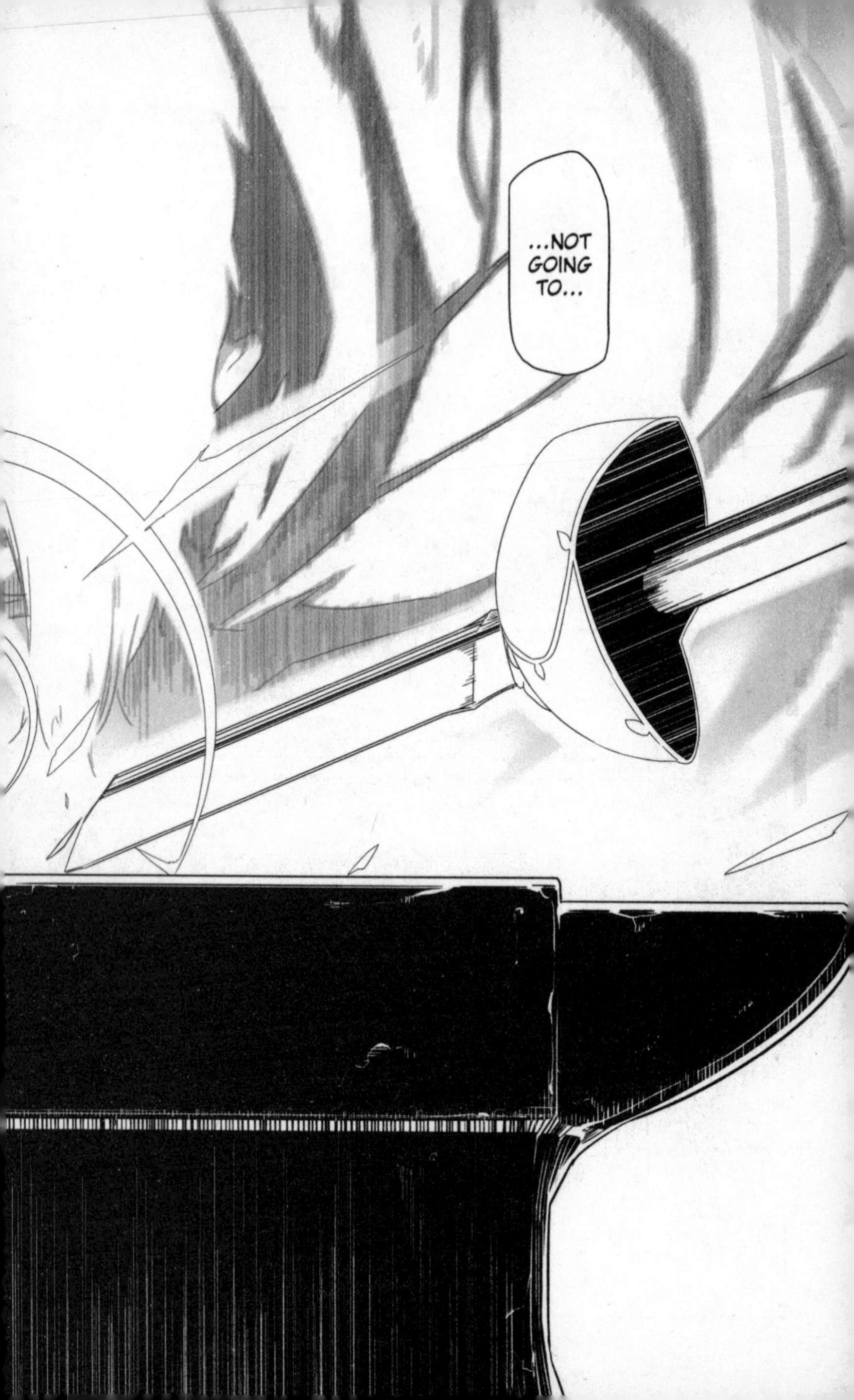
...NOT GOING TO...

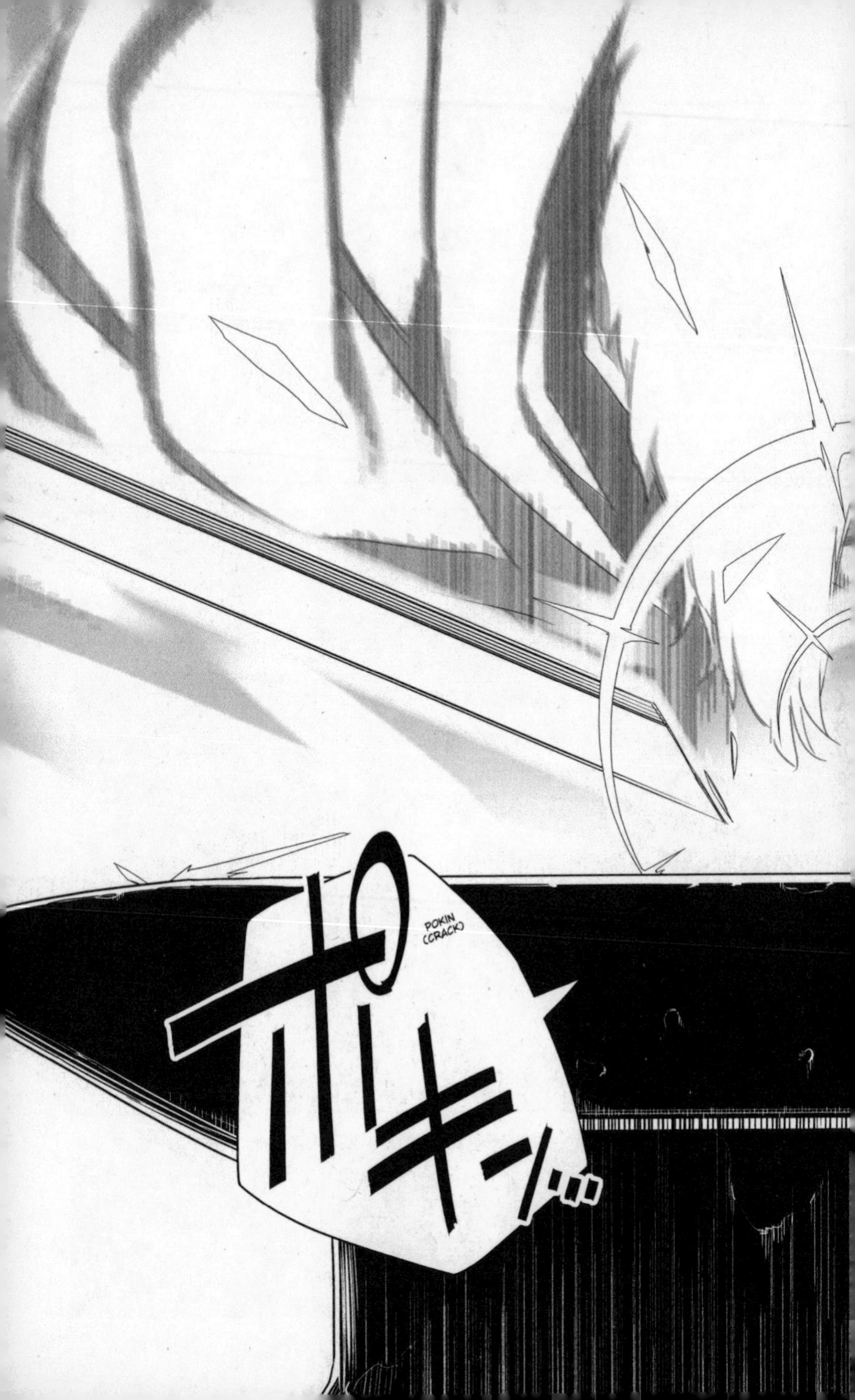
ポキーン…
POKIN (CRACK)

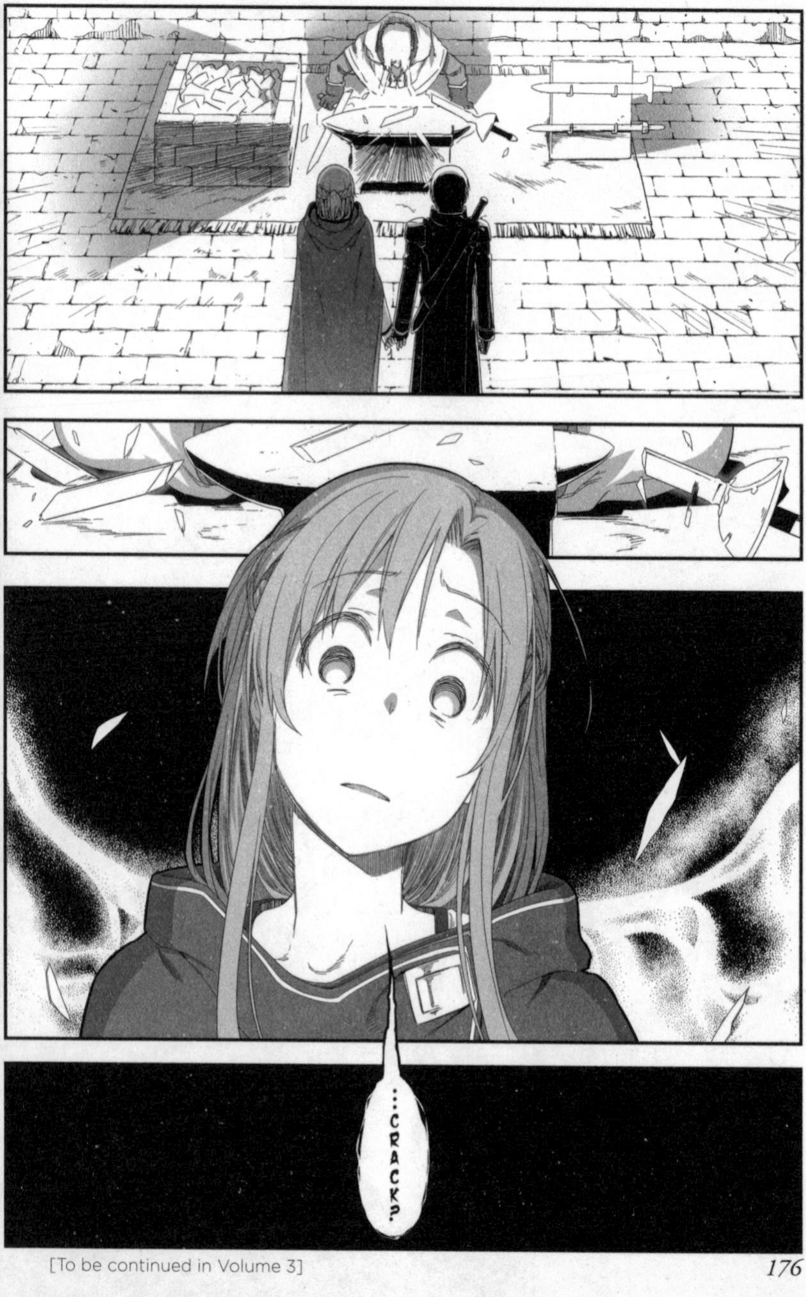
...CRACK?

[To be continued in Volume 3]

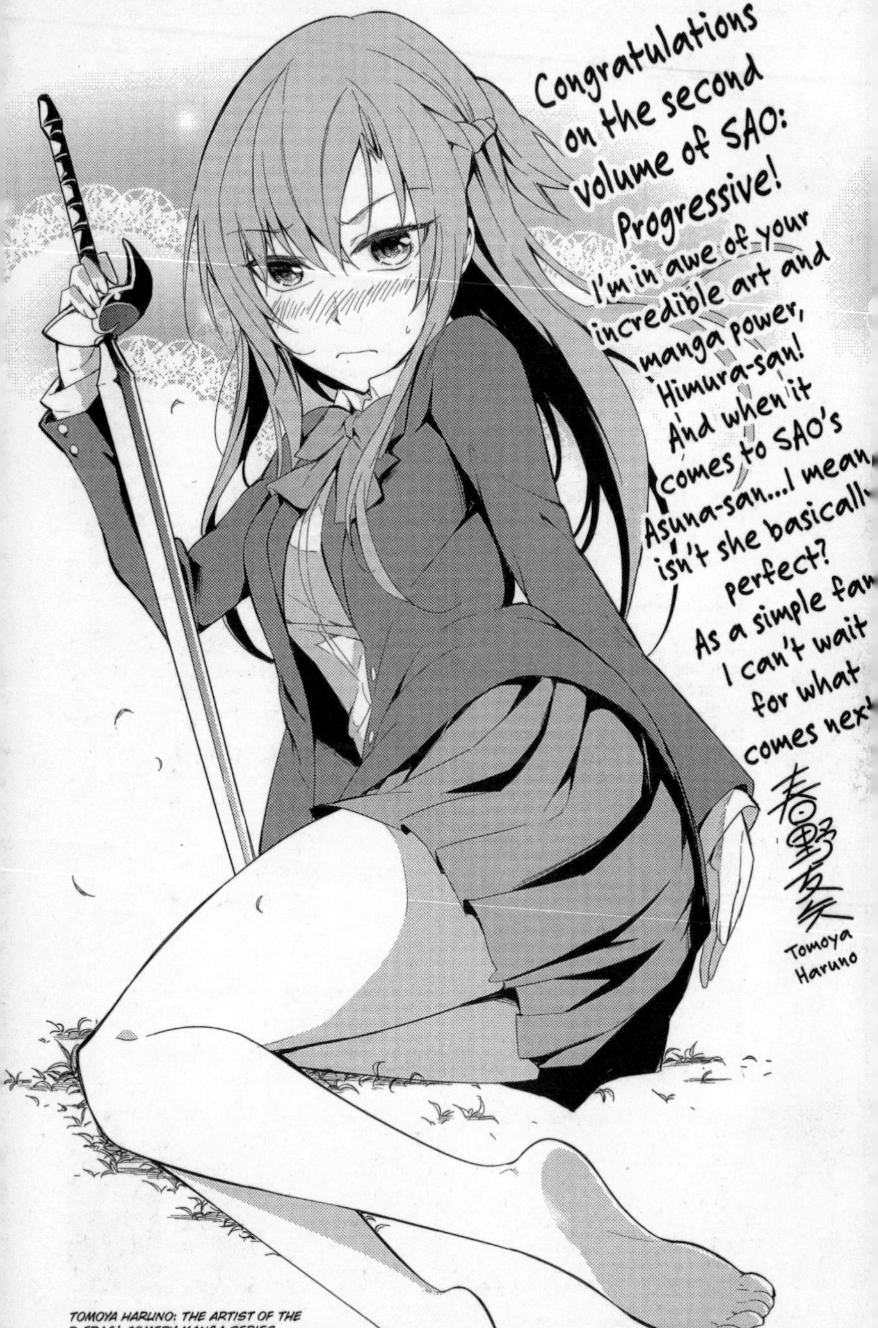

Congratulations on the second volume of SAO: Progressive! I'm in awe of your incredible art and manga power, Himura-san! And when it comes to SAO's Asuna-san...I mean, isn't she basicall perfect? As a simple fan I can't wait for what comes nex
Tomoya Haruno

TOMOYA HARUNO: THE ARTIST OF THE D-FRAG! COMEDY MANGA SERIES.

SWORD ART ONLINE: PROGRESSIVE

ART: KISEKI HIMURA
ORIGINAL STORY: REKI KAWAHARA
CHARACTER DESIGN: ABEC

Translation: Stephen Paul
Lettering: Brndn Blakeslee & Lys Blakeslee

SWORD ART ONLINE: PROGRESSIVE
© REKI KAWAHARA/KISEKI HIMURA 2014
All rights reserved.
Edited by ASCII MEDIA WORKS
First published in Japan in 2014 by KADOKAWA CORPORATION, Tokyo.
English translation rights arranged with KADOKAWA CORPORATION, Tokyo, through Tuttle-Mori Agency, Inc., Tokyo.

English translation © 2015 by Hachette Book Group, Inc.

Yen Press
Hachette Book Group
1290 Avenue of the Americas
New York, NY 10104

www.HachetteBookGroup.com
www.YenPress.com

Yen Press is an imprint of Hachette Book Group, Inc. The Yen Press name and logo are trademarks of Hachette Book Group, Inc.

The publisher is not responsible for websites (or their content) that are not owned by the publisher.

First Yen Press Edition: April 2015

ISBN: 978-0-316-38377-6

10 9 8 7 6 5 4 3 2 1

BVG

Printed in the United States of America